ALine

M

SPORT PSYCHOLOGY:

LINKING THEORY AND PRACTICE

Ronnie Lidor, Ph.D.
Michael Bar-Eli, Ph.D.
Wingate Institute
Netanya, Israel

Editors

Fitness Information Technology, Inc. • P.O. Box 4425 •
Morgantown, WV 26504-4425 • USA

Library of Congress Card Catalog Number: 98-74827

ISBN 1-885693-15-X

Cover Design: Bellerophon Productions
Copy Editor: Sandra R. Woods
Developmental Editor: Geoffrey C. Fuller
Production Editor: Craig Hines
Printed by: Bookcrafters
Printed in the United States of America
10 9 8 7 6 5 4 3 2 1

Fitness Information Technology, Inc.
P.O. Box 4425, University Avenue
Morgantown, WV 25504 USA
(800) 477-4348
(304) 599-3482 (phone/fax)
Email: fit@fitinfotech.com
Web Site: www.fitinfotech.com

About the Editors

Ronnie Lidor

Ronnie Lidor is the head of the Motor Behavior Laboratory at the Zinman College of Physical Education and Sport Sciences at the Wingate Institute and a lecturer at the School of Education at Haifa University (Israel). Dr. Lidor has published about 60 articles, book chapters and proceedings chapters in English and Hebrew. He has published (as author, coauthor, and editor) 8 books in the Hebrew language. Among these books are *Motor Development in Childhood, Motor Learning, Talent Detection in Sport, Thoughts and Behavior in Tennis,* and *Measurement and Evaluation in Physical Education and Sport.* He has published more than 100 articles in professional journals for coaches, physical educators, and administrators. Dr. Lidor is the president of the Israeli Society for Sport Psychology and Sociology. In addition, he was elected in 1997 as a member of the managing council of the ISSP (International Society of Sport Psychology).

Michael Bar-Eli

Michael Bar-Eli, born 23/1/1953, is an associate professor in the Department of Business Administration, School of Management, Ben-Gurion University of the Negev, Beer-Sheva; and Senior Researcher in the Ribstein Center for Sport Medicine Sciences and Research, Wingate Institute, Netanya, Israel. He studied psychology and sociology in Israel and sport psychology and sociology in the German Sport University, Cologne. Bar-Eli has published about 90 international refereed journal articles and book chapters, and numerous journal articles, book chapters and books in Hebrew. He is the current "Social Aspects" section editor of the *International Journal of Sport Psychology.* He served in senior positions in the psychological organs of the Israel Defense Forces and has often acted as psychological consultant to athletes, primarily in team sports. Bar-Eli is past president of the Israeli Society for Sport Psychology and Sociology, vice president of ASPASP, and managing council member of FEPSAC. He served as guest professor at the Norwegian Sport University, Oslo, Norway, in 1995.

Table of Contents

Part I: Historical Perspectives

Part II: Basic Concepts of Sport Psychology

Part III: Cognitive Aspects of Skilled Motor Behavior

Part IV: Motivation and Emotion

Part V: The Interface Between Behavioral Sciences and Society

Contributing Authors

Isabel Balaguer

Isabel Balaguer is professor of social psychology in the Faculty of Psychology at the University of Valencia, Spain, where she teaches graduate and undergraduate courses in social psychology and social psychological aspects of sport and exercise. Dr. Balaguer received her Ph.D. in psychology from the University of Valencia. One line of her research concerns the psychological predictors of performance among elite athletes. She also has done work on the youth sport experience with a particular interest in the interplay between social psychological factors, participation in physical activities, and adolescents' lifestyles. Dr. Balaguer is the director of the sport psychology research group at the University of Valencia and director of the master course on high performance in sport at the same university. She has worked with athletes and coaches as a consultant with the Spanish Tennis Federation for many years. Dr. Balaguer is a member of the Spanish Society of Psychology, the Valencian Society of Social Psychology, the International Society of Sport Psychology, the North American Society for the Psychology of Sport and Physical Activity, and the Association for the Advancement of Applied Sport Psychology.

Reinoud J. Bootsma

Reinoud J. Bootsma obtained his Ph.D. in human movement sciences from the Vrije Universiteit of Amsterdam in 1988. As a fellow of the Royal Dutch Academy of Sciences, he spent a year in the Department of Kinesiology of the University of Waterloo in Canada before returning to Amsterdam. In 1992 he moved to France, where he currently holds a full professorship at the Faculty of Sport Sciences of the University of the Mediterranean in Marseille. His research focuses on the coupling between information and movement in a large variety of tasks (catching, hitting, aiming, navigating) and seeks to identify the principles by which goal-directed movement is produced in complex environments.

Celia Brackenridge

Celia Brackenridge is professor of sport and leisure at Cheltenham College of Higher Education in the UK where she is head of the Leisure and Sport Research Unit. She began her career as a teacher of physical education before moving into lecturing and researching. Her major research interests are gender equity and child protection in sport and leisure. She coached and captained the English women's lacrosse team, was the first chair of the Women's Sports Foundation (UK) and was a founding member of *WomenSport International.*

Brenda Light Bredemeier

Dr. Brenda Light Bredemeier has been studying sociomoral development and behavior in physical activity contexts for nearly 20 years at the University of California at Berkeley. She coauthored the book *Character Development and Physical Activity* and has authored or coauthored 40 articles and book chapters on this topic. She currently serves on editorial boards for *Quest, The Journal of Applied Sport Psyhchology,* and the *International Journal of Sport Psychology* as section editor for sociomoral development and behavior. She enjoys the woods and the water, both in solitude and as places to play with family and friends. Hiking, canoeing, swimming, and camping are some of her favorite activities.

Gunnar Breivik

Gunnar Breivik, born 8/4/1943, is a professor in social sciences at the Norwegian University of Sport and Physical Education in Oslo, Norway. He has studied philosophy, theology, sociology, and sport and has been instructor in various outdoor sports. He has been a visiting scholar in Tübingen, Germany, and at the University of California, Berkeley. Breivik is teaching philosophy, theory of science, ethics and sociology; his research interests have especially been related to the following areas: (a) personality, sensation seeking and risk taking in sports; (b) sports as part of the sociocultural process—empirical studies of values, attitudes, and behavior; (c) rationality in sports—game theoretical analyses of doping; (d) tacit knowledge and the epistemology of sport; (e) career development, life quality, and performance in elite sport. Breivik is current past-president of the Philosophic Society for the Study of Sport.

Joan L. Duda

Joan L. Duda (Ph.D., University of Illinois at Urbana-Champaign) is a professor of sport and exercise psychology in the Department of Health, Kinesiology and Leisure Studies and an adjunct professor in the Department of Psychological Sciences at Purdue University, West Lafayette, Indiana. Dr. Duda has been a member of the executive boards of the North American Society for the Psychology of Sport and Physical Activity, the Sport Psychology Academy, and the International Society for Sport Psychology and is a Fellow of the

American Academy of Kinesiology and Physical Education. She was editor of the *Journal of Applied Sport Psychology* and is on the editorial board of the *Journal of Sport and Exercise Psychology*. Dr. Duda has published over 80 papers focused on the topic of sport motivation and the psychological dimensions of sport and exercise behavior. She is certified as a sport psychology consultant by the Association for the Advancement of Applied Sport Psychology and is listed on the U.S. Olympic Registry.

Gerard Joseph Fogarty

Gerard Fogarty completed his Ph.D. in the Department of Psychology at the University of Sydney in 1984. His dissertation was on the structure of human abilities. While working on his dissertation, he became interested in the topic of psychological measurement. This topic, along with the broader topics of statistics and research design, has formed the basis of his teaching career at the University of Southern Queensland, where he is currently the head of the Psychology Department. Dr. Fogarty has published in the fields of differential psychology, sport psychology, and organizational psychology. Research techniques with which he is particularly familiar include Rasch analysis and structural equation modelling. He is a member of the College of Sport Psychology of the Australian Psychological Society and teaches research methods to postgraduate students seeking to join the college.

Dieter Hackfort

Since 1991 Prof. Dr. Dieter Hackfort has been professor for sport psychology at the University of the Federal Defence in Munich, and head of the Institute for Sport Science and Sports. He earned his doctoral degree from the German Sports University at Cologne. From 1984 to 1985, he was a visiting professor at the Center for Behavioral Medicine and Health Psychology at the University of South Florida in Tampa. From 1986 to 1991 he was a professor at the University of Heidelberg. His main areas of research are the development of action theory and empirical methods within the framework of this perspective; emotions in sports, so-called "negative" emotions (especially anxiety), as well as "positive" emotions (fun, pride, etc.); self-presentation; and issues referring to health in sports as well as health by sports. He is a past president of the ASP (the national sport psychological association in Germany), counselor for various national teams/Olympic teams, and editor/coeditor of national and international book series in sport science. He has been honored with various awards and grants for his research. Dr. Hackfort was a keynote speaker at the 8th World Congress of Sport Psychology (1993) in Lisbon. He has authored or edited a dozen books, the main ones in English being *Anxiety in Sports: An International Perspective* (with Charles D. Spielberger) and *Research on Emotions in Sport.* Dr. Hackfort is married and the father of two boys, and his favorite sports are tennis, skiing, and golf.

Yeshayahu Hutzler

Yeshayahu Hutzler completed in 1986 his Ph.D. research on movement actions of wheelchair users at the Faculty of Social and Behavioral Sciences of the Heidelberg University, Germany. Since 1987 he has been a senior staff member (tenured in 1989) of the Zinman College at the Wingate Institute, Israel, and a scientific counselor of the Israeli Sport Center for the Disabled. He has published 3 books and more than 20 articles in refereed international and national journals. During the last 4 years he has served as chairman of the Israeli Organization of Sport Therapy. He is also active in the International Federation of Adapted Physical Activity, and for 2 years he has served as representative of the Middle East Region in the board. During his work he has permanently linked research and academic work into practical application at the Israeli Sport Center for the Disabled in Ramat Gan and the Center for Disability Sport at the Zinman College. His recent involvement in practice includes developing modern assessment and intervention programs, redesigning methodological approaches in adapted physical activity, and conceptualizing inclusive programs.

Sandra Kirby

Sandra Kirby is a professor in the Department of Sociology at the University of Winnipeg in Canada. She has done extensive advocacy work for equity both in and beyond sport and has been an active member of CAAW+S and of WomenSport International. Her major research interests include qualitative research methods and gender and sexuality equity. She was an Olympic rower at the 1980 Moscow Games. In 1997 she was a visiting scholar in the Leisure and Sport Research Unit of Cheltenham and Gloucester College of Higher Education in the United Kingdom.

Yotam Lurie

Yotam Lurie, born 30/8/1964, is affiliated with the School of Management and the Department of Social Work at Ben-Gurion University of the Negev, Beer-Sheva, Israel. He studied philosophy, political science, and sport in Israel and received a Ph.D. in philosophy from the University of Illinois at Urbana-Champaign in 1996. Lurie teaches philosophy, applied ethics, and social and political theory as well as track and field. His major research interests and publications are in these areas.

Vincent Nougier

Vincent Nougier is a professor at the Department of Sport Sciences, University Joseph Fourier-Grenoble 1 (France). He is also head of the Department of Sport Sciences. He is a member of the Sport and Motor Performance Laboratory. His work is mainly focused on the integration of sensorimotor information in complex motor skills, such as sport skills.

Iris Orbach

Iris Orbach is completing her Ph.D. in sport psychology in the Department of Exercise and Sport Sciences at the University of Florida. Her scholarly interests are entwined with practical concerns, and her main goal is to contribute to the development of applied sport psychology as a scholar, a teacher, and a consultant. Ms. Orbach's research interests focus on competitive stress and anxiety, athlete motivation, and their relationship with exercise/sport performance. Ms. Orbach has consulted with athletes in a variety of collegiate sports, such as track and field, volleyball, and triathlon. She was a professional track and field athlete in Israel, and today she enjoys a variety of fitness activities, including running, biking, and racquetball.

Stéphane Perreault

Stéphane Perreault received his Ph.D. in social psychology from l'Université de Québec à Montréal. He also received an M.A. in sport psychology and a B.A. in psychology from McGill University. He is presently pursuing post-doctoral studies under the guidance of Dr. Robert Vallerand at l'Université de Québec à Montréal. He has taught sport psychology and research methods in physical education at McGill University as well as the psychology of motivation at l'Université de Québec à Montréal. His research interests include motivation, wheelchair populations, and intergroup relations in sport. During his leisure time, he enjoys running and playing basketball.

Bruna Rossi

Bruna Rossi was a professor of psychology at the Department of Sport Sciences, University of Roma (Italy). She moved to the Sport and Motor Performance Laboratory (University Joseph Fourier-Grenoble 1, France). Her work is mainly focused on attentional processes. As the sport psychologist of different Italian national teams (modern pentathlon, volleyball, water polo), she has seen her teams win different gold medals in various world and Olympic championships. In addition, Rossi is the sport psychologist of one of the most famous Italian soccer clubs.

John H. Salmela

Dr. Salmela is a sport psychology professor at the University of Ottawa, where he teaches and conducts research in the field of human expertise development. He has approximately 150 professional and scholarly publications, including 13 edited or written books, the most recent being *Great Job Coach* (1996). He has served as journal editor for the *International Journal of Sport Psychology* and presently for *Avante,* and has served on the executive boards of both the ISSP and AAASP. In the former position, he documented the development of sport psychology worldwide in *The World Sport Psychology Sourcebook* (1992). Dr. Salmela was a recipient of the ISSP Honor Award in 1993. His current interests are in the acquisition of expertise by exceptional coaches and athletes and the structure of their knowledge.

Claudine Sherrill

Claudine Sherrill completed her Ed.D. degree at Columbia University, New York, in 1961. Since then she has been teaching and is currently a professor in the Department of Kinesiology at Texas Woman's University. She has published 10 books, 29 chapters in books, and more than 80 articles in various professional periodicals. Currently she is the editor of the *Adapted Physical Activity Quarterly,* the official journal of the International Federation of Adapted Physical Activity (IFAPA). She is past president of the National Consortium on Physical Education and Recreation for the Handicapped, a Fellow in the American Academy of Kinesiology and Physical Education, and in 1979 she received the National Honor Award from the American Alliance for Health, Physical Education, Recreation and Dance (AAHPERD). In 1989 she was elected Vice President of the IFAPA and in 1991 was the first recipient of the Elly D. Friedmann Award for Outstanding Service by the IFAPA. Since 1992 she also has functioned as board member of the Cerebral Palsy-International Sports and Recreation Association.

Robert N. Singer

Dr. Robert N. (Bob) Singer is chair and professor in the Department of Exercise & Sport Sciences at the University of Florida. He is a past president of the International Society of Sport Psychology, the Division of Exercise and Sport Psychology of the American Psychological Association, and the American

Academy of Kinesiology and Physical Education. He is well-known and recognized as a leader and visionary in sport psychology. For over 3 decades, he has published numerous research articles, books, chapters in books, and professional articles, with one of the most respected books being *The Handbook of Research on Sport Psychology* (1993), for which he served as editor. Among his many awards is the Distinguished Sport Psychology Award, presented to him by the International Society of Sport Psychology in 1997. For many years, Bob has consulted with numerous high-level athletes representing different sports and headed up the first Sport Psychology Division of the USOC. He himself has been an active athlete in a variety of sports as long as he can remember, still trying to apply those mental skills he teaches others to use in competition!

Ronald E. Smith

Ronald E. Smith is a professor of psychology at the University of Washington. Dr. Smith has served as director of clinical psychology training, as head of the social psychology and personality area, and as co-director of the sport psychology graduate training program. He also co-directs Husky Sport Psychology Services, which provides performance-enhancement services to the University of Washington Department of Intercollegiate Athletics, and has worked extensively as a consultant in professional baseball. His major research interests are in personality, stress and coping, and sport psychology and performance-enhancement research and intervention. Dr. Smith is a past president of the Association for the Advancement of Applied Sport Psychology. He is the recipient of a Distinguished Alumnus Award from the UCLA Neuropsychiatric Institute for his contributions to the field of mental health.

Jeffery J. Summers

Jeff Summers received his Ph.D. in 1974 from the University of Oregon and then moved to Australia where he spent 18 years at the University of Melbourne. In 1993 he took up the position of Foundation Professor of Psychology at the University of Southern Queensland. In 1998 he moved to the University of Tasmania (Australia). He has published extensively in the field of human motor control and learning, particularly in issues relating to the coordination of movement. In recent years he has been using the tools and concepts from dynamical systems theory in an attempt to gain a deeper understanding of the principles and laws of human motor control, with particular emphasis on the application of dynamical models to the study of movement disorders and movement rehabilitation. In the sport psychology field, his research interests include attentional mechanisms in sport, the stress-performance relationship, predisposition to injury, and exercise addiction.

Gershon Tenenbaum

Dr. Gershon Tenenbaum is an associate professor in the Department of Psychology at the University of Southern Queensland, Australia. Until 1994 he was the director of the Ribstein Center for Research and Sport Medicine Sciences at the Wingate Institute in Israel. He is a graduate of the Zinman College, Tel-Aviv University, and the University of Chicago, where he received a Ph.D. in measurement, evaluation and statistical analysis. He is currently serving as the president of the International Society of Sport Psychology (ISSP). He has published more than 100 articles and chapters in refereed journals and books. His main fields are (a) psychometrics and methodological issues in sport sciences, (b) cognition and sport performance, and (c) motivation in sport: field-driven theory.

Robert J. Vallerand

After receiving his Ph.D. from the Université de Montréal, Dr. Vallerand pursued postdoctoral studies in experimental social psychology at the University of Waterloo. He is presently full professor and Director of the Laboratoire de Recherche sur le Comportement Social in the Department of Psychology at the Université de Québec à Montréal, where he teaches experimental social psychology and human motivation. Dr. Vallerand has written three books and more than 100 articles and book chapters mainly in the area of motivation. He has served as chair of the psychology department, president of the Quebec Society for Research in Psychology, chair of both the social psychology and the sport psychology sections of the Canadian Psychological Association (CPA), associate editor of the Canadian Journal of Behavioural Sciences, and editorial board member of several journals including the *Journal of Applied Sport Psychology* and the *Journal of Personality and Social Psychology*. Dr. Vallerand is a Fellow of the Canadian Psychological Association. He has also received the Sport Science Award from the International Olympic Committee. During his leisure time, he enjoys reading and playing basketball.

Preface

The idea of developing this book emerged about one year before the 1997 ISSP (International Society of Sport Psychology) World Congress. This congress was held in Israel on July 5–9 and was organized by the Wingate Institute for Physical Education and Sport and the Zinman College of Physical Education and Sport Sciences, in conjunction with the 15th Maccabiah Games. Our initial intention was to include in the book only the contributions from the keynote speakers who had been invited to the Congress to deliver their scientific messages. Each invited speaker was asked to submit a lengthy paper on his or her topic; most of the speakers agreed to do so, some of them collaborating with other authors in preparing their manuscripts.

After some progress had been made in developing a tentative outline for the book, it was decided to extend its scope by addressing other leading scholars in sport psychology, asking them to contribute chapters. This was done for two main reasons: (a) to add some important topics that we believed were highly relevant for emphasizing the link between theory and practice in sport psychology and (b) to strengthen the international perspective of the book by providing leading experts in sport psychology from other parts of the world with the opportunity to present their ideas. Thus, instead of producing a book that includes only topics covered within the 1997 ISSP World Congress, this book reflects a much wider scope on its theme "Innovations in sport psychology: Linking theory and practice". The keynote speakers were asked to substantially extend and update their contributions after the congress. Each chapter was reviewed by highly qualified experts on each particular area. Based on the comments and the suggestions made by the expert reviewers, the authors were asked to revise their manuscripts. Naturally, this careful review process improved the quality of the chapters even beyond their original excellence.

The book contains five parts. Except for Part I, which presents some historical perspectives on sport psychology, an attempt was made to emphasize the link between theory and practice within various specific areas of sport psychology; each part focuses on one such area. Part I includes chapter 1, which is entitled "The Antonelli Era of Sport Psychology: Inspiration, Improvisation, and Angst." The author (John H. Salmela) describes the early development of the ISSP as well as the establishment of the *International Journal of Sport Psychology*.

Part II of the book deals with some basic concepts of sport psychology. These concepts, presented in chapters 2, 3, and 4, can be applied to many topics in sport psychology and may be implemented by the researcher and the practitioner as well. Chapter 2 is entitled "The Sport Psychologist as Scientist-Practitioner: Reciprocal Relations Linking Theory, Research, and Intervention" (author: Ronald E. Smith). This chapter presents the author's unique view of the intimate relations between theory and practice in sport psychology. Chapter 3, entitled "Rationality in Sport: A Psychophilosophical Approach" (authors: Michael Bar-Eli, Yotam Lurie, and Gunnar Breivik), demonstrates how philosophy can help in clarifying important sport-psychological issues. In Chapter 4, entitled "Moving With the Times: Keeping Up With Trends in Statistical Analysis and Research Design" (authors: Gershon Tenenbaum and Gerard Fogarty), the authors discuss some central recent developments in methodology and statistics in sport psychology.

Four chapters (chapters 5, 6, 7, and 8) are included in Part III that examine various cognitive aspects of skilled motor behavior. The scientific emphases in the area of motor behavior have dramatically changed in the past few decades. More specifically, the focus of the studies on skill acquisition has shifted from "behaviorally oriented" to "cognitively and control oriented" designs; the chapters included in this part reflect this trend. Chapter 5, by Jeffery J. Summers, entitled "Skill Acquisition: Current Perspectives and Future Directions," may serve as a general introduction to this topic. Chapter 6, entitled "Learning Strategies and the Enhancement of Self-Paced Motor Tasks: Theoretical and Practical Implications" (author: Ronnie Lidor), describes the application of cognitive strategies in motor skill acquisition. The last two chapters included in this part, namely "Orienting of Attention: From Perception to Action" (chapter 7, authors: Vincent Nougier and Bruna Rossi) and "Information and Movement in Interception Tasks" (chapter 8, author: Reinoud J. Bootsma), present different perspectives of examining the relationship between perception and action in motor skill acquisition.

Part IV, Motivation and Emotion, includes four chapters (chapters 9, 10, 11, and 12). The first three chapters, "Persistence, Excellence, and Fulfillment" (chapter 9, authors: Robert N. Singer and Iris Orbach), "Intrinsic and Extrinsic Motivation in Sport: Toward a Hierarchical Model" (chapter 10, authors: Robert J. Vallerand and Stéphane Perreault), and "Toward an Integration of Models of Leadership with a Contemporary Theory of Motivation" (chapter 11, authors: Joan L. Duda and Isabel Balaguer), focus on the issue of motivation, which has always been central to sport psychologists. A general overview of the relationship between motivation and human motor performance is presented in chapter 9. The intrinsic and extrinsic facets of human motivation are discussed within the authors' unique model in chapter 10; finally, the implications of current motivation theory to the issue of leadership are examined in chapter 11. The last chapter in this part, "The Presentation and Modulation of Emotions" (chapter 12, author: Dieter Hackfort), presents the author's unique paradigm for research on athletic emotion, including some recent data.

The last part of the book (Part V) contains three chapters (chapters 13, 14, and 15) that discuss various facets of the interface between behavioral sciences and society. The first two chapters, namely "Character in Action: The Influence of Moral Atmosphere on Athletes' Sport Behavior" (chapter 13, author: Brenda Light Bredemeier) and "Protecting Athletes From Sexual Abuse in Sport: How Theory can Improve Practice" (chapter 14, authors: Celia H. Brackenridge and Sandra Kirby), focus on two issues that are often subject to vehement societal debate: moral behavior in sport settings (chapter 13) and sexual abuse in sport (chapter 14). The last chapter of the book (chapter 15, authors: Yeshayahu Hutzler and Claudine Sherrill), entitled: "Disability, Physical Activity and Psychological Well-Being: A Life-Span Perspective," examines some substantial psychological aspects in sports for disabled people. This chapter reflects the current growing interest in adapted physical activity and sport, an interest that is important from both scientific and practical perspectives.

This book represents the fruits of the scientific and applied work of some of the world's leading sport psychologists. Its content is highly relevant, not only for researchers and students of sport psychology, but also for practitioners, such as coaches and athletes interested in the application of this exciting and evolving discipline to their particular areas. Thus, we do hope that many of the domains of sport psychology presented here will be implemented in reality by academicians and practitioners for research, teaching, consultation, and application. In this way, the link between theory and practice—which is the focus of the book—will not remain only a hypothetical one.

The Editors,

Ronnie Lidor, Ph.D.

Michael Bar-Eli, Ph.D.

Acknowledgments

Editing a book is a team effort, in which many individuals were involved and were willing to contribute. The editors would like to express their deepest appreciation for any effort and assistance given to them. More specifically, we would like to acknowledge the work done by all the reviewers, who contributed to improving the quality of the book through their fruitful comments and suggestions. The reviewers were (in alphabetical order):

Mark Anshell (U.S.A.)
Stuart Biddle (United Kingdom)
Celia H. Brackenridge (United Kingdom)
Brenda Light Bredemeier (U.S.A.)
James H. Cauraugh (U.S.A.)
P. Chelladurai (U.S.A.)
Richard L. Cox (United Kingdom)
Charmain DeFrancesco (U.S.A.)
Joan L. Duda (U.S.A.)
Naomi Fejgin (Israel)
Ema Geron (Israel)
Yuri Hanin (Finland)
Keith Henschen (U.S.A.)
Herb Marsh (Australia)
Hubert Ripoll (France)
Richard M. Ryan (U.S.A.)
Guido Schilling (Switzerland)
Robert N. Singer (U.S.A.)
Ronald E. Smith (U.S.A.)
Gloria B. Solomon (U.S.A.)
Marit Sorensen (Norway)
Jeffery J. Summers (Australia)
Gershon Tenenbaum (Australia/Israel)
Robert J. Vallerand (Canada)

The editors would like to thank Shulamit Ben-Arie for her assistance in preparing this manuscript. Her efforts in this time-consuming task are deeply appreciated. In particular, we would like to emphasize the contribution of Dinah Olswang for her effort and enthusiasm during the preparation of this book. Without her, the preparation of this book would have been impossible.

Finally, we would like to extend our appreciation to Dr. Andrew Ostrow and his staff at Fitness Information Technology, Inc., for providing us with the opportunity to produce this book. His involvement, valuable advice, and encouraging support assisted us in the completion of this project. We hope that the outcome of this book meets his expectations.

Part I

Historical Perspectives

In the past three decades, sport psychology has emerged as a distinct scientific discipline. It has been well established by researchers and practitioners that psychological as well as physiological elements contribute to the achievement of a high proficiency level in sport settings. In their work, sport psychologists attempt to explore the mental states of athletes, teams, coaches, and referees before, during, and after practice and competition. Cognitive processes, social interactions, intervention techniques, and behavioral observations are of primary interest to both researchers and practitioners in this field.

The history and development of sport psychology are areas that have been neglected in the sport and exercise sciences. To better understand the current perspectives of sport psychology, it is necessary to look at the beginning of this professional discipline. Chapter 1, entitled "The Antonelli Era of Sport Psychology: Inspiration, Improvisation, and Angst," provides the readers with an insightful look into the establishment and early stages of the International Society of Sport Psychology (ISSP) and the *International Journal of Sport Psychology* (IJSP). Both the society and the *Journal* have played a major role in the initiation of sport psychology around the world.

1

The Antonelli Era of Sport Psychology: Inspiration, Improvisation, and Angst

John H. Salmela
School of Human Kinetics
University of Ottawa, Canada

The beginning of any professional discipline, perhaps more so at the international level, is often marked by serendipity, improvisation, and opportunism. Such was the case for the field of sport psychology, which was deemed into formalized, global existence by Ferruccio Antonelli, an Italian psychiatrist. Thus, the International Society of Sport Psychology (ISSP) was created in 1965 in Rome, prior to the existence of most national societies, without having formal membership structures, and not even rudimentary guidelines to direct this field of study. Three years later, Antonelli founded the *International Journal of Sport Psychology (IJSP),* the first journal devoted only to sport psychology in the world, in a void of worldwide contributors, established editorial policies, and financial backing. Such were the pioneering efforts in early international sport psychology of one man, Antonelli, who initially shouldered considerable responsibilities single-handedly amidst considerable posturing and protest from his colleagues. The purpose of this contribution is to provide an account of these Antonelli years as reconstructed from extant documents on the organization of the ISSP.

The Inaugural Rome Congress

The academics. In 1965, over 500 participants from 40 countries attended the First International Congress of Sports *[sic]* Psychology in Rome, mainly through the efforts and considerable persuasive skills of Antonelli, in collaboration with the powerful Italian Sport Medicine Association and the Italian Olympic Committee. A call for papers was distributed worldwide without guarantees of foreign attendance. However, it seems that the announcement of this international event struck a chord with the collective spirit of individuals already working independently in psychiatry, psychology, pedagogy, and sport in various countries. Antonelli became an important catalyst by assembling noted researchers from Bulgaria (Genov, Geron), Czechoslovakia (Vanek), Romania (Epuran), the Soviet Union (Puni, Roudik), Spain (Cagigal) and the United States (Cratty, Ogilvie, Slater-Hammel).

During this inaugural meeting, Antonelli pointed out that the original idea for the ISSP was not his, but that of his friend, a fellow psychiatrist, José Ferrer Hombravella, some 4 or 5 years earlier in Barcelona. At this earlier meeting of the Fédération Internationale de Medécine Sportive (FIMS), the directorate of FIMS authorized Antonelli to pursue the unification of the specialized interests, mainly in psychiatry and sport, of individuals who were presently working in Spain, France, and Italy. Thus the inaugural Congress had a very clinical tone because many of Antonelli's colleagues in psychiatry dabbled in sport and certainly had many interesting insights. Antonelli's influence in Rome was so powerful that the Congress members were actually granted an audience with the Pope. In 1966, Antonelli published a proceedings of 1,296 pages in Italian, English, French, and German (Schilling, 1992), a landmark both in scholarship and globalism for the newly developed field of sport psychology.

The politics. On April 20 during that inaugural congress, at the business meeting chaired by Antonelli, the ISSP was founded, an event orchestrated within severe time constraints. "Now, if we start discussing the Constitution point by point, we would waste too much time to the detriment of a [session] that has to begin in about half an hour's time" (Antonelli, 1966, p. 31). Thus, the ISSP was born with Antonelli as its founding President, and the events that follow took place in less than 30 minutes!

In anticipation of continuing this academic and professional legacy, 3 years later in Washington, DC, a slate of officers was proposed for the managing council (MC), or the executive board, by Hombravella based not strictly on academic competence, but rather on geography and language skills. This preselected list of candidates included some leading academics of the time whereas others were virtually unknown, but were selected based upon their language skills and geographical origins: English (Arthur Slater-Hammel, USA), French (Henry Périe, France), German (Jose Recla, Austria), Eastern Europe (Paul Kunath, GDR), Scandinavia (A. Morgan Olsen, Norway), and the United States (Warren Johnson, USA). Hombravella added: "Finally, to coordinate all, from Italy, as the first President of the Society, Professor Antonelli" (Antonelli, 1970b, p. 3). No real discussion transpired on the selections, except for the addition of the Portuguese-speaking Athayde Ribeiro da Silva from Brazil. Antonelli had already nominated his friend Hombravella as the secretary and representative for Spanish countries. Thus, the first MC of the ISSP was formed with Professor Venerando's proclamation: "If you agree with this list, raise your hand. Whoever does not agree with this list, raise your hand. One [person in opposition]. The list is approved by the vast majority!" (Antonelli, 1970b, p. 3).

Of interest, Hombravella broke his own language rule for MC representation to the MC during this Cold War era and provided additional places on the slate for the Communist bloc with Paul Kunath and for the United States with Warren Johnson. Apparently, Antonelli also added Miroslav Vanek for the Slavic countries as an afterthought, at the end of the meeting, to appease a dissenting Eastern Europe: "It was a little bit naive, e.g., Vanek represented Slavian [sic] countries which did not exist. Only Kunath was nominated to represent East European countries. Such an ostrich policy shortly caused a heavy and long-lasting crisis in the ISSP, especially because the ISSP was in reality a European society, even though having two U.S. representatives" (Vanek, 1994, p.24). Criticisms aside, this vision, dedication, and frequent improvisation shown by Antonelli, during his stewardship from 1965–1973, single-handedly directed international sport psychology through the realization of three world congresses and the creation of its own specialized journal.

Less is known about the events leading up to the second ISSP congress in Washington, an interim period that should have been one filled with regular, structured annual meetings of the newly elected MC to create policies and provide direction for this fledgling field. Vanek (1994), however, reported that "improvisational" MCs were held in Lisbon, Barcelona, Prague, and Rome.

> The ISSP MC never met together as the original team. The agenda for "Business Meetings" were short and without discussions, while often improvisational in nature. The leadership of Antonelli, as the president of ISSP MC, was strong and decisions were deeply influenced by him.
>
> —Vanek, 1994 (p.24)

No minutes of these meetings were ever published. The formation of the ISSP was a direct precursor to the founding of the North American Society for the Psychology of Sport and Physical Activity (NASPSPA) in 1967: "The origins of NASPSPA were, in effect, the result of a bit of crisis management by the pioneers of SP in the United States, and especially by A. Slater-Hammel, the Founding President, who were rushed into Organizing the second ISSP Congress" (Salmela, 1993, p. 121), held 3 years later in Washington.

The Second Washington Congress

The academics. The Washington congress was more typical of what would be seen in North America during the 1970s with the emergence of a newly trained generation of doctoral graduates who were making their first academic strides in sport psychology. "There were really good scientists studying human movement behavior as the product of the U.S. competitive university system. They showed friendly acceptance of others, critical thinking, and high self-confidence" (Vanek, 1994, p. 25). However, the academic strength of this English-only congress later influenced the development of international sport psychology during these formative years.

Vanek (1994) reported:

> The second ISSP Congress in Washington, DC, in 1968 raised expectations for the quality of the meetings due to the high level of status of the USA. But the reality was a general shortage of everything: no simultaneous translations, a small staff, no sponsors, no celebrities. I was sorry for Arthur Slater-Hammel, the lonely man. He was expected to provide direction for this Congress. At least the professional standard of the North American papers was very high. (p. 25)

The 878-page congress proceedings of 101 contributions was totally in English and was published as an empirically, rather than clinically based reference text, in contrast to the multilingual, clinically based Rome proceedings (Schilling, 1992).

The politics. The lack of clarity in dealing with this new society was reflected in Antonelli's 1968 inaugural address at the second ISSP congress in which he referred to the ISSP as the International Sport Psychology Society. The Washington meeting was colored by tensions from the 1968 Prague Spring invasion of Czechoslovakia by the Soviet bloc army. Antonelli (1970b) also foreshadowed this crisis, which would plague the ISSP for, at least, the next decade: "I bring to you the general dismay at the absurd neo-colonialism of the Eastern countries" (p. 5). Within the MC, a new structure was extemporaneously thrown together with the reelections of Antonelli as president, Olsen and Slater-Hammel as vice presidents, Ferrer-Hombravella as secretary, and Athayde da Silva and Miroslav Vanek as members-at-large. Newly elected members were Michel Bouet (France), John Kane (Great Britain), and Peter Roudik (Soviet Union) as members, and José Cagigal (Spain), Ema Geron (Bulgaria), and Arthur Sheedy (Canada) as members-at large. Cold War political pressures on Antonelli from Soviet bloc colleagues in Bucharest who were not in attendance in Washington resulted in Paul Kunath of the GDR being "appointed" by Antonelli as a member-at-large on October 1, 1969, and in the midterm promotion of Vanek to secretary on December 7, 1970. Thus, the ineffectual and meetingless MC now had two secretaries: "Dr. Ferrer Hombravella will take care of any kind of ISSP's interests in Latin European Countries, Middle and South America; Prof. Vanek in Middle and Eastern Europe, North America and elsewhere" (Antonelli, 1970b, p. 5). This extemporaneous organization continued up to the third ISSP congress in 1973 in Madrid, a barren interim period filled with political tensions and more improvisation.

The creation of the Fédération Européenne de Psychologie des Sport et des l'Activités Corporelles (FEPSAC), the European counterpart to the ISSP, was a direct fallout of two events at the Washington meeting, and this split the newly developing field of sport psychology. First, Eric de Winter, a French physiotherapist, abruptly left Washington before the congress even began, ostensibly because congress communication was to be only in English. Vanek (1994) continues:

> He participated in the MC meeting a day prior to the Congress in Washington. Then he left and reacted by founding FEPSAC. What were the reasons behind the problematic relationship between de Winter and the ISSP? They included economic and troubles of organizations, the U.S. concept of congresses, the nature of the U.S. universities and traditional competition, and especially the pre-congress dabble in politics. (p. 25)

Second, because of Cold War tensions and the 1968 occupation of Czechoslovakia, the Soviet Union and its satellite countries did not send delegates to Washington. Therefore, on June 4 1969, "the foundation of a socialistic FEPSAC as an antipode of the capitalistic ISSP was created" in Vittel, France (Vanek,1994, p. 26). Ema Geron of Bulgaria, since emigrated to Israel, was elected president along with MC representatives from eastern bloc countries of Czechoslovakia, Poland, Romania, GDR, and the USSR, with four other Western European countries. Of some interest was the election of Hombravella as Honorary President of FEPSAC and Secretary of the rival "antipode," the ISSP. Antonelli also attended the Vittel meeting, but did not run for office.

Little has been reported about the events between 1968 and 1973, but Vanek (1994) recalled:

> My reflection of the period between the end of the '60s and '70s is influenced by the re-Sovietization of my country and an isolation of all affairs of the ISSP. There was surely some activity in the restoration of the fragile relations between the Eastern bloc countries and the free world, between ISSP and FEPSAC. (p. 26)

In 1972, the FEPSAC congress in Cologne helped fill the interim and rebuild the sport psychology activity in Europe, which was more stagnant than similar activity in North America, where congresses were held annually both in Canada and the United States since 1969.

The Third Madrid Congress

The academics. The third ISSP Congress was scheduled 5 years later in 1973 in Madrid so that it would not be in conflict with the 1972 Munich Olympics and their own scientific congress, a suggestion by the Professor José Maria Cagigal, the congress organizer. The Madrid congress was more in the mold of the event in Rome with simultaneous translation, a Latin flavor, and representation from both Eastern Europe and North America. An undisclosed number of participants were present, and the scientific exchange resulted in a three-volume publication of 1,094 pages in English, Spanish, German, and French (Schilling, 1992).

The politics. Perhaps due to the perceived lack of control of the MC members with Antonelli at the helm during the period between Washington and Madrid and exacerbated by the East-West political tensions of the Cold War, Vanek (1994) reported that during the Madrid annual general assembly, there was

> . . . a contra Antonelli "revolution". The absolute chaos could not be controlled, especially when the only formal statute was useless. Finally, based on common sense the presidential elections were improvised. My being elected President was commentated on by a Spanish colleague as a communist putsch. This was absurd, as the Congress was held in Madrid and there was but a small participant group from the Eastern bloc. It was just the Antonelli's loss. (p. 26)

The Antonelli era was over after 8 turbulent years. Vanek (1994) continues:

> The situation of ISSP at that time was nebulous. There was a low image by others but a relatively heroic self-image especially of the MC members. The international tendencies and balances determined an unbelievable increase of the MCs. In Rome in 1965, there were 9 members plus one at large on the MC. In Washington, there were 9 members plus 4 at large (2 of them were not present—Kunath and Geron). In Madrid, 14 officials were on the MC, including 2 General Secretaries. The first MC meeting held in Madrid brought two important decisions. Herman Rieder accepted my proposal to work as the Secretary General. Also, Antonelli achieved to be given the position of Honorary President even though this was a very unusual protocol. In order to overcome the many

ISSP difficulties, there was only one way: hard work and modesty. (pp. 26–7)

Antonelli had successfully sowed the seeds for international sport psychology during a difficult era, and the ISSP stood on his shoulders and embarked upon a new trajectory with an Eastern European slant under Vanek's guidance.

To better understand perhaps the most significant contribution of Antonelli, let us backtrack to 1968 and the General Assembly of the congress in Washington. Antonelli (1970b) suggested that the ISSP had now 1,500 (unpaid) members from 49 countries and "expressed the need to publish a review" (p. 3). Once again this Roman psychiatrist embarked upon another mission that again underlined his passion, commitment, and single-mindedness regarding international sport psychology and his role within it.

The International Journal of Sport Psychology

The *International Journal of Sport Psychology (IJSP)*, the brainchild of Antonelli in 1970, was the first journal in the world solely dedicated to sport psychology and predated the *Journal of Sport Psychology* by 9 years. Although the *IJSP* has suffered the criticism of scholars because of publication delays, uneven quality of submissions, and a plethora of typographical errors, its role in the development of sport psychology worldwide cannot be denied. As a former editor of the *IJSP* with Alberto Cei from 1988–1995, I directly felt the stings of ire regarding the *IJSP*. However, a closer analysis of the journal's functions in these early years provides a much kinder picture of what was accomplished by Antonelli's foresight and the *IJSP*'s very existence.

The *IJSP* was initially meant to be published in Norway with A. Morgan Olsen as head of the editorial board (EB), but a contract with the publisher was not honored. Antonelli then asked his bridge partner and friend, Luigi Pozzi, to add the *IJSP* to his list of European medical publications. In 1970, he was "at last able to deliver this sweat-stained first issue to the press" (Antonelli, 1970a, p. 4). It was indeed a historic event, because no unifying, international vehicle in sport psychology existed at that time.

Indeed, the single-minded determination of Antonelli in creating this enterprise was idealistically carried out without any financial guarantees of its success:

In promising this new Review, I feel a little ashamed. For $10 a year I am able to offer only two small unpretentious issues. I must therefore reveal another fact. When the ISSP subscription was free, I received 1,500 applications for memberships. When I asked $10 a year, not for the ISSP, which has no expenses and therefore needs no money, but for the membership subscription, only 10% replied by sending the due fee. I found a very understanding publisher, who disclaimed all profit, and I therefore publicly and most heartily thank; but the press and postal costs are enormous. With the taking so far received I am able to print and dispatch the first issue. And I am sending it to all 1,500 members. Now that it has been launched, the Review will keep going. I shall keep it going, if need be, at my own expense. (Antonelli, 1970a, p. 4)

The intentions of Antonelli were indeed heroic. Antonelli, a committee of one, was perhaps the best solution for directing the development of this fledgling enterprise.

On paper, there was an EB composed of Antonelli as chief-editor; eight associate editors, who with the exception of Bryant J. Cratty, four of whom were members of the basically nonfunctional MC of the ISSP. In addition, there were 40 national correspondents, who were probably individuals who had corresponded with Antonelli or whom he had met at various sport psychology functions. To the best of my knowledge, after having been an EB member from 1986–87, no submissions were ever reviewed by the EB. The composition of the EB was but a Potemkin village created by Antonelli to assuage the egos of these international figureheads, most of whom never had academic impact in the field. The academic content of the *IJSP* from 1970–73 was very thin and probably was not of sufficient volume to require the review process, except by Antonelli. In 1987, when I was nominated to coedit the *IJSP* with Cei, some of the listed members of the EB had been deceased for a number of years! This fact spurred Antonelli to allow us to rotate off the EB members whom Antonelli did not wish to offend and select active, young scholars.

Contents of the IJSP

The *IJSP* was launched in 1970, with two volumes of about 80 pages each. The title on the cover read *International Journal of Sport Psychology* and underneath, "Official Journal of the International Society of Sports [*sic*] Psychology". This discrepancy on the cover between the use of sport and sports remained until the October-December 1990 issue. In 1987, the descriptor changed to "An Official Journal," when the ISSP also claimed *The Sport Psychologist* as another ISSP journal, a status that discontinued in 1995. Within the orange cover rectangle appeared the Greek character *psi*, the symbol for psychology, over the official rings of the International Olympic Committee (IOC). This practice ended in 1990 when the legal department of the IOC warned the ISSP that the use of this logo was a copyright infringement.

The first issue of the *IJSP* began with an editorial by Antonelli in which the evolution of the ISSP and the genesis of the *IJSP* were outlined. The first published article was by William P. Morgan entitled "Pre-Match Anxiety in a Group of College Wrestlers." A total of three empirical articles, one opinion piece, and one overview made up the original scholarly content of the first issue. In the second issue, there was but one empirical article and two overviews. Thus, in the 1970 volume, only 34% of the total pages were devoted to empirical work and 18% to overviews. To put these figures into perspective, the 1995 volume of the *IJSP* had 79% of original articles, 5% of professional matters, and 15% of overviews.

One interesting feature that continued in this first issue of the *IJSP,* presumably because of a shortage of submissions, was the creation of an "Abstracts" (11%) rubric. Sport psychology article résumés were published in this section from either American or European sport science journals or from recent sport psychology congresses. Perhaps the most important section of the journal for the international development of sport psychology was the last part of each issue, which included "Book Reviews," "Meetings," "Forthcoming Events," and "News" (37%). It was here that Antonelli provided the precursor to the "electronic highway" for sport psychology in the 1970s. Everything that was printable in sport psychology from 19 countries around the world appeared in this section in the first issue of the *IJSP.* The professional impact of the *IJSP* was enormous, and the global direction of the field was single-handedly orchestrated by Antonelli from 1970–73, in a unique fashion for an academic journal (Figure 1.1).

The prevailing, negative North American view of the *IJSP* was fueled by what Vanek referred to as the self-confidence of Americans, which characterized the early scholars of this burgeoning field, who were equipped with new research tools and ideas. In defense of the *IJSP* beyond this North American

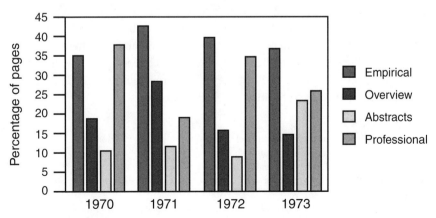

Figure 1.1. Distribution of content areas in the *IJSP* (1970–73).

perspective was evidence of the facilitation of professional development in sport psychology throughout the world by means of these professional rubrics in the *IJSP* and of Antonelli's vision, selflessness, and dedication. Over this 4-year period, 39 empirical or overview articles were published from authors from 15 countries, 19 of whom were from North America.

There was a North American bias in research contributions, due mainly from publication in the English language. But, from the start, there were résumés for each article in French in 1970–72, in Spanish in the first number of 1973, and in French, Spanish, and German when the *IJSP* went to three issues in 1973. The *IJSP* reported on activities in sport psychology from 25 different societies, many of which, including NASPSPA, were a direct result of Antonelli's initiatives with the 1965 Rome congress. In the second 1973 issue, Antonelli published a 27-page volume that perhaps was his most important. In this issue, which had *no* original contributions, there was an article written in French by Mihai Epuran of Romania on "Terminology in Sport Psychology" with 25 collaborators from six European countries, who attempted to demystify current jargon in the field. There was also a section in the "News" section, where Antonelli listed the addresses of collaborators from 57 countries, from which 18 national societies were created as the result of the ISSP, 12 of which were authentic national entities, rather than phantom organizations (Salmela, 1993).

The *IJSP*, from its earliest years, was the major force in the world in the development of sport psychology. Now under the independent editorial control of the ISSP MC, the quality and regularity of its production have improved considerably, while maintaining its broad international and multilingual perspectives. However, despite its warts, the earliest years of the *IJSP* may still have been the finest and the most effective tool during this period of growth in international sport psychology. The ISSP has also reached maturity with an effective, functioning MC that has effectively brought change to the field through initiatives with a global impact, such as publishing position statements, effectively coordinating the *IJSP*, and organizing congresses with speakers on the cutting-edge field. However, the pioneering initiatives of Ferruccio Antonelli should not be lost during this era when research and professional practice appears to be attaining full stride.

References

Antonelli, F. (1966). Seduta organizzativa del comitato scientifico. In F. Antonelli (Ed.), *Psicologia dello sport*. Rome: Federazione Medico-sportiva Italiana.

Antonelli, F. (1970a). Editorial. *International Journal of Sport Psychology, 1,* 3–5.

Antonelli, F. (1970b). Opening address. In G. S. Kenyon, & T. M. Grogg (Eds.), *Contemporary psychology of sport* (pp. 3–6). Washington, DC: Athletic Institute.

Salmela, J.H. (1993). *The world sport psychology sourcebook.* Champaign, IL: Human Kinetics.

Schilling, G. (1992). State-of-the-art review of sport psychology. *Sport Science Review,1,* 1–12.

Vanek, M. (1994). Reflections on the inception, development, and perspectives of ISSP's image and self-image. In S. Serpa, J. Alves, & V. Pataco (Eds.), *International perspectives on sport and exercise psychology* (pp. 21–34) Morgantown, WV: Fitness Information Technology.

Part II

❖

Basic Concepts
of
Sport Psychology

The science of sport psychology has advanced rapidly in the past few decades, during which time its basic fundamentals have been conceptualized, structured, and revised. Every scientific domain is based upon philosophical, theoretical, and methodological concepts. Many of these are adapted from other disciplines, but they are unique to the domain itself. This observation also applies to the area of sport psychology. Major concepts have been borrowed from other disciplines such as general psychology, philosophy, and research methodology. However, specific concepts have been developed within the body of knowledge of sport psychology that reflect various areas of interest unique to this professional discipline.

The three chapters included in Part II of this book provide us with an in-depth look at some basic concepts of sport psychology: Chapter 2, entitled "The Sport Psychologist as Scientist-Practitioner: Reciprocal Relations Linking Theory, Research, and Intervention," explores ways in which theory development, research, and applied interventions can reinforce one another in order to produce a discipline that meets high standards of scientific and social accountability.

Chapter 3, entitled "Rationality in Sport: A Psychophilosophical Approach," discusses some of the philosophical bases of rationality, both in general and specifically in the domain of sport. In addition, an attempt is made to demonstrate some of the consequences for sport psychology.

Chapter 4, entitled "Moving With the Times: Keeping Up With Trends in Statistical Analysis and Research Design," presents a review of current major controversies in statistics and measurement, including their potential implications for research in sport psychology.

2

The Sport Psychologist as Scientist-Practitioner: Reciprocal Relations Linking Theory, Research, and Intervention

Ronald E. Smith
University of Washington
Seattle, Washington, USA

The theme of the ninth World Congress of Sport Psychology, "Linking Theory and Practice," captures several important themes in contemporary sport psychology. One is its interdisciplinary nature, which encourages interaction among sport scientists, sports medicine professionals, and psychologists. My own activities as a sport psychologist have been enriched in many ways by these interactions, and I have learned a great deal from my sport science and sports medicine colleagues.

A second hallmark of our discipline is the opportunity to forge linkages between scientific and practical endeavors. As a person whose own training in clinical psychology was based on the so-called scientist-practitioner model, I have long favored this model as a means of advancing both the frontiers of knowledge and the contributions of sport psychology to human betterment (Smith, 1989a). The present chapter focuses this second aspect of our field and explores some ways in which theory development and testing, research, and applied interventions can mutually reinforce one another and help produce a discipline that meets high standards of scientific and social accountability.

An Integrative Working Model

A distinction is sometimes made between basic and applied science. Basic science is usually defined as the development of theories and the discovery of knowledge for its own sake, whereas applied science involves the applications of knowledge derived from basic science for the solution of practical problems. This dichotomy is convenient from a conceptual perspective, but the distinction blurs when we consider relations among theory development and testing, empirical research, and interventions designed to have practical impact. These relations do not simply involve a one-way causal path from knowledge or theory to application. Instead, they are more likely to involve the kinds of interactions shown in Figure 2.1. This model shows reciprocal interactions between theory, research, and interventions, meaning that each of the three facets has a causal impact on the others and is, in turn, influenced by them.

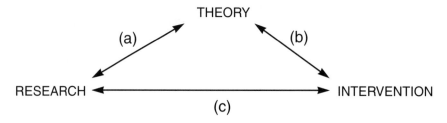

Figure 2.1. Reciprocal relations involving theory, research, and interventions in sport psychology.

To illustrate the implications of the reciprocal influence model, let us consider the topic of anxiety, one that continues to receive considerable scientific and applied attention in sport psychology throughout the world (Hackfort & Spielberger, 1989). Sport psychologists have long been interested in understanding anxiety, its antecedents and consequences, the mechanisms whereby it affects sport behavior, and ways of minimizing its negative effects on performance, enjoyment of competition, and physical well-being, and reliable means for measuring it (e.g., Martens, Vealey, & Burton, 1990; Scanlan, 1996; Smith, Smoll, & Schutz, 1990; Spielberger, 1989). We now have theoretical models of both trait and state anxiety that deepen our understanding and help guide our research. However, our theories are themselves influenced by the results of our research (which, hopefully, help us to build better theories). Thus, Link A is a reciprocal one, with theory and research affecting one another. Our theories also affect the anxiety reduction interventions we develop (e.g., Smith, 1989b), but the success of these interventions, in turn, affect theory development, for the success of these interventions reflect in part on the adequacy of our theory. That is, if our theory predicts that a particular intervention will work and it does not, either the theory needs to be revised or the intervention was not carried out correctly. Thus, Link B is also reciprocal. Finally, Link C, connecting intervention and research, is a reciprocal one. Our research provides leads for intervention, and sound outcome research allows us to assess the efficacy of the interventions and, perhaps, to identify which aspects of the intervention are responsible for its success. In turn, the nature of the intervention dictates the outcome variables that we focus on and the way the evaluation is conducted.

This model not only provides a useful schema for conceptualizing scientific and applied aspects of sport psychology, but attending to the three basic linkages also helps to ensure that our conceptual frameworks, research, and applied activities will support one another and advance our field as a scientific and applied discipline. Where interventions are concerned, adherence to the model helps ensure that they are based on firm theoretical and research foundations and that they will be evaluated in a manner that conforms to standards of scientific accountability.

I shall now relate the working model to two lines of theory development, research, and intervention to illustrate the linkages in more concrete terms. The first project involves the study of coaching behaviors and how they affect young athletes, whereas the second involves psychosocial factors that influence athletic injuries.

Coaching Behaviors and Self-Esteem

As a clinical psychologist who specialized in working with children and as a former playground and social center director who had worked his way through college by doing a lot of coaching, it is probably not surprising that I became interested in studying the effects of coaching behaviors on young athletes. In fact, the work that developed from this interest marked the beginning of my professional identity as a sport psychologist. I was fortunate to find a colleague with similar interests in the University of Washington's Kinesiology Department, and Frank Smoll and I have collaborated for more than 25 years.

The major thrust of our collaborative work has been (a) to discover how specific coaching styles affect children's reactions to their athletic experience and (b) to use this information to develop an intervention program for training coaches in how to create a positive psychosocial environment that would enhance sport outcomes. This work, described in greater detail elsewhere (Smith & Smoll, 1996), was guided by a theoretical model that specified linkages among coaching behaviors, athletes' perceptions of those behaviors, and athletes' evaluative reactions to the coaching behaviors as experienced. The model also identified situational as well as coach and individual difference factors in coaches and athletes that were expected to affect the behaviors, perceptions, and evaluative reactions, as well as the linkages among them (Smoll & Smith, 1989). This conceptual model is shown in Figure 2.2.

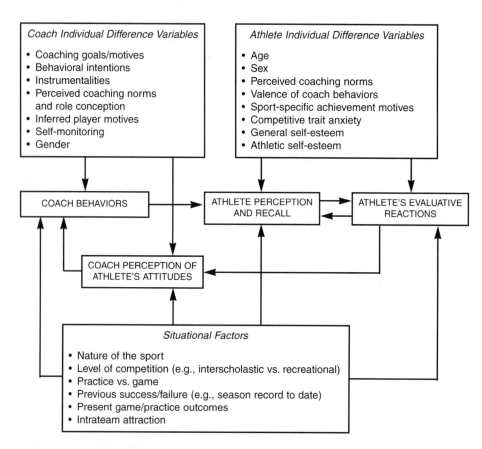

Figure 2.2. A theoretical model of coaching behaviors, their antecedents, and their effects on athletes, with hypothesized relations among situational and individual difference variables that are thought to influence the base relations.

The model, which was itself influenced by previous leadership and sport research, was important to us because it guided our methods for identifying and measuring the variables we thought to be important. For example, we developed a behavioral assessment instrument known as the Coaching Behavior

Assessment System (CBAS) to directly observe and code the overt coaching behaviors (Smith, Smoll, & Hunt, 1977), as well as self-report instruments to measure the athletes' perceptions of the coaching behaviors and their evaluative reactions to the coach, the sport experience, and themselves (Smith, Smoll, & Curtis, 1978). In accordance with the model, we have sought to determine how observed coaching behaviors, athletes' perception and recall of the coach's behaviors, and player attitudes are interrelated. We have also explored the manner in which player and coach individual difference variables might serve as moderator variables and influence the basic behavior-attitude relations. I will focus on one of those variables, namely, the athlete's level of self-esteem, to illustrate an important linkage between theory, research, and intervention.

Self-Esteem and Attraction: Self-Verification or Self-Enhancement?

The way in which personal characteristics affect responses to other people has long been a topic of interest in psychology. Of the personality variables that have been studied in this regard, self-esteem has received the greatest amount of theoretical and empirical attention (Swann, 1985; Wylie, 1979). Much of the research concerned with the influence of self-esteem on reactions to others has been inspired by consistency theories (e.g., Lecky, 1945; Rogers, 1951), which assert that people are most comfortable with personally relevant information that is consistent with their self-concept. Presumably such information is more predictable, familiar, and uncertainty reducing, and it produces less dissonance than does inconsistent information (Swann, Griffin, Predmore, & Gaines, 1987). It serves to reinforce the correctness of one's self-concept, a process that is known as self-verification. Consistency models that stress the importance of self-verification thus lead to the prediction that people will react most positively to others who treat them in a manner that is consistent with their self-concept.

An alternative model, self-enhancement theory (Tesser & Campbell, 1983), asserts that people are primarily motivated not by consistency needs, but by a general desire to achieve and maintain positive self-regard. Self-enhancement needs are thought to be especially strong in those people having low self-esteem because such people are most in need of positive self-relevant experiences. Enhancement models, like consistency theories, thus address the issue of how self-esteem is related to people's responses to others who provide them with evaluative feedback. However, as Swann (1996) and Shrauger (1975) have noted, the two models lead to very different predictions concerning the reactions that people low in self-esteem will have to supportive vs.

unsupportive others. When a person low in self-esteem is treated well, consistency and self-enhancement influences are presumably pitted against one another. Consistency theories lead to the prediction that low self-esteem individuals will respond more positively to people who treat them poorly than to those who treat them well because unsupportive acts from others are consistent with their poor opinion of themselves and therefore satisfy the need for self-verification. Indeed, Rogers (1951) has asserted that people with poor self-concepts will actually deny or distort positive feedback so as to maintain congruence between self and experience. In contrast with the prediction derived with consistency theory, the self-enhancement model predicts that low self-esteem people should particularly like others who respond positively to them because positive interpersonal feedback helps satisfy their desire for an enhanced self-view (Shrauger, 1975; Swann, 1996).

Consistency and enhancement models are thus pitted against one another in studies concerned with the effects of positive and negative interpersonal feedback on subsequent evaluative responses of people who vary in self-esteem. The crucial condition in such studies is that in which participants low in self-esteem are given positive feedback. The results of such studies, though not totally consistent, have tended to favor the enhancement model, particularly when the evaluative responses have an affective component, such as degree of liking for the person who gave the positive or negative feedback (Shrauger, 1975; Swann et al., 1987; Wylie, 1979). For example, Dittes (1959) selected college students who were low, moderate, and high on a global self-esteem scale and assigned them to experimental conditions in which they received feedback that their acceptance by a group was either well below average, average, or far above average. Consistent with the notion that low self-esteem people have especially strong self-enhancement needs that negate consistency influences, Dittes found that although all self-esteem groups responded most positively to the group in the high-acceptance condition, the difference in attraction responses as a function of degree of acceptance was especially large for the low self-esteem participants. Such people were strongly attracted to the group that had provided positive feedback and exhibited negative reactions to the group that had provided negative feedback, a pattern of results that was consistent with self-enhancement needs. A strict consistency model would predict that low self-esteem people would react negatively to feedback that was inconsistent with their unfavorable self-image.

Although many studies have been performed to test the relative influence of consistency and self-enhancement tendencies, most of them were performed under laboratory conditions involving single interactions between people who were probably not very important to one another and, in many instances, never even met face to face. However, the self-theories that stimulated this line of research are most concerned with longer-term interactions with others whose reactions are important to the individual. Moreover, most of the research has involved college samples, and we know relatively little about how consistency and self-enhancement processes operate in other age-groups, such as children.

The youth sport setting is one that offers some significant advantages for approaching this theoretical issue because young athletes interact within a restricted setting and over an extended period of time with an adult coach who is often an important figure in their lives. Moreover, these coach-athlete interactions occur during a developmental period when self-confirmation and social evaluation are thought to be particularly important to the child's self-esteem (Rosenberg, 1979; Scanlan, 1996). To approach this issue within the youth sport setting, we assessed the attitudes of young athletes toward coaches who differed in their tendency to exhibit supportive behaviors.

The study involved 51 Little League baseball teams whose coaches were observed and their behaviors coded using the Coaching Behaviors Assessment System (CBAS; Smith et al., 1977). The CBAS contains 12 behavioral categories developed through content analysis of verbal descriptions of observed coaching behaviors. Factor analyses of the 12 categories in the CBAS system have consistently yielded four factors that we have labeled Activity Level, Supportiveness, Punitiveness, and Instructiveness, respectively. The Supportiveness factor accounts for about 20% of the total behavioral variance of coaches. Coaches high on the Supportiveness dimension provide high levels of positive feedback for desirable behaviors and effort, and they tend to respond to mistakes with support and encouragement rather than with punitive responses.

During the course of the season, the coaches were observed during a total of 202 complete games. These observations yielded an average of more than 1,100 coded behaviors per coach, and a factor analysis of the observed behaviors yielded the usual supportiveness factor. Factor scores on Supportiveness were then generated for each of the coaches. At the end of the season, 542 of the children who had played for the 51 coaches were interviewed and administered questionnaires in their homes by trained interviewers. Among the variables assessed were attitudes toward the coach they had played for and a measure of general self-esteem (Smith & Smoll, 1990).

The results of the study are shown in Figure 2.3, which shows the attraction responses of children differing in level of self-esteem to coaches who fell either one standard deviation above or one standard deviation below the mean on the Supportiveness dimension. The results clearly favor predictions derived from the self-enhancement model. In line with the self-enhancement assumption

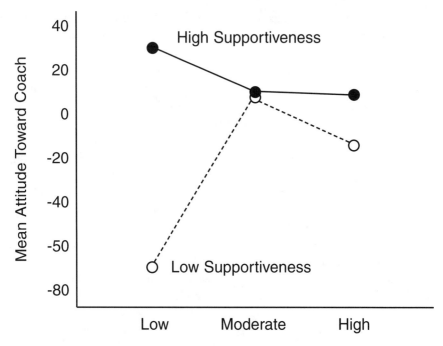

Figure 2.3. Mean attraction factor scores of children having low, moderate, and high self-esteem scores toward coaches who were high or low on the Supportiveness factor.

that people low in self-esteem are especially responsive to variations in evaluative feedback from others, the attraction responses of the low self-esteem children were most strongly influenced by differences in coaches' supportiveness. Low self-esteem children responded most positively to highly supportive coaches and most negatively to those who were low in supportive behaviors. Indeed, our results almost directly paralleled those obtained by Dittes (1959) in his laboratory experiment with college students, indicating an impressive consistency of this self-enhancement pattern across different settings and age-groups.

    The practical implications of this finding may be quite important, for it appears that variations in supportive coaching behaviors may have the greatest impact on children who are low in self-esteem. If this is indeed the case, then it might be possible to enhance the self-esteem of low self-esteem children by training coaches to create a supportive environment in which such children receive plenty of encouragement and positive feedback. In terms of our working model, we now see how theory and research results suggest an intervention.

Coach Effectiveness Training: Increasing Self-Esteem

In the second phase of the research, the results from the observational study formed the basis for a cognitive-behavioral intervention program designed to train coaches to provide a more positive and socially supportive athletic environment for their young athletes (Smith & Smoll, 1996; Smith et al., 1979). Our theoretical model as well as the results of the observational study led us to hypothesize that if coaches could be trained to create a sport environment in which children feel accepted and supported, then we might expect that children would respond more positively to the coach, their teammates, and their sport experience. Perhaps most important, we might also find an increase in general self-esteem, especially among children who are low in self-esteem prior to playing for the coaches.

To test these hypotheses, we randomly assigned youth baseball coaches to an experimental (training) or to a no-treatment control group. During the preseason intervention program, which we called Coach Effectiveness Training, behavioral guidelines derived from the initial research were presented and modeled by the trainers. In addition to the information-modeling portion of the program, behavioral feedback and self-monitoring procedures were employed in an attempt to increase the coaches' self-awareness of their behaviors and to encourage them to comply with the behavioral guidelines. Behavioral feedback took the form of profiles based on 400 to 500 behaviors coded during early-season games, and self-monitoring of key target behaviors involving supportiveness was carried out by coaches after each of 10 games during the season.

To assess the effects of the experimental program, CBAS data were collected throughout the season, and behavioral profiles were generated for each coach. Outcome measures were obtained from the children after the season in individual data-collection sessions in their homes. On both behavioral and player perception measures, the trained coaches differed from the controls in a manner consistent with the coaching guidelines. The trained coaches gave more reinforcement in response to good performance and effort, and they responded to mistakes with more encouragement and technical instruction and with fewer punitive responses. These behavioral differences were, in turn, reflected in their players' attitudes. Although the average won-lost percentages of the two groups of coaches did not differ, the trained coaches were better liked and were rated as better teachers. Additionally, players on their teams liked one another more and enjoyed their sport experience more. In a word, they had more fun. These results are thought to reflect the more socially supportive environment created by the trained coaches. Perhaps most encouraging was the fact that children who played for the trained coaches exhibited a significant increase in general self-esteem as compared with scores obtained a year earlier, whereas those who played for the untrained coaches showed no significant change (Smith et al., 1979). In a later study focused primarily on low self-esteem children, we found that these children showed a significant increase in self-esteem if they played for trained coaches, but not if they played for untrained coaches (Smoll, Smith, Barnett, & Everett, 1993). Thus, the outcome research provides support not only for the efficacy of the Coach Effectiveness Training intervention, but also for the broader theoretical model that was in part inspired by the self-enhancement theory of self-esteem. We thus see in this example how theory, research, and intervention can mutually influence one another.

Although we formulated the coaching behavior model two decades ago, we feel that we have barely scratched the surface in terms of testing it. An initial attempt to test the hypothesis that athletes' perceptions mediate relations between coaching behaviors and athletes' evaluative reactions to the coach provided some supportive evidence (Smoll, Smith, & Hunt, 1978), but the analysis was done using a regression methodology that is quite unsophisticated by today's structural equation modeling standards. The latter approach would make it possible to test the hypothesized causal links in a more powerful and systematic manner. Likewise, although current results indicate that the Coach Effectiveness Training intervention produces a range of positive outcomes, a number of important research questions remain. For example, dismantling studies are needed to assess the relative contributions of the various components of the training program, which included didactic instruction, modeling and role-playing of desired behaviors, training in self-monitoring of coaching behaviors, and behavioral feedback. Such research could help to establish the necessary and sufficient components for an effective program and could facilitate the development of improved training programs. Moreover, such research can address basic issues of behavior change in a nonclinical population in the same manner that more traditional behavior therapy research does with clinical populations.

Let us now turn to a second example of sport-related research, this one addressing the role of psychosocial factors in athletic injuries in adolescents. In this project, as in the coaching research, we are proceeding in a two-stage sequence in which theory and basic research serve as the basis for intervention.

Psychosocial Factors and Athletic Injuries

Health psychology is one of the most active areas of theory development, research, and intervention within contemporary psychology. Within sport psychology a converging area of interest is the role of psychological factors in athletic injuries and in the injury rehabilitation process. From a basic research perspective, the athletic environment offers advantages to investigators interested in the study of accidents and injuries. First, injuries occur with high frequency. Epidemiological studies indicate that in the United States alone, 3–5 million athletic injuries occur each year (Kraus & Conroy, 1984), with injury rates approaching 50–70% in some collision sports like football (Garrick & Requa, 1978). Moreover, such injuries frequently occur within restricted athletic settings where they can be observed, and the injuries and their rehabilitation are often monitored by athletic trainers and team physicians who can provide research data. Finally, the athletes are readily accessible for psychological measurement and intervention purposes.

Although many of the causal factors in athletic injuries are primarily physical or biomechanical in nature, there is mounting evidence that psychosocial factors may also contribute to injury risk. Among the factors that may be involved are stressful life events (Bramwell, Masuda, Wagner, & Holmes, 1975); personality variables, such as anxiety, locus of control, self-esteem, and sensation seeking (Bergandi, 1985); and deficits in psychosocial assets, such as psychological coping skills and social support (Hardy, Richman, & Rosenfeld, 1991; Williams, Tonymon, & Wadsworth, 1986). Andersen and Williams (1988) have advanced a conceptual model that highlights a number of hypothesized psychosocial variables, and this model has stimulated considerable research over the past decade.

Of the psychosocial factors studied to date, life change has received the greatest amount of empirical attention. In an early study performed at the University of Washington, Bramwell, Masuda, Wagner, and Holmes (1975) modified the Social Readjustment Rating Scale (Holmes & Rahe, 1967) and added items relevant to the athletic environment (e.g., "Problems with the coach," "Significant athletic accomplishments"). Using life-change units as the predictor variable in a prospective study of college football players, Bramwell et al. found injury rates of 30%, 50%, and 73%, respectively, in college football players who reported low, moderate, and high levels of life change over the previous year. Using the same life-change measure, Cryan and Alles (1983) reported similarly impressive differences in injury rates between groups of football players who differed in life change units. In contrast, however, later prospective studies of life change and athletic injuries using improved life-event measures that distinguish between positive and negative events have yielded weak and inconsistent results (Passer & Seese, 1983; Williams et al., 1986).

The Role of Moderator Variables

The inconsistent pattern of results obtained in studies of life events and athletic injuries suggests the possibility that other variables may affect the relation between life change and injuries. One of the most consistent findings within the life-stress literature is the variability in well-being that people exhibit in response to stressful life events. Constructs like vulnerability and resiliency reflect attempts to identify social, situational, and individual difference variables that increase or decrease the likelihood that people will exhibit negative reactions to stressful events (Garmezy, 1981; Kessler & McLeod, 1984). Research on vulnerability and resiliency factors was stimulated in part by low and inconsistent relations between life events and outcome measures. Although statistically significant relations between negative life events and self-report measures of physical and psychological well-being have frequently been reported, seldom has more than 10 to 15% of the outcome variance been accounted for in studies using prospective designs. When objective outcome measures of physical well-being have been used, thereby eliminating the potential role of self-report biases, the amount of variance accounted for has often shrunk to 1 to 5% (Rabkin & Streuning, 1976; Schroeder & Costa, 1984).

The inconsistent pattern of results obtained in studies of life events and athletic injuries suggests the possibility that, as in the case of other medical and psychological outcomes, certain moderator variables may influence the relation between life events and injury vulnerability. Based on prevailing theories of stress and coping (e.g., Garmezy, 1981; Lazarus & Folkman, 1984) and research results (e.g., Rosenbaum & Ben-Ari, 1985; Sarason, Sarason, Potter, & Antoni, 1985), we might expect that psychosocial assets, such as social support and coping skills, would influence the extent to which athletes are affected by stressful life events. In particular, we were interested in the possibility that these two classes of psychosocial assets might operate in combination with one another. Elsewhere, we have suggested that the term *conjunctive moderation* be used to describe instances in which two or more moderator variables must combine in a particular pattern in order to produce an optimal moderator effect (Smith, Smoll, & Ptacek, 1990). In the present instance, evidence that coping skills and social support operate in a conjunctive manner requires that some combination of these variables (most logically, low levels of both) result in a notable increment in the amount of injury variance accounted for by life-event scores over that accounted for when either moderator is considered alone. This approach thus involves searching for interactions among moderator variables themselves in terms of how they affect relations between other classes of variables.

To study the potential effects of life events, social support, and coping skills on athletic injuries, we conducted a prospective study that involved 13 Seattle-area high schools and a total of 41 teams in the sports of basketball, wrestling, and gymnastics. Within a prospective research design, the athletes completed a series of questionnaires prior to the beginning of the sport season. Recent life events were assessed by means of a modified version of the Adolescent Perceived Events Scale (Compas, Davis, Forsythe, & Wagner, 1987) that allowed us to measure positive and negative life events of a minor or major nature as perceived by the athletes. The athletes also completed a measure of the amount and quality of social support available to them from 20 different individuals, such as parents, coach, teachers, best friend, and from groups, such as their teammates and clubs or religious groups to which they belonged. Self-perceived adequacy of coping skills was assessed by means of a preliminary form of the Athletic Coping Skills Inventory (Smith, Schutz, Smoll, & Ptacek, 1995). This scale is designed to measure a range of general coping skills within a sport context, including the ability to control arousal and to concentrate and think clearly under stress, the tendency to set specific goals and engage in problem-solving strategies, and the ability to relate effectively to authority figures and to profit from corrective feedback. Finally in order to obtain a measure of injury independent of the subject's retrospective self-report, the coaches of the 41 teams served as paid research assistants for the project and provided daily injury data over the course of the sport season. The total number of days of nonparticipation because of injury over the course of the season served as the injury measure.

How well did life stress predict later injuries? As in a number of other studies, virtually no predictive relation was found. Correlations between the various classes of preseason life events and the injury time loss measure yielded no significant relations. Indeed, none of the correlations between positive and negative events of a major and minor nature exceeded .10 for the total sample of athletes.

Again, however, our model suggested that social support and/or coping skills might influence the stress-injury base relation. In a series of moderator variable analyses, we then assessed the role of differences in social support and coping skills, both singly and in combination with one another, on the relations between the life-event scores and subsequent injury. Although social support and coping skills were themselves unrelated to injuries, they combined to exert a strong effect on the relation between major negative events and injuries.

Social support considered alone did not exert a significant moderator effect. Coping skills fared somewhat better; the correlation between negative life events and subsequent injury was significant for athletes who reported low levels of coping skills, whereas no relation existed for athletes who fell within the upper third of the coping skills distribution. However, the most noteworthy result occurred when possible conjunctive moderator effects of social support *and* coping skills were assessed. Here, our results provided strong support for a conjunctive moderator influence. Consistent with our hypothesis, athletes low in both psychosocial assets exhibited the strongest correlation between major negative life events and subsequent injuries. Among athletes who fell in the lower quartiles of both the social support and coping skills distributions, a correlation of +.55 was found between the number of major negative life events they reported prior to the season and the amount of subsequent time loss during the season due to injury. In this group, therefore, 30% of the injury variance was accounted for by differences in life stress. For the other three combinations of social support and coping skills, none of the correlations approached significance.

Our results thus identified a subgroup of athletes that appears quite vulnerable to the impact of major negative life events. It appears that only athletes who are low in both classes of psychosocial assets are vulnerable to the impact of negative life events. When this group of athletes experiences a high number of stressful life events, their risk of injury increases substantially. The amount of injury variance accounted for by differences in life stress within this group far exceeds the 1–5% typically accounted for by life-events measures in other prospective studies involving objective well-being measures. The result is all the more striking in that injuries would appear less likely to be influenced by psychological stress than would many illnesses that are not dependent upon the physical/biomechanical factors that undoubtedly play a central role in injuries.

The mechanism whereby stressful events might increase vulnerability to injury is unknown, but two hypotheses have been advanced. One hypothesis is that stress disrupts attentional processes and concentration, resulting in poorer vigilance to cues signaling physical danger (Andersen & Williams, 1988). A second hypothesis is that stress produces physiological arousal that increases muscular tension and reduces motor coordination and fluidity of movement, thereby increasing risk of injuries (Nideffer, 1983). In relation to these proposed mechanisms, it is worth noting that our coping-skills measure contains items that assess the ability to concentrate and avoid distracting thoughts, as well as the ability to control arousal through relaxation and self-instructions. Athletes who lack these psychological skills could be more vulnerable to cognitive and/or physiological mechanisms that increase injury risk. Low levels of perceived social support could serve to increase the threat value of negative life events and their actual or anticipated consequences, thereby increasing both preoccupation and arousal. Whatever the mechanisms involved in the life event-injury relation, our results suggest that only events appraised as major negative ones increased the injury vulnerability of athletes low in these psychosocial assets.

Interest in person-situation interactions has stimulated renewed attempts to identify moderator variables and to study their influence. Seldom, however, have such analyses proceeded beyond the study of a single moderator at a time. Our results suggest the importance of theory-driven hypotheses in selection of conjunctive moderator possibilities because vulnerability and resiliency may involve specific patterns of moderator variables. The study of conjunctive moderators can also provide us with valuable information regarding the manner in which personality variables interact with one another to effect behavior and thereby extend the scope of our inquiry beyond the currently fashionable approach of studying personality variables one at a time. Because of the complexity of personality, we have tended to study individual dimensions, with little attention being paid to questions of how the dimensions interact to create the gestalt that constitutes personality patterns.

A Model of Psychosocial Factors and Potential Interventions

The data just presented, derived from basic research, suggest that a certain subgroup of athletes—those low in both social support and psychological coping skills—may be at increased risk for injury if they have experienced recent major stressors. However, these data also showed that if athletes were high in either perceived social support or psychological coping skills, the positive relation between stress and injury found in the low coping skills/low social support group disappeared. Thus, where resiliency is concerned, we are not dealing with a conjunctive effect of social support and coping skills, but rather a disjunctive one. That is, adequate levels of *either one* of these variables appears to render the athlete resilient to the impact of stressors. The intervention implications of this finding are fairly clear: Resiliency should be increased through either an increase in social support, an increase in coping skills, or both. A model of the variables and processes that we hypothesized as potential mediators of relations between life stress and injuries, together with the foci of two interventions intended to address these resiliency factors, is shown in Figure 2.4. In contrast to the coaching behavior research, where an intervention has already been evaluated, the final links involving the suggested interventions remain to be tested.

Let us first consider social support enhancement. Social support increases

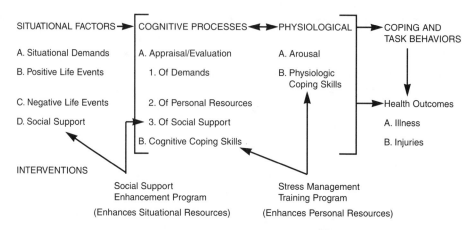

Figure 2.4. A model showing variables and processes thought to mediate relations between life stress, coping, and health outcomes, together with the potential foci of interventions designed to enhance social support and coping skills.

within the athletic environment can be brought about in a number of ways. For example, we have recently begun to view the Coach Effectiveness Training program as, in part, a social support intervention, and it has been demonstrated that the socially supportive behaviors of athletic coaches can be increased significantly through this relatively brief training program (Smoll et al., 1993). Thus, one means of enhancing social support, at least within the athletic environment, would be to train coaches to be more socially supportive. We have also suggested ways in which the Coach Effectiveness Training program could be part of a broader program of "team building," complementing procedures such as those described by Nideffer (1981) to increase team cohesion and mutual support among teammates (Smith & Smoll, 1997). Training coaches to be more supportive and enhancing team cohesion would both serve to increase the amount of social support available to the athlete and, according to our model, could help to buffer the impact of life stressors.

A second potential approach to injury prevention suggested by our research results and the theoretical model they inspired is to enhance the psychological coping skills of the athletes. A number of cognitive-behavioral programs have already been developed to teach athletes stress-management coping skills, such as relaxation, cognitive problem solving, goal setting, and meditation skills (Smith, 1980, 1989b). A major benefit of such training is that the kinds of skills taught in such programs should be highly generalizable across a variety of life situations and should therefore increase the athlete's range of *life skills.* Such skills have the potential for not only enhancing performance and adjustment within sport, but also helping sport to fulfill its stated goal of helping prepare the athlete to deal more effectively with life.

Concluding Comment

Significant opportunities exist in exercise and sport psychology for fruitful interdisciplinary activities. Many issues related to sport, exercise, and health promotion invite interactions between psychologists, exercise physiologists, biomechanics specialists, and sports medicine professionals. An excellent example of such interaction has occurred in the area of exercise and mental health. Here, psychologists have collaborated with other scientists to examine a wide spectrum of issues related to the role of exercise in health maintenance and in therapeutic programs directed at psychological problems such as depression (Morgan, 1997; Sime, 1996). As sport psychology matures as a scientific and applied field, the interchange with other disciplines and with other specialties within psychology will undoubtedly continue to grow. The resulting epistemic yield, both for a better understanding of sport and for advances in theory and research on basic psychological processes, justifies the attention that sport is now receiving from psychologists.

I have tried to emphasize the intimate relations that should exist between theory development, research, and application as the field of sport psychology continues to mature. Although I have focused on the areas of coaching behaviors and athletic injuries, many other areas of sport psychology invite similar approaches to developing and testing theoretical models, doing basic research, and developing and testing interventions. With the accelerating interest in applied sport psychology, we must not neglect the relations between theory and application. I have always felt that program evaluation is one of the best ways to test the practical value of a theory. This is possible, however, only if the intervention is explicitly enough linked to the theory so that the results of a program evaluation can be applied to the underlying theoretical propositions. Likewise, applications should be based on soundly designed basic research, and accountability demands that interventions be rigorously evaluated. In this way, the sport environment can be a natural laboratory in which our understanding of causal factors in behavior is continually tested and refined.

References

Andersen, M. B., & Williams, J. M. (1988). A model of stress and athletic injury. *Journal of Sport and Exercise Psychology, 10,* 294–306.

Bergandi, T. A. (1985). Psychological variables relating to the incidence of athletic injury: A review of the literature. *International Journal of Sport Psychology, 16,* 141–149.

Bramwell, S. T., Masuda, M., Wagner, N. N., & Holmes, T. H. (1975). Psychological factors in athletic injuries: Development and application of the Social and Athletic Readjustment Rating Scale (SARRS). *Journal of Human Stress, 1,* 6–20.

Compas, B. E., Davis, G. E., Forsythe, C. J., & Wagner, B. (1987). Assessment of major and daily stressful events during adolescence: The Adolescent Perceived Events Scale. *Journal of Consulting and Clinical Psychology, 55,* 534–541.

Cryan, P. D., & Alles, W. F. (1983). The relationship between stress and college football injuries. *Journal of Sports Medicine, 23,* 52–58.

Dittes, J. E. (1959). Attractiveness of group as a function of self-esteem and acceptance by group. *Journal of Abnormal and Social Psychology, 59,* 77–82.

Garmezy, N. (1981). Children under stress: Perspectives on antecedents and correlates of vulnerability and resistance to psychopathology. In A. I. Rabin, J. Aronoff, A. M. Barclay, & R. A. Zucker (Eds.), *Further explorations in personality* (pp. 196–269). New York: Wiley.

Garrick, J. G., & Requa, R. K. (1978). Injuries in high school sports. *Pediatrics, 61,* 465–473.

Hackfort, D., & Spielberger, C. D. (Eds.). (1989) *Anxiety in sports: An international perspective.* New York: Hemisphere.

Hardy, C. J., Richman, J. M., & Rosenfeld, L. B. (1991). The role of social support in the life stress/injury relationship. *The Sport Psychologist, 5,* 128–139.

Holmes, T. H., & Rahe, R. H. (1967). The Social Readjustment Rating Scale. *Journal of Psychosomatic Research, 11,* 213–218.

Kessler, R. C., & McLeod, J. D. (1984). Sex differences in vulnerability to undesirable life events. *American Sociological Review, 49,* 620–631.

Kraus, J. F., & Conroy, C. (1984). Mortality and morbidity from injuries in sports and recreation. *Annual Review of Public Health, 5,* 163–192.

Lazarus, R. S., & Folkman, S. (1984). *Stress, appraisal, and coping.* New York: Springer.

Lecky, P. (1945). *Self-consistency: A theory of personality.* New York: Island Press.

Martens, R., Vealey, R. S., & Burton, D. (1990). *Competitive anxiety in sport.* Champaign, IL: Human Kinetics.

Morgan, W. P (Ed.). (1997). *Physical activity and mental health.* Washington, DC: Taylor & Francis.

Nideffer, R. M. (1981). *The ethics and practice of applied sport psychology.* Ithaca, NY: Mouvement Publications.

Nideffer, R. M. (1983). The injured athlete: Psychological factors in treatment. *Orthopedic Clinics of North America, 14,* 373–385.

Passer, M. W., & Seese, M. D. (1983). Life stress and athletic injury: Examination of positive versus negative events and three moderator variables. *Journal of Human Stress, 9,* 11–16.

Rabkin, J. G., & Streuning, E. L. (1976). Life events, stress, and illness. *Science, 194,* 1013–1020.

Rogers, C. R. (1951). *Client-Centered therapy.* Boston: Houghton-Mifflin.

Rosenbaum, M., & Ben-Ari, K. (1985). Learned helplessness and learned resourcefulness: Effect of noncontingent success and failure on individuals differing in self-control skills. *Journal of Personality and Social Psychology, 48,* 198–215.

Rosenberg, M. (1979). *Conceiving the self.* New York: Basic Books.

Sarason, I. G., Sarason, B. R., Potter, E. H., & Antoni, M. H. (1985). Life events, social support, and illness. *Psychosomatic Medicine, 47,* 156–163.

Scanlan, T. K. (1996). Social evaluation and the competition process: A developmental perspective. In F. L. Smoll & R. E. Smith (Eds.), *Children and youth in sport: A biopsychosocial perspective.*(pp. 298–308). Madison, WI: Brown & Benchmark.

Schroeder, D. H., & Costa, P. H. (1984). Influence of life event stress on physical illness: Substantive effects or methodological flaws? *Journal of Personality and Social Psychology, 46,* 853–863.

Shrauger, J. S. (1975). Responses to evaluation as a function of initial self-perceptions. *Psychological Bulletin, 82,* 581–596.

Sime, W. (1996). Guidelines for clinical applications of exercise therapy for mental health. In J. L. Van Raalte & B. W. Brewer (Eds.), *Exploring sport and exercise psychology* (pp. 159–188). Washington, DC: American Psychological Association.

Smith, R. E. (1980). A cognitive-affective approach to stress management training for athletes. In C. H. Nadeau, W. R. Halliwell, K. M. Newell, & G. C. Roberts (Eds.), *Psychology of motor behavior and sport-1979* (pp. 54–72). Champaign, IL: Human Kinetics.

Smith, R. E. (1989a). Applied sport psychology in an age of accountability. *Journal of Applied Sport Psychology, 1,* 166–180.

Smith, R. E. (1989b). Athletic stress and burnout: Intervention strategies. In D. Hackfort & C. D. Spielberger (Eds.), *Anxiety in sports: An international perspective* (pp. 217–234). New York: Hemisphere.

Smith, R. E., Schutz, R. W., Smoll, F. L., & Ptacek, J. T. (1995). Development and validation of a multidimensional measure of sport-specific psychological skills: The Athletic Coping Skills Inventory-28. *Journal of Sport and Exercise Psychology, 17,* 379–398.

Smith, R.E., & Smoll, F.L. (1990). Self-esteem and children's reactions to youth sport coaching behaviors: A field study of self-enhancement processes. *Developmental Psychology, 26,* 987–993.

Smith, R. E., & Smoll, F. L. (1996). The coach as a focus of research and intervention in youth sports. In F. L. Smoll & R. E. Smith (Eds.), *Children and youth in sport: A biopsychosocial perspective* (pp. 125–141). Dubuque, IA: McGraw-Hill.

Smith, R. E., & Smoll, F. L. (1997). Coach-mediated team building in youth sports. *Journal of Applied Sport Psychology, 9,* 114–133.

Smith, R. E., Smoll, F. L., & Curtis, B. (1978). Coaching behaviors in Little League Baseball. In F. L. Smoll & R. E. Smith (Eds.), *Psychological perspectives in youth sports* (pp. 173–201). Washington, DC: Hemisphere.

Smith, R. E., Smoll, F. L., & Curtis, B. (1979). Coach Effectiveness Training: A cognitive-behavioral approach to enhancing relationship skills in youth sport coaches. *Journal of Sport Psychology, 1,* 59–75.

Smith, R. E., Smoll, F. L., & Hunt, E. B. (1977). A system for the behavioral assessment of athletic coaches. *Research Quarterly, 48,* 401–407.

Smith, R. E., Smoll, F. L., & Ptacek, J. T. (1990). Conjunctive moderator variables in vulnerability and resiliency research: Life stress, social support and coping skills, and adolescent sport injuries. *Journal of Personality and Social Psychology, 58,* 360–370.

Smith, R.E., Smoll, F.L., & Schutz, R.W. (1990). Measurement and correlates of sport-specific cognitive and somatic trait anxiety: The Sport Anxiety Scale. *Anxiety Research, 2,* 263–280.

Smoll, F.L., & Smith, R.E. (1989). Leadership behaviors in sport: A conceptual model and research paradigm. *Journal of Applied Social Psychology, 19,* 1522–1551.

Smoll, F. L., Smith, R. E., Barnett, N. P., & Everett, J. J. (1993). Enhancement of children's self-esteem through social support training for youth sport coaches. *Journal of Applied Psychology, 78,* 602–610.

Smoll, F. L., Smith, R. E., & Hunt, E. (1978). Toward a mediational model of coach-player relationships. *Research Quarterly, 49,* 528–541.

Spielberger, C. D. (1989). Stress and anxiety in sports. In D. Hackfort & C. D. Spielberger (Eds.), *Anxiety in sports: An International perspective* (pp. 3–17). New York: Hemisphere.

Swann, W. B., Jr. (1985). The self as architect of social reality. In B. Schlenker (Ed.), *The self and social life* (pp. 100–125). New York: McGraw-Hill.

Swann, W. B. (1996). *Self-traps: The elusive quest for higher self-esteem.* San Francisco: Freeman.

Swann, W. B., Jr., Griffin, J. J., Predmore, S. C., & Gaines, B. (1987). The cognitive-affective cross-fire: When self-consistency confronts self-enhancement. *Journal of Personality and Social Psychology, 52,* 881–889.

Tesser, A., & Campbell, J. (1983). Self-definition and self-evaluation maintenance. In J. Suls & A. G. Greenwald (Eds.), *Psychological perspectives on the self* (Vol. 2, pp. 1–31). Hillsdale, NJ: Erlbaum.

Williams, J. M., Tonymon, P., & Wadsworth, W. A. (1986). Relation of stress to injury in intercollegiate volleyball. *Journal of Human Stress, 12,* 38–43.

Wylie, R. C. (1979). *The self-concept* (Vol. 2). Lincoln: University of Nebraska Press.

3

Rationality in Sport: A Psychophilosophical Approach

Michael Bar-Eli
Department of Business Administration, School of Management,
Ben-Gurion University of the Negev, Beer-Sheva, Israel
Ribstein Center for Sport Medicine Sciences and Research,
Wingate Institute, Israel

Yotam Lurie
Department of Business Administration, School of Management,
Ben-Gurion University of the Negev, Beer-Sheva, Israel

Gunnar Breivik
Institute of Social Sciences, Norwegian University of Sports
and Physical Education, Oslo, Norway

I don't like players who don't do what I say, and I don't like players who do exactly what I say.

—Larry Bird, Coach of the NBA team Indiana Pacers
Cited in the Israeli newspaper "Maariv", 22/10/97, p. 7

Introduction

Rationality is a central concept in the Western cultural tradition. Accordingly, rationality is also embedded in contemporary sport and exercise psychology, be it explicitly or implicitly. For example, in elite sport, sport psychology strives to maximize athletes' performances by optimizing their arousal states (Gould & Krane, 1992; Zaichkowsky & Takenaka, 1993). Sport psychologists are expected to help minimize children's dropping out from competitive sport by utilizing methods such as the positive approach to coaching (Smith, 1993; Smith & Smoll, 1996). Exercise psychologists attempt to convince people to adhere to physical exercise because it contributes to mental health maximization and, conversely, to mental illness minimization (Biddle, 1995; Dishman, 1993). Basically, then, sport and exercise psychology perceives its subjects of research and application as people who would act according to logical, common-sense principles—that is, rational human beings.

A closer look at sport and exercise behavior raises the question, however, whether such behavior can really be defined as rational. One of the most conspicuous examples that comes to mind would be the alarming epidemiological numbers of sport and exercise injuries, which are also connected with amazingly high financial damage claims in many Western economies (Kirkby, 1995; Williams & Roepke, 1993). Some years ago, Bar-Eli (1984) argued that cognitive and emotional variables interact to distort and disturb the making of optimal decisions in competitive sport, for example, when coaches are concerned. Accordingly, he suggested that decision-aid systems be used, which could relieve such decision makers of cognitive and emotional difficulties related to the process of judgment and decision making, helping them to use available information more optimally. In a more recent work, Bar-Eli (1991) questioned the entire concept of rationality in sport-psychological interventions, arguing that processes that are seemingly illogical may have rational consequences, and vice versa. Thus, sport psychology is in need of a more thorough discussion of the concept of rationality.

In this chapter we will first discuss some of the philosophical bases of rationality, in general and in the specific domain of sport. In addition, an attempt will be made to demonstrate some of the consequences for sport psychology.

The Nature of Rationality

The Heritage

The roots of the modern Western rationality concept can be traced back to ancient Greece. The Greek culture—as expressed in the views of Plato and Aristotle—placed heavy emphasis on the human as a living being that was a carrier of logos (Copleston, 1963). Logos meant both the spoken word, the reason behind it, and the greater logos, that is, the logos of the cosmos (because humans—as a microcosmos—were supposed to reflect the macrocosmos). Thus, the logos structure of cosmos and man was presupposed in Greek philosophy, from Pythagoras to the Stoics. During Hellenism, the concept of a universal logos lived on in the cosmopolitan views of philosophic schools like the Cynic.

In the Greek context, it is more appropriate to speak of reason than of rationality. In Greek philosophy, reason, will, and emotion were the three faculties in humans that should work together in a harmonious whole, with reason as the guide (Plato, 400 B.C./1945). According to Aristotle (350 B.C./1976), man's life should be guided by wise decisions. The golden rule of this approach tells us that one should choose the middle road between extremes. For instance, one should be courageous but not a daredevil or a coward. The goal in life is to reach happiness, with reason as a guide to good and right actions.

In Roman translation the Greek logos became ratio; Aristotle's definition of man became in Latin animal rationale. As a result, something of the richness in logos got lost in ratio, which became associated with a more narrow, cool way of reasoning, that is, with calculation. It should be noted that Weber's (1919/1946) later distinction between rationality of means and ends (*Zweckrationalität* vs. *Handlungsrationalität*) reflected the ancient Greek concept, which included both forms of rationality in a more general theory of practical reason.

The idea of the human as a "rational animal" was reflected in many different contexts and senses, continuing through the Middle Ages to modern times, such as, for example, the French Enlightenment's proclamation of the autonomy of reason and its celebration of the methods of the natural sciences. In these different contexts, the notion of rationality was often used in rather vague senses with rather complex connections with one another. Nonetheless, in one central usage, to be rational means to be committed to reason rather than to faith, prejudice, habit, passion, or any other, so-called irrational, sources of conviction. Hence, in the context of Greek culture, when Plato (400 B.C./1945) and Aristotle (350 B.C./1976) emphasized that the human is a rational animal, they were claiming that the human being has the ability to deliberate and to be propelled to action by reasons rather than by cultural habits or national desires and passions. Similarly, the philosophers of the French Enlightenment, who were primarily concerned with epistemological issues, viewed knowledge as being obtained by relying on reason alone, without the distractions of irrational sources of belief, such as religious faith and superstition.

It should be noted, however, that some philosophers challenged the notion of reason or rationality as the guide to right actions. Hume (1740/1978), for example, argued that the ends are determined by emotions, with reason being a pure servant that helps realize the ends. According to this approach, in our emotions we find the motivating power and the goal for our actions, and through our reasoning and rationality we find the best means and instruments to reach our goals. Thus, the challenge to the rationality of humans is not entirely new (Wilson, 1991).

Modern Concepts of Rationality

Rationality is a concept that is currently used with a variety of meanings. For example, Elster (1982) distinguished between more than 20 different meanings of "rationality," applied in various disciplines, such as philosophy, sociology, psychology, and economics. According to Føllesdal (1988), a modern theory of rationality will have to discern between at least four basically different notions or aspects of rationality, which will be discussed now in brief (in line with Elster, 1982, 1991).

The first notion is of *rationality as logical consistency*. According to this notion, we expect persons to act in accordance with beliefs that are logically compatible with each other. However, one cannot be sure whether the relevant beliefs are objectively or subjectively available to a person in a particular situation, and therefore, whether the relevant beliefs are those that actually cause one's respective actions. A major problem is related to the question of what is actually meant by consistency: Do we mean that no belief should be a negation of another belief or that the consequences of all our beliefs should not be incompatible with each other—a demand which is particularly hard to meet?

The second notion is of *rationality as good evidence*. This notion goes one step further by arguing that the consistency demand is a necessary but not a sufficient condition for rationality. Therefore, rationality should also imply that beliefs should be based on good evidence. According to this approach, if a belief is accepted as rational, there should be some evidence for it and not better evidence for any other competing belief. Thus, rationality includes considerations not only of quality, quantity, and relevance of evidence, but also of sufficiency of evidence for some given purposes. Do we need better and more evidence in order to take a particular course of action, or should we act upon the evidence we already have?

The third notion is of *rationality as well-grounded values*. In addition to the widely accepted notion of rationality of means (see below, "rationality as effectiveness of actions"), one can also ask whether there is a rationality of ends. Here we ask whether our normative views or value systems can be viewed as more or less rational, in other words, whether evidence can be found for a certain ordering of values or norms. As indicated before, it was Hume (1740/1978) who believed that all ends are based on emotions and therefore one can argue for or against ends only in relation to means. Weber's (1919/1946) concept of *Wertrationalität* (i.e., value rationality) implied some commitment to particular values, but not a rationality in the sense of a piece of evidence for (or against) certain values and a respective ordering of values. As opposed to this view, some modern philosophers follow the ancient Greek tradition by being somewhat more optimistic about rational arguments for certain values. For example, both Plato (400 B.C./1945) and Aristotle (350 B.C./1976) thought of ends as ultimate Ideas or Forms that had objective existence and could be identified through correct reasoning. In line with this notion, Føllesdal (1988) believes that the most promising way of arguing for certain value orderings is to use the method of reflexive equilibrium developed by philosophers such as Rawls (1971) and Habermas (1990). The basic idea here is that our general values should be adjusted to each other and to more special evaluations in specific areas until we feel satisfied and an equilibrium has been reached.

The fourth notion is of *rationality as effectiveness of actions*. The basic idea here is that an individual has a certain goal that he or she wants to realize and that a course of action is chosen that most effectively brings about the realization of that goal. In order to make this general idea more precise, normative theories of decision were developed in philosophy and economy, which probably give the clearest picture of what rationality of action can mean. For example, according to game theory, a decision consists of a two-step process. The first step is actually a process of scanning for alternative courses of action, in which persons tend to concentrate on the alternatives that seem to have the highest positive or negative utilities. The second step is a process of weighing the alternatives, with both the utilities and the probabilities of the various outcomes being considered. The utilities—multiplied by their probabilities—are then added to produce the total value of each alternative course of action. Because objective utilities are hard or even impossible to measure, decision theory has concentrated on subjective expected utilities of outcomes; thus, a person is supposed to choose the course of action that will give him or her the higher subjective utility. It should be noted that, empirically, the construction of utility scales, the weighing of alternatives, and the calculation of utility scores are extremely complicated tasks. Accordingly, game theory of decision should best be considered as an ideal type, which may give a fairly good model of what rationality can mean in certain real-life situations.

In one way or another then, the meaning of rationality is connected to the notion of having a **reason** *for believing or acting*; a person is deemed rational if he or she believes or does something because he or she has a reason for believing or doing this. In contrast, irrational persons are said to form their beliefs or acts because of so-called irrational sources conviction, such as inspiration, imagination, faith, habit, or passion. Among other things, philosophers focused on the evaluation of good and bad reasons (i.e., on people's degrees of rationality) and on the complex problem of distinguishing between reasons and all other nonrational sources of conviction. This can be demonstated by considering, for example, the intellectuals of the scientific revolution, who believed that only reasons that are public and observable should be the basis of knowledge, because they are objective and thus not as likely to be irrational sources of conviction in disguise.

It is quite common to confuse the notion of rationality and the notion of "getting it right." Rationality has to do with the quality of one's reasoning and not necessarily with the question of whether one has the right answer or not. It is possible, for example, to distinguish between a rational and an irrational argument for communism without this having any bearing on the question of whether communism is right or wrong. Thus, a rational argument might result in false beliefs, or, by mere coincidence, an irrational argument might "hit the nail on the head." Similarly, a basketball coach, for example, may manage a game rationally and lose (e.g., because his or her most important player was injured), whereas another, irrational coach may win by coincidence.

It should also be noted that one can definitely acknowledge that another person is rational without necessarily agreeing with the other's actions or beliefs. For example, suppose Dan consumes huge amounts of ice cream because he is on a diet and because he believes that ice cream is cold and therefore nonfattening. Even though Ron may believe that Dan is wrong and may completely disagree with Dan's claims about the dietary quality of ice cream, Ron can still agree that (based on Dan's beliefs) Dan's behavior might indeed be rational (in the sense of logical consistency). In the same way, to someone who has grasped no more about soccer than that there are two opposing teams trying to kick a ball into each other's net, it would seem quite irrational for a player to stop playing just as he or she was about to score, just because he or she heard a whistle blown. It is only with the assumption that one recognizes and accepts the rules of soccer (and thus grasps the notion of a referee) that the sound of a whistle seems like a relevant reason for the player to stop. However, even after one understands what the sound of a whistle in soccer means, it is possible to hear a distant whistle blow and thus understand why the player stopped playing, without agreeing with him or her.

Manifestations of Rationality in Sport: Philosophical Considerations

Sport: From Expressivity to Science

As mentioned above, rationality is a central concept in the Western cultural tradition. It is not at all self-evident, however, that sport is a realm where rationality reigns. It can be argued that sport is one form of human activity—along with several other forms of human activity, such as singing, dancing, worshipping, and fighting—that may be better understood as an expressive form of human activity (Berlin, 1982). More specifically, sport can be viewed as a tribal affair where old traditions are reaffirmed and where men—and in recent times women as well—join together either as a group or as individuals, giving expression more to their passions and their physical abilities than to their rational reason. For example, one can think about South American farmers playing soccer on their day off or about African-American kids shooting hoops in the parking lot in a big urban ghetto. Thus, much of what happens in sport is tied to habits and circumstances; it has to do with local traditions and with fun and games, and hence, at least intuitively, it is not self-evidently rational. Understood in this manner, sport has little to do with concepts such as reason and rationality.

Moreover, if we suppose for a moment that what we mean by sport coincides at least in part with the notions of games and playing, then the case for rationality in sport becomes even more grim. According to Suits (1978), games are situations in which people attempt to overcome unnecessary obstacles by adopting means that are relatively inefficient for completing a task that they could otherwise complete much faster and easier. For example, the riders of the Tour de France travel all around France on a bicycle. Riding a bicycle all around France, however, is a less efficient way of completing the task of traveling around France to Paris than is driving the same route to Paris by car. Along the same lines, archery is a sport in which people attempt to hit a target with a bow and arrow from a distance. The problem that the task presents is obviously not necessary, and the means that archers adopt in order to complete this task (i.e., hit the target) are clearly less efficient and less precise than just walking up to the target and sticking an arrow in it. Thus, at least according to Suits (1978), in games we use inefficient and hence less rational ways of attempting to complete unnecessary tasks.

The fare of rationality in play is not much better than that in games. According to some views (e.g., Huizinga, 1995; Suits, 1978), in comparison to games, an important feature of play has to do with the fact that to play is to pretend or make believe. Thus, playing stands outside of ordinary life and is, therefore, perceived as not real or serious. In addition, players often prefer the activity itself and are less concerned with its outcome, as long as it does not affect the quality of their experiences. In this respect, the outcome of play is not important in terms of its effect (Huizinga, 1995). According to Kretchmer (1994) "play is fundamentally prerational. Something is prerational when it is done in the absence of calculation, not because of it (rational) and not in spite of it (irrational)" (p. 210).

In contrast to this conception of sport as related to the notions of game and play, much of contemporary sport life as it is manifested in competitive sport and in physical education programs is permeated with rationality. Thus, it is disconnected from old traditions and self-expression and appears to be very carefully planned and calculated, that is, as a product of scientific thinking.

Consider the following examples of rationality in sport, outlined by Kretchmer (1994):

1. The coach or sport instructor learns his or her trade in a professional and/or academic setting. When questioned, he or she claims that he or she does not prepare the team in an intuitive or capricious manner, but rather makes use of fairly advanced theories derived from various scientific disciplines, such as biomechanics, physiology, or psychology. The coach claims to be an expert with a unique body of knowledge that allows him or her to prepare his or her team in a cautious, well-planned and rational manner. Thus, the athletes following the coach's instructions are said to be doing whatever empirical science has shown to be correct in order to improve their performance.

2. Many physical educators strive to build programs around what is scientifically considered as right or good. Only infrequently are programs built around what makes good sense historically or culturally. For example, activities such as softball or soccer that in particular cultures are often connected with students' day-to-day lives might be altogether eliminated from a physical education program for health considerations, which are considered highly rational.

3. Many physical education and adult exercise programs that take place in gyms and exercise rooms are often conducted by the clock with a lesson plan loaded with good outcomes. Thus, people do not want to "waste time" on mere play and games, so they put play to work for them to ensure that it serves rationally defensible ends, such as fitness, health, relaxation, and moral or social development.

4. The focus of all too many physical education programs is on *Cities, Altos, Forties* (faster, stronger, higher), never mind what the negative side effects might be and/or questions of right and wrong. This entails that programs make use of reason and the sciences of sports as a sledgehammer in order to design a program that will improve on the athletes' ability to run faster, become stronger and reach higher, often without being concerned for the price.

What these examples bring into focus are some of the ways in which Western culture has tried to modify more traditional and expressive approaches to sport in favor of an approach to sport that is fabricated rationally, primarily according to the scientific credo of "I will do whatever empirical science has shown to be correct in order to improve the athlete's performance." In the following sections, we will further elaborate on various facets of the rationality concept in sport.

Rationality in Sport as Practical Reasoning

Since Aristotle (350 B.C./1976), a distinction has been made in philosophy between theoretical reasoning, such as philosophical argument or scientific debate, and practical reasoning by which we mean reasoning that is somehow bound with action, such as that which takes place when considering what to do in a particular situation. More specifically, philosophers such as Von Wright (1963) and Habermas (1974) have sought to clarify the notion of theoretical reasoning by speaking of a rational argument as an argument in which the conclusion is well supported by the premises or an argument that proceeds logically from the premises. In the case of practical reasoning, we can speak of rational behavior as behavior that is based on good reasons. The distinction between theoretical reasoning and practical reasoning is related to classical contrast between theory and practice. It is clear that rationality and irrationality can both be displayed in theoretical and practical reasoning (Habermas, 1974; Von Wright, 1963).

Theoretical reasoning and practical reasoning differ from one another in more than just the subject matter with which they are concerned; they actually proceed differently. Theoretical reasoning often has to do with chains of proof where the specific conclusion follows from some kind of universal premises. Practical reasoning has to do with the contingent changing circumstance of the actual world and thus often involves a wider range of factors than just formal deductions. In the case of practical reasoning, one is trying to deal with a certain problem and must draw on the outcomes of previous experience, carrying over the procedures used to resolve earlier problems and reapplying them in new problematic situations. Universal rules and abstract principles are often inadequate in cases of practical reasoning, and thus one must reason by using one's experience with past cases as a paradigm for the present situation. Dealing with practical reasoning depends, therefore, on how closely the present situation resembles past cases with which one is familiar (Toulmin & Jonsen, 1988).

Practical reasoning is usually taught by what has come to be known as the case method, which is typically used in law schools, business schools, medical schools, and in the study of applied ethics. In the case method, general principles and rules are downplayed because of their inadequacy for practical reasoning. Instead, actual and hypothetical cases involving concrete problems and changing situations are used so as to develop skills of deliberation, decision making and the ability to weigh competing considerations in reaching a decision. The focus is put on concrete problems or dilemmas and how to deal with them, while making no assumption that there is a right answer to any of the problems that has to be memorized; there are just more or less successful ways of handling the problems. By analyzing different cases, each posing a different kind of problem or dilemma, the student develops certain skills and learns how to utilize these skills in a contingent world. Usually these skills cannot be applied mechanically, and hence the student is expected to develop the ability to think and act intelligently and rationally under complex and changing circumstances. The point is to develop the students' ability to grasp problems and devise novel solutions that work out in the given context (Beauchamp & Bowie, 1993).

The issue of rationality in sport has to do with practical reason. A related idea that can help us shed more light on rationality in sport as practical reasoning is suggested by Oakeshott (1962), who distinguished between technical and practical knowledge. According to this notion, every scientific, artistic, or practical activity requiring skills involves knowledge of two sorts—technical and practical. *Technical knowledge* is knowledge of a technique; for example, driving a car requires knowledge of the techniques of driving, which have been collected and formulated and can be found in sources such as a highway driving code booklet. However, through reading a highway driving code booklet, one usually does not become a good driver; similarly, learning the specific techniques required in a certain sport and/or the tactical and strategic principles of that sport is not sufficient to make one an elite athlete. What is usually missing is practical knowledge; it exists only in use and cannot be formulated in the same way as technical knowledge. Practical knowledge has to do with skill and with the mastery of a technique; it is shared and becomes public, not through formulation but through various forms of practice, practical training, and apprenticeship, often under the guide of a mentor, an instructor or a coach. Thus, technical knowledge can usually tell only *what* is to be done, whereas practical knowledge tells *how* it is to be done.

To illustrate this distinction with regard to the activity of coaching, let us take Peter Coe, Sebastian Coe's father and coach; under Peter Coe's guidance, the British runner Sebastian Coe dominated the middle distance runs and was the world record holder for the 800m and 1500m runs in 1979. Peter Coe (1982) argued that

> Coaching is an art. Although it is science-based it is still an art. Whereas in science one can fall back on formulas and repeatable experiments, art relies on sensitivity of feelings. The athlete is a unique individual and cannot be seen in the same way as a piece of matter where the predictability of the whole embraces the behavior of the individual molecule. (p. 6)

Thus, coaching consists not merely of a list of technical instructions that can be formulated and applied as general rules, because each athlete in each sport presents a unique case, which also requires a substantial amount of practical knowledge in coaching.

Instrumental Reasoning vs. Critical Thinking

Before an important competition, one might hear a coach say to his or her athletes, "If you want to win you will have to play (or run or swim) **smart**. You will have to examine the situation on the court (or field or track) and to **use your heads**. If you play **foolishly** you will lose." At first glance it seems pretty clear that the coach is trying to tell the athletes that a good athlete should be smart (i.e., rational) in order to win. Being rational in this context, however, may have two possible senses that actually complement one another: The first has to do with the notion of instrumental rationality, which basically means choosing the course of action that most effectively brings about the realization of a goal. The second has to do with the notion of critical thinking and with the idea of not accepting the dogmas of tradition. In fact, these seem to be the two facets of "being smart on the field."

Instrumental rationality has to do with the effectiveness of one's application of means towards the accomplishment of a certain goal. However, sport is a rule-governed behavior; within any sport there are "constitutive rules" that are game defining and "regulative rules" that are penalty invoking (Black, 1962; Shwayder, 1965). More recently, the concept of "strategic rules" has been suggested to account for the notion of "rule" in a much broader sense (Baker & Hacker, 1984; Kripke, 1982).

An athlete must of course accept and obey the constitutive rules of the sport that define what it actually means to participate, but he or she is often expected to challenge and push the limits of certain regulative rules as well in order to succeed. Thus, considered as a matter of instrumental rationality, what athletes do is to use the means available to them, including the (regulative) rules of their sport, in the most efficient manner to achieve a goal that is preset by the (constitutive) rules of that sport. Because the situation is practical, athletes are said to reason in a practical manner by trying to deal with the problem and achieve the goal through the adaptation and application of past experiences to the present situation.

The second facet of "being a smart athlete" has to do with being a critical thinker. According to Descartes (1641/1987), the rationalist, understood as a critical thinker, stands for independence of mind, for thought free from obligation to any authority or prejudice save the authority of reason. He or she should, therefore, be the enemy of all that is habitual, traditional or customary, being optimistic, sceptical, and individualistic. In other words, the rationalist is a person who is also committed to the notion of evaluating behavior in a critical and reflective manner, hoping to find ways of behaving that are well justified, based on good and coherent reasons. Along these lines, "being a smart athlete" also has to do with a critical assessment of one's thoughts and actions. According to this conception, a rational athlete is often one who breaks with tradition and invents new ways of meeting an old challenge; he or she is creative and nondogmatic in his or her thinking. A well-known example of this idea is Dick Fosbury, who—in the Mexico Olympics, 1968—instead of trying to excel in the high jump by utilizing old means (as all other high jumpers were trying to do), broke with tradition and invented a radically new approach to the high jump, later called the "Fosbury Flop."

Psychological Aspects of Rationality in Sport

Optimization

Recently Bar-Eli (1997a, 1997b) reviewed the research on psychological performance crisis in competition. Among other things—and in line with earlier work (Bar-Eli, 1984)—a formal framework for diagnosis was suggested with reference to the development of an athlete's psychological performance crisis in competition. The probabilistic measure of diagnostic value used for this purpose was based on the Bayesian approach (Edwards, Lindman, & Savage, 1963; Rapoport & Wallsten, 1972; Slovic & Lichtenstein, 1971). Bayes's theorem has been used extensively in expert systems, for example, to help geologists look for mineral deposits (Duda et al., 1976) and to provide probabilities for medical diagnosis (Eddy, 1982; Schwartz, Baron, & Clarke, 1988).

Quite often, people seem to have substantial difficulties in weighing and combining (i.e., aggregating) information as a result of their limited information-processing and decision-making capability (see, for a review, Tenenbaum & Bar-Eli, 1993). Accordingly, judgment tasks have often been decomposed into a number of presumably simpler estimation tasks (Armstrong, Denniston, & Gordon, 1975). Edwards (1962) attempted to circumvent aggregation difficulties by having people estimate separate components and letting a computer system combine them. In this way, a probabilistic diagnosis may be substantially facilitated (Edwards, 1962; Slovic, Fischoff, & Lichtenstein, 1977; Slovic & Lichtenstein, 1971).

The use of these principles for diagnostic purposes has been repeatedly recommended within various contexts that involve thought and decision processes (Baron, 1994). In sport psychology, Bar-Eli (1984) introduced the use of the Bayesian approach, applying it to the crisis model. In order to carry out a diagnosis of crisis development in the individual athlete during competition, factors that are diagnostic in this respect were identified. Through these factors, the problem of diagnosing an athlete's psychological state in competition (e.g., crisis) could be decomposed. Each such factor includes several components (i.e., Bayesian data) that can be separately assessed by experts with regard to their probability of occurrence when a crisis or a noncrisis is given. Later on, the ratio of these probabilities can be computed via Bayes's rule (see also Tenenbaum & Bar-Eli, 1993, 1995a).

The Bayesian approach—originally described by Reverend Thomas Bayes in 1763—is thoroughly embedded within the framework of decision theory. Its basic tenets are that opinions should be expressed in terms of subjective probabilities and that the optimal revision of such opinions, in the light of relevant new information, should be accomplished via Bayes's theorem, particularly when it leads to decision making and action (Edwards, 1966). Because of this concern with decision making, the output of a Bayesian analysis is not always a single prediction but rather a distribution of probabilities over a set of hypothesized states of the world. These probabilities can then be used, in combination with information about payoffs associated with various decision possibilities and states of the world, to implement any of a number of decision rules. Bayes's theorem is thus also a normative model. It specifies certain internally consistent relationships among probabilistic opinions and serves also to prescribe, in this sense, how people should think (Rapoport & Wallsten, 1972; Slovic & Lichtenstein, 1971). Central to this approach, then, is the concept of optimality, closely associated with rationality. In other words, such an approach may, in principle, be used to aid optimizing people's thought processes, thereby contributing to the maximization of their performances in a particular area, such as elite sport.

At least two questions may be asked as to the assumption of rationality of such probabilistic models, both of them related to the probability estimates. First, it could be argued that subjective probabilistic responses are, in fact, "common sense judgments" and, as such, are vulnerable to distortions and biases (Kahnemann, Slovic, & Tversky, 1982; Nisbett & Ross, 1980). A possible solution to this problem is to make sure that highly experienced and qualified experts in any subject matter are used, who are—by definition —characterized by a unique knowledge base, built on variables such as formal educational and practical experience (Peters & Waterman, 1982). Experts have "professional vocabularies" of cognitive patterns at their disposal (Simon, 1979), which imply a considerably better perceptual and motor task performance of experts in comparison to novices or "naive" subjects (Abernethy, 1993). In addition, experts are less vulnerable to judgmental errors in their field of expertise (Tenenbaum & Bar-Eli, 1993). For such reasons, it is worth using such experts to create efficient decision aids, together with a further tapping into these experts' unique knowledge. In addition, it is highly important to study the relations between subjective and observational behavioral dimensions, to validate the subjective model's predictions.

A second interesting question relates to the probability estimates mentioned above, which contain a somewhat unnoticed paradoxical or absurd element. Let's take, for example, a person who provides a probability estimate of 50% with regard to a particular event (e.g., "heads" or "tails"). From an information-processing standpoint, this would mean as if this person would say that "I am 100% certain that this probability is 50%" or—if we take this argument *ad absurdum*— "I am completely sure that I am completely unsure" about this particular event. This supposedly absurd situation occurs because people usually neglect the so-called "second order probability", which was defined by Einhorn and Hogarth (1981) as "one's uncertainty about a probabilistic estimate" (p. 66). A possible solution to this problem would be to treat "first-order" probability estimates as some kind of "central tendency measures" and to use ambiguity measures (Curly, Yates, & Abrams, 1986; Fox & Tversky, 1996; Frisch & Baron, 1988; Heath & Tversky, 1991) to account for second order probabilities. This would make, however, the entire process of probability estimation—in the context of building decision aids—quite complex. Therefore, we act as if such second-order probabilities do not exist—in particular, also, because according to the same logic, we could think about "3rd-, 4th-, 5th- or Nth-order probabilities."

The question of whether probabilistic aggregation aids would be used by coaches, for instance, to diagnose athletes' psychological states during actual competitions, depends not only on the scientist's ability to provide the coach with appropriate computerized diagnostic tools, but also on the coach's readiness to accept such consultation. As noted by Bar-Eli and Tenenbaum (1989), coach-psychologist collaboration is often disturbed as a result of different utility concepts of both professions. For example, whereas the psychologist—acting as a consultant—should consider only scientific subject matter (i.e., from an "internal" perspective) and treat it probabilistically (according to the regular state of scientifically based knowledge), the coach often considers such subject matters both "internally" and "externally" (that is, includes also considerations that are not scientific, though important) and needs deterministic answers, required to enhance athletes' performance. As a result, when a sport psychologist is asked by a coach to recommend a plan of action for an athlete, he or she is actually expected to supply a deterministic action plan, which would rely on "internal" as well as "external" considerations. The best line of action the psychologist—acting as a scientific consultant—could recommend would be, however, only "internal" and probabilistic in nature. Thus, it may disappoint the coach and/or be perceived as the psychologist's failure, hence leading to possible disputes and misperceptions between the two. A continuing coach-psychologist collaboration could contribute to reducing the difference in their utility concepts and improving the results of their mutual collaboration.

It should be noted that the principle of performance optimization has been widely used in management science, particularly in the area of operations research. Quantitative methods of systems analysis have been applied to many fields of human endeavour, including sport (see, for review, Gerchak, 1994; Ladany, 1996). Recently, Mehrez, Friedman, Sinuany-Stern and Bar-Eli (1997) analyzed the problem of programming in elite sports. More specifically, this study focused on threshold optimization in multistage sport disciplines, such as weight lifting, pole vault, and high jump. From an applied perspective, it was demonstrated that elite athletes often fail due to taking an inefficient policy according to which, for example, a too difficult goal (i.e., threshold) is set. To aid these athletes, Mehrez et al. (1997) suggested an operation-research based model and concluded that applying the main principles derived from their model may help athletes in sport disciplines, such as weight lifting, pole vault, and high jump, in optimizing their mental preparation for future competitions, taking into account their past achievements. As mental preparation includes important components such as goal setting and decision making, which have been shown to require optimization also from a sport-psychological point of view (Bar-Eli, 1995; Tenenbaum & Bar-Eli, 1993), this approach may substantially contribute in this respect, if appropriately applied by practitioners. Thus, management science could, in principle, provide sport psychology with rational models, which may be used as optimal aids for performance enhancement.

Irrational Rationality, Rational Irrationality

It was previously mentioned that one of the central modern concepts of rationality is that of rationality as effectiveness of actions. Within this framework, game theory was briefly discussed. Basically, game theory of decision may be considered as an ideal type, which can provide a quite reasonable model of real-life situations. However, participants in such games, who supposedly act according to rational principles, may sometimes end up being locked in a completely irrational game.

One example of this idea is the problem of doping in sport. It has been long established that in itself, doping in various forms seems to be effective for increasing athletic success (e.g., Macintyre, 1987; Schwenk, 1997; Wagner, 1991). However, modern doping increases economic costs for athletes and sport organizations, possibly damages the athletes' health, and presents several moral problems (Hoberman, 1992). In a series of studies, Breivik (1987, 1991, 1992) discussed the problem of doping from a game theoretical point of view. Breivik assumed that each athlete has a choice between dope and no-dope as two different strategies. Breivik made no distinction between different forms of doping or different quantities and qualities, but assumed that a doping strategy will enhance the performance of the athlete, or at least that athletes think so. According to this approach, athletes are supposed to have different values and therefore different preferences between outcomes in sport. They are also supposed to have different values and preferences regarding the use of doping means. This means that there would be different preference structures in sport related to doping.

Central to Breivik's analyses (1987, 1991, 1992) was the assumption that athletes will act rationally to reach their goals. In other words, it was assumed that they would try to maximize their subjective expected utility when they are choosing between alternative strategies. In line with Nozick (1981), Breivik (1992) argued that there may be several reasons and causes, even evolutionary ones, why rationality will be preferred in certain areas of life, including sport. Based on these assumptions, he made an attempt to identify and analyze some of the most prevalent preference structures regarding doping. For example, Breivik (1987) analyzed the doping dilemma and found—for two-person games—that the so-called "prisoner's dilemma" exists in sport and that there are strong and widespread preference structures among athletes that inevitably lead to doping. Later, Breivik (1992) broadened his view and analyzed n-person versions (in both symmetrical and asymmetrical situations), which according to Parfit (1986) are more relevant for real-life situations. Based on his own analyses and on Axelrod's (1984) ideas, Breivik (1991) also discussed some possibilities for cooperation against doping.

A simple illustration of this approach may be derived from the basic version of the so-called "prisoner's dilemma" (Hamburger, 1979; Luce & Raiffa, 1957). Breivik (1991) gives the following example: The two best 100-meter sprinters in the United States, who happen also to be the best in the world, will come up against each other in the next championship. For years, both have focused all their effort on becoming the best: the UCLA man (U) and the man from San Jose State University (S). Several outcomes are possible. One of them could use doping and the other not, in which case the doper would get the highest possible payoff (5), whereas the other would lose and get the worst (0). If both used a no-doping strategy, competition would be hard and winning uncertain but fair for both. The moral, health, and career costs would be less. That would, for both, be the second-best result (3). If both used doping, competition would be hard and fair, winning uncertain, and the costs greater. That means the third-best outcome (1). This payoff matrix is illustrated in Figure 3.1.

U

	No Dope	Dope
No Dope	(3,3)	(0,5)
Dope	(5,0)	(1,1)

S (shown to the left, spanning the two row labels)

Figure 3.1. Illustration of the "Prisoner's Dilemma" applied to the problem of doping in sport.

The preferences of the sprinters are obviously regulated by two principles:

1. Winning is more important than fairness. Therefore, a certain but unfair victory is preferred to an uncertain and fair competition.
2. Fairness without costs is preferred to fairness with costs, even if absolute performance decreases.

The question now is whether these athletes will dope or not in the championship. To reach the no-dope outcome (3,3) in the Championship, cooperation is needed. However, the danger that one's opponent will defect (dope) and make one a sucker is there all the time.

What would the athletes do in such a game? Suppose you are the UCLA sprinter. You think the San Jose man will cooperate and not use doping. This means that you may get a reward (3) for cooperating (the No-dope strategy). But you may get your best outcome, a probable victory, by defecting and choosing Dope (5). So it pays to defect if the San Jose sprinter cooperates.

Suppose you think the San Jose sprinter will defect and choose Dope. By choosing defection yourself, you get a payoff of 1. But you are even worse off if you choose to cooperate (No-dope) and get the sucker's payoff (0). This means that whatever the San Jose sprinter does, you are better off choosing Dope and defecting from a cooperative No-dope strategy. The San Jose sprinter will reason in exactly the same way. Both athletes will end up choosing defection and Dope, which gives them their third-best payoff (1,1). The paradox here is that by mutual cooperation they could have reached their second-best outcome (3,3).

In his series of studies, Breivik (1987, 1991, 1992) elaborated on this basic paradigm and discussed several "doping games," which differ from one another with respect to their basic guiding rationale and the players' structures of preferences. Breivik identified three types of games that will encourage doping (the Lombardian, Machiavellian, and Brownian games) and two types of games that will result in a decrease in doping (the Coubertinian and Naessian games), all of them derived from the basic "prisoner's dilemma." The central idea is, however, that under some conditions, a behavior that is seemingly rational may lead to irrational consequences.

This very idea was also discussed in Bar-Eli's (1991) work on paradoxical interventions. Bar-Eli assumed that people usually perceive themselves as rational, acting according to logical, common-sense principles. For example, in order to better control the behavior of a rebellious athlete, a coach may nag him or her about his or her performance. However, this may lead the athlete to play hookey more often. In reaction, the coach may escalate the nagging and threats. Through their "common-sense" solution of the problem, both sides find themselves trapped in a problem cycle, referred to as the "more of the same" syndrome (Watzlawick, Weakland, & Fisch, 1974). Thus the "logical solutions" paradoxically perpetuate the problem. This happens because if we view event "E" as undesired, we "rationally" tend to solve it by using the "common-sense" solution "not-E." However, as long as the solution is sought within the dichotomy "E" or "not-E", the person is trapped in an illusion of alternatives (Weakland & Jackson, 1958).

Whatever alternative he or she may choose, the actual problem is not solved but reinforced. This results from the persisting illusion that either "E" or "not-E" must be chosen in order to solve the problem. The possibility of choosing neither "E" nor "not-E" is neglected in this problem-solving process. Philosophically viewed, the person insists on moving between thesis and antithesis instead of trying to move toward synthesis, which stands beyond this dichotomy (Hegel, 1812–16/1929; Wittgenstein, 1958) and, in fact, may suggest a new way of considering the situation (Kuhn, 1962). From a psychological point of view, what is needed is a transition from "first-" to "second-order" cognitive change processes, which seem to be paradoxical (Bateson, 1972, 1979). Thus a seemingly logical solution leads us to an illogical state of an everlasting problem. In contrast, a seemingly illogical (i.e., paradoxical) solution, which is based on choosing neither "E" nor "not-E," may lead to the logical state of solving the actual problem through changing the structure of the system under consideration (e.g., the system of coach-athlete relationship). This is the very basic conception behind using paradoxical interventions in counseling and coaching in sport, as demonstrated by Bar-Eli's (1991) detailed examples.

Conclusion

In this chapter, an attempt was made to discuss some of the philosophical bases of rationality in general as well as in the specific domain of sport. In addition, we discussed some of the consequences for sport psychology.

Of course, this chapter suffers from some limitations. For example, it is evident that different people are involved in sport in very different ways: Many sport lovers take part in the sport they fancy by sitting in front of a television; that is, they play the role of spectators. Other sport lovers make a living of sport as sport administrators and officials; and finally others are participating athletes. In asking about rationality in sport, we were here concerned primarily with participating athletes. In addition, we made no attempt to define what exactly is meant by the notion of sport; that is a big philosophical question that is beyond the scope of this chapter. It will suffice in this context to rely on what might be considered a common-sense and quite loose understanding of sport, to avoid any diversion from our main issue.

It is also important to note that the questions we were dealing with were rather different from the question of the rationality of sport or the rationality of a sport, that is, the question of whether or not engagement in a certain sport is rational. The rationality of sport is a difficult ethical question that has to be discussed from within the context of a person's life considered as a whole. Thus, for example, a question such as whether it is rational for a person to participate in the sport of boxing (considering the danger of mental damage due to injury, but also the possibility of monetary rewards and personal satisfaction one might gain as a boxer) deserves a separate discussion, which is beyond the scope of this chapter. However, for sport psychology, such a discussion will probably be necessary in the future, considering the issue of the extremely high direct and indirect damages that are connected to sport and exercise injuries (Kirkby, 1995; Williams & Roepke, 1993).

In principle, this chapter may provide impetus for future empirical research into various issues discussed here. For example, game theory has not been used much in sport science (see however, Suits, 1978), including sport psychology. This is quite amazing not only because the theory of games was introduced about 55 years ago (Von Neumann & Morgenstern, 1944), but also because concepts such as the prisoner's dilemma have been intensively studied in general social psychology, especially within the framework of research on cooperation and competition, already in the 1960's and early 1970's (see, for review,

Rubin & Brown, 1975). Because cooperation (vs. competition) is highly important, for example, in elite team sports (Widmeyer, Carron, & Brawley, 1993), the present discussion may have further implications beyond the question of doping. Similarly, empirical research is needed also on the effectiveness of paradoxical interventions in sport. For this purpose, traditional research methods would probably be inappropriate, as indicated before (Bar-Eli, 1991). Thus, investigators in this area would probably have to be somewhat "irrational" themselves (in the sense discussed here) and to adapt somewhat unconventional research methods (such as the ones suggested by Tenenbaum and Bar-Eli, 1992, 1995a), to achieve maximal (i.e., "rational") effects.

In sport psychology, interdisciplinary work is already quite common in areas such as psychophysiology and sport medicine; however, in other areas, such interdisciplinary endeavors are still lacking. Thus, from a broader perspective, it would be rational for sport psychologists to start integrating concepts and paradigms from other scientific disciplines, as has been demonstrated here not only with regard to philosophy, but also with regard to management science.

Finally, there is also a more general reason for examining the relationship between sport and rationality, because it can be asked whether sport education contributes to the development of rationality. It is clear that one of the chief aims of education in general is the development of rationality (Baron, 1993). It is also clear that there are many important payoffs to sport education. It is not yet clear, however, whether sport education contributes to the development of rationality. By teaching children to appreciate and to participate in athletic activities, they not only play and have fun, but they also develop physical fitness as well as certain personal characteristics and values that are believed to be important for a person's well-being. In principle, these may be viewed as ethical payoffs of sport education. However, if there is any rational facet to participation in sports, then both sport education in physical education programs and training at the club level may have an additional focus beyond sheer physical excellence; whatever rationality might mean, these programs should consider the development of one's skills not only an as intelligent athlete (Tenenbaum & Bar-Eli, 1995b), but also as a rational human being.

References

Abernethy, B. (1993). Attention. In R. N. Singer, M. Murphey, & L. K. Tennant (Eds.), *Handbook of research on sport psychology* (pp. 127–170). New York: Macmillan.

Aristotle (1976). *Ethics* (J. A. K. Thomson, Trans.). London: Penguin. (Original work published 350 B.C.)

Armstrong, J. S., Denniston, W. B., & Gordon, M. M. (1975). The use of the decomposition principle in making judgments. *Organizational Behavior and Human Performance, 14,* 257–263.

Axelrod, R. (1984). *The evolution of cooperation.* New York: Basic.

Baker, G., & Hacker, P. (1984). *Skepticism, rules and language.* Oxford: Basil Blackwell.

Bar-Eli, M. (1984). *Zur Diagnostik individueller psychischer Krisen im sportlichen Wettkampf—Eine wahrscheinlichkeitsorientierte, theoretische und empirische Studie unter besonderer Berücksichtigung des Basketballspiels* [Diagnosis of individual psychological crisis in sports competition. A probabilistically oriented, theoretical and empirical study giving special attention to the game of basketball]. Unpublished doctoral dissertation, Deutsche Sporthochschule, Cologne.

Bar-Eli, M. (1991). On the use of paradoxical interventions in counseling and coaching in sport. *The Sport Psychologist, 5,* 61–72.

Bar-Eli, M. (1995). Goal setting as a motivational tool in sport and exercise: Research and application. In F. H. Fu & M-L. Ng (Eds.), *Sport psychology: Perspectives and practices toward the 21st century* (pp. 111–123). Hong Kong: Baptist University.

Bar-Eli, M. (1997a). A multiple facetisation of psychological performance crisis in competition. In R. Lidor & M. Bar-Eli (Eds.), *IX ISSP World Congress of Sport Psychology: Part I. Innovations in sport psychology: Linking theory and practice* (pp. 19–21). Netanya, Israel: Wingate Institute.

Bar-Eli, M. (1997b). Psychological performance crisis in competition, 1984–1996: A review. *European Yearbook of Sport Psychology, 1,* 73–112.

Bar-Eli, M., & Tenenbaum, G. (1989). Coach-psychologist relations in competitive sport. In A. D. Le-Unes, J. S. Picou, & W. K. Simpson (Eds.), *Applied research in coaching and athletics, Annual* (pp. 150–156). Boston, MA: American Press.

Baron, J. (1993). Why teach thinking?—An essay. *Applied Psychology, 42,* 191–237.

Baron, J. (1994). *Thinking and deciding* (2nd ed.). New York: Cambridge University Press.

Bateson, G. (1972). *Steps to an ecology of mind.* New York: Ballantine.

Bateson, G. (1979). *Mind and nature: A necessary unity.* New York: Bantam.

Beauchamp, T. L., & Bowie, N. W. (1993). *Ethical theory and business.* Englewood Cliffs, NJ: Prentice Hall.

Berlin, I. (1982). *Against the current.* London: Penguin.

Biddle, S. J. H. (Ed.) (1995). *European perspectives on exercise and sport psychology.* Champaign, IL: Human Kinetics.

Black, M. (1962). *Models and metaphors.* Ithaca, NY: International Library of Philosophy.

Breivik, G. (1987). The doping dilemma: Some game theoretical and philosophical considerations. *Sportwissenschaft, 17,* 83–94.

Breivik, G. (1991). Cooperation against doping? In J. Andre & D. N. James (Eds.), *Rethinking college athletics* (pp. 183–193). Philadelphia, PA: Temple University Press.

Breivik, G. (1992). Doping games: A game theoretical exploration of doping. *International Review for the Sociology of Sport, 27,* 235–255.

Coe, P. (1982). Training a world class 800/1500 athlete. In J. W. Alford (Ed.), *Running the IAAF Symposium* (pp. 6–15). New York: IAAF.

Copleston, G. (1963). *A history of philosophy.* New York: Doubleday.

Curly, S. P., Yates, J. F., & Abrams, R. A. (1986). Psychological sources of ambiguity avoidance. *Organizational Behavior and Human Decision Processes, 38,* 230–256.

Descartes, R. (1987). *Meditations on first philosophy* (E. S. Haldane and G. R. T. Ross, Trans.). New York: Cambridge University Press. (Original work published 1641).

Dishman, R. K. (1993). Exercise adherence. In R. N. Singer, M. Murphey, & L. K. Tennant (Eds.), *Handbook of research on sport psychology* (pp. 779–798). New York: Macmillan.

Duda, R. O., Hart, P. E., Barrett, P., Gashnig, J., Konolige, K., Reboh, R., & Slocum, J. (1976). *Development of the prospector consultation system for mineral exploration.* Menlo Park, CA: AI Center, SRI International.

Eddy, D. M. (1982). Probabilistic reasoning in clinical medicine: Problems and opportunities. In D. Kahnemann, P. Slovic, & A. Tversky (Eds.), *Judgment under uncertainty: Heuristics and biases* (pp. 249–267). New York: Cambridge University Press.

Edwards, W. (1962). Dynamic decision theory and probabilistic information processing. *Human Factors, 4,* 59–73.

Edwards, W. (1966). *Nonconservative probabilistic information processing systems* (Report No. ESD-TR-66–404). Wright Patterson Air Force Base, OH: U. S. Air Force Decision Sciences Laboratory.

Edwards, W., Lindman, H., & Savage, L. J. (1963). Bayesian statistical inference for psychological research. *Psychological Review, 70,* 193–242.

Einhorn, H. J., & Hogarth, R. M. (1981). Behavioral decision theory: Processes of judgment and choice. *Annual Review of Psychology, 32,* 53–88.

Elster, J. (1982). Rationality. In G. Flistad (Ed.), *Contemporary philosophy: A new survey* (Vol. 2, pp. 111–131). The Hague: Nijhoff.

Elster, J. (1991). *Sour grapes: Studies in the subversion of rationality.* New York: Cambridge University Press.

Føllesdal, D. (1988). Hva er rasjonalitet? [What is rationality?]. *NFT, 10,* 203–212.

Fox, C. R., & Tversky, A. (1996). Ambiguity aversion and comparative ignorance. *Quarterly Journal of Economics, 110,* 22–35.

Frisch, D., & Baron, J. (1988). Ambiguity and rationality. *Journal of Behavioral Decision Making, 1,* 149–157.

Gerchak, Y. (1994). Operations research in sports. In S. M. Pollock (Ed.), *Operation research and management science* (Vol. 6, pp. 507–527). Amsterdam, The Netherlands: Elsevier Science.

Gould, D., & Krane, V. (1992). The arousal-athletic performance relationship: Current status and future directions. In T. S. Horn (Ed.), *Advances in sport psychology* (pp. 119–141). Champaign, IL: Human Kinetics.

Habermas, J. (1974). *Theory and practice.* London: Penguin.

Habermas, J. (1990). *Moral consciousness and communicative action.* Oxford: Polity.

Hamburger, H. (1979). *Games as models of social phenomena.* San Francisco: Freeman.

Heath, C., & Tversky, A. (1991). Preference and belief: Ambiguity and competence in choice under uncertainty. *Journal of Risk and Uncertainty, 4,* 5–28.

Hegel, G. W. F. (1929). *Science of logic* (W. H. Johnston & L. G. Struthers, Trans.). Woking: Unwin. (Original work published 1812–1816)

Hoberman, J. (1992). *Mortal engines: The science of performance and the dehumanization of sport.* New York: The Free Press.

Huizinga, J. (1995). The nature of play. In W. J. Morgan & K. V. Meier (Eds.), *Philosophic inquire in sport* (pp. 5–8). Champaign, IL: Human Kinetics.

Hume, D. (1978). *A treatise of human nature* (L. A. Selby Bigge, Ed.). Oxford: Oxford University Press. (Original work published 1740)

Kahnemann, D., Slovic, P., & Tversky, A. (Eds.). (1982). *Judgment under uncertainty: Heuristics and biases.* New York: Cambridge University Press.

Kirkby, R. (1995). Psychological factors in sport injuries. In T. Morris & J. Summers (Eds.), *Sport psychology: Theory, applications and issues* (pp. 456–473). Brisane: Wiley.

Kretchmer, R.S. (1994). *Practical philosophy of sport.* Champaign, IL: Human Kinetics.

Kripke, S. (1982). *Wittgenstein on rules and private language.* Oxford: Basil Blackwell.

Kuhn, T. (1962). *The structure of scientific revolutions.* Chicago: University of Chicago Press.

Ladany, S. P. (1996). Sports. In S. I. Gass & C. M. Harris (Eds.), *Encyclopedia of operations research and management science* (pp. 639–643). Boston, MA: Kluwer.

Luce, R. D., & Raiffa, H. (1957). *Games and decisions.* New York: Wiley.

Macintyre, J. G. (1987). Growth hormone and athletes. *Sports Medicine, 8,* 129–142.

Mehrez, A., Friedman, L., Sinuany-Stern, Z., & Bar-Eli, M. (1997). Programming in elite sport: Threshold optimization in multistage sport games. In R. Lidor & M. Bar-Eli (Eds.), *IX ISSP World Congress of Sport Psychology: Part II. Innovations in sport psychology: Linking theory and practice* (pp. 482–484). Netanya, Israel: Wingate Institute.

Nisbett, R. E., & Ross, L. (1980). *Human inference: Strategies and shortcomings of social judgment.* Englewood Cliffs, NJ: Prentice Hall.

Nozick, R. (1981). *Philosophical explanations.* Cambridge, MA: Harvard University Press.

Oakeshott, M. (1962). *Rationalism in politics and other essays.* Indianapolis: Liberty Press.

Parfit, D. (1986). *Reasons and persons.* Oxford: Oxford University Press.

Peters, T. J., & Waterman, R. H. (1982). *In search of excellence.* New York: Harper & Row.

Plato (1945). *The republic* (F. M. Cornford, Trans.). Oxford: Oxford University Press. (Original work published 400 B.C.).

Rapoport, A., & Wallsten, T. S. (1972). Individual decision behavior. *Annual Review of Psychology, 23,* 131–176.

Rawls, J. (1971). *A theory of justice.* Cambridge, MA: Harvard University Press.

Rubin, J. Z., & Brown, B. R. (1975). *The social psychology of bargaining and negotiation.* New York: Academic Press.

Schwartz, S. M., Baron, J., & Clarke, J. R. (1988). A causal Bayesian model for the diagnosis of appendicitis. In J. F. Lemmer & L. N. Kanal (Eds.), *Uncertainty in artificial intelligence* (Vol. 2, pp. 423–434). Amsterdam: North Holland.

Schwayder, D. (1965). *The stratification of behavior.* London: Routledge & Paul.

Schwenk, T. L. (1997). Psychoactive drugs and athletic performance. *Physician and Sportsmedicine, 25,* 32–46.

Simon, H. A. (1979). Information processing models of cognition. *Annual Review of Psychology, 30,* 363–396.

Slovic, P., Fischhoff, B., & Lichtenstein, S. (1977). Behavioral decision theory. *Annual Review of Psychology, 28,* 1–39.

Slovic, P., & Lichtenstein, S. (1971). Comparison of Bayesian and regression approaches to the study of information processing in judgment. *Organizational Behavior and Human Performance, 6,* 649–744.

Smith, R. E. (1993). A positive approach to enhancing sport performance: Principles of positive reinforcement and performance feedback. In J. M. Williams (Ed.), *Applied sport psychology: Personal growth to peak performance* (2nd ed., pp. 25–35). Mountain View, CA: Mayfield.

Smith, R. E., & Smoll, F. L. (1996). Psychosocial interventions in youth sport. In J. L. Van Raalte & B. W. Brewer (Eds.), *Exploring sport and exercise psychology* (pp. 287–315). Washington, DC: American Psychological Association.

Suits, B. H. (1978). *The grasshopper: Games, life and utopia.* Toronto: University of Toronto Press.

Tenenbaum, G., & Bar-Eli, M. (1992). Methodological issues in sport psychology research. *The Australian Journal of Science and Medicine in Sport, 24,* 44–50.

Tenenbaum, G., & Bar-Eli, M. (1993). Decision making in sport: A cognitive perspective. In R. N. Singer, M. Murphey, & L. K. Tennant (Eds.), *Handbook of research on sport psychology* (pp. 171–192). New York: Macmillan.

Tenenbaum, G., & Bar-Eli, M. (1995a). Contemporary issues in exercise and sport psychology research. In S. J. H. Biddle (Ed.), *European perspectives on exercise and sport psychology* (pp. 292–323). Champaign, IL: Human Kinetics.

Tenenbaum, G., & Bar-Eli, M. (1995b). Personality and intellectual capabilities in sport psychology. In D. H. Saklofske & M. Zeidner (Eds.), *International handbook of personality and intelligence* (pp. 687–710). New York: Plenum.

Toulmin, S., & Jonsen, A. (1988). *The abuse of casuistry.* Los Angeles, CA: University of California Press.

Von Neumann, J., & Morgenstern, O. (1944). *Theory of games and economic behavior.* Princeton, NJ: Princeton University Press.

Von Wright, G. H. (1963). *Norm and action.* Ithaca, NY: International Library of Philosophy.

Wagner, J. C. (1991). Enhancement of athletic performance with drugs: An overview. *Sports Medicine, 12,* 250–265.

Watzlawick, P., Weakland, J. H., & Fisch, R. (1974). *Change*. New York: Norton.

Weakland, J. H., & Jackson, D. D. (1958). Patient and therapist observations on the circumstances of a schizophrenic episode. *Archives of Neurology & Psychiatry, 79*, 554–574.

Weber, M. (1946). Politics as a vocation. In H. H. Gerth, & C. W. Mills (Eds.), *From Max Weber: Essays in sociology* (pp. 77–156). New York: Oxford University Press. (Original work published 1919)

Widmeyer, W. N., Carron, A. V., & Brawley, L. R. (1993). Group cohesion in sport and exercise. In R. N. Singer, M. Murphey, & L. K. Tennant (Eds.), *Handbook of research on sport psychology* (pp. 672–692). New York: Macmillan.

Williams, J. M., & Roepke, N. (1993). Psychology of injury and injury rehabilitation. In R. N. Singer, M. Murphey, & L. K. Tennant (Eds.), *Handbook of research on sport psychology* (pp. 815–839). New York: Macmillan.

Wilson, B. R. (Ed.) (1991). *Rationality*. Oxford: Blackwell.

Wittgenstein, L. (1958). *Philosophical investigations* (2nd ed.). (G. E. M. Anscomb, Trans.). New York: Macmillan.

Zaichkowsky, L., & Takenaka, K. (1993). Optimizing arousal level. In R. N. Singer, M. Murphey, & L. K. Tennant (Eds.), *Handbook of research on sport psychology* (pp. 511–527). New York: Macmillan.

4

Moving With the Times: Keeping Up With Trends in Statistical Analysis and Research Design

Gershon Tenenbaum and Gerard Fogarty
University of Southern Queensland, Australia

In this chapter, we review some current controversies in statistics and measurement and suggest what they might mean for research in sport psychology. The first section of the chapter deals with the debate on the use of null hypothesis testing, a debate that has gathered considerable momentum over the past 5 years. Because most research in our field still relies on conventional tests of significance—after all, that is the approach still advocated in most textbooks—it is important that we review the arguments for and against significance testing and consider whether we need to change the way we do things. Our own summation of the debate is that it comes down to a question of reliability: the faith one has in one's experimental outcomes. We suggest a number of ways in which researchers in sport psychology can improve the confidence they have in the results of single studies.

Furthermore, we suggest alternative methods of data collection and treatment of data. We strongly believe that the concepts of measurement and research methods in sport and exercise psychology that we used are not sufficient to advance this domain. We approach first the consequences of null hypotheses significance testing (NHST). Then, to improve validity and reliability, we show how research in sport psychology can be performed by using measures and observations from various sources in order to arrive at sound conclusions. We also argue for more "ecological" (i.e., domain-specific) paradigms that may lead us to account more for athletes and exercisers. Two examples illustrate these concepts. We strongly believe that the latent-trait concepts of measurement, such as the Rasch Analysis, have more to offer to the measurement of human behaviors than do the traditional concepts. Improving the measurement tools results in higher reliability and consequently higher validity of the theoretical concepts we are looking for. We briefly introduce and illustrate this concept that relatively was not widely used in sport and exercise psychology. Finally, we feel that practitioners do not share with us their real experiences. We remind them how to do it for the benefit of all of us. These methodological and measurement concepts, when adequately implemented, will undoubtedly advance the sport and exercise psychology domain.

Rethinking the Null Hypotheses Significance Testing (NHST)

Recently one of our papers has returned from a review process. The response of one of the reviewers is used here to signify the concern that several leading statisticians in the behavioral and social sciences have with what is termed "null hypothesis significance testing" (NHST). The reviewer wrote,

> With three dependent variables, a repeated measures MANOVA would be the appropriate analysis for this data. At least with an experiment-wise Bonferroni adjustment of ANOVA p values, significance criterion would be actually around .016, putting most results in doubt, and definitely attenuating the discussion presented of already non-significant results. MANOVA would also provide a report on sphericity compliance in multivariate data—supporting or rejecting the use of RM degrees of freedom (360 in the denominator) in what are already, at least, only marginal F values.

It should be noted, before we discuss further the NHST, that the effect sizes obtained in the study ranged between 0.40 and 1.71, and although the procedures suggested by the reviewer would reduce experimentwise error rate, they would also reduce the power of the study. There is nothing technically wrong with the advice of the reviewer, but we wish to make the point that this sort of advice is driven by a concern for strict adherence to the NHST approach. We have to ask: Is "significance level" really an additional amendment that should be added to the 10 amendments already published in the old testament? We shall now address this concept in more depth.

According to J. Cohen (1994), who quotes Morrison and Henkel (1970) and earlier researchers, the NHST "has not only failed to support the advancement of psychology as a science but also has seriously impeded it" (p. 997). It is mainly the 0.05 significance level on which Ho is rejected that concerns Cohen. The common neglect of "base-rates" before testing any hypothesis, advocated by Bayesian theorem, results in a substantial error as a consequence of adopting a low and arbitrary probability such as 0.05. G.F. Loftus (1996) further argues that "reliance on NHST has channelled our field into a series of methodological cul-de-sacs, and it has been my observation over the years . . . that conclusions made entirely or even primarily based on NHST are at best severely limited, and at worst highly misleading" (p. 162).

To make sense out of NHST, one should specify what is meant by a "difference" between two or more means of the population. The probability that the means will be identical is zero, and therefore "meaningful" differences should be proposed. Thus, instead of asking whether there are differences between two or more means, the questions should be "How big are the differences? Are they big enough for the investigator to care about and, if so, what pattern do they form?" (G.F. Loftus, 1996, p. 163). When simply testing for mean differences, "rejecting a typical null hypothesis is like rejecting the proposition that the moon is made of green cheese . . . Well, yes, okay, but so what" (G.F. Loftus, 1996, p. 163). The null hypothesis, according to Schmidt (1992), is always false, and therefore the rate of Type I error is zero, resulting only in Type II error. Thus, our science is going nowhere due to false results that rely on significance levels rather than magnitudes of effects. "Amounts" are more important than "directions" when verifying a theory. It is for this reason that regression coefficients are more stable than correlation coefficients and therefore recommended.

G.F. Loftus (1996) argues that

> investigators, journals, journal editors, reviewers, and scientific consumers often forget . . . and behave as if the .05 cutoff were somehow real rather than arbitrary. Accordingly, the world of perceived psychological reality tends to become divided into "real effects" (p < = .05) and "non-effects" (p > .05) . . . no wonder there is an epidemic of "conflicting" results in psychological research. (p. 164)

It is for this reason that meta-analytical studies end up with zero effect-size. When appropriate measures are applied and magnitudes estimated, baserates could be determined and used for testing hypotheses. The 0.05 level of significance would no longer be the ultimate criterion for accepting or rejecting theories.

What then should we do in order to advance the domain of sport and exercise psychology? We advocate that instead of imitating other domains, we should develop statistical procedures that better account for the behaviors observed in our field. We summarize the recommendations made by J. Cohen (1994) and G.F. Loftus (1996) in Table 4.1.

Table 4.1.
Recommendation to Improve the Statistical Procedures in the Social and Behavioral Sciences.

J. Cohen (1994)	G.F. Loftus (1996)
(1) Use graphical presentation.	1) Plot data rather than present in tables plus F and *p* values.
(2) Use effect sizes to show magnitudes and confidence intervals (CI) to replace *p* values in NHST. The smaller the CIs the greater the power.	(2) Provide confidence intervals (CI) to assess the statistical power of the results. It visually shows how the pattern of means reflects the population means-pattern (see Loftus & Masson, 1994, for review).
(3) Decide upon a "good enough" range to test hypotheses. Determine differences in units such as effect-size; logits; etc. (see Seplin & Lapsley, 1993, for review).	(3) Compute effect sizes for single studies and overall ES plus variation and CI for a set of studies. Control for independent variables such as gender, culture, instrumentation, ego, type of task/treatment, duration of interventions, etc.
(4) Challenge the results with alternative explanations (perceptual control over independent variables).	(4) Set a quantitative hypothesis about the underlying pattern of means (i.e., assign weights) and correlate with observed means (i.e., "planned comparison").
(5) Add likelihood ratios and Bayesian methods (Goodman, 1993; Greenwald, 1975).	(5) When interaction emerges, instead of focusing on differences between the dependent variable at a fixed level of the independent variables (vertical differences), look at differences between the independent variable (horizontal differences) at a fixed level of the dependent variable.
(6) Rely on replication.	

These are all good suggestions and are echoed by others in the literature. Hammond (1996), for example, advocates the use of confidence intervals and effect sizes. He also recommends the use of replication to improve reliability. Gonzalez (1994) lists four principles to guide psychological research:

- The theoretical model should play a central role in guiding the analysis.
- The theoretical model should suggest parameters to estimate.
- The researcher should create a design that permits proper estimation of the parameters.
- Intervals should be placed around parameter estimates.

Gonzalez goes on to advocate the use of a Bayesian approach wherein one has to estimate one's *prior belief* in an hypothesis and then compute a *posterior belief* on the basis of data gathered in the study. The essence of the Bayesian approach is the moderation of one's beliefs in the light of empirical data. Gregson (1997) argues that the problem is more serious than simply replacing a "significance" test by a confidence interval and also agrees with Gonzalez that a Bayesian approach is the preferred option.

Grayson, Pattison, and Robins (1997) made an interesting contribution to the debate when they summarized the alternatives as follows:

- continue as at present with objective tests of null hypotheses that severely limit what we can say about the results of a study;
- move towards a Bayesian approach that is intuitively appealing but where the requirement for prior knowledge poses some difficulties;
- adopt some intermediate position, such as a commensense approximation to Bayesian confidence intervals in the absence of prior knowledge.

Grayson and his colleagues stopped short of recommending any particular approach, preferring instead to urge researchers to be more flexible in their thinking about the role of statistical inference in research:

> We also believe that the context of a problem may well affect the interpretive position that one might wish to adopt. In one situation, meta-analysis of existing, focused, pertinent research may be very useful; in another scientifically new, exploratory context, the null hypothesis could well be a very important speculation at which to address evidence; in another well-studied situation, a more quantitative Bayesian approach to inference about parameter values may be especially valuable. (p. 70)

The important point made by Grayson et al. (1997) is that there is unlikely to ever be any resolution of the debate over preferred statistical approaches and that scientists should not adopt a passive role, waiting to see which side emerges the victor. Rather, scientists should recognize that they are in the best position to judge how data should be interpreted.

Considering Implications for Sport Psychology

It would be pointless if we were to advise researchers in our field to abandon the NHST when it is still so widely accepted (and expected) by journal editors and reviewers. Nor would we wish to do so. The NHST is so well entrenched that it is likely to take many years before it ceases to be the dominant paradigm. Certainly it will retain this status whilst the textbooks continue to favour the NHST position. Instead, we would urge researchers to take the not-quite-so-adventurous steps of reporting effect sizes and confidence intervals rather than relying solely on a test of the null hypothesis. This will give researchers wider scope for the interpretation of research findings. We would also argue that the real crux of the NHST debate hinges on the question of reliability: It is a debate not so much about alpha levels and confidence intervals as it is about the confidence we are prepared to place in our own experimental findings. Basically, with the NHST approach, one can make two kinds of errors: a Type I error where one has rejected the null hypothesis when it was inappropriate to do so or a Type II error where one failed to reject the null hypothesis when it should have been rejected. These errors will be detected only with replications that fail to support the original decisions; hence Hammond's (1996) emphasis on replication. To improve the reliability of research outcomes, we agree with Hammond that replication is important, but we would disagree that it is the only way of improving reliability. Another way of improving reliability is by improving the measures one uses in a study and also by increasing the number of measures. We will illustrate both of these principles in research conducted in our own laboratories.

Improving Validity and Reliability of the Research Procedures by Collecting Multiple Measures

Kirker (1997) investigated how aggression and violence develop in basketball and ice hockey. He assumed that aggression is most likely a result of a combination of factors, and therefore the more causal factors that are present, the greater the likelihood that an aggressive act will occur. Also the severity of the aggressive acts is believed to be a function of the number and intensity of actors present. The sequence or combination of causal variables is not easily specified, and factors may operate simultaneously. Thus multivariate causal traces should be considered.

Kirker believed that self-report and introspective measures alone have limited value in understanding sport aggression in real competitive settings. Such tools are best applied in conjunction with more ecologically valid and objective measures (i.e., naturalistic observation). The observation of behavior in a natural setting provides opportunities for researchers to better understand the complex dynamics of aggressive behavior in sport. Aggression is best studied in real time and in the context it occurs. Practical constraints, such as the need for extensive training of observers, expense, and lengthy data analysis, have traditionally been the main barriers to observational research. Today, through the use of the computer and video technology, these logistic difficulties can be overcome, and observational analysis can be used in a more sophisticated manner.

In Kirker's study (1997), questionnaires were constructed to assess the attitudes of players and officials towards aggression, to determine relevant aspects of histories of aggression, and generally to gain some insight into the factors found to be related to aggression in sport but not directly observable and thus not able to be analyzed through observational coding.

With observational analysis, intentionality is essentially inferred. In this study, such inferences were made under rigorous conditions by experts through repeated replays of sport-specific behavioral typologies, incorporating hypothesized typical intention and severity of actions. This approach advances on the use of single measures, such as officials' ratings of penalized behaviors made without the aid of video replays and without supplementary data from the athletes themselves (Russell & Russell, 1984; Widmeyer & Birch, 1984). In the determination of causality, the use of observational analysis, questionnaire data, and players' and officials' comments on a video replay of behaviors of interest advances on previous methodologies.

Experts have been used previously to assess the nature of aggressive-like behaviors (Bar-Eli & Tenenbaum, 1989; Teipel, Gerisch, & Busse, 1983; Widmeyer & Birch, 1984). In these previous studies, the experts used were not directly involved in the behaviors under investigation. They were using their personal experience to infer intention behind acts committed in general (Widmeyer & Birch, 1984) or by others (Bar-Eli & Tenenbaum, 1989; Teipel et al., 1983). Here, experts involved in the observed behaviors of interest were used. Furthermore, the role of the experts was expanded so that they became involved in the categorization of behaviors (taxonomies for coding), questionnaire development, observation of behaviors, and inferences of causation.

To carry out the study the following measures were taken:

- The histories of games between the teams involved were reviewed and recorded.
- Four experts, two in each sport, were recruited to develop two taxonomies of violations and aggressive acts based on the literature and their experiences and the official game regulations. Taxonomies consisted of several dimensions and classifications of severity.
- Attitudes Toward Aggression Questionnaires and single items were provided to players and officials at training sessions prior to filming games.
- Four games, two ice hockey and two basketball, were filmed. A CAMERA (Computer Acquisition of Multiple Ethnological Records and Analysis) video-coding equipment was used for observational analysis.

The CAMERA system contains PC-compatible computer software that records the sequence of distinct behavioral events occurring in real time, each with start and stop times. Complex interactions were broken down to manageable segments and sessions. For each game, two cameras were used: one directed to the play, the other to the court/rinkside behavior of coaches and substitutes. Also, microphones were placed on officials and on the sidelines to pick up comments from the bench and crowd.

- Classification, considerations of causation, and rating-like behaviors were recorded by the experts individually on the computer while watching the games on video. The taxonomies were used as references.
- The players exhibiting the aggressive behaviors were invited to observe their acts on video and reflect on the reasons behind these acts.
- The most severe aggressive acts were selected and referenced as "zero" point. Up to 4 minutes of footage before and after each act from each game was analyzed. Details of players exhibiting these behaviors and recipients of the behaviors were recorded on the computer output, along with game score, time phase, and any other relevant information.

The single analysis for each aggressive act enabled Kirker (1997) to integrate the information collected and generalize the findings across the two games in each of the two sports. His conclusions are presented in Tables 4.2 and 4.3.

When such procedures are adopted, more meaningful conclusions can be made as to how aggressive acts are developed and subsequently how we can modify or minimize their occurrence. The use of multiple measures was instrumental in achieving the aims of this particular study.

Another way of improving the validity and reliability of the research procedures involves the use of measures that are ecologically valid. One of the most frustrating experiences that social and behavioral scientists undergo is the low amount of dependent variable variance accounted for by the independent variables. This can be improved by the use of more ecological paradigms in which performance is measured according to some objective criteria in addition to the self-ratings that seem to form the bases of so many studies in sport psychology.

We argue that when the dependent variable is measured under conditions that completely mimic the real world, more variance of this dependent variable will be accounted for by other psychological variables. Again, this is easier to demonstrate by referring to another research project in our laboratory.

In exercise physiology, measures such as oxygen uptake and anaerobic threshold account for the majority of the variance of long-distance running times. The nonaccounting variance is sometimes attributed to psychological variables. Recent psychological theories (see Tenenbaum, 1996, for review)

Table 4.2.
Summary of Causal Factors Associated With Severe Aggression in the Two Case Studies From Basketball Games.

Preceding Punch and Swinging Arm	
Observed Events	**Other Variables**
• Other physical aggressive acts of less severity.	• Little time left in game.
• Lost possession/missed shots.	• Score differential within 6 points (close).
• String of points by one team.	• Preexisting grudges between players involved in aggression.
• Immediate behavior eliciting retaliation to source of behavior.	• Official does not act when should have.

Following Punch and Swinging Arm	
Observed Events	**Other Variables**
• Crowd reaction.	• Teammate/crowd support; physical retaliation or verbal response to act.
• Team that was target of aggression scores more points than team that commits act.	• Official correctly penalizes judged instigator.

have postulated that goal orientation interacts with environmental conditions to influence effort and adherence in exertive-type tasks. Perceived ability, self-efficacy, self-control, and determination are also believed to be important mediators of behavioral outcomes. Two studies have examined this theory using real-life exertive conditions to measure consistency and adherence under such conditions. Calcagnini (1996) asked nonactive participants and anaerobic and aerobic athletes to squeeze the handbar of a dynamometer at 50% of their maximal squeezing strength as much as they could until a decrement of 10% of their designated value occurred. Freeman (1997) asked his participants to run on a treadmill as much as they could for 90% of their maximal oxygen uptake. Measures of the psychological variables were taken prior to and after the completion of the tasks. The dependent variable was how much time participants could sustain in the zone of exertive tolerance. In each study, the "time in the zone of exertive tolerance" was the dependent variable whereas physical activity, goal orientation, coping strategies, and determination were the predicting clusters in a hierarchical regression procedure. The results are presented in Table 4.3(a, b).

Table 4.3.
Summary of Hierarchical Regression Predicting "Time in Zone of Exertive Tolerance" in Aerobic (a) (Running) and Strength (b) (Squeezing a Dynamometer) Tasks.

Variable	Step	mult R	R^2	ΔR^2
(a)				
Activity type (aerobic, anaerobic, untrained)	1	0.33	0.11	-
Goal orientation (task, ego)	2	0.55	0.31	0.20
Coping strategies (self-control, self-efficacy, perceived ability)	3	0.61	0.38	0.07
Determination	4	0.69	0.48	0.11
(b)				
Activity type (aerobic, anaerobic, untrained)	1	0.33	0.11	-
Goal orientation (task, ego)	2	0.56	0.31	0.21
Coping strategies (self-control, self-efficacy, perceived ability)	3	0.65	0.43	0.12
Determination	4	0.76	0.59	0.16

As expected, the results in both studies revealed that psychological variables play an important role in determining how one can tolerate exertive conditions. Though the participants' activity type determined 11% of the exertion tolerance variance, goal orientation added 20% and 21% additional explained variance, whereas coping strategies added an additional 7% and 12%, and determination 11% and 16%, respectively. A total of 48% and 59% of variance was accounted for. These values are far above those that are common in social and behavioral research. We use these studies to illustrate our point that this line of research should be encouraged and applied.

Improving Measurement Operations

There is yet another way of improving the reliability of individual studies that we can address here. It concerns the measurement process itself, a theme to which we have alluded elsewhere (Tenenbaum & Fogarty, 1998). J. Cohen (1994) stated that to work constructively with "raw" regression coefficients and confidence intervals, psychologists have to start respecting the units they work with, or develop measurement units they can respect enough so that researchers in a given field or subfield can agree to use them. In this way, there can be hope that researchers' knowledge can be cumulative. . . . A beginning in this direction comes from meta-analysis . . . but imagine how much more fruitful the typical meta-analysis would be if the research covered used the same measures for the constructs they studied. (p. 1001)

Meta-analyses would undoubtedly be more useful if the studies all used the same measures, but they would be doubly useful if the measures themselves satisfied basic measurement properties. As early as 1928, Thurstone stated that scales are not sufficient if they do not satisfy the requirement of having an "origin" or a defined "zero-point" with units of measurement that extend from the origin in a linear fashion. To achieve this, Thurstone (1928) stipulated that there should be a systematic attempt to select items that in fact do elicit a linear response from "low" to "high". The requirement for a zero origin poses some difficulties for the classical measurement model. A score of zero tells us little because it does not indicate that the individual has zero ability, it simply indicates that the individual did not get any of the items in the test correct or, in the case of an attitude scale, did not select any option with a value above zero. Nor can we easily make interpretations about the intervals between different total scores. Classical measurement processes do not satisfy the requirement for a zero origin and equal units of measurement in the way stipulated by Thurstone.

The essential prerequisites for constructing such a measure comprise (a) a consistent definition of the domain of investigation (Thurstone, 1928), (b) selection of items that best represent the domain and share a common content classified under a single heading (Guttman, 1944), and (c) administration of the resulting scale to a sample of the relevant population in order to examine the response patterns. Andrich (1981) argued that the requirements outlined by Thurstone and Guttman that define the concept of psychological scaling are solved by the Rasch model. In Andrich's (1981) words,

The most important distinguishing feature of Rasch's models is that, when they hold within some specified frame of reference, they provide explicit comparisons of person parameters which are independent of other persons to be compared and also independent of the parameters of the questions or items used to obtain the required responses. In achievement testing these parameters are the abilities of persons and the difficulty of items, while in attitude measurement they may be termed respectively attitudes and, following Thurstone, affective values. The explicit separation distinguishes these models from other psychometric models, generally called latent trait models, within which framework the Rasch models are often placed. (p. 2)

The Rasch method yields person measures and item values that are independent of each other. Both represent points on linear continuums, and both rely on measurement units called *logits* that have a true zero point with equal units of measurement extending in either direction.

There are many benefits to using Rasch measurement, some of which were described in Tenenbaum and Fogarty (1998). In this section, we will show how Rasch analysis can be used to check whether a scale is suited to the population being studied. In this study, the Task and Ego Orientation in Sport Questionnaire (TEOSQ: Duda & Nicholls, 1992) was administered to 91 athletes participating in an aerobic task. The TEOSQ measures task and ego orientation in competitive activities and has quite a lot of supporting psychometric data gathered using the classical test model approach. That is, there is evidence that the TEOSQ does measure two independent factors and that scales developed on the basis of these two factors are reliable and relate in a meaningful way to external constructs. What else could we learn by using a Rasch approach?

One requirement for good measurement is that a test instrument should be appropriate for the population. Among other things, it should be neither too easy nor too difficult. This requirement also applies to attitude scales, such as the TEOSQ, where it is possible to translate "difficulty" into terms of how easy respondents find it to agree with the items. Where a Likert scale is used, as is the case with the TEOSQ, easy items are ones that respondents feel inclined to rate highly. If the items in a test are too easy, they will not discriminate among the respondents. If they are too difficult, the same applies. The problem of matching a test with respondents is illustrated in Figure 4.1.

In this illustration, the test is too easy for the respondents: The items are all tapping the low end of the ability continuum whereas the respondents are located at the upper end. In a research situation, such a test would not be able to discriminate among the respondents. Administering the test would be a

Figure 4.1. Illustration of mismatch between tests and persons.

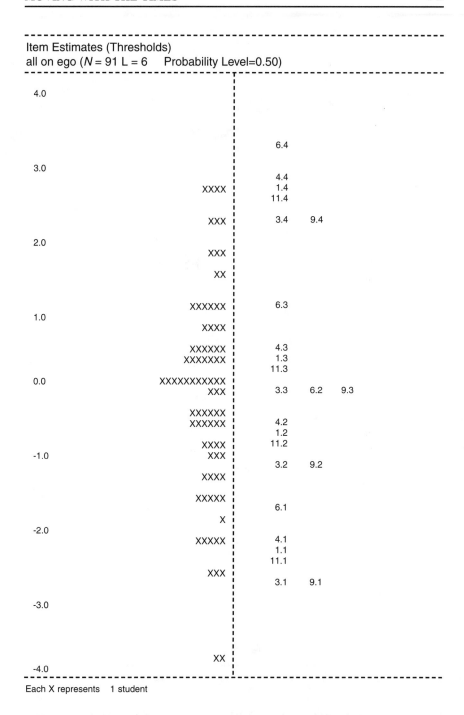

Figure 4.2. Rasch analysis of TEOSQ (ego): Person and item locations.

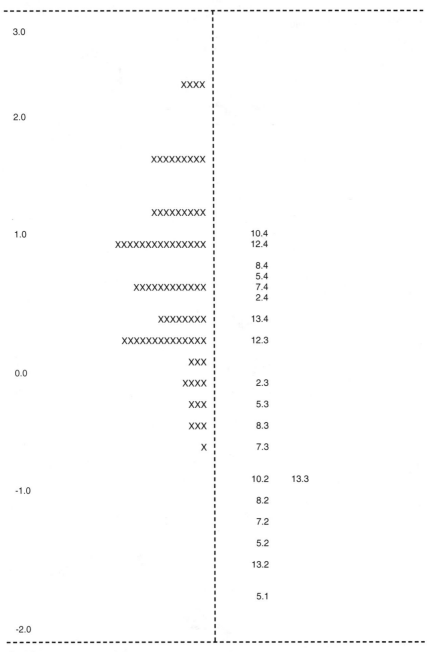

Each X represents   1 student

Figure 4.3. Rasch analysis of TEOSQ (task): Person and item locations.

complete waste of time. One of the most basic applications of Rasch analysis enables researchers to draw maps showing where both items and respondents are located on the underlying ability continuum (or affectivity continuum in the case of an attitude scale). Analyses of this type can be very useful. The item-respondent map for the TEOSQ ego scale is shown in Figure 4.2.

The map may be a little hard to read if you haven't seen one before, so we will explain it carefully. The line down the middle represents the affectivity continuum. People with a high ego orientation are represented by crosses towards the top left-hand side of the diagram. Item locations are shown on the right-hand side of the diagram. Because the TEOSQ uses a 5-point Likert scale, the Rasch analysis shows four locations for each item. The locations represent the thresholds among the five categories. Thus, 3.1 on the bottom right of Figure 4.2 represents the amount of the latent trait (ego orientation) required before one marks the second Likert option rather than the first for Item 3. Moving up the right-hand side of the diagram, it can be seen that an affectivity value of approximately -1.0 represents the threshold between Category 2 and Category 3 of this same item. People with lower amounts of ego orientation will select Option 2 or Option 1, people with higher amounts will select Option 3 or higher. To select the highest option for Item 3, one would need a value above 2.0 on the affectivity continuum. We can see from the crosses on the left-hand side that only seven people marked Option 5. Overall, the ability span of the items and the persons who are responding match very well. There are items that will discriminate among most respondents. This is a favorable outcome.

The map for the task scale of the TEOSQ paints a somewhat different picture. It is shown in Figure 4.3.

Here, there is a slight mismatch between the items and the respondents. The mismatch can be summed up by saying that the respondents found the items too easy. There are no items that can discriminate reliably among the top 20 or so respondents in this study.

The Scientific-Practitioner Approach

Though the role of the practitioner in the development of the behavioral and social sciences was debated for a long period of time, and much progress has been made since then, the scientific-practitioner approach is still underprivileged. Barlow, Hayes, and Nelson (1984) suggested methodologies that enable practitioners to empirically collect data on the interventions they use with their clients so that behavioral changes can be better accounted for and evidence of their effectiveness be more sound. Accordingly, the scientific side of practice consists of three interrelated activities: (a) Practitioners consume research findings on techniques they can apply when necessary; (b) practitioners use their own intervention using empirical methods to increase accountability; and (c) practitioners become researchers by producing new data from their own observations and measures to advance the scientific domain.

It is evident though that the prevailing experimental techniques, which are based on large groups of participants, means and significance levels, and comparisons and predictions in determining treatment effectiveness, widen the scientific-practitioner gap (Barlow et al., 1984). About 21 years ago L.H.Cohen (1976), in a review of educational and health professionals, reported that fewer than 20% of research articles have some applicability to field practitioners. Moreover, about 40% of mental health professionals believe that **no** research exists that is relevant to practice. Though L.H. Cohen (1981) raised the difficulty in defining research utilizition, this concern remains today, and we strongly believe that it is evident in the sport and exercise psychology domain. It is a common finding that observations made by clinicians were disregarded by scientists, and research findings were perceived as inappropriate or trivial by practitioners (Strupp, 1968). Thus it seems that both scientists and practitioners seem to be insensitive to each other's work.

To overcome the disputes between practitioners and scientists, Barlow et al. (1984) suggest to practitioners an integrated model of applied research that has the potential to narrow the gap and contribute substantially to any domain that involves human and social interactions. We believe that if these principles were appropriately applied to the sport and exercise psychology domain, better models which are field driven would be established, and more accountability for interventions would be evident. Therefore, we shall briefly introduce the principles of this integrated model.

The first stage involves an assessment of current interventions suggested in the literature. Such a review can lead practitioners to develop or enhance one or more of these interventions. In the next stage, a short-term study on the effectiveness of these techniques is necessary. Some initial comparisons are needed to establish alternative or modified interventions for specific problems. Then, long-term outcome studies should take place in order to test for intervention efficacy. This procedure is necessary in order to compare the findings reported by researchers and the findings in typical clinical settings (Agras & Berkowitz, 1980). At this stage, long-term outcomes and systematic field-testing are substantially missing. Therefore, the extent of effectiveness and generalizability of the reported findings concerning intervention and treatment are very limited.

To solve some of the methodological problems associated with practice, practitioners are encouraged to treat large numbers of athletes or exercisers in diverse settings. Care should be given particularly to successes and failures as the series progresses and, subsequently, to the **reasons** for these outcomes. In particular those alterations and/or additions that have been made to secure intervention success are to be accounted for. Failures, through the process of clinical replication, and their **reason** should also be reported. At this stage the use of different measures is essential along with appropriate application of single-case experimental design (see chapters 8–10 in Barlow et al., 1984). A schematic representation of the various stages of this approach is displayed in Figure 4.4.

Time-series methodology is recommended to practitioners because variability attributed to other sources than that of treatment can be identified at the individual level, and therefore, more reliable rules can be generated that relate particular client or therapist characteristics to outcome. Thus single-subject designs should be used with many individuals so that generalizability can be identified. Such a methodology, in contrast to group-comparison methodology, may offer more possibilities for applications but "it is only through the work of many practitioners that the development of rules of generalizability, based on the analysis of the individual, become practical" (Barlow et al., 1984, p. 66). Thus large-scale, multicluster, clinical collaborative studies are believed to become an alternative to the classical positivistic approach.

An essential component in the empirical practitioner approach is accountability. Accountability can be achieved only when good **measures** are sufficiently valid and sensitive to the treatment provided to the clients. Each athlete, coach, or exerciser should be provided with realistic "measures of change." Only through sufficient measures can the practitioners evaluate their efforts. Though hundreds of measures were developed in recent years (see Ostrow, 1996), one should be cautious before choosing an appropriate measure or any observational procedure to (a) evaluate or measure changes associated with any problem, trait, and/or state, and (b) estimate "**changes**" in certain behavior/s. Many surveys in the past indicated that a substantial number of measurement tools are impractical in the applied setting (Ford & Kendall, 1979; Wade, Baker, & Hartmann, 1979). Thus, in the sport and exercise domain, we suggest that both practitioners and scientists first read the items before submitting questionnaires to their clients, then, if necessary, submit the questionnaire to clients and question for clarity and appropriateness. Treatments can be improved substantially by being aware of measurement problems, measuring different aspects that treatment is aimed at, and enhancing accountability (Barlow et al., 1984).

Next we briefly specify the guidelines and principles suggested by Barlow et al. (1984) for collecting measures in practical settings. These guidelines,

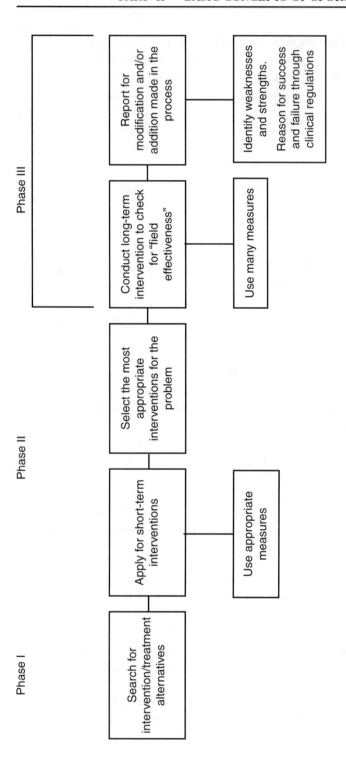

Figure 4.4. A schematic display of the integrated model of the scientific-practitioner approach.*

* This figure consists of ideas introduced by Barlow, Hayes, and Nelson (1984).

through their scientific perspective, may advance any social/behavioral field and establish better ecological theories. These guidelines are as follows:

1. State client's problems or concerns in **specific** terms. Specific terms are measureable or observed. Ask clients about their specific goals and wishes. Use problem-oriented record (POR) and obtain subjective data (S), objective data (O), assessment (A), and plan (P), (SOAP). Goal-attainment scaling (i.e., for each goal establish a scale) is a recommended procedure.

2. Specify several problem behaviors. Behaviors and interventions are complex and should be broken down into dimensions and segments. Quantified measures should be obtained for each problem, regardless of its importance. In several cases, measures that are unrelated to the treatment can also be applied.

3. Obtain multiple measures for each problem behavior. One measure is sometimes insufficient for diagnosis. Sometimes measures of the same trait/state are in accordance with each other. Thus, through clinical replications, the "best" measure for the "particular situation" can be determined. Inconsistency among measures can be then attributed to "method variance." Frequency in reported asynchrony among motoric, physiological, and self-report measures is due to confounded measurement methods and the content being measured (Cone, 1979).

4. Select measures that are both sensitive and meaningful. Choose molecular measures that are very sensitive to intervention changes though lacking in construct validity (i.e., smiles, violent acts, eye contact, etc.) along with molar measures that have high construct validity but lack sensitivity (i.e., many of the introspective questionnaires in use). Molecular measures should be tested very frequently whereas molar measures should be tested on a monthly or longer basis.

5. Collect measures early in the course of treatment. This secures a substantial baseline for late treatment accountability. At baseline, it is recommended that many measures be used to detect problems and concerns.

6. Some measures should be taken repeatedly prior to, during, and following treatment to account for **reasons** and **outcomes**. Such measures are used to provide feedback for the psychologist as to the effectiveness of the treatment/technique and to indicate when alteration is necessary.

7. Comparisons should be made within a specific measure only if data are collected under similar conditions, to enable valid comparisons to be made across measurement. Irrelevant factors (time of talk, etc.) that occur during the intervention are kept constant to enable later cause-effect conclusions. It is of vital importance to insure that changes in

behaviors are due to real events rather than uncontrolled conditions, as behavior is situation specific. Measures should be sensitive to situational changes.

8. Quantitative data should be presented graphically. On the time axis, different measures should be displayed in parallel along with remarks of changes and alterations that have taken place in specific points of time. Graphs provide a convenient means of data storage that can be used later for subsequent analysis and conclusions.

9. Convenient measures should be measured more frequently than inconvenient measures. Some measures that may supply additional information do not have to be collected frequently, though they may supply evidence for different aspects associated with the interventions.

10. Selection of good and accurate measures is essential. Multiple methods and measures are recommended. Though psychometrically sound measures are recommended, use of "real" measures of what clients do in their natural environment is necessary. These behaviors should be recorded by trained observers to secure accuracy. The quality of the self-monitoring data can be improved if clients are aware that their reliability can be detected. Thus, "reliability check-ups" are also important. The selection of instruments that have "functional utility" is therefore required.

Once these procedures are adopted, the domain of sport and exercise psychology may be recognized as a "target domain" in which the practitioner-scientist gap has been narrowed and ecological theories have been developed.

References

Agras, W.S., & Berkowitz, R. (1980). Clinical research in behavior therapy: Halfway there? *Behavior Therapy, 11,* 472–488.

Andrich, D. (1981). *Rasch's models and Guttman's principles for scaling attitudes.* Paper presented at the International Conference on Objective Measurement, Chicago.

Bar-Eli, M., & Tenenbaum, G. (1989). Observations of behavioral violations as crisis indicators in competition. *The Sport Psychologist, 3,* 237–244.

Barlow, D.H., Hayes, S.C., & Nelson, R.O. (1984). *The scientist practitioner: Research and accountability in clinical and educational settings.* New York: Pergamon.

Calcagnini, N. (1996). *An investigation of the psychological mediators of pain/discomfort tolerance in physically demanding tasks.* Unpublished master's thesis, University of Southern Queensland.

Cohen, J. (1994). The earth is round (p < .05). *American Psychologist, 49,* 997–1003.

Cohen, L.H. (1976). Clinicians' utilization of research findings. *JSAS Catalog of Selected Documents in Psychology, 6,* 116.

Cohen, L.H. (1981). *Research utilization by clinical psychologists.* Paper presented at the annual convention of the American Psychological Association, Los Angeles, CA.

Cone, J.D. (1979). Confounded comparisons in triple response mode assessment research. *Behavioral Assessment, 1,* 85–95.

Duda, J.L., & Nicholls, J.G. (1992). Dimensions of achievement motivation in schoolwork and sport. *Journal of Educational Psychology, 84,* 290–299.

Ford, J.D., & Kendall, P.C. (1979). Behavior therapists' professional behaviors: Converging evidence of a gap between theory and practice. *The Behavior Therapist, 2,* 37–38.

Freeman, G. (1997). *An integrated motivational approach applied to account for variability in aerobic exertive tasks.* Unpublished master's thesis, University of Southern Queensland.

Gonzalez, R. (1994). The statistical ritual in psychological research. *Psychological Science, 5,* 321–325.

Goodman. S.N. (1993). P values, hypothesis tests, and likelihood implications for epidemiology: Implications of neglected historical debate. *American Journal of Epidemiology, 137,* 485–496.

Grayson, D., Pattison, P., & Robins, G. (1997). Evidence, inference, and the "rejection" of the significance test. *Australian Journal of Psychology, 49,* 64–70.

Greenwald, A.G. (1975). Consequences of prejudice against the null hypothesis. *Psychological Bulletin, 82,* 1–20.

Gregson, R.A.M. (1997). Signs of obsolescence in psychological statistics: Significance versus contemporary theory. *Australian Journal of Psychology, 49,* 59–63.

Guttman, L. (1944). A basis for scaling quantitative ideas. *American Sociological Review, 9,* 139–150.

Hammond, G. (1996). The objections to null hypothesis testing as a means of analysing psychological data. *Australian Journal of Psychology, 49,* 104–106.

Kirker, B. (1997). *Investigating the causal dynamics underlying aggression in sport: Naturalistic observations of ice-hockey and basketball.* Unpublished master's thesis, University of Southern Queensland.

Loftus, G.F. (1996). Psychology will be a much better science when we change the way we analyze data. *Current Directions in Psychological Sciences, 54,* 161–170.

Loftus, G.F., & Masson, M.E.J. (1994). Using confidence intervals in within-subject designs. *Psychonomic Bulletin & Review, 1,* 476–490.

Morrison, D.E., & Henkel, R.E. (Eds.). (1970). *The significance test controversy.* Chicago: Aldine.

Ostrow, A.C. (1996). *Directory of psychological tests in the sport and exercise sciences.* Morgantown, WV: Fitness Information Technology.

Russell, G.W., & Russell, A.M. (1984). Sports penalties: An alternative means of measuring aggression. *Social Behavior and Personality, 12,* 69–74.

Schmidt, F.L. (1992). What do data really mean? Research findings, meta-analysis, and cumulative knowledge in psychology. *American Psychologist, 47,* 1173–1181.

Seplin, A.A., & Lapsley, D.K. (1993). Rational appraisal of psychological research and the good-enough principle. In G. Keren & C. Lewis (Eds.), *A handbook for data analysis in the behavioral sciences* (pp.199–228). Hillsdale, NJ: Erlbaum.

Strupp, H.H. (1968). Psychotherapists and (or versus?) researchers. *Voices, 4,* 28–32.

Teipel, D., Gerisch, G., & Busse, M. (1983). Evaluation of aggressive behavior in football. *International Journal of Sport Psychology, 14,* 228–242.

Tenenbaum, G. (1996). Theoretical and practical considerations in investigating motivation and discomfort during prolonged exercise. *Journal of Sports Medicine and Physical Fitness, 36,* 145–154.

Tenenbaum,G., & Fogarty, G. (1998). Applications of the Rasch Analysis to sport and exercise psychology measurement. In J. Duda (Ed.), *Advances in sport and exercise psychology movement* (pp. 409–421). Morgantown, WV: Fitness Information Technology.

Thurstone, L.L. (1928). The measurement of opinion. *Journal of Abnormal and Social Psychology, 22,* 415–430.

Wade, T.C., Baker, T.B., & Hartmann, D.P. (1979). Behavior therapists' self-reported views and practices. *The Behavior Therapist, 2,* 3–6.

Widemayer, W.N., & Birch, J.S. (1984). Aggression in professional ice hockey: A strategy for success or a reaction to failure? *The Journal of Psychology, 117,* 77–84.

Part III

❖

Cognitive Aspects of
Skilled Motor Behavior

It is a well-established fact that mental preparation can assist athletes in attaining a high level of performance and that the level of skill achieved throughout the competition or game will affect the performance outcome. Therefore, scientists, coaches, and physical educators alike have shown an increasing interest in theoretical and practical aspects of motor skill acquisition.

In the early years of research on skill acquisition, emphasis was placed on the behavioral aspects of motion, such as the observed outcome of a motor act. During the last two decades, however, the interest of researchers has shifted towards the cognitive facets of skilled motor behavior. Thus, the internal processes that occur during acquisition and performance of motor skills have become of special interest. The four chapters included in this part reflect this specific trend.

Chapter 5, entitled "Skill Acquisition: Current Perspectives and Future Directions," presents and evaluates the research on skill acquisition and discusses the extent to which this research is applicable to the performance of sporting activities.

The topic of chapter 6 is "Learning Strategies and the Enhancement of Self-Paced Motor Tasks: Theoretical and Practical Implications." This chapter examines the effectiveness of learning strategies in self-paced motor skills. Empirical evidence for strategy utilization is provided, combined with practical recommendations for sport psychologists and practitioners interested in motor skills.

Chapter 7, entitled "Orienting of Attention: From Perception to Action," focuses on the contribution of attentional mechanisms to information processing. In addition, the interaction between orienting of attention and information processing is discussed from both theoretical and practical perspectives.

In chapter 8, entitled "Information and Movement in Interception Tasks," an attempt is made to explain the different ways in which information and movement may be brought together. By drawing on relevant empirical stuides, the feasibility of some of these ways is examined.

5

Skill Acquisition: Current Perspectives and Future Directions

Jeffery J. Summers
School of Psychology
University of Tasmania, Australia

Understanding the processes and conditions underlying the acquisition and maintenance of skill is of vital importance to sport scientists, coaches, teachers and therapists involved in movement rehabilitation. In the sporting arena, for example, although sport psychologists can assist an athlete to achieve the optimal mental state to perform up to their potential, it is ultimately the level of skill attained by the athlete that will determine the result. However, despite a relatively long history of research into motor skill learning the field has failed to produce a widely accepted comprehensive, coherent theory of skill acquisition. One reason for the lack of consensus among theoreticians may lie in the vast array of human activities that have been studied under the label of skill. A common assumption of much of the skill research has been that the processes involved in the development of common everyday skills such as reading, driving and typing are also involved in the achievement of expertise in sporting, musical and intellectual endeavors (e.g., Proctor & Dutta, 1995).

As a consequence, models such as Fitts' (1964) three-stage characterization of skill acquisition are used to account for both the development of "cognitive skills", for example, skill in academic subjects (e.g., mathematics) and games (e.g., chess, bridge), and the learning of activities in which skill involves the execution of a complex sequence of movements often in response to some environmental event, such as is the case in many sporting activities. Although cognitive and motor skills undoubtedly share some of the same processes the tendency to transport experimental paradigms from the cognitive domain to the motor domain has, arguably, impeded the progress in understanding motor skill acquisition.

The aim of the present chapter is to examine the current perspectives and future directions in skill acquisition research. In evaluating the research a primary consideration will be the extent to which it is readily applicable to the performance of sporting activities. First, however, a brief historical overview of the field will be presented to provide a context for current perspectives on the acquisition of skill.

Historical Overview

In the history of experimental psychology, interest in skill learning was evident quite early. The classic work of Bryan and Harter (1897, 1899) on the acquisition of telegraphy is often cited as the beginning of research into motor skill learning. Three aspects of their research laid the groundwork for some of the current thinking about the development of expertise (Lee & Swinnen, 1993). First, Bryan and Harter compared the performance of experts and novices and examined changes in performance over relatively long practice periods (e.g., 40 weeks). For example, one characteristic of the learning curves of operators receiving Morse code was the occurrence of plateaus during which there was little change in performance. Bryan and Harter argued that skill acquisition in such tasks involves the development of a hierarchy of habits, and plateaus represent periods when transitions to higher order habits are occurring. Although the existence and cause of performance plateaus produced much debate, they appear to be mainly evident in skills such as telegraphy and typing involving components that have a clear hierarchical organization (e.g., letters, words, phrases, etc.).

The second contribution relates to the importance of the concept of automaticity. Bryan and Harter believed that advance to a higher order habit was facilitated when a lower order habit became automated. The development of automaticity is a key feature in current information processing models of skill acquisition. The third important contribution of Bryan and Harter's work was the examination of within message and between message variability in performance outcomes (Lee & Swinnen, 1993). The meaning of performance variability and whether it is a positive or negative feature of skill acquisition are issues that are currently the subject of much debate (see Newell & Corcos, 1993).

A general feature of learning in these simple repetitive skills is that performance appears to improve indefinitely with the greatest gains occurring early in practice and improvement over time becoming smaller as the level of practice increases. These systematic changes with practice can be best described by a power function and have been observed in a variety of motor and cognitive tasks (Newell & Rosenbloom, 1981), the best known being Crossman's (1959) naturalistic study of the operators of cigar-making machines. The generality of the power law of practice has provided evidence for a common set of principles of learning. Newell (1991), however, has argued that the continuous power-law function may represent a special rather than a general case of motor learning, a consequence of the narrow range of tasks that have been studied. He agreed with Bernstein (1967) that systematic discontinuous changes in motor performance are frequently observed. Discontinuities in learning are a fundamental assumption of the ecological perspective on perception and action.

After the initial burst of interest in motor skill acquisition research activity was sparse until the advent of World War II when applied psychologists were given the task of devising optimal methods for the selection and training of military personnel. Much of the work was concerned with identifying the underlying motor, perceptual and intellectual abilities and devising test batteries to determine possible success in tasks requiring high levels of skill and attention. During the post-war period research continued to be task-centered and was concerned with the effects of various practice variables (e.g., structuring of practice sessions, scheduling of knowledge of results) on skill acquisition. Other major influences in the 1950s and 1960s were Craik's (1948) notions about central intermittency and the analogy between the brain and a computer, Welford's (1952) single channel hypothesis, and the view arising from cybernetics that motor behavior should be regarded as an error-nulling activity. The latter idea stressed the role of error detection and correction processes in skill learning and the importance of the establishment of an internal reference of correctness within the learner. A common assumption that is still held today is that as learning progresses there is a shift from a closed loop to an open loop form of control.

A particularly important development during the 1950s was the application of information theory (Shannon & Weaver, 1949) to the systematic study of the motor system in terms of capabilities and limitations in information processing. Paul Fitts (1954), for example, examined the relationship between movement time and accuracy in simple hand movements leading to the development of Fitts' Law. However, the emergence of cognitive psychology as a viable alternative to the behaviorist tradition led to massive changes not only in research paradigms in experimental psychology but also in the field of motor control and learning. In particular, the orientation of research in motor behavior changed from examining the effect of various variables (e.g., fatigue, practice schedules) on task performance to a focus on the mental and neural processes underlying the learning and execution of skilled movements.

Current Perspectives on Skill Acquisition

The Information Processing Approach

The change from an applied to a theoretical orientation led to a decrease in research directly examining the learning of complex real-world skills. This was partly due to the new emphasis on motor control which stressed neurophysiological mechanisms and the popularity of information processing models in psychology. As Adams (1987) in his historical review of motor learning noted, neither approach had much interest in learning. Rather researchers focused on the processes underlying simple movements, how movement information was stored and represented in memory and how movements were planned prior to execution. This approach to the study of motor behavior has been strongly influenced by the philosophical underpinnings and experimental paradigms of traditional cognitive psychology.

Perhaps the most important fundamental assumption shared by all cognitive approaches is that of animal-environment dualism and the associated premise that mind and body are separate distinct entities. The interaction between the mind, body and the environment in this formulation requires the existence of some form of internal representation of an intended movement and a hierarchical control system in which the body slavishly carries out the commands issued by higher levels in the CNS (Abernethy, Burgess-Limerick, & Parks, 1994).

A second major influence on cognitive approaches has been the analogy between the brain and a high speed computer. The computer analogy has been most clearly expressed in information processing models that assume the processing of information through serial stages, typically involving stimulus identification, decision making and response selection, and response programming and execution. As a consequence, perceptual processes, decision making, and the preparation and programming of movement have tended to be studied as independent entities and the linking of perception to action has been assigned to an homunculus-like entity, the "executive."

The most influential conceptualization of the skill learning process emanating from the information processing perspective has been Fitts' (1964) three phase model, incorporating an early or cognitive stage, an intermediate or associative stage and a late or autonomous stage. In the early phase the learner attempts to understand the task requirements, and various performance strategies are tried out. There is heavy involvement of cognitive processes and observational learning and verbal instructions play an important part during this initial phase. With continued practice the learner moves into the associative phase of learning. This stage is usually typified by a refinement of movement patterns, a decrease in errors and diminished need for verbal mediation of movements. These outcomes reflect the development of efficient strategies for linking perception to the rapid retrieval of information and responses. The length of the associative phase will vary depending on the complexity of the skill being learned. Eventually through extensive practice the learner moves into the late phase which is typified by a reduction in the attentional demands of performing the task and an ability to time-share the automated task with other activities. It is a contentious issue as to whether in the performance of complex tasks one can ever reach a level of automaticity that allows the task to be performed completely without conscious control. The notion of the development of automaticity with practice, however, is a basic assumption inherent in most information processing models of skill learning (e.g., motor program models) despite the fact that there is "no evidence of a shift from controlled to automatic processing for motor behavior" (Adams, 1987, p. 66).

Although there has been little research directly evaluating Fitts' general description of skill learning, it remains the dominant conceptualization of the learning process for both motor and cognitive skills (Ericsson & Oliver, 1995). Anderson (1982) has provided three learning mechanisms corresponding to the three stages of Fitts' model. The first stage, similar to Fitts' cognitive phase, involves the development of declarative knowledge (i.e., facts and information about the task) which is gradually changed through a process of knowledge compilation (equivalent to Fitts' associative phase) into procedural knowledge. In the third stage procedural knowledge becomes represented as a set of procedures (also called productions) specific to the task at hand. Although Anderson's model was primarily concerned with the acquisition of cognitive skills, it has also been used as a framework by proponents of a knowledge based view of motor expertise. Furthermore, in recent work by Keele and colleagues on sequence learning (see Keele, Davidson, & Hayes, 1998, for review) the existence of two sequence learning mechanisms has been proposed, one called attentional because it requires freedom from distraction and may equate to Fitts' cognitive stage of skill learning, and the other nonattentional because learning occurs even with substantial distraction and may be equated with the autonomous stage of Fitts' model. Support for the presence of these two independent and parallel sequence-learning systems has come from PET scan analyses indicating different neural loci for attentional and nonattentional sequence learning.

Motor Program Models

Much of the early work in the information processing approach was concerned with the relative contribution of peripheral and central mechanisms in the control of movement. Adams (1971) proposed a closed-loop theory in which motor learning was seen as a process of acquiring the capability to detect and correct errors. Although research from a closed-loop perspective clearly demonstrated the importance of feedback processes in the learning of slow positioning movements, the theory had limited generality to the acquisition of skills involving rapidly executed sequences of movements. In response to these limitations it was proposed that with extensive practice the sequencing and timing components of a skill become represented centrally in the form of a motor program which can operate in an open loop mode (see Summers, 1989, for a detailed discussion of motor programs).

In recent years, to accommodate for the tremendous flexibility evident in skilled behavior, motor control theorists have moved away from the view that the program specifies every detail in the response, to the conceptualization of the program as a multi-level or hierarchical system. The production of skilled movements is seen as a constructional or generative process in which abstract descriptions of an action represented at high levels in the CNS are transformed into specific patterns of movements at lower levels in the system (Keele, 1981; Schmidt, 1975; Summers, 1989). This reformulation of the motor program concept led to a great deal of research attempting to identify those aspects of a skill that are represented at the highest levels (i.e., the invariant features) and those features or parameters that can be varied to meet specific task and environmental demands. Furthermore, in recent conceptualizations of the motor program feedback processes play a vital role in monitoring the movement to ensure that performance is progressing as planned and for the updating or changing of programs (Summers, 1989).

Although motor learning was on the research agenda, the issue of how motor programs are acquired was rarely addressed. For example, Schmidt's (1975) theory of schema development assumes the prior existence of generalized motor programs. One of the few descriptions of the development of a motor program was offered by Keele and Summers (1976). It was argued that the initial stage of learning a skill involved the development in the learner of a template or internal model of how feedback should appear if the skill is performed correctly (expected sensory consequences). In most instances the learner will use an external model (e.g., watching someone perform the skill) and extrinsic and intrinsic feedback from their initial attempts to guide the establishment of the internal model. Whether the template can be acquired independent of overt practice (e.g., through mental practice) has been an issue of some debate. Eventually, the model will be firmed up and stored in memory. The development of a motor program for the activity then involves the production of a series of movements via centrally issued commands to the musculo-skeletal system and a matching of kinesthetic and exteroceptive feedback arising from these movements to the template. Any discrepancy between current feedback and the template leads to a modification of the movement sequence. With practice an internal representation (the motor program) of the skill will be established that will produce the appropriate spatial-temporal pattern of movements.

This view suggests, therefore, that a key ingredient in skilled performance is the ability to generate the required sequence of motor commands from a generalized source of movement information, the motor program. Furthermore, the assumption that the system that generates movements (the motor program) and the system that evaluates ongoing feedback (the template or comparison center) are separable units has some interesting implications for skill learning. For example, Keele (1977) suggested that an artificial template and feedback source could be used to assist the building of a motor program and described as examples some visual feedback substitution techniques that have been used as aids in the learning of a foreign language and in training the deaf to speak. In the learning of motor skills loop films could be used to portray a model and the learners' attempts videotaped to provide feedback to be used in the comparison process. Attempts to apply these ideas to learning the skills of discus throwing and fly-casting were reported by Keele (1977) and recently Cauraugh (1997) has examined the effectiveness of modeling and split-screen video analysis in modifying soccer kicking movement patterns and the fine motor actions involved in surgical techniques.

Although the motor programming perspective has prompted extensive research on factors than influence motor skill learning, such as the type and schedule of information feedback and practice trials (see Magill, 1993 for review), much of the work has suffered from a lack of ecological validity. Strongly influenced by the research paradigms of experimental psychology, movement scientists opted for carefully controlled laboratory experiments involving the acquisition of simple "novel" tasks, (e.g., unidirectional rapid arm movements, sequences of finger movements, rotary pursuit, reaction time) with performance being measured often by relatively simple outcomes scores such as movement time, interresponse time, accuracy, and errors. Furthermore, because of the type of skill examined and the research philosophy of large N experiments, few studies were conducted in the Bryan and Harter (1899) legacy of examining changes in performance over long time periods. As it is now generally recognized that the development of expertise in many domains requires at least ten years of intense practice (Ericsson, Krampe, & Tesch-Romer, 1993), the applicability of the learning and practice principles developed from artificial laboratory tasks to the acquisition of sports skills may be limited.

A great deal of research effort was also spent on obtaining support for the concept of pre-programming inherent in motor program theory. While many of these studies were elegant in design and spawned equally elegant models of the planning process (e.g., Hierarchical Editor Model, Rosenbaum, Inhoff, & Gordon, 1984), the extent to which the findings from this type of research can be generalized to response planning in dynamic sporting environments is debatable (Handford, Davids, Bennet, & Button, 1997). Proponents of the programming approach, however, argue that the class of skills they are trying to understand involve elementary motor acts that may occur more than once in a string of events and that such sequencing requirements are an integral part of skills such as typing, playing music, phoneme sequencing in speech and the assembly of a set of actions as in woodworking. In contrast, critics of the motor program approach go as far as stating that:

> . . . one can question whether there have been *any* advances in human motor learning and control within this framework (cognitive approach) during the same 15 year period (1981–1996)? Many of the established issues and experimental protocols seem about where they were 15 years ago (e.g., reaction time and programming, schema), and the new ideas of connectionism and neural nets have not had any strong impact on the theoretical or empirical work on human motor learning and control, although there are a few preliminary signs that this could occur. (Newell, 1998; brackets mine)

Modular Approach to Skill

Before leaving our discussion of the motor program theory, brief mention should be made of a recently developed modular approach to skill (see Jones, 1993 for review). This approach is interesting because it revives the long-debated issue of the role of underlying general abilities in motor expertise. Although acknowledging the importance of task-specific experience in the development of expertise, Keele and colleagues (e.g., Keele, Cohen, & Ivry, 1990) have argued that some general underlying abilities can also contribute to task performance. Specifically, they propose that a small number of separable elementary components or abilities, each controlled by a different module (an anatomically distinct neural computation) in the brain, make up a motor program for any given task (e.g., piano playing, gymnastic routine, riding a bicycle etc). The three modular functions that have received greatest experimental support are sequencing, timing, and force regulation, although the existence of general coordination and attention switching abilities have been proposed for complex task performance (Jones, 1993).

The implication of the modular view for skill acquisition is that it predicts that individual differences in the performance of each module will determine the level of task performance ultimately achieved. An interesting corollary of this view is that if performance is being impaired by a low level in a particular ability then specific training may improve the functioning of the module in question. Jones (1993) reports a partially successful attempt to train the timing module.

Expert—Novice Approach

Deliberate Practice Theory

In recent years dissatisfaction with the generalizability of the research on the learning of simple laboratory based skills to the skills exhibited by an expert musician or sportsperson, has led researchers in the motor domain to turn to the field of cognitive science and the study of expert systems. Two basic assumptions dominate this work: The first is that unlike most laboratory learned skills the achievement of expertise in many real-world cognitive and physical skills requires at least 10 years of intensive practice. The second assumption is that the acquisition of expertise involves the development of domain specific knowledge structures.

With regard to the role of practice in expertise Ericsson and colleagues (e.g., Ericsson et al., 1993; Ericsson & Charness, 1994) have conducted a detailed examination of the practice history of experts and lesser skilled individuals in the music domain. The similarity in the practice profiles for violinists and pianists led Ericsson et al. (1993), to conclude, "Across many domains of expertise, a remarkably consistent pattern emerges: The best individuals start practice at earlier ages and maintain a higher level of daily practice" (p. 392). While few of us would disagree with the premise that practice is a necessary factor in the attainment of expertise, Ericsson et al. adopt the radical position that practice is the cause of expertise and that innate abilities play no important role in its achievement. The key to expertise in this approach is the amount of what is termed 'deliberate practice' engaged in by the performer. That is, the level of performance obtained by an individual is a monotonically increasing function of the amount of deliberate practice he or she has accumulated. Ericsson et al. define deliberate practice as a specific activity designed for an individual by a skilled instructor (e.g., a coach) which is explicitly designed to improve the current level of performance. Furthermore, deliberate practice is assumed to be effortful and not intrinsically enjoyable.

In their theory of deliberate practice Ericsson et al. (1993) identified three distinct stages, similar to those proposed by Bloom (1985), in the development of expertise (Figure 5.1).

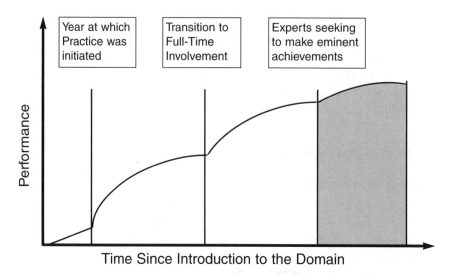

Figure 5.1. The phases in the development of Expertise. From Ericsson, K. A., & Charness, N. (1994). *Expert performance: Its structure
and acquisition.* American Psychologist, 49, 725–747. Copyright
1994 by the American Psychological Association. Reprinted with
permission.

In the initial phase the individual, usually a child, is introduced to the domain through play and appears to exhibit some "talent" which is recognized by
the parents. This often leads to the parents arranging formal lessons for the
child and the start of deliberate practice (Phase II). The second phase can extend over long periods of time and the individual is seen to enter the final phase
when a full-time commitment is made to the activity. The final phase (Phase
III) involves even more intense deliberate practice and ends when the individual either becomes a professional performer in the domain or terminates full-
time involvement in the activity. Ericsson et al. propose an extension of this
framework to a fourth phase to accommodate those individuals who go beyond
the knowledge of their instructors and achieve eminence in their domain.

Although Ericsson et al.'s (1993) view of the development of expertise has
considerable intuitive appeal, it remains to be seen whether the findings from
the practice schedules of musicians can be directly applied to athletes on
whom the type and constraints on practice are very different. For example, for
musicians the activity that best meets the deliberate practice criteria is practicing alone, an activity that has few practical constraints. In contrast, in the
sport domain athletes often need to train with a team or partner and at a specific time and venue (e.g., football ground, gymnasium, swimming pool). In

one of the few studies of the deliberate practice hypothesis in the sporting arena, Hodges and Starkes (1996) examined past and current practice levels and type of practice activities engaged in by international and club wrestlers. In general, the wrestling data lend support to the application of deliberate practice to sport. Retrospective estimates of practice levels over the wrestler's career were consistent with previous studies of musicians, with wrestlers reaching their peaks after about 10 years of practice and the international group accumulating a greater number of hours of practice (M = 5882) than the club group (M = 3571). Somewhat surprising, however, was the finding from a second study of no difference in current practice levels between international and club wrestlers. For both groups the ideal deliberate practice for wrestlers is sparring with a partner of similar size and ranking. Interestingly, this posed major problems for the international group often requiring much time during the week traveling to and from suitable venues.

The application of deliberate practice theory to sport looks promising. Although many researchers may object to the view that innate talents contribute little to skill acquisition (e.g., Gardner, 1995), a recent analysis of the evidence by Howe, Davidson, and Sloboda (1998) has also concluded that environmental factors, such as early experiences, opportunities, training and practice are the real determinants of expertise in a domain. Clearly, deliberate practice theory has major implications for early talent identification programs on which many sporting organizations are spending large amounts of money. Rather than searching for innately talented young people, a primary task of such programs should be to identify young athletes who exhibit the necessary psychological qualities (e.g., high levels of motivation and commitment) required to engage in countless hours of deliberate practice in order to become an expert.

In a recent extension of the framework, Krampe and Ericsson (1996) have suggested that in addition to deliberate practice being essential for the development of expertise it is also necessary for the continued maintenance of expert performance during adulthood. Support for this hypothesis, termed the selective maintenance account, came from a comparison of age-related decline in general processing and domain-specific skills in a group of older expert and amateur pianists (M = 60 years). While both groups exhibited large age-related decline in tasks measuring general processing speed, in the performance of music-related tasks only the older amateur pianists showed significant decline in performance relative to young pianists. Furthermore, the best predictor of the degree to which older experts maintained relevant musical skills was the amount of deliberate practice they had engaged in during the last 10 years. Again, the extent to which these data are applicable to the sport domain is debatable because it is unlikely that deliberate practice will be able to overcome the inevitable decline in physiological processes confronting the older athlete.

Skilled-Memory Theory

Within the cognitive approach, the commonly held view is that extensive practice on a skill leads to the acquisition in memory of declarative and procedural knowledge relevant to the domain of expertise. Support for skilled memory theory has come from a number of studies showing the superiority of experts in recognizing complex, meaningful patterns within their domain of expertise (see Abernethy, 1994 for review). Much of this work was stimulated by the classic study of expertise in chess by Chase and Simon (1973). In that study master level chess players exhibited superior memory for briefly presented midgame configurations of pieces, but similar memory performance to lesser accomplished players when the pieces were placed randomly on the board. The superior recognition memory of experts for domain specific information has been interpreted as indicating that practice leads to the efficient encoding of relevant information into large meaningful chunks and the development of retrieval strategies enabling rapid access to the stored information. The development of efficient storage and retrieval processes was convincingly illustrated in a study of a subject SF who practiced a digit span task for two years (Ericsson, Chase, & Faloon, 1980). Over the two year period SF increased his digit span from 7 to 82 digits through the development of a sophisticated system of storage and retrieval cues.

Researchers interested in the acquisition of motor expertise have tended to adopt the paradigms and models used by cognitive psychologists to examine expertise in activities such as playing chess, solving physics problems, diagnosing X-ray pictures, computer programming and typing. These have included the pattern-recognition paradigm discussed above and think-aloud protocols to examine the representation of declarative and procedural knowledge. Although sport experts are faster and more accurate in recognizing patterns from within their domain of expertise than nonexperts and exhibit superior declarative and procedural knowledge (see Starkes & Allard, 1993), there are a number of limitations that should be acknowledged in the direct application of cognitive paradigms to the motor domain (Abernethy, Burgess-Limerick, & Parks, 1994). For example, the use of static slides to present stimulus patterns in the recognition paradigm fails to capture the dynamic nature of the environmental information available to the performer in normal sporting situations. Furthermore, the meaning of procedural knowledge in the motor domain is not clear and the use of self-report methods to examine processes that theoretically have been automatized are some of the problems with knowledge-based paradigms (see Abernethy et al., 1994, for review).

Perhaps the most serious issue confronting the expert-novice approach to skill acquisition relates to the relevance of the findings obtained. As McLeod and Jenkins (1991) point out, it is hardly surprising that domain specific practice leads to the formation of memory structures that allow experts to better understand, recognize, and predict what will happen in sporting situations than non-experts. What is somewhat surprising, however, is how small the effects are in many laboratory studies of expert-novice differences. The key question, therefore, is whether these differences are the cause of the large performance differences evident between experts and novices in real game situations. McLeod and Jenkins suggest that

> The task for sport scientists is not to go on showing expert/novice differences in yet more sports. Their mere existence is neither surprising nor interesting. What is required is to show whether the differences that do exist are sufficient to explain the dramatic differences in performance between experts and novices or whether we should be looking elsewhere (pp. 290–291).

In sum, researchers from the cognitive approach to skill learning are returning to the legacy of Bryan and Harter (1897, 1899) and examining the acquisition of real world skills over long practice periods. However, the whole-hearted adoption of methods and "explanations" from cognitive psychology has meant a focus on the knowledge structures and cognitive architecture underlying skilled performance with little concern for movement execution processes. Whether this approach will prove a profitable endeavor in the understanding of motor skill learning remains to be seen. We now turn to a radically different approach to motor learning that has its roots in ecological psychology and offers new paradigms for the study of motor expertise.

Ecological Approaches to Skill Acquisition

The ecological approach to perception and action was developed partly in response to perceived inadequacies in the cognitive approach to explain motor control and learning. In particular, ecological theorists reject the reliance of the cognitive approach on internal knowledge structures which are coordinated by an homunculus-like "executive". In the words of Turvey, Fitch, and Tuller (1982):

> When trying to explain how it is that a person can, for instance, play tennis, you do not want in your explanation a person inside the head playing tennis. Our understanding of the control and coordination of

movement will be directly correlated with the degree to which we can
eliminate from our explanation an entity that has the abilities approxi-
mating those of a fully fledged animal—that is, to the degree we can
trim down the homunculus concept. (p. 243)

To achieve this goal, the assumption of mind-body dualism characteristic of
the cognitive approach is replaced by animal-environment reciprocity as the
foundation of an overriding principle of ecological realism. Rather than seeking explanations of expertise in the acquisition of knowledge structures, the
ecological perspective sees skill as an emergent consequence of the direct
mapping between the biomechanical system and environmental information.
Central to this approach is the work of Gibson on direct perception (e.g., Gibson, 1979) and Bernstein on movement coordination (Bernstein, 1967), the
application of nonequilibrium thermodynamics to self-organisation in biological systems (e.g., Kugler & Turvey, 1987) and the concepts of synergetics to
the problem of pattern formation in complex systems (e.g., Kelso, 1995). As a
full exposition of the ecological perspective is beyond the scope of the present
chapter, sport scientists are referred to an excellent "readable" account of the
approach by Davids, Handford, and Williams (1994). In the remainder of this
presentation I will focus on those aspects of the ecological approach that have
most relevance to skill acquisition.

Direct Perception

The central tenet of mutual dependency between perception and action has led
researchers to search for the environmental information available to our perceptual systems that specifies directly and unambiguously everything needed
for the control of action. Gibson argued that energy patterns (perceptual flow
fields) within the environment provide the necessary information directly to
the perceiver about the layout of objects and surfaces as well as information
about the environment in relation to the observer. Key concepts in this approach are *invariants* and *affordances*. Invariants are higher order properties
of the perceptual flow fields that remain constant across changes associated
with the perceiver, the environment, or both. However, rather than perceiving
directly the invariant energy patterns, the organism perceives the affordances
of objects or events in the environment. Affordances represent the possibilities
for action in the environment and, as such, are neither strictly a property of the
perceiver or the environment but reflect the interaction between the two. Thus,
in the ecological perspective *information* refers to the energy patterns specifying affordances that are detectable by the perceptual systems and serve as
the substrate for the coupling of actions to objects and events (Michaels,

1993). As affordances can be perceived directly there is no need for stored representations or mediation by a central 'executive'.

Although there are flow fields associated with each sensory system, Gibson described in detail the light waves making up the visual flow field, termed the *optic array*. He argued that in performing any activity three kinds of information are available in optic array. Firstly, as light is structured in characteristic ways by properties of the environment such as objects and surfaces off which it reflects, information about the layout of the environment is directly available in the optic array. Secondly, local changes in the optic array can also provide proprioceptive information about the relationship between body parts. For example, when one swings a tennis racket local changes in the visual information in the region of the racket head will provide information to the player regarding the position of the racket with respect to the body. Fitch, Tuller, and Turvey. (1982) suggest that part of learning a skill such as tennis involves becoming attuned to this type of proprioceptive information. The third type of information, provides information about the environment in relation to the observer (Fitch et al., 1982). That is, when a person moves in a stable environment a specific invariant pattern of change in the global optic array will accompany each type of movement. For example, moving forward will produce a global expansion of the array, moving backward a contraction in the optic array. Likewise, if a person is stationary and an object, say a ball, moves towards toward that person its approach will be signaled by a local expansion in the array in the region of the object.

From the direct perception perspective, therefore, the learning of skill involves becoming sensitive to the invariant perceptual flow patterns specific to that activity. In ball sports, for example, part of skill acquisition may involve discovering the relationship between the local and global changes in the optic array accompanying movement of the self, other players and the ball (see Davids et al., 1994). Within this framework, practice in a sport leads to the development of smart perceptual mechanisms that are attuned to the higher order invariants specific to that sport.

A higher order invariant in the optic array that has been mathematically quantified is *tau* (the inverse of the relative rate of expansion of the image of an approaching object on the retina) specifying the time-to-contact between an approaching object and an observer. Time-to-contact information has been implicated in the control of interceptive actions in a variety of sporting activities involving catching, hitting, and jumping (see Davids et al., 1994, for review). For example, in a study of elite long jumpers, Lee, Lishman, and Thompson (1982) found that rather than adopting a constant stride pattern in the run-up phase, jumpers made adjustments to the stride pattern in the last few strides prior to hitting the take-off board. Lee et al. (1982) argued that these highly skilled jumpers were using time-to-contact information specified in the optic array to modify their stride pattern. Interestingly, a similar stride profile has recently been found in a group of novice long-jumpers (Scott, Li, & Davids, 1997) supporting the view that the stride modification pattern was not a learned "strategy" but a response to time-to-contact information.

Although there have been some recent criticisms of the "tau" concept and its measurement (e.g., Wann, 1996), the existence of invariants in the optic array onto which actions can be directly mapped remains appealing (see Bootsma in this volume for an in depth discussion of tau and other optical variables).

Dynamical Systems

While the notions of direct perception are being used to solve the homunculus problem on the perceptual side, the concept of self-organization has been invoked on the motor side to reduce the role of an executive in movement production. The dynamical systems perspective has been strongly influenced by Bernstein's (1967) characterization of the problem of coordinating movements in complex activities as "the degrees of freedom problem." He recognized that the production of even simple movements involves many elements within the body (e.g., motor units, muscles, joints) interacting in complex ways with each other and the environment, making the regulation of each element separately an impossible task even for a super homunculus. Bernstein's solution to the problem was the linking together of elements in the system into larger task-specific functional units, thereby reducing the degrees of freedom that have to be controlled. Within the dynamical systems approach these functional units or special purpose devices have become known as *coordinative structures* or synergies. According to this perspective then, an important part of skill acquisition is the development of a coordinative structure that is specific to the task at hand (Vereijken, Emmarik, Bongaardt, Beek, & Newell, 1997).

The major goal of dynamical systems theorists, therefore, has been to discover the mechanisms by which order can be achieved in complex dynamical systems without the influence of an external agent. A key theoretical thrust was the proposal that biological systems can be modeled as self-organizing systems using principles from modern physics, particularly nonequilibrium thermodynamics (see Kugler & Turvey, 1987). From this perspective coordinative structures could be modeled as non-linear, limit-cycle oscillators which exhibit self-sustaining properties and mutual synchronization or entrainment. These properties provided a mechanism for the coordination of coordinative structures "for free", that is without requiring mediation by some higher level control system. Demonstrations of entrainment in human neuromuscular systems (e.g., interactions among concurrent bimanual activities) have provided strong support for this approach.

More recently, the problem of how coordinative structures or synergies are formed has begun to be addressed through the application of principles from synergetics by Haken, Kelso, Schoner, and colleagues (see Haken, 1990; Kelso, 1995). This approach sees skilled performance in terms of the formation and change of spatiotemporal patterns (Kelso, 1995) and aims to mathematically model the pattern formation process. Accordingly, at any instant a dynamical system can be in a region of stability (i.e., an attractor state) or exhibiting a loss of stability (a phase transition) as it moves into another stable configuration. An attractor state can be regarded as equivalent to a particular coordinative relationship between parts of the body, such as in-phase or anti-phase relations (Handford et al., 1997). Phase transitions by which a system's behavior changes qualitatively are the simplest form of self-organization known in physics (Turvey, 1990). Evidence in support of this view has come from sudden transitions between forms of motor coordination observed in the gait patterns of horses (e.g., trot to gallop) and humans (e.g., walk to run), and bimanual actions (i.e., anti-phase to in-phase coordination).

The application of synergetics to movement behavior also allows the identification of a macroscopic quantity called an order parameter or collective variable which captures the current organizational state of the system and through which qualitative changes in the movement dynamics are indexed. Research on interlimb coordination, for example, has suggested relative phasing between the limbs as an appropriate order parameter. The movement of a system through its various attractor states is a function of non-specific *"control parameters."* In interlimb coordination frequency appears to be an appropriate control parameter, for when cycling frequency of bimanual anti-phase movements is gradually increased a sudden spontaneous transition to in-phase coordination occurs at a critical driving frequency. Environmental information or intentions may also act as control parameters moving the system to new stable states.

A key feature of the dynamical systems approach to skill acquisition is the explicit recognition that new learning always occurs against a background of existing capabilities. While the cognitive approach attempted to cope with this problem by having subjects learn artificial novel tasks, the dynamical systems perspective has modeled learning as a "specific modification of already existing behavioral patterns in the direction of the task to be learned" (Kelso, 1995, p. 161). Specifically, dynamic system theorists distinguish between *intrinsic dynamics* which refer to the existing capabilities the learner brings to the task and *extrinsic dynamics* which are to-be-learned movement patterns. Skill learning is seen as the extrinsic dynamics acting on (cooperating or compet-ing with) the intrinsic dynamics. If the required behavioral pattern is consis-tent with the intrinsic dynamics then learning should be facilitated and pattern stability enhanced. However, if the required pattern does not correspond to ex-isting intrinsic dynamics, competition will arise between the intended and in-trinsic patterns and the learner must overcome the influence of pre-existing patterns resulting in increased learning time and reductions in the stability of the new pattern. Support for this characterization of the learning process has come from recent studies of bimanual coordination. In these studies the ease of learning new coordination patterns was determined by their relationship to two inherently stable coordination patterns (attractor states), in-phase (0° rel-ative phase) and anti-phase (180° relative phase) (e.g., Byblow, Bysouth-Young, Summers, & Carson, 1998; Swinnen, Dounskaia, Walter, & Serrien, 1997; Zanone & Kelso, 1992).

Skill Acquisition: Coupling Perception and Action

The ecological approach offers a radically different perspective on skill learn-ing. Whereas cognitive approaches have tended to focus on the outcome of the learning process, the ecological approach is primarily concerned with the learning process itself.

Stages of Learning

Although the terms *coordination, control,* and *skill* have been used interchange-ably in the motor skill literature, to ecological theorists these terms reflect changes (stages) in movement organization over the course of skill learning.

Coordination. From an ecological perspective, the initial problem in learn-ing a skill is gaining control over the redundant degrees of freedom produced by movement of the various body parts. For example, for the learner trying to produce a movement involving a number of biomechanical links, the body parts may seem to have a will of their own as forces produced by movement in one link lead to unwanted and unexpected movement in other links (Turvey et al., 1982). Furthermore, the learner needs to discover the relationship be-tween the task demands and their intrinsic dynamics, as discussed previously. This stage is characterized by the learner attempting to simplify the control problem by eliminating some of the degrees of freedom by keeping as much of the body as possible rigid. As a consequence of this freezing of degrees of freedom, novice performance is inflexible and inefficient.

The achievement of *coordination* then can be seen as the constraining of the degrees of freedom into a temporary coordinative structure (assemblage of muscle synergies) in which only a few parameters are free to vary. In this stage, the role of the teacher/coach is to help the learner "discover" the relevant task and coordination dynamics by constraining the learning situation to facilitate the optimal discovery environment (Handford et al., 1997). In fact, Handford and colleagues suggest that in the very early stages of skill acquisition there should be minimal interaction between coach and learner so that the true dynamics of the movement can be revealed through discovery.

Control. Once the basic form of the movement pattern has been established the control phase involves the manipulation of the free parameters and discovery of the appropriate *control parameters* that drive the system through its stable states and emergent movement patterns (Newell,1996). As the learner becomes more skilled several degrees of freedom are unfrozen, integrated and incorporated into larger functional units or coodinative structures. Handford et al. (1997) suggest that during this phase the coordinative structure becomes task specific and directly related to perceptual information, thereby setting up the required perception-action coupling. The role of the teacher/coach is to assist the learner to tune into the perceptual consequences of their movements, and thereby the interfacing of perception and action.

Skill. For Bernstein (1967) a skilled performer is one who is exploiting nonmuscular forces rather than trying to minimize or compensate for them. By learning to work with existing reactive forces, the need for active muscular force is reduced and the movements of the highly skilled performer are not only energy efficient but appear effortless. The skilled performer also exhibits flexibility in changing the movement coordination and control solution to accommodate changes in the performer-environment interaction and task goals.

A nice demonstration of the progression of the learner through the coordination, control and skill phases has come from a series of studies by Vereijken and colleagues (e.g., Vereijken, Emmarik, Whiting, & Newell, 1992) examining the acquisition of slalom-like movements on a ski apparatus. In the initial stage subjects were seen to freeze out degrees of freedom by fixating the ankle, knee and hip joints resulting in relatively rigid movements on the ski apparatus that resembled an unstable inverted pendulum. With practice, angular movements of the joints increased and became increasingly uncoupled suggesting a release of degrees of freedom. Finally, control over all the degrees of freedom was achieved and the coordinative structure had the characteristics of a compound hanging pendulum. Furthermore, subjects were able to exploit the available reactive forces and thus "ride the dynamics" of the apparatus (Verijken et al., 1997).

Searching the Perceptual-Motor Workspace

The ultimate aim of the ecological approach is "to formulate laws or law-like statements about perception and action that express regularities among observable quantities" (Michaels & Beek, 1995, p. 263). Central to the achievement of this aim is an understanding of how an appropriate task-specific mapping of perception and movement is established. The dynamical interface between the information in the perceptual kinematic flow fields and the kinetic flow fields produced by movement dynamics has been termed *the perceptual-motor workspace.*

Newell and colleagues (e.g., Newell, 1986, 1996; Newell & McDonald, 1994) have presented a framework for examining the perceptual-motor workspace shown in Figure 5.2. A key concept in this formulation is that the coordinated movement patterns that arise to meet a task goal are a function of the interaction between three sources of constraint—the organism, the environment, and the task.

The organism brings constraints at many levels of analysis (biochemical, neurological, biomechanical, psychological, etc.) to the task situation. For example, in some sports important organismic constraints may include the percentage of fast- or slow-twitch muscles, the physical dimensions of the individual (e.g., height in basketball) and the level of anxiety experienced by the performer. The environment also provides many sources of constraint to action that help to shape the emergent movement pattern. The perceptual flow fields, discussed earlier, as well as gravitational forces, temperature, altitude etc. can be regarded as environment based constraints. Finally, task constraints refer to the goal of the action and other factors such as rules that constrain the movement patterns allowed to achieve those goals. Task constraints

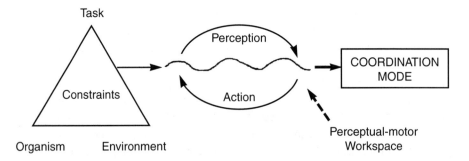

Figure 5.2. A schematic showing the relationship between the constraints on action, the perceptual-motor workspace and coordination mode. From Newell, K. M., & McDonald, P. V. (1994). *Learning to coordinate redundant biomechanical degrees of freedom.* **In S. Swinnen, H. Heuer, J. Massion, & P. Casaer (Eds.), Interlimb coordination: Neural, dynamical, and cognitive constraints (pp. 515–536). New York: Academic Press. Reprinted with permission.**

are particularly obvious in sports like gymnastics, diving and ice skating, but the no-hands (except the goalkeeper) rule in soccer and other similar rules in many sports restrict the number of movement solutions available to the performer. Coaches frequently use modified game situations during training to constrain the movements available to the performers. Constraints then, contribute to solving Bernstein's (1967) degrees of freedom problem.

The view of the learning process portrayed in Figure 5.2, characterizes the learner as involved in a search for an appropriate solution to the task demands through a perceptual-motor workspace which is constrained by the interaction between constraints within the learner, the environment, and the task. Recent research is attempting to identify search strategies adopted by the learner to explore the perceptual-motor workspace (e.g., McDonald, Oliver, & Newell, 1995). In searching for task specific solutions the learner is faced with a dual control problem (Newell, 1996), that is trying to discover the dynamics of the system while simultaneously trying to control the system. Although exploring the boundaries of stability and instability (e.g., errors) in a system is necessary to fully determine the dynamical characteristics of the task-specific system, in some activities the cost of instabilities (e.g., a crash, fall) may preclude such search strategies. Learning to hang-glide while at the same time trying not to crash is a good example of the dual-control problem (Newell, 1996). From the coaching perspective the role of the coach is to enhance the search process of the learner by manipulating constraints to optimize the exploration of the perceptual-motor workspace (Handford et al., 1997).

Future Directions

The ecological approach offers an alternative framework for the study of skill acquisition that may provide new insights into motor expertise. Although the approach is still in its infancy, recent work suggests that applying the ecological paradigm to complex motor skills such as juggling (e.g., Beek, 1989) and sport-related activities will be a worthwhile endeavor (see Davids et al., 1994; Bootsma & Hardy, 1997). Furthermore, the adoption of a constraints driven view of skill acquisition suggests a radically different practice strategy for teachers and coaches (see Handford et al., 1997).

There are, however, a number of problems facing the ecological approach that need to be addressed before it can be regarded as a viable alternative to the more traditional cognitive perspective (see Michaels & Beek, 1995; Summers, 1998). At present, there have been few, if any, data that have supported an ecological interpretation to the exclusion of a cognitive interpretation. Perhaps, the greatest obstacle facing ecological theorists is to provide a satisfactory account of "cognitive processes," such as strategic planning, decision

making, attention and intention, that are an essential part of any sport performance. For example, recent studies of the acquisition of bimanual coordination patterns, such as polyrhythms (e.g., Summers, Ford, & Todol,1993; Summers, Rosenbaum, Byrns, & Ford, 1993), suggest that cognitive processes
play a role in overriding or modifying the intrinsic dynamics to allow the establishment of the to-be-learned coordination. Although an integration of the
two theoretical approaches may be necessary, as some have argued (e.g., Summers, 1992), the modeling of cognition as a subset of dynamics must be the
goal of ecological theorists. It seems that cognitive functions may be best
viewed as control parameters that constrain the dynamical system in specific
ways to produce specific behavior (Turvey, 1990).

Another challenge facing the ecological approach is providing a satisfactory alternative(s) to notions of internal representations and memory that seem
particularly important in the more "cognitively" mediated skills such as typing, handwriting, speech and musical performance. Although the concept of
an affordance appears to remove the need for representations "inside the
head" the concept is still ill-defined and remains unconvincing to many critics
of the ecological approach. There is also a need for ecological theorists to go
beyond metaphorical descriptions and relate the proposed variables to underlying physiological mechanisms (Summers, 1998).

To date, the strongest support for the ecological approach has come from
relatively simple overlearned activities involving rhythmical or continuous
movements and "minimal" cognitive mediation. The application of the approach to the learning and performance of complex sport-related skills will
provide a major test of the explanatory power of the theoretical perspective.

References

Abernethy, B. (1994). The nature of expertise in sport. In S. Serpa, J. Alves, & V. Pataco (Eds.), *International perspectives on sport and exercise psychology* (pp. 57–68). Morgantown, WV: FIT.

Abernethy, B., Burgess-Limerick, R., & Parks, S. (1994). Contrasting perspectives to the study of
motor expertise. *Quest,* 46, 186–198.

Adams, J. A. (1971). A closed loop theory of motor learning. *Journal of Motor Behavior,* 3, 111–150.

Adams, J. A. (1987). Historical review and appraisal of research on the learning, retention, and transfer of human motor skills. *Psychological Bulletin,* 101, 41–74.

Anderson, J. R. (1982). Acquisition of cognitive skill. *Psychological Review,* 89, 369–406.

Beek, P. J. (1989). Timing and phase locking in cascade juggling. *Ecological Psychology,* 1, 55–96.

Bernstein, N. A. (1967). *The coordination and regulation of movements.* Oxford: Pergamon.

Bloom, B. S. (1985). Generalizations about talent development. In B. S. Bloom (Ed.), *Developing talent in young people* (pp. 507–549). New York: Ballantine.

Bootsma, R. J., & Hardy, L. (Eds.) (1997). Perception and action in sport. *Journal of Sports Sciences,*
(Special Issue), 15.

Bryan, W. L., & Harter, N. (1897). Studies in the physiology and psychology of the telegraphic language. *Psychological Review,* 4, 27–53.

Bryan, W.L., & Harter, N. (1899). Studies on the telegraphic language. The acquisition of a hierarchy of habits. *Psychological Review, 6*, 345–375

Byblow, W. D., Bysouth-Young, D., Summers, J. J., & Carson, R. G. (1998). Performance asymmetries and coupling dynamics in the acquisition of multifrequency bimanual coordination. *Psychological Research, 61*, 56–70.

Cauraugh, J. H. (1997). Skill acquisition and modeling: Split-screen analyses. *Proceedings of the IX World Congress in Sport Psychology* (pp. 184–185A). Netanya, Israel.

Chase, W. G., & Simon, H. A. (1973). Perception in chess. *Cognitive Psychology, 4*, 55–81.

Craik, K. J. W. (1948). Theory of the human operator in control systems: II. Man as an element in a control system. *British Journal of Psychology, 38*, 142–148.

Crossman, E. R. F. W. (1959). A theory of the acquisition of a speed-skill.*Ergonomics, 2*, 153–156.

Davids, K., Handford, C., & Williams, M. (1994). The natural physical alternative to cognitive theories of motor behaviour: An invitation for interdisciplinary research in sports science. *Journal of Sports Sciences, 12*, 495–528.

Ericsson, K. A., & Charness, N. (1994). Expert performance: Its structure and acquisition. *American Psychologist, 49*, 725–747.

Ericsson, K. A., Chase, W. G., & Faloon, S. (1980). Acquisition of a memory skill. *Science, 208*, 1181–1182.

Ericsson, K. A., Krampe, R. Th., & Tesch-Romer, C. (1993). The role of deliberate practice in the acquisition of expert performance. *Psychological Review, 100*, 363–406.

Ericsson, K. A., & Oliver, W. L. (1995). Cognitive skills. In N. J. Mackintosh & A. M. Coleman (Eds). *Learning and skills* (pp. 37–55). London: Longman.

Fitch, H. L., Tuller, B., & Turvey, M. T. (1982). The Berstein perspective: 111. Tuning of coordinative structures with special reference to perception. In J. A. S. Kelso (Ed.), *Human motor behavior: An introduction.* (pp. 271–281). Hillsdale, NJ: Erlbaum

Fitts, P. M. (1954).The information capacity of the human motor system in controlling the amplitude of movement. *Journal of Experimental Psychology, 47*, 381–391.

Fitts, P. M. (1964). Perceptual motor skill learning. In A. W. Melton (Ed.) *Categories of human learning* (pp. 234–285). New York: Academic Press.

Gardner, H. (1995). Why would anyone become an expert? *American Psychologist, 50*, 802–803.

Gibson, J. J. (1979). *The ecological approach to visual perception.* Boston, MA: Houghton Mifflin.

Haken, H. (1990). Synergetics as a tool for the conceptualization and mathematization of cognition and behavior-How far can we go? In H. Haken & M. Stadler (Eds.), *Synergetics of cognition* (pp. 2–31). Berlin: Springer.

Handford, C., Davids, K., Bennet. S., & Button, C. (1997). Skill acquisition in sport: Some applications of an evolving practice ecology. *Journal of Sports Sciences, 15*, 621–640.

Hodges, N. J., & Starkes, J. L. (1996). Wrestling with the nature of expertise: A sport specific test of.Ericsson, Krampe and Tesch-Romer's (1993) theory of deliberate practice. *International Journal of Sport Psychology, 27*, 400–424.

Howe, M.J.A., Davidson, J.W., & Sloboda, J.A. (1998). Innate talents: Reality or myth? *Behavioral and Brain Sciences, 21*, 399–442.

Jones, S. K. (1993). A modular approach to individual differences in skill and coordination. In J. L. Starkes and F. Allard (Eds). *Cognitive issues in motor expertise* (pp.273–293). Amsterdam: Elsevier.

Keele, S.W. (1977). Current status of the motor program concept. In D. M. Landers, & R. W. Christina, (Eds.) *Psychology of motor behavior and sport. Volume I* (pp.2–16). Champaign, IL: Human Kinetics.

Keele. S. W. (1981). Behavioral analysis of motor control. In V. B. Brooks (Ed.), *Handbook of physiology, Section1, Vol. 2: motor control* (pp. 1391–1413), Bethesda, MD: American Physiological Society.

Keele, S.W., Cohen, A., & Ivry, R. (1990). Motor programs: Concepts and issues. In M. Jeannerod (Ed.), *Attention and performance XIII: Motor representation and control* (pp. 77–110), Hillsdale, NJ: Erlbaum.

Keele, S., Davidson, M., & Hayes, A. (1998). Sequential representation and neural basis of motor skills. In J. Piek (Ed.) *Motor control and human skill: A multi-disciplinary perspective,* (pp. 3–28) Champaign, IL: Human Kinetics.

Keele S. W., & Summers, J. J. (1976). The structure of motor programs. In G. E. Stelmach (Ed.), *Motor control: Issues and trends,* (pp. 109–142). New York: Academic Press.

Kelso, J. A. S. (1995). *Dynamic patterns: The self-organization of brain and behavior.* Cambridge, MA: MIT Press.

Krampe, R. Th. & Ericsson, K . A. (1996). Maintaining excellence: Deliberate practice and elite performance in young and older pianists. *Journal of Experimental Psychology: Human Perception and Performance,* 125, 331–359.

Kugler, P. N. & Turvey, M. T. (1987). *Information, natural law, and the self-assembly of rhythmic movement.* Hillsdale, NJ: Erlbaum.

Lee, D. N., Lishman, J. R., & Thompson, J. A. (1982). Regulation of gait in long jumping. *Journal of Experimental Psychology: Human Perception and Performance,* 8, 448–459.

Lee, T. D., & Swinnen, S. P. (1993). Three legacies of Bryan and Harter: Automaticity, variability and change in skilled performance. In J. L. Starkes, & F. Allard (Eds.). *Cognitive issues in motor expertise* (pp. 295–315). Amsterdam: North-Holland.

Magill, R. A. (1993). *Motor learning: Concepts and applications.* 4th ed. Dubuque, IA: Brown & Benchmark.

McDonald, P. V., Oliver, S. K., & Newell, K. M. (1995). Perceptual-motor exploration as a function of biomechanical and task constraints. *Acta Psychologica,* 88, 127–165.

McLeod, P., & Jenkins, S. (1991). Timing, accuracy, and decision time in high-speed ball games. *International Journal of Sport Psychology,* 22, 279–295.

Michaels, C. F. (1993). Defining compatibilty, affordances, and coding rules: A reply to Proctor, Van Zandt, Lu, and Weeks. *Journal of Experimental Psychology: Human Perception and Performance,* 19, 1121–1127.

Michaels, C.F., & Beek, P. (1995). The state of ecological psychology. *Ecological Psychology,* 7, 259–278.

Newell, A., & Rosenbloom, P. S. (1981). Mechanisms of skill acquisition and the law of practice. In J.R. Anderson (Ed.), *Cognitive skills and their acquisition* (pp. 1–55). Hillsdale, NJ: Erlbaum.

Newell, K. M. (1986). Constraints on the development of coordination. In M. Wade, & H. T. A. Whiting (Eds.). *Motor development in children: Aspects of coordination and control* (pp. 341–359). Dordrecht: Martinus Nijhoff.

Newell, K. M. (1991). Motor skill acquisition. *Annual Review of Psychology,* 42, 213–237.

Newell, K. M. (1996). Change in movement and skill: Learning, retention, and transfer. In M. L. Latash & M.T. Turvey (Eds.). *Dexterity and its development* (pp. 393–429). Mahwah, NJ: Erlbaum.

Newell, K. M. (1998). Action and ecological psychology: A winters view from Summers. In J. Piek (Ed.). *Motor control and human skill: A multi-disciplinary perspective* (pp. 410–412). Champaign, IL: Human Kinetics

Newell, K. M., & Corcos, D. M. (Eds.) (1993). *Variability and motor control.* Champaign, IL: Human Kinetics.

Newell, K. M., & McDonald, P. V. (1994). Learning to coordinate redundant biomechanical degrees of freedom. In S. Swinnen, H. Heuer, J. Massion, & P. Casaer (Eds.). *Interlimb coordination: Neural, dynamical, and cognitive constraints* (pp. 515–536). New York: Academic Press.

Proctor, R. W., & Dutta, A. (1995). *Skill acquisition and human performance.* London: Sage.

Rosenbaum, D. A., Inhoff, A. W., & Gordon, A. M. (1984). Choosing between movement sequences: A hierarchical editor model. *Journal of Experimental Psychology: General,* 113, 372–393.

Schmidt, R. A. (1975). A schema theory of discrete motor skill learning. *Psychological Review,* 82, 225–260.

Shannon, C. E., & Weaver, W. (1949). *The mathematical theory of communication.* Urbana, IL: University of Illinois Press.

Scott, M. A., Li, F. X., & Davids, K. (1997). The regulation of gait in long-jumping: Expert-novice differences. *Journal of Sports Sciences,* 15, 597–605.

Starkes, J. L., & Allard, F. (Eds.) (1993). *Cognitive issues in motor expertise.* Amsterdam: North-Holland.

Summers, J. J. (1989). Motor programs. In D. Holding (Ed.), *Human skills* (pp. 49–69). Chichester: Wiley.

Summers, J, J. (1992) Movement behaviour: A field in crisis? In J. J. Summers (Ed.), *Approaches to the study of motor control and learning* (pp. 551–562). Amsterdam: North-Holland.

Summers, J. J. (1998). Has ecological psychology delivered what it promised? In J. Piek (Ed.), *Motor control and human skill: A multi-disciplinary approach* (pp. 385–402). Champaign, IL: Human Kinetics.

Summers, J. J., Ford, S. K., & Todd, J. A. (1993). Practice effects on the coordination of the two hands in a bimanual tapping task. *Human Movement Science,* 12, 111–118.

Summers, J. J., Rosenbaum, D. A., Burns, B. D., & Ford, S. K. (1993). Production of polyrhythms. *Journal of Experimental Psychology: Human Perception and Performance,* 19, 416–428.

Swinnen, S. P., Dounskaia, N., Walter, C., & Serrien, D. J. (1997). Preferred and induced coordination modes during the acquisition of bimanual movements with a 2:1 frequency ratio. *Journal of Experimental Psychology: Human Perception and Performance,* 23, 1087–1110.

Turvey, M. T. (1990). Coordination. *American Psychologist,* 45, 938–953.

Turvey, M. T., Fitch, H. L., & Tuller, B. (1982). The Bernstein perspective: 1. The problems of degrees of freedom and context-conditioned variability. In J.A.S. Kelso (Ed.). *Human behavior: An introduction* (pp. 239–270). Hillsdale, NJ: Erlbaum.

Vereijken, B., van Emmerik, R. E. A., Bongaardt, R., Beek, W.J., & Newell, K. M. (1997). Changing coordinative structures in skill acquisition. *Human Movement Science,* 16, 823–844.

Vereijken, B., van Emmerik, R.E.A., Whiting, H. T. A., & Newell, K. M. (1992). Free(z)ing degrees of freedom in skill acquisition. *Journal of Motor Behavior,* 24, 133–142.

Wann, J. P. (1996). Anticipating arrival: Is the tau margin a specious theory? *Journal of Experimental Psychology: Human Perception and Performance,* 22, 1031–1048.

Welford, A. T. (1952). The "psychological refractory period" and the timing of high speed perfromance: A review and a theory. *British Journal of Psychology,* 43, 2–19.

Zanone, P. G., & Kelso, J. A. S. (1992). Evolution of behavioral attractors with learning: Nonequilibrium phase transitions. *Journal of Experimental Psychology: Human Perception and Performance,* 18, 403–421.

6

Learning Strategies and the Enhancement of Self-Paced Motor Tasks: Theoretical and Practical Implications

Ronnie Lidor
The Motor Behavior Laboratory
The Zinman College of Physical Education and Sport Sciences
Wingate Institute, Israel

It is strange that we expect students to learn yet seldom teach them about learning. We expect students to solve problems yet seldom teach them about problem solving. . . .We need to develop the general principles of how to learn, how to remember, how to solve problems . . .

(Norman, 1980, p. 97)

In a typical learning situation, after formal instruction is completed, students must undertake the activity on their own, independent of supervision. They may have to adjust to new conditions, to transfer previous knowledge and skills to related learning situations, and to cope with demands not previously experienced.

To anticipate the future needs of students, instructors may need to pay more attention to enhancing the effect of learning processes and appropriate strategies (e.g., learning strategies) during formal instructional programs. Behaviors and thoughts that learners use during acquisition, and that are intended to influence information-processing processes, should be taught by instructors (Lee, Swinnen, & Serrien, 1994; Weinberg & Gould, 1995; Weinstein & Mayer, 1986). By directing learners in the use of task-relevant strategies, teachers can assist them in activating appropriate cognitive processes at the appropriate time. Ultimately and ideally, students would know more about how to manage their own cognitive processes, and how to analyze themselves and the situational demands in order to improve performance and to adopt future related situations once a formal instructional program has been completed.

In educational psychology, an emphasis on cognitions and human information processing has led to research on effective learning strategies and how these strategies may be taught to individuals who do not use them spontaneously. The prominent finding that has emerged from these studies is that task-relevant cognitive and metacognitive strategies facilitate learning (e.g., Garner, 1990).

Although motor skills appear to be acquired in a manner similar to that of cognitive skills (e.g., Anderson, 1987, 1990; Crossman, 1959; MacKay, 1982), not much attention has been focused on research on learning strategies in the motor domain. It is true that some relevant issues about effective practice conditions are abundant in many specific areas related to teaching and learning motion acts. Some examples are (a) the ideal distribution of practice, such as massed versus distributed practice (Lee & Genovese, 1988, 1989) and blocked versus random practice (Magill & Hall, 1990; Shea, Kohl, & Indermill, 1990); (b) the amount and timing of knowledge of results given to learners during or after performance (Lee & Carnahan, 1990; Salmoni, Schmidt, & Walter, 1984; Swinnen, 1996); and (c) the role of the teacher in terms of setting goals, modeling and demonstrating the desired task, and providing instructions and directions (McCullagh, 1993; McCullagh, Weiss, & Ross, 1989).

However, it seems that instructional guidelines that are related to the thought processes involved in motor skill acquisition have been somewhat neglected in the motor learning/sport psychology literature. By emphasizing strategy instructions throughout the process of skill acquisition, learners may benefit in similar ways as they do when acquiring a cognitive skill. Thus, the purpose of this chapter is to examine the effectiveness of learning strategies in aiding learners in achieving skilled performance of self-paced motor tasks. More specifically, the chapter focuses on (a) psychological definitions of the term *learning strategy,* (b) characteristics and effectiveness of learning strategies in educational psychology in general and in motor learning/sport psychology in particular, (c) empirical evidence for strategy usage, (d) practical implications for sport psychologists and other practitioners concerned with motor skills, and finally, (e) future considerations for strategy research. These considerations appear to strengthen the ecological validity of the paradigms used in strategy studies.

A Learning Strategy Defined

Although the term *learning strategy* has been defined in several ways, it seems that there are many similar practical implications among these interpretations. Singer (1988) defined a learning strategy as a form of guidance for learners to acquire skill, as well as an approach that should be helpful for individuals in selecting performance strategies and building or repairing them. According to Logan and Zbrodoff (1982), a strategy is an optimal organization of cognitive processes designed to achieve a goal or a task. Additionally, Good and Brophy (1990) stated that strategies are general principles of problem-solving and learning-to-learn skills.

The improvement of learning ability necessitates development not only of specific learning skills but also of "an executive control mechanism that automatically accesses and combines learning skills whenever they are needed" (Derry & Murphey, 1986, p.1). For Gagné (1985), a learning strategy is a form of problem-solving ability, and for Bruner, Goodnow, and Austin (1956), the term describes an intellectual capability that enables individuals to control the way in which they think in problem-solving situations.

For some scholars (e.g., Flavell, 1979), the term learning strategy contains concepts such as metacognition, metacognitive awareness, and metamemory, which emphasize higher order internal processes associated with using a strategy. Metacognition, according to Singer (1988), is defined as one's knowledge about one's cognitive processes and one's ability to direct them. Good and Brophy (1990) have added that this knowledge is also about how cognitive processes function. *Metacognitive awareness* has been defined as a person's conscious monitoring of his or her own cognitive strategies during the process of applying them (Kail & Hagen, 1982), and *metamemory* as knowledge about how memory works and how to memorize effectively (Flavell & Wellman, 1977).

Considering these interpretations, a learning strategy is the overall plan one formulates for accomplishing particular achievement goals with a learning task, and the knowledge about the usefulness of this plan. In addition, strategies refer to the behaviors and thoughts that a learner activates during learning in an attempt to influence information-processing processes and, in turn, level of achievement in an activity.

Characteristics and Effectiveness of Learning Strategies

Norman (1980) has proposed that "we need to develop the general principles of how to learn, how to remember, and how to solve problems" (p. 97). In addition,

Weinstein and Mayer (1986) have stated that good teaching includes teaching students how to learn, how to remember, how to think, and how to motivate themselves to learn. It seems that results of studies that examined the effectiveness of strategies in educational psychology and motor learning may provide appropriate techniques for instructors (and learners) to improve these capabilities (e.g., Kurtz & Borkowsky, 1984; Lidor, Tennant, & Singer, 1996; Singer, DeFrancesco, & Randall, 1989; Singer, Lidor, & Cauraugh, 1993, 1994).

For the learning of academic subject matter, Weinstein and Mayer (1986) have identified five general types of learning strategies: (a) rehearsal (being involved in actively preparing by either saying or writing the material or focusing attention on key parts of it); (b) elaboration (being involved in making connections between the new material and more familar material); (c) organization (involvement in imposing structure on the material by subdividing it into parts or clusters); (d) comprehension-monitoring (being involved in remaining aware of what one is trying to accomplish during a learning task, keeping track of the strategies one uses and the degree of success achieved with them, and adjusting behavior accordingly); and (e) effectiveness (being involved in eliminating undesirable effects and preparing to learn).

Considering the educational psychology research, two primary characteristics of an effective strategy have been described in the literature:

1. Two classes of strategies have been categorized: Primary and supportive. According to Dansereau (1978, 1985), a primary strategy assists learners to acquire a specific task (for example, task-specific encoding and retrieval of information), whereas a supportive strategy helps learners improve the operation of the primary strategy (for example, a self-management technique). Furthermore, a supportive strategy may improve learners' attitudes toward the learning and performance of the task and help learners cope with external or internal distractions (Chen & Singer, 1992).

2. The degree of specificity or general potential of strategies has been characterized. A strategy may facilitate learning and performance of (a) a specific task (such as how to write the English letters in alphabetical order) or (b) a category of related activities (such as how to memorize key sentences in a paragraph). According to Dansereau (1985), a specific strategy can be termed as a content-dependent strategy. In the motor domain, Singer and Cauraugh (1985) recommended that learners be taught generalizable strategies more frequently in order to apply them across different tasks in subsequent learning situations.

For each of these strategies, there is evidence to illustrate its effectiveness during learning and performance. In educational psychology settings, for example, Richards and August (1975) found that students who were asked to underline sentences in a passage (rehearsal strategy) were able to substantially recall more information than were students who simply read the passage without underlining. Reese (1977) observed that an imposed imagery (elaboration strategy) tends to improve paired-associate learning performance for kindergartners and first graders. In addition, Moely, Olsen, Howles, and Flavell (1989) have shown that children who were taught how to apply an organizing strategy to list learning were able to enhance their recall performance.

Situations in which learners have been taught task-relevant learning strategies (specific and general) that have resulted in better learning and performance are not found only in educational psychology. The usefulness of learning strategies has been determined in motor learning and sport psychology research as well. Most of the strategy characteristics that were illustrated in the educational psychology literature can also be observed in the motor domain. However, learning strategies that have been developed for the execution of self-paced motor tasks also reflect the state of awareness of a learner/performer. In general, two approaches have been proposed to assist individuals in coping successfully with some learning behaviors, for instance, cognitive and psychological demands of the acquired activity: An awareness approach and a nonawareness approach for learning and performing self-paced motor tasks.

A self-paced task has been defined as a motor skill that is executed in a stable environment in which the initiation of the act is determined by the performer. The act is performed when the performer is physically and mentally ready to execute (Schmidt, 1991; Singer, 1988). For example, a free-throw in basketball, a 7-m penalty throw in team handball, and an opening serve in tennis are self-paced tasks that are performed at the pace of the player. If the performer knows when he or she is going to initiate the act, a learning strategy can be implemented before, during, and even sometimes after the execution. Furthermore, if most of the conditions of the self-paced activity can be accurately anticipated, a routinized strategy can be integrated within the immediate preparation stage and during the execution stage. The two approaches for learning and performing self-paced motor skills, that is, an awareness approach and a nonawareness approach, can be applied as learning strategies by learners who attempt to perform any self-paced task (Lidor, 1996).

An Awareness Approach

Although in many motor-learning situations, skills are performed without conscious attention or thought, it is apparent that beginners frequently think about the activity that they are learning and do pay attention to what they are doing. Even more highly skilled individuals frequently attempt to think about what they are doing.

In most learning and performing situations, many external and internal cues are potentially available for yielding essential or irrelevant information. The challenge is to determine the most minimal, relevant cues at a particular time immediately prior to and during an act. For example, while a squash player serves the ball, he or she can feel the movement and be aware of body parts and their location and timing, in relation to the requirements of the objective. There is visual information as to where the ball landed on the front wall, with what force, and what happened afterwards. Finally, it is possible to attempt to hear the sound generated either by the racquet (when the ball hits the racquet) or by the wall (when the ball hits the wall) to evaluate the quality of the serve.

In another situation, a jockey may be aware of his or her riding position or the distance between his or her horse and the other horses and use this information to plan a new strategy. In these cases, there is a deliberate awareness of specific cues in the situation that may be used to assess how well one is performing and whether any subsequent modifications are needed. It appears that different sources of information can be used to improve performance during the execution of motor skills. These sources are dependent upon (a) the task to be performed, (b) the environment, and (c) the ability of the learner to perceive relevant information at the right time as well as to use it to initiate appropriate actions.

Research was initiated earlier in this century in which participants were asked indirectly to pay attention to and to be aware of what they were doing in learning situations. Cox (1933) directed a group of children and two groups of adults to perform an industrial task (assembling, wiring, and stripping an electrical lamp holder). The children and one group of adults were given a general explanation about the task. The other adults were instructed to pay attention to the (a) manner of holding the parts, (b) visual and kinesthetic cues, and (c) control of attention and effort. Participants who used visual and kinesthetic cues performed better than did the participants who were given general instructions. Although there were some methodological problems with this study (e.g., the instruction was included in such a way that the group receiving it was allotted additional time), it seems that Cox's findings have added another dimension to the investigation of instructional programs. Various kinds of instruction were compared to make learning more meaningful. Performance in a motor task was facilitated best when kinesthetic and visual cues were emphasized.

In an earlier study, Goodenough and Brian (1929) gave three different sets of instructions to participants. The participants in one group did not receive any instructions, whereas participants in another group were given a brief preliminary demonstration and a subsequent verbal feedback of the general types of errors made. A third group was provided with the same set of instructions as the second group and, in addition, was taught to follow a specific procedure in throwing. The greatest amount of improvement was shown by the third group, followed by the second group. In this study, participants in the second and third groups received (a) additional but essential information about the task and (b) directions (although indirectly) as to how to be aware of the correct way to execute the movements (throwing rings onto a post).

In a similar study, Parker and Fleishman (1961) also manipulated three different sets of instructions. However, they emphasized the importance of task analysis. In this experiment, participants in one group received only a brief description of the task, with no formal training, whereas participants in another group received explanation, guidance, assistance, and critiques of performance (a common-sense program). A third group of participants, in addition to the instructions that were given to the second group, received instructions on how to use special ability demands of the task to develop special training procedures. The authors found that participants in the third group performed better than those in the second group, who performed better than those in the first group. Apparently, directing learners how to use specific cues and details that are related to performance may lead to a better understanding of the task. In other words, if learners are able to use more sources of information during performance and are instructed as to how to become aware of them, better performance can be achieved.

From another perspective, Holding and Macrae (1964) showed that physical guidance, as a way of directing students how to perform a task, can help to develop skill. It is not uncommon, for example, for a tennis coach to take the arm of a player learning tennis, and to guide it through the desired movement pattern. By following this procedure, learners may increase their movement awareness of the correct way to execute the skill. Not only may direct and indirect instructions develop awareness in learners, but it may also be developed when learners talk to themselves about the directions/instructions that were introduced before practice began. Holding (1965), for example, found that at the very early stage of practice, better beginning learners tend to mutter to themselves. By doing this, they may increase their awareness of the (a) instructions, (b) specific demands of the task, and (c) particular ways in which the potential number of errors may be reduced.

Also, practical advice (not necessarily based on research evidence) has been offered on how awareness of performance can lead to better achievement. Gallwey (1981) has proposed that a good instructor is "one who engages the student in learning from experience and increases his self-trust" (p.12). Gallwey called this awareness instruction and defined it as a mode of learning in which individuals are requested to attempt to feel what is happening. He proposed that learners should be asked to (a) feel their movements, (b) listen to the sound of the happening event, and (c) pay attention to the direction of the movements.

So far, an attempt has been made to describe awareness and awareness instructions at the beginning of the learning process. However, it also seems that experienced performers, if instructed to do so, are able to develop a state of awareness during performance. Ravizza (1986) stated that the skilled athlete should "be encouraged to become aware of his or her one ideal performance state and routine behaviors . . ." (p. 151) to focus attention on the task. According to Ravizza, awareness is developed in sport, and experience and practice can help athletes to be aware of their optimal emotional and arousal levels. In addition, it has been shown by Laszlo and Bairstow (1983) that kinesthesis sensitivity can be trained and that once kinesthetic awareness has been established, the ability to use kinesthetic information is retained.

In summary, beginners may consciously try to attend to environmental cues and specific details during the act. They attempt to be aware of what they are doing. In most instructional settings, beginners are usually taught to think about the execution of the movements and how to use movement-produced feedback. However, in sport settings, skilled athletes have reported that they did not pay attention to what they were doing when they executed at their best. They seemed to perform without awareness. They were relaxed and presumably let the movements flow. The movements appear to be exhibited as if the athlete was in a state of automaticity, performing without any conscious attention. This state of awareness is reflected in the nonawareness approach to learning and performance.

A Nonawareness Approach

One of the characteristics that seemingly is related to excellence in the execution of any sport act appears to be performance without deliberate conscious attention to self or situation. Furthermore, more complicated externally paced activities, as in ongoing tennis play, require the automatization of routine skills so that attention can be freed for anticipation and decision making. According to Abernethy (1993), the mastery of any skill, whether a routine daily task or a highly refined talent, depends on the ability to perform it as if sub consciously, effectively meeting the challenge of the situation with minimal effort.

When performers attain a state of automaticity, it appears that they do not have to think about what they are doing, and movements are sub consciously executed. Generally, when skilled athletes, dancers, or musicians are asked afterward what they thought about during their best performances, they typically report that they remember very little. After initiating the activity, the body seems to take over and everything "just happens". They "relax their mind" and perform with minimum conscious effort.

In exploring the state of mind associated with this feeling, sport psychologists (Loehr, 1982, 1990; Suinn, 1976) agree that words and phrases such as "automatic," "unconscious," "without thought," and "focus on the present" characterize athletes during peak performance. Garfield and Bennett (1984) suggest that athletes lose all conscious thought of what has been learned about "how to use the mind and body" (p. 179) when they perform at their best. They use the term *letting go* to indicate the mental state that athletes experience, and point out that learning to "let it happen" rather than "trying to make it happen" is the major step in achieving this performance state.

Apparently, athletes have minimal thoughts about what they should do or how they should do it during an outstanding competitive performance. They may feel (a) isolated from all distractors, (b) so involved in the action that there is not even a question of confidence or the lack of it, and (c) possessed of all the time they need to respond accurately. According to Singleton (1988), tennis players should learn to relax and let their "mind function to its ability" (p. 50). He recommends that athletes not think about their strokes when they play. Instead, they should relax and "let their mind automatically make the shots" (p. 50).

When working with tennis and golf players, Gallwey (1976, 1981) observed that players develop a unique approach during a practice or match: They hit the ball through an automatic process that seemingly does not require thinking. The athletes may be aware of the sight, sound, or the tactical situation, but they seem to know what and how to perform without thinking about it. Based on this state, a mental technique associated with the ability to perform skills (such as a serve in tennis) without thinking about or being aware of the actual act was introduced by Gallwey (1976).

Excellence in performance has been studied in other situations besides sports. By asking people to think out loud as they attempt to solve a problem, it is possible to study how they use their knowledge, for example, in playing chess or solving physics problems (Good & Brophy, 1990; Welker, 1991). Research in this area involves comparing the thinking of skilled and experienced experts with that of novices. The purpose of this kind of investigation is to describe "how the experts do it" and to identify the nature of problems that the novices experience (Ericsson & Charness, 1994; Greeno, 1980). Such knowledge may be used as a basis for instruction designed to move novices toward expert status more quickly by teaching them to think as experts do and by teaching them to achieve more expediently.

Expert-novice studies have revealed differences in problem perception. Experts respond faster and more accurately than novices do when the knowledge is relevant in specific situations (Ericsson & Charness, 1994; Good & Brophy, 1990; Welker, 1991). For example, expert chess players perceive board positions of actual chess games in terms of patterns of board arrangement, whereas novices cannot construct this arrangement and try to keep track of each individual piece (Chase & Simon, 1973). It seems that experts plan their journey and are able to see the whole picture, whereas novices may depend on specific cues and must think about each position separately.

Ericsson and Charness (1994) pointed out that experts bring a much broader, deeper, and better organized body of specific knowledge to problems than novices do. They do this by relying on chunking strategies and by activating familiar strategy schemes. Novices tend to focus on specific features of problems and try to link them to specific information stored in their memory. Additionally, experts have extraordinarily fast and accurate pattern-recognition capabilities for these specific activities.

If implementing a nonawareness approach, beginners should try to perform without deliberately attending to what they are doing. They should attempt to imitate the mode of operation of skilled performers. This strategy of approaching the task may be too difficult for the novice learner who is involved in a very initial stage of learning. As a result, an individual may need to first go through the awareness approach, and after gaining some experience with the activity, he or she would be more able to use the nonawareness strategy.

In order to assist learners to overcome the transition between the awareness and the nonawareness approaches, a third learning strategy is presented. This strategy contains five sequential steps that are utilized before, during, and after the execution of a self-paced motor task.

The Five-Step Approach

The Five-Step Approach (5-SA) (Singer, 1988) is a global strategy that contains five steps: Readying, imaging, focusing attention, executing, and evaluating. It has been proposed as a facilitator in learning as well as performing all types of self-paced skills (Singer, 1988). The effect of the strategy across different self-paced motor tasks is due to its containing five substrategies that intuitively seem to be beneficial for achievement. In addition, each substrategy has been subjected to a fair amount of scientific scrutiny. The procedures of each step are outlined next.

Step 1: Readying

When executing any motor skill, the learner must be psychologically and physically ready to perform at his or her best. For example, ideally the person should know how to control and direct emotions and motivations in order to achieve an optimal arousal condition for the task to be learned/performed (Weinberg & Gould, 1995).

In fact, research on the relationship between arousal and performance has indicated that performance is better when the arousal level is appropriate for the task (Gould, Horn, & Spreeman, 1983; Powell & Verner, 1982). A person with low arousal is typically unmotivated whereas a person with high arousal is overwhelmed and disorganized. Under these conditions, optimal performance will not be achieved.

Bandura has proposed (1990, 1997) that self-beliefs of efficacy influence how people feel, think, and act. In other words, the actual performance will be predicted by the individual's belief in personal competence. Thus, it is recommended that performers convince themselves that they can successfully execute the task.

Additionally, Weinberg (1997) and Locke and Latham (1985) have reported that individuals may set learning and performance goals. The goals must be specific, difficult but realistic, and positive. Thus, by having appropriate expectations, learners may (a) be ready mentally to perform the activity (knowing what they can do at their best and what they want to do), (b) be motivated to achieve better, and (c) increase the probability of success.

With regard to this research, Singer (1986) has emphasized four points to consider by teachers and learners in the psychological and cognitive preparatory state of the learner:

1. Previous experience, familiarity, and skill level in the present activity.
2. Previous best performance in the same or similar events.
3. Cognitive style (personal approaches to addressing and solving problems).
4. Attitude and feeling toward and in the situation.

Hence, at this stage, learners should try to attain a constructive preparatory routine, and to develop consistency in its use. In addition, positive thinking about the coming event, the act, or the outcome can benefit performance.

Step 2: Imaging

Imaging has been defined as a process in which the performer visualizes him or herself performing the event to the best of his or her ability (Gould & Damarjian, 1997). In addition, to enhance imaging, a kinesthetic awareness of the movement may be included or even a form of self-talk (Singer & Cauraugh, 1984). Ryan and Simons (1982) have proposed that the more clearly and vividly a learner can form the mental presentation of the event, the better the act will be executed.

Research in sport psychology and motor learning has shown that imagery practice can be effective in enhancing achievement (Epstein, 1980; Meichenbaum, 1976; Weinberg, Seabourne, & Jackson, 1981). In these studies, learners who were instructed on how to appropriately use imagery techniques seemed to benefit from it while acquiring a new skill.

There are, however, different ways to imagine. For example, a distinction has been made between the terms "internal" and "external" imagery. Internal imagery involves seeing or feeling something from the performer's point of view. In other words, learners image themselves performing the act. On the other hand, external imagery occurs when performers see themselves from the point of view of an external observer. Both internal and external imagery techniques can assist learners (Weinberg & Gould, 1995). However, internal imagery techniques may be more desirable because proprioceptive mechanisms can be involved in the process, possibly leading to strengthening of the visual presentation (Epstein, 1980).

Pursuing this line of reasoning, internal imagery is recommended for the 5-SA (Singer, 1988). Learners should not only mentally picture themselves doing the act at their very best, but also try to feel the movements being performed.

Step 3: Focusing Attention

According to Shiffrin (1989), the term *attention* has been used to refer to all aspects of human cognition that people can control and have to do with limited resources or capacity. Additionally, Singer, Cauraugh, Murphey, Chen, and Lidor (1991) have pointed out that attentional processes are associated with many stages in information processing. For instance, focusing on the most relevant cue of those available at a particular point of time is important in order to execute a task successfully. Of course, it may be necessary to divide attention among cues, depending on the performance concept and the level of the performer. Irrelevant sources of information need to be ignored and nonattended.

Singer, Cauraugh, Tennant, et al. (1991) have reviewed concepts and research on distractors and attentional processes in relation to the performance of motor skills. They have postulated that there are no clear-cut conclusions with regard to distractor effects on performance, although it is generally believed that distractors can potentially disrupt performance unless appropriate attentional-focusing techniques are used. Few studies have been undertaken on attentional programs and distractors.

In this context, applied sport psychologists, such as Gallwey (1981), Nideffer (1993), and Orlick (1990), have developed training programs for assisting athletes to improve their ability to direct their attention appropriately during performance. Although more research is needed to determine the effectiveness of such programs, it has been reported that learners seem to benefit from such experience. For example, in Gallwey's program, golfers are asked to (a) focus their attention on a very specific cue (such as listening to the sound of the ball impacting the golf club), (b) relax, and, (c) let the movement go (Gallwey, 1981). With this procedure, beginners as well as skilled performers may (a) reduce their information-processing activity, (b) block out any potential distractors (internal or external), and (c) perform the task without conscious attention, as if in a state of automaticity.

While performing a self-paced task, individuals have the time to select the appropriate cue and focus their attention correctly. When the same activity is repeated under almost the same conditions, learners should be able to develop an optimal state of concentration. This in itself may lead to a reduced negative effect of any potential distractors, thereby resulting in better performance (Abernethy, 1993; Hardy, Jones, & Gould, 1996).

For the 5-SA, Singer (1988) has provided the following guidelines to be followed during the performance of an act:

1. Concentrate intensely on one relevant feature.
2. Think only of this specific cue.
3. Try to block out any other internal or external thoughts.

Step 4: Executing

In this step, the learner should perform without thinking of the act or the outcome of the act (Singer, 1988). When the appropriate focus of attention has been attained, the self-paced task (which is self-initiated) should then be executed. Singer (1988) has pointed out that "the self-mechanism seems to say 'do it'" (p. 58).

The execution step of the strategy is salient. The fourth step considers the actual behaviors and thoughts of the learner while performing the motor task. During the first three steps of the strategy, learners are asked to prepare themselves for performing the task. They are told that by following these preparation stages (readying, imaging, and focusing attention) performance will be facilitated. However, in the fourth step, learners are directed to execute the movement without thinking of anything. They are asked to perform the task without being aware of what they are doing—just do it (Singer, 1988). This state of the strategy seems to represent how skilled performers, performing at their best, approach a situation.

Step 5: Evaluating

If time permits between attempts at the task, the learner should analyze (a) the quality of the performance and (b) the effectiveness of each substrategy (Singer, 1988). However, if time does not permit, this step should be omitted. Time is typically available during practice or training sessions but may not be so under real performance conditions.

Learners can use their own movement-generated feedback to evaluate their performance (Magill, 1993). In most self-paced tasks, performers are able to see the outcome of their performance. For example, basketball players can see if a foul shot was successfully made during the game. If they missed the target, they are then able to (a) use visual information to evaluate their last trial, (b) analyze what the causes were for this poor performance, (c) suggest to themselves a better way to shoot the ball, and (d) perform better in the next trial. In this case, self-feedback mechanism can be used by the person without any need of feedback from an external source, such as a coach (Magill, 1993).

However, inadequate execution may be due to factors other than poor mechanics. Besides feedback information to evaluate performance outcome, the ability to correctly evaluate how well the processes associated with the previous four steps of the strategy were activated is also important, although very infrequently considered. If there is sufficient time, as in practice, the contribution of each of the steps to the quality of the performance of an act can be assessed. It is impossible for instructors to evaluate the learner's cognitive and psychological state in producing the desired state for each of the steps. The extent that the learner images, ideally immediately prior to an act, can be determined only by the learner. A verbal report can be given by the individual to the instructor after the performance is completed (Christina & Corcos, 1988). The better one can analyze and evaluate the contribution of each substrategy to the actual performance, the more likely that appropriate corrective steps can be taken. For example, if a lack of focused attention is a problem, emphasis should be placed on improving this phase in the overall sequence of events (Nideffer, 1993).

An attempt to determine the usefulness of the 5-SA as well as of the awareness approach and the nonawareness approach has been made in motor learning and sport psychology research. Although most of the empirical evidence has emerged from laboratory investigations (e.g., Singer, et al., 1994), there have been a few attempts (e.g., Lidor, 1997; Lidor & Tenenbaum, 1994) to study the usage of these strategies in field settings.

Empirical Evidence for Strategy Usage

In most studies, participants have been given strategy training sessions before practice and are asked to apply them when learning a primary task and possibly subsequent related tasks. In addition to the ability to enhance the acquisition of a primary motor task, the strategies are examined in a transfer design (Schmidt, 1991). A learning situation that demands that learners use the acquired knowledge in a new but related condition further indicates the contribution of a task-pertinent learning strategy. Typically, the effectiveness of the strategies has been studied under controlled conditions, (i.e., laboratory settings), in which the control over the independent variable and the strategy procedures to be followed by the participants is almost optimal. Most of the strategy guidelines have been derived from laboratory investigations.

Laboratory Inquiry

Attempts have been made to examine the effectiveness of the 5-SA under laboratory conditions vs. controlled conditions, (e.g., a no-strategy effect) and the effectiveness of the 5-SA, the awareness approach, and the nonawareness approach vs. control conditions.

When studying the effect of the 5-SA on skill attainment in self-paced motor tasks, Singer and Suwanthada (1986) and Singer, DeFrancesco, and Randall (1989) found that participants who were taught the strategy achieved at a higher level of performance than those who did not use it. In Singer and Suwanthada's (1986) study, the value of the 5-SA as a general task-referenced strategy was investigated. Participants were asked to perform three different tasks: (a) a specific task (underhand dart throwing), (b) a very related task (dart throwing), and (c) a less related task (soccer foul shooting). The commonality among the three tasks was that they were self-paced. Two prominent findings emerged from this investigation. First, all participants in the strategy groups (the strategy was introduced under different conditions to different groups of participants) performed better than did the control participants across all three learning tasks. Second, participants who were taught the strategy as content independent (without reference to any one specific task) achieved better in the transfer tasks than did participants who were provided with directions that introduced the strategy as content dependent (with specific reference to only the primary task).

In addition, when the experimenter reminded the participants to use the particular strategy, performance was facilitated. Reminders are apparently necessary to focus learners' attention on relevant cues of the performance. In this case, participants were aware of strategy usage in different contexts and were able to transfer the five sequential strategies (readying, imaging, focusing attention, executing, and evaluating) efficiently across three tasks.

Singer, DeFrancesco, and Randall (1989) further investigated the transferability of the 5-SA. More specifically, the effectiveness of the strategy on achievement in laboratory and simulated self-paced sport tasks was investigated. Participants were instructed to perform (a) either a laboratory task (a novel but complex motor task requiring speed and accuracy in movement) or an applied sport task (a modified table-tennis serve) as a primary task and (b) a transfer task (seated underhand dart throwing). Participants who were instructed to use the strategy accomplished more than did participants who did not use it in the primary task as well as in the transfer task. It was concluded that the 5-SA enhanced achievement in an artificial laboratory task as well as a modified sport task.

In line with these and similar results (e.g., Singer, Flora, & Abourezk, 1989), it is important to note two things. First, learners can benefit from learning strategy usage in different learning situations when they utilize the strategy properly. If this knowledge can be applied across different motor tasks, then learners would have an advantage as they attempt to acquire new but related skills.

Second, in general, individuals will probably need to be reminded to initiate relevant strategy usage throughout the early stages of learning. It is easy to forget when confronting the performance demands in a situation. If one of the purposes of learning strategy usage is to direct learner behaviors and thoughts during learning, instructors may have to remind learners to remember what to do physically as well as psychologically. However, it seems that after some practice, learners should be able to initiate appropriate strategies spontaneously.

The results of these laboratory studies were supported in a recent study in which the effectiveness of the 5-SA was investigated on achievement in psychomotor tasks varying in degree of cognitive activity involved (Kim, Singer, & Radlo, 1996). In this study (Experiments 1 and 2), participants were guided to perform several laboratory tasks, for instance, a brain scrambler, a golf putting and a card sorting, which were seemingly different in the amount of cognitive activity engaged during performances. The findings revealed that the 5-SA-enhanced performance of tasks contained a greater number of motor elements than did those having a high number of cognitive elements.

When comparing the effectiveness of the 5-SA and the awareness and the nonawareness approaches to learning and performance of self-paced motor tasks vs. a nonstrategy condition, it has been found that all strategies facilitated achievement in a variety of laboratory-designed tasks. For example, participants who were directed how to implement the strategies performed a ball-throwing task (Singer, et al., 1993) and a key-pressing task (Singer, et al., 1994) faster and more accurately than did participants who were provided with only a technical explanation on how to perform. In other words, the global strategy, for instance, the 5-SA, as well as the narrower oriented approaches, for example, the awareness and the nonawareness strategies, enhanced speed and accuracy of self-paced motor tasks. Furthermore, the strategies also facilitated performance under a dual-task condition in which participants were guided to execute two tasks simultaneously. A motor task was administered as the primary task, and a cognitive task, for instance, listening to 5-item sequences of one-digit numbers was given as a secondary task. The primary task, that is, ball throwing to a target (Singer, et al., 1993) and a key-pressing task (Singer, et al., 1994), were performed faster and more accurately by the strategy learners compared with the control learners. The strategies did not enhance performance in the secondary tasks. It was proposed that the learners who were guided on how to organize their thoughts before, during, and after execution of a movement were able to achieve a higher level of proficiency than were learners who were not given this guidance, no matter what their state of awareness. All strategy groups were provided with the cognitive plan to be more focused and task oriented.

More interestingly, a between-strategies comparison indicated that participants who were taught the 5-SA and the nonawareness guidelines achieved better than those who were administered the awareness approach (Singer, et al., 1993, 1994). The strategies that experts seem to typically use when they achieve their best (e.g., the 5-SA and the nonawareness) were favorable procedures for beginning learners to adopt. The traditional belief in sport that beginners must go through a process of trial-and-error learning was not supported in these laboratory findings. Apparently, novices could successfully use mental approaches associated with experts during the execution of laboratory self-paced motor tasks.

When asking strategy and control participants to perform a sequence of two similar tasks, the 5-SA was found to be a better learning strategy than the awareness and the nonawareness strategies. Participants who were guided to use the strategies and then to perform a primary task (e.g., ball throwing) and a secondary task (e.g., dart throwing) were more accurate and consistent than were the control participants. However, only those who applied the 5-SA achieved the highest level of proficiency in both tasks (Lidor et al., 1996). Whereas learners were asked to transfer cognitive knowledge from one learning situation to a related but different situation, the components of the awareness and the nonawareness strategies might not be sufficient for performance enhancement. It was suggested that the 5-SA provided participants with more relevant and specific information in performing a consecutive set of tasks. In this case, the usage of a global strategy resulted in a better performance compared with the implementation of some of its sub components.

Field Investigations

The effectiveness of learning strategies has been studied mainly under laboratory conditions that eliminated any potential distractors that may appear in field investigations. The instructional program differs greatly in field settings when compared to the laboratory. For example, under laboratory conditions, usually one participant at a time is instructed on how to use the strategy. In contrast, during field settings many learners are instructed at the same time, as for example in physical education classes. Although the methodological control over the laboratory conditions strengthens the design of the research, it decreases the environmental (ecological) validity of the results (Thomas & Nelson, 1996).

Two field investigations were undertaken to study the usefulness of learning strategies under more real-world conditions. The first study focused on the implementation of the 5-SA in sport settings, for instance, basketball practice, whereas the second study examined the usefulness of the 5-SA during physical education classes as part of the school curriculum. In the first study (Lidor & Tenenbaum, 1994), the 5-SA was introduced to a 16-year-old basketball player who was taught how to implement the strategy during six training sessions. A case-study design was conducted in order to examine (a) the accuracy of shooting performance and (b) the preparation time, that is, the time that it took the player to initiate the throw. It was found that shooting accuracy was higher in the last session than in the first pre treatment session. In addition, the time interval required to execute the shots during the last treatment session was longer compared with the time interval during the first session. It was concluded that the 5-SA could be efficiently used as a pre performance routine to attain a high level of shooting achievement.

In the second study (Lidor, 1997), the 5-SA was introduced to third grade (Experiment 1) and seventh grade (Experiment 2) children. The control conditions provided the young participants with additional technical information about the tasks. A bowling simulation task was used in Experiment 1, and a team handball throw was introduced in Experiment 2. Illustrated guidelines of the strategy were uniquely designed for young children. For example, in Experiment 1, the children were exposed to the strategy instructions by taking part in activity stations in which different throwing, catching, running, and jumping drills were introduced. In each activity, a different step of the strategy, for example, readying, was practiced. In Experiment 2, a colored poster was introduced to the children who could clearly read the strategy directions. These procedures helped the children to better understand the strategy. Experiments 1 and 2 indicated that performance accuracy of the bowling and the throwing tasks improved by using the 5-SA. A learning strategy, if designed and introduced appropriately, can also facilitate the learning of self-paced tasks that are undertaken by young learners.

Considering the results obtained from laboratory as well as field investigations, individuals attempting to master any self-paced activity should receive instructions as to how to think, what to think about, and when to think prior to and during the performance. Learners need to be guided as to what to do with their thought processes. Thus, instructors should direct them on how to plan their action, to block internal thoughts, and to perform the task without paying attention to internal and external details. In order to achieve this, instructors may use the 5-SA as a global learning strategy or the awareness and the non-awareness appoaches as substrategies.

Practical Implications for Sport Psychologists and Practitioners

The proficiency demonstrated by participants experiencing relevant strategies in a variety of studies in general, and the superiority of the 5-SA and the non-awareness approach in particular, may require a re-evaluation of traditional instructional programs. Typically, instructors and coaches direct students and players to pay attention to what they are doing and to be aware of their performance. The data indicate that the 5-SA and the nonawareness strategy may be considered as useful techniques in benefiting the learning and performance of self-paced motor activities. Instructors and sport psychologists should consider teaching either the 5-SA or the nonawareness strategy, depending upon the situational demands and the time available.

For example, during a practice session, instructors can direct learners on how to use the 5-SA appropriately, as a global strategy for learning and performance. More time would be spent on the third and fourth steps of the strategy in which a reflection of what individuals should actually think about (or not think about) during execution is stressed. Although the 5-SA is a more comprehensive, time-consuming, and complicated technique than is the nonawareness approach, both make an impact on learners.

From a practical point of view, four main recommendations are offered to sport psychologists as well as practitioners:

1. Learners should learn to use task-pertinent strategies to enhance learning and performance of self-paced motor tasks as part of their instructional program.

2. Beginners should attempt to approach a learning situation more like skilled performers typically do.
3. If time permits, a global and comprehensive learning strategy should be taught to assist learners to cope with potential internal and external distractors that may appear during a skill acquisition.
4. Considerations should be made for teaching strategies relevant for transfer of knowledge and skills to future conditions, once formal instruction is completed.

Further Considerations for Strategy Research

On the basis of this review, the following suggestions are offered for future investigations that may be conducted in this area:

- The transferability effect in learning is a major issue not only in the literature of motor learning and sport psychology but also in educational psychology and counseling. The generalizability effect of learning strategies across similar as well as different self-paced motor activities needs to be examined more thoroughly, as well as the concept of near-transfer and far-transfer task situations.
- In most learning-strategy investigations, an attempt has been made to study the influence of a learning strategy (e.g., the 5-SA) on achievement in the early stages of practice. For example, in one study (Lidor et al., 1996), participants were given 60 trials with one task and then 48 trials with a secondary task. Furthermore, the strategy instruction was administered in only one training session. It would be interesting to examine (a) the influence of learning strategies on achievement at an advanced phase of practice, that is, 1,000 or 1,500 trials, and (b) the effect of several strategy training sessions on achievement.
- Although the effectiveness of learning strategies in dual-task performance situations has been examined in a few studies (e.g., Singer, et al., 1993, 1994), the use of strategies in which learners are guided to perform two tasks simultaneously needs to be further examined. The reason for this is that individuals very often perform more than one task at the same time in routine daily-life activities as well as in sport events. Hence, further investigation is recommended on the use of particular learning strategies for simultaneous effective performance of primary and secondary tasks.
- Although each substrategy of the 5-SA has been subjected to a fair amount of scientific scrutiny, it is suggested that to be effective, each component of a multicomponent strategy should be tested in terms of its overall "worth" (Levin, 1986). There is evidence (DeFrancesco, 1989)

to suggest that when the 5-SA was compared to each substrategy used in isolation, its effectiveness was debatable. Thus, more studies are needed to evaluate the contribution of each component of the strategy to its overall contribution.

Considering these suggestions for future research, more investigations in motor learning and sport psychology should be conducted in order to understand what learners need to think about prior to and during execution of a learning task. Good educators, trainers, and coaches seem to be very competent in explaining to learners how to perform the task of interest and what techniques and tactics should be implemented (Schmidt, 1991; Singer, 1980). They also know how to evaluate performance and what kind of feedback to provide at the completion of the activity (Swinnen, 1996). However, do they really know how to guide learners to control their thoughts prior to and during execution? Can they explain to individuals what to think about while they actually undertake the activity? Furthermore, are they able to offer learners such useful strategies that can be applied in the future as to what to do when they are on their own in subsequent learning situations? With more research on these and related questions, instructional and training programs should be improved, and learners should be better prepared to use practice time more economically and successfully.

References

Abernethy, B. (1993). Attention. In R.N. Singer, M. Murphey, & L.K. Tennant (Eds.), *Handbook of research on sport psychology* (pp. 127–170). New York: Macmillan.

Anderson, J.R. (1987). Skill acquisition: Compilation of weak-method problem solutions. *Psychological Review, 92*, 192–210.

Anderson, J.R. (1990). *Cognitive psychology and its implications* (3rd ed.). New York: Freeman.

Bandura, A. (1990). Perceived self-efficacy in the exercise of personal agency. *Journal of Applied Sport Psychology, 2*, 128–163.

Bandura, A. (1997). *Self-efficacy: The exercise of control.* New York: Freeman.

Bruner, J., Goodnow, J., & Austin, G. (1956). *A study of thinking.* New York: Wiley.

Chase, W.G., & Simon, H.A. (1973). Perception in chess. *Cognitive Psychology, 4*, 55–81.

Chen, D., & Singer, R.N. (1992). Self-regulation and cognitive strategies in sport participation. *International Journal of Sport Psychology, 23*, 277–300.

Christina, R.W., & Corcos, D.M. (1988). *Coaches guide to teaching sport skills.* Champaign, IL: Human Kinetics.

Crossman, E.R.F.W. (1959). A theory of the acquisition of speed-skill. *Ergonomics, 2*, 153–166.

Cox, J.W. (1933). Some experiments on formal training in the acquisition of skill. *British Journal of Psychology, 24*, 67–87.

Dansereau, D.F. (1978). The development of learning strategies curriculum. In H.F. O'Neil, Jr. (Ed.), *Learning strategies* (pp. 1–29). New York: Academic Press.

Dansereau, D.F. (1985). Learning strategy research. In J. Segal, S. Chipman, & P. Glaser (Eds.), *Thinking and learning skills: Relating instruction to basic research* (Vol. 1, pp. 209–240). Hillsdale, NJ: Erlbaum.

DeFrancesco, C. (1989). The effectiveness and transferability of four learning strategies on achievement in self-paced discrete, serial and continuous motor tasks. (Doctoral dissertation, Florida State University, 1988). *Dissertation Abstracts International, 49,* 3655A.

Derry, S.J., & Murphey, D.A. (1986). Designing systems that train learning ability: From theory to practice. *Review of Educational Research, 56,* 1–39.

Epstein, M.L. (1980). The relationship of mental imagery and mental rehearsal to performance. *Journal of Sport Psychology, 2,* 211–220.

Ericsson, K.A., & Charness, N. (1994). Expert performance: Its structure and acquisition. *American Psychologist, 49,* 725–747.

Flavell, J.H. (1979). Metacognitive and cognitive monitoring: A new area of cognitive development inquiry. *American Psychologist, 34,* 906–911.

Flavell, J.H., & Wellman, H. (1977). Metamemory. In R. Kail & J. Hagen (Eds.), *Perspective on the development of memory and cognition* (pp. 3–33). Hillsdale, NJ: Erlbaum.

Gagné, R.N. (1985). *The conditions of learning and theory of instruction* (4th ed.). New York: Holt, Rinehart & Winston.

Gallwey, T.W. (1976). *Inner tennis.* New York: Random House.

Gallwey, T.W. (1981). *The inner game of golf.* New York: Random House.

Garfield, C.A., & Bennett, H.Z. (1984). *Peak performance: Mental training techniques of the world's greatest athletes.* Los Angeles: Tarcher.

Garner, R. (1990). When children and adults do not use learning strategies: Toward a theory of settings. *Review of Educational Research, 60,* 517–529.

Good, T.L., & Brophy, J.E. (1990). *Educational psychology: A realistic approach* (4th ed.). New York: Longman.

Goodenough, F.L., & Brian, C.R. (1929). Certain factors underlying the acquisition of motor skills by pre-school children. *Journal of Experimental Psychology, 12,* 127–155.

Gould, D., & Damarjian, N. (1997). Imagery training for peak performance. In J.L. Van Raalte & B.W. Brewer (Eds.), *Exploring sport and exercise psychology* (pp. 25–50). Washington, DC: American Psychological Association.

Gould, D., Horn, T., & Spreeman, J. (1983). Competitive anxiety in junior elite wrestlers. *Journal of Sport Psychology, 5,* 58–71.

Greeno, J. (1980). Psychology of learning, 1960–1980: One participant observation. *American Psychologist, 35,* 713–728.

Hardy, L., Jones, G., & Gould, D. (1996). *Understanding psychological preparation for sport: Theory and practice of elite performers.* New York: Wiley.

Holding, D.H. (1965). *Principles of training.* London: Oxford Press.

Holding, D.H., & Macrae, A.W. (1964). Guidance, restriction and knowledge of results. *Ergonomics, 7,* 289–295.

Kail, R., & Hagen, J. (1982). Memory in childhood. In B. Wolman (Ed.), *Handbook of developmental psychology* (pp. 350–366). Englewood Cliffs, NJ: Prentice-Hall.

Kim, J., Singer, R.N., & Radlo, S.J. (1996). Degree of cognitive demands in psychomotor tasks and the effects of the five-step strategy on achievement. *Human Performance, 9,* 133–169.

Kurtz, B.E., & Borkowsky, J.G. (1984). Children's metacognition: Exploring relations among knowledge, process, and motivational variables. *Journal of Experimental Child Psychology, 37,* 335–354.

Laszlo, J.I., & Bairstow, P.J. (1983). Kinaesthesis: Its measurement, training and relationship to motor control. *Quarterly Journal of Experimental Psychology, 5A,* 411–421.

Lee, T.D., & Genovese, E.D. (1988). Distribution of practice in motor skill acquisition: Learning and performance effects reconsidered. *Research Quarterly for Exercise and Sport, 59,* 277–287.

Lee, T.D., & Genovese, E.D. (1989). Distribution of practice in motor skill acquisition: Different effects for discrete and continuous tasks. *Research Quarterly for Exercise and Sport, 60,* 59–65

Lee, T.D., Swinnen, S.P., & Serrien, D.J. (1994). Cognitive effort and motor learning. *Quest, 46,* 328–344.

Levin, J.R. (1986). Four cognitive principles of learning-strategy instruction. *Educational Psychologist, 21,* 3–17.

Lidor, R. (1996). Awareness and nonawareness approaches to motor learning and performance: How to organize thoughts during execution of motor tasks. *Studies in Physical Culture and Tourism, 4,* 77–93.

Lidor, R. (1997). Effectiveness of a structured learning strategy on acquisition of game-related gross motor tasks in school settings. *Perceptual and Motor Skills, 84,* 67–80.

Lidor, R., & Tenenbaum, G. (1994). Applying learning strategy to a basketball shooting skill: A case study report. In R. Lidor, D. Ben-Sira & Z. Artzi (Eds.), *Proceedings of the World Congress of FIEP* (pp. 53–59). Israel: Wingate Institute.

Lidor, R., Tennant, K.L., & Singer, R.N. (1996). The generalizability effect of three learning strategies across motor task performances. *International Journal of Sport Psychology, 27,* 22–36.

Locke, E.A., & Lathman, G.P. (1985). The application of goal setting to sports. *Journal of Sport Psychology, 7,* 205–222.

Loehr, J.E. (1982). *Mental toughness training for sports.* New York: Greene.

Loehr, J.E. (1990). *The mental game.* New York: Greene.

Logan, G.D., & Zbrodoff, N.J. (1982). Constraints on strategy construction in a speeded discrimination task. *Journal of Experimental Psychology: Human Perception and Performance, 8,* 502–520.

MacKay, D.G. (1982). The problem of flexibility, fluency, and speed-accuracy trade-off in skilled behavior. *Psychological Review, 89,* 483–506.

Magill, R.A. (1993). Augmented feedback in skill acquisition. In R.N. Singer, M. Murphey & L.K. Tennant (Eds.), *Handbook of research on sport psychology* (pp. 193–212). New York: Macmillan.

Magill, R.A., & Hall, K.G. (1990). A review of the contextual interference effect in motor skill acquisition. *Human Movement Science, 9,* 241–289.

McCullagh, P. (1993). Modeling: Learning, developmental, and social psychological considerations. In R.N. Singer, M. Murphey & L.K. Tennant (Eds.), *Handbook of research on sport psychology* (pp. 106–126). New York: Macmillan.

McCullagh, P., Weiss, M.R., & Ross, D. (1989). Modeling considerations in motor skill acquisition and performance: An integrated approach. In K.B. Pandolf (Ed.), *Exercise and sport science review* (Vol. 17, pp. 475–513). Baltimore: Williams & Wilkins.

Meichenbaum, D.H. (1976). *Cognitive-behavior modification: An integrative approach.* New York: Plenum.

Moely, B., Olsen, F., Howles, T., & Flavell, J.H. (1989). Procedural deficiency in young children's clustered recall. *Developmental Psychology, 1,* 26–34.

Nideffer, R.N. (1993). Attention control training. In R.N. Singer, M. Murphey & L.K. Tennant (Eds.), *Handbook of research on sport psychology* (pp. 542–556). New York: Macmillan.

Norman, D.A. (1980). Cognitive engineering and education. In D.T. Tume & F. Reif (Eds.), *Problem solving and education* (pp. 96–107). Hillsdale, NJ: Erlbaum.

Orlick, T. (1990). *The pursuit of excellence.* Champaign, IL: Human Kinetics.

Parker, J.F., & Fleishman, E.A. (1961). Use of analytical information concerning task requirements to increase the effectiveness of skill training. *Journal of Applied Psychology, 45,* 295–302.

Powell, F.M., & Verner, J.P. (1982). Anxiety and performance relationships in first time prarchutists. *Journal of Sport Psychology, 4,* 184–188.

Ravizza, K. (1986). Increasing awareness for sport performance. In J.W. Williams (Ed.), *Applied sport psychology* (pp. 149–158). Mountain View, CA: Mayfield.

Reese, H.W. (1977). Imagery and associative memory. In R.V. Kail & J.W. Hagen (Eds.), *Perspective on the development of memory and cognition* (pp. 113–175). Hillsdale, NJ: Erlbaum.

Richards, J., & August, G. (1975). Generative underlining strategies in pros recall. *Journal of Educational Psychology, 67,* 860–865.

Ryan, E.E., & Simons, J. (1982). Efficacy of mental imagery on enhancing mental rehearsal of motor skills. *Journal of Sport Psychology, 4,* 41–51.

Salmoni, A.W., Schmidt, R.A., & Walter, C.B. (1984). Knowledge of results and motor learning: A review and critical reappraisal. *Psychological Bulletin, 95,* 355–386.

Schmidt, R.A. (1991). *Motor learning and performance: From principles to practice.* Champaign, IL: Human Kinetics.

Shea, C.H., Kohl, R., & Indermill, C. (1990). Contextual interference: Contributions of practice. *Acta Psychologica, 73,* 145–157.

Shiffrin, R.M. (1989). Attention. In R.C. Atkinson, R.J. Herrnstein, G. Lindzey, & R.D. Luce (Eds.), *Steven's handbook of experimental psychology* (2nd ed., pp. 739–811). New York: Wiley.

Singer, R.N. (1980). *Motor learning and human performance* (3rd ed.). New York: Macmillan.

Singer, R.N. (1986). *Peak performance and . . . more.* Ithaca, NY: Mouvement

Singer, R.N. (1988). Strategies and metastrategies in learning and performing self-paced athletic skills. *The Sport Psychologist, 2,* 49–68.

Singer, R.N., & Cauraugh, J.H. (1984). Generalization of psychomotor learning strategies to related psychomotor tasks. *Human Learning, 3,* 215–225.

Singer, R.N., & Cauraugh, J.H. (1985). The generalizability effect of learning strategies for categories of psychomotor skills. *Quest, 37,* 103–119.

Singer, R.N., Cauraugh, J.H., Murphey, M., Chen, D., & Lidor, R. (1991). Attentional control, distractors, and motor performance. *Human Performance, 4,* 55–69.

Singer, R.N., Cauraugh, J.H., Tennant, K.L., Murphey, M., Chen, D., & Lidor, R. (1991). Attention and distractors: Considerations for enhancing sport performance. *International Journal of Sport Psychology, 22,* 95–114.

Singer, R.N., DeFrancesco, C., & Randall, L.E. (1989). Effectiveness of a global learning strategy practiced in different contexts on primary and transfer self-paced motor tasks. *Journal of Sport & Exercise Psychology, 11,* 290–303.

Singer, R.N., Flora, L.A., & Abourezk, T. (1989). The effect of a five-step cognitive learning strategy on the acquisition of a complex motor task. *Journal of Applied Sport Psychology, 1,* 98–108.

Singer, R.N., Lidor, R., & Cauraugh, J.H. (1993). To be aware or not aware? What to think about while learning and performing a motor skill. *The Sport Psychologist, 7,* 19–30.

Singer, R.N., Lidor, R., & Cauraugh, J.H. (1994). Focus of attention during motor skill performance. *Journal of Sports Sciences, 12,* 335–340.

Singer, R.N., & Suwanthada, S. (1986). The generalizability effectiveness of a learning strategy on achievement in related closed motor skills. *Research Quarterly for Exercise and Sport, 57,* 205–214.

Suinn, R.N. (1976). Body thinking: Psychology for Olympic champs. *Psychology Today, 7,* 38–43.

Swinnen, S.P. (1996). Information feedback for motor skill learning: A review. In H.N. Zelaznik (Ed.), *Advances in motor learning and control* (pp. 37–66). Champaign, IL: Human Kinetics.

Thomas, J.R., & Nelson, J.K. (1996). *Research methods in physical activity* (3rd ed.). Champaign, IL: Human Kinetics.

Weinberg, R.S. (1997). Goal setting in sport and exercise: Research to practice. In J.L. Van Raalte & B.W. Brewer (Eds.), *Exploring sport and exercise psychology* (pp. 3–24). Washington, DC: American Psychological Association.

Weinberg, R.S., & Gould, D. (1995). *Foundations of sport and exercise psychology.* Champaign, IL: Human Kinetics.

Weinberg, R.S., Seabourne, T.G., & Jackson, A. (1981). Effects of visuo-motor behavior rehearsal, relaxation, and imagery on karate performance. *Journal of Sport Psychology, 3,* 228–238.

Weinstein, C.E., & Mayer, R.E. (1986). The teaching of learning strategies. In M.C. Wittrock (Ed.), *Handbook of research on teaching* (pp. 315–327). New York: Macmillan.

Welker, R. (1991). Expertise and the teacher as expert: Rethinking a questionable metaphor. *American Educational Research Journal, 28,* 19–35.

7

Orienting of Attention: From Perception to Action

Vincent Nougier
Bruna Rossi
Université Joseph Fourier, Grenoble, France

Introduction

In sport practice, attention is a very common concept. However, this does not mean that this concept is well-defined and possesses a similar significance for all of those interested and involved in sport, such as sport psychologists, sport educators, trainers, or athletes. As emphasized by Parasuraman and Davies (1984) in their book, there are varieties of attention. Thus, in order to avoid any confusion or misinterpretation, it is necessary within a given community (in the present case, the sport community) not to have a unique definition of attention, but at least a common language, each one specifying what he or she means by attention.

In the present chapter, we will focus on orienting of visual attention (Posner, 1980). This process can be considered as a controlling process that modulates information processing without actually working at a specific stage (Keele & Hawkins, 1982). That is, orienting attention towards a given source of information should facilitate the processing of this source of information and, at the same time, should inhibit the processing of the others. It has been shown that this orientation of attention can be realized either voluntarily or automatically (Jonides, 1981). That is, two somewhat distinct mechanisms underlie these two attentional modes (Müller & Rabbitt, 1989), mechanisms that can work either successively or simultaneously and can both contribute to the efficiency of subjects' performances.

From another point of view, orienting of attention processes is very similar to orienting of those processes involved in motor preparation. Requin (1985) underlined that attention mainly plays a role at the perceptual stages of information processing whereas motor preparation mainly contributes to facilitate the programming and execution stages. Requin also suggested that it may be legitimate to use the notion of perceptual preparation to define the selection process of sensory information, and that of motor attention to define the selection process of motor outputs. As pointed out by Kahneman and Treisman (1984), the interest in the behavioral function of selective attention has gradually shifted, during the last two decades, from perceptual to motor processing. In the following sections, the contribution of these different processes to information processing and their possible interactions will be considered, both from theoretical and sport practice points of view.

Orienting of Attention and Perception

Voluntary Orienting of Attention

Following the most common assumption, attention is a voluntary process (Posner, 1980). This means that a subject can pay more or less attention, that is, can orient attention to specific events and/or stimuli, as a function of the task to be performed and of his or her own goal or intention. Paying more or less attention to process some information suggests that orienting of attention is an optional and costly mechanism. In other words, one can decide how much attention has to be devoted to a given task (Klein, 1994). For example, the a priori subjective or objective knowledge of the respective probabilities of different events is typically the basis of a voluntary orienting of attention. The higher the probability of a specific event, the greater should be the attention paid to it. In the basic paradigm (Posner & Snyder, 1975; Posner, Snyder, & Davidson, 1980), a central cue presented at fixation (for example, an arrow) orients subjects' attention towards a stimulus location. In 80% of the trials, the stimulus is presented in the cued location (valid condition) whereas in the remaining 20% of the trials, the stimulus is presented in the uncued location (invalid condition). Subjects are instructed to respond as fast as possible to the stimulus. Generally, both reaction time (RT) and accuracy are measured. In an additional condition, subjects' attention is not cued towards a specific location (neutral condition). It is generally shown that valid RTs are shorter than neutral RTs, which are also shorter than invalid RTs. The greater efficiency for processing the information to which attention is paid is called an *attentional benefit*. Conversely, the diminished efficiency for processing the information to which attention is not oriented is called an *attentional cost* with respect to the neutral condition in which no attention is paid at all. The magnitude of the attentional costs and benefits (i.e., the magnitude of the attentional effects) has been viewed as an indication of subjects' attentional flexibility (Keele & Hawkins, 1982), that is, the ability to quickly switch attention from one source of information to another one. The smaller the costs and benefits, the greater should be the attentional flexibility. This flexibility may be one of the cognitive factors contributing to a high level of performance.

The manipulation of other factors, such as the utility or significance of some of the available information with respect to the task, should also increase the attention paid to this information, independently of its probability (Klein, 1994). However, attention cannot be allocated for an unlimited period of time. For example, it has been shown that when the delay between the cue and the target is longer than 200/300 ms, the initial facilitation observed for the cued location becomes an inhibition of the cued location in favor of the uncued one (Posner & Cohen, 1984; Possamaï, 1986). This observation suggested that attention is initially oriented and engaged on the cued location. However, after few hundred milliseconds, attention is disengaged and reoriented spontaneously back towards the central fixation point, which is a very useful start point for exploring the visual space.

Different models of attention have been proposed to explain the observed effects: the so-called spotlight model, zoom-lens model, and gradient model. Following the original spotlight model (Posner, 1980), attention is assimilated to a beam of light that can move through the visual space, facilitating the processing of attended (cued) stimuli. From one location to another one, attention has (a) to be disengaged from a source of information, (b) to move towards the new attended source of information, and (c) to be engaged on this new stimulus location. It remains unclear, however, whether the attentional beam moves at a constant (Tsal, 1983) or proportional speed within the visual space (Eriksen & Murphy, 1987).

According to the zoom-lens model, attention can be either distributed or focused, on a continuum between these two extremes (Eriksen & Yeh, 1985). In this model, the efficiency of processing is inversely proportional to the size of the attention beam (Castiello & Umiltà, 1990; Eriksen & St. James, 1986). Furthermore, according to these authors, there is a partial enhancement of processing efficiency in the area surrounding the focused region.

Finally, the gradient model of attention (La Berge & Brown, 1989) proposes different assumptions about the efficiency of processing outside the attended area. According to this model, the gradient of allocated attentional resources is proportional to the size of the attended area. The larger the size of the attended area, the broader are the gradient of allocated resources and the decrease of processing efficiency outside the attended area (Henderson, 1991; La Berge, Brown, Carter, Bash, & Hartley, 1991).

In sport, different studies have shown that attentional costs but also benefits were smaller for elite athletes when compared to those of control subjects (e.g., Castiello & Umiltà, 1992; Nougier, Ripoll, & Stern, 1989; Nougier,

Stein, & Bnnel, 1991; Pesce Anzeneder & Bösel, in press). This result is somewhat counterintuitive because greater benefits could have been expected. The main explanation was that elite athletes prefer to pay proportionally less attention to highly probable events and more attention to less probable events, in order to minimize the attentional costs in the most difficult situations. In other words, they would prefer to expect the unexpected, which may have greater positive or negative effects on their motor performance. This suggests that the elite athletes do not strictly follow the a priori probabilities in order to organize their attentional behavior. Conversely, control subjects seem to be more dependent on the real probabilities. Similar patterns of response have been observed when comparing the attentional behavior of elite young athletes to that of elite adult athletes (Nougier, Azémar, Stein, & Ripoll, 1992). More specifically, it was shown that exogenous factors, such as learning, and endogenous factors, such as development, may interact and that experience through learning can accelerate the development of attention. Figure 7.1 illustrates the typical attentional effects observed for expert and nonexpert tennis players, according to tennis players' age.

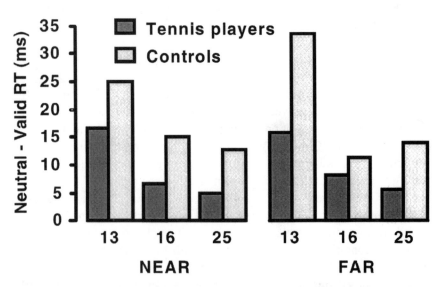

Figure 7.1. Attentional benefits for expert and nonexpert tennis players, according to players' age (13, 16, and 25 years old) and stimuli eccentricity (near = 8 deg and far = 12 deg, on each side of the central fixation point). Adapted from Nougier et al. (1992).

Automatic Orienting of Attention

As indicated in the introduction, attention can be also oriented automatically (Jonides, 1981), by way of a different mechanism. It is a characteristic event or stimulus that can direct subjects' attention to a given location, rather independently of his or her own wish. In the basic paradigm, a cue (called "peripheral cue") is directly presented at a stimulus location. In the valid condition, the stimulus is presented at the cued location, whereas in the invalid condition, the target is presented at the uncued location. In other words, in the voluntary mode (central cues), information about the location of stimuli that may occur on each side of a central fixation point is presented at fixation. In the automatic mode (peripheral cues), the cue is presented at one of the presumed stimuli locations whereas the eyes are directed towards the fixation point. It is generally shown that attentional effects are larger when using peripheral rather than central cues, that is, when attention is drawn automatically rather than voluntarily. Abrupt signals can also draw subjects' attention automatically with respect to signals presented more progressively (Jonides & Yantis, 1988). Such an automatic orienting mechanism has both negative and positive effects on a subject's behavior. The negative effects are that attention may be directed towards a source of information that is not presently significant for the subject. For example, in a tennis match, an unexpected sound, flash of light, or movement of a spectator can perturb the athlete in his/her concentration and execution of a movement (e.g., the service). In this situation, the athlete's attention has been unexpectedly drawn towards a perturbing stimulus. Conversely, this automatic mechanism allows an athlete to quickly orient attention towards a given location in which unexpected but useful information is available. This is typically the case in situations of emergency in which there is a high time pressure requiring rapid decisions. This may be the case, for example, in sport field situations in which an opponent is unexpectedly arriving from the left or right or a partner is calling for the ball.

In a recent experiment (Nougier, Rossi, Alain, & Taddei, 1996), we manipulated both the automatic and the voluntary modes of orienting of attention. This was done, on the one hand, by orienting subjects' attention with peripheral cues (automatic orienting) and, on the other hand, by manipulating in different blocks of trials the probability of cued and uncued signals (voluntary control of attention). More precisely, the probability of cued and uncued signals was respectively 80%/20%, 50%/50% and 20%/80%. In the 80%/20% probability condition, automatic orienting of attention and voluntary control of attention were complementary. In the 50%/50% probability condition, only the automatic orienting processes were investigated because cued and uncued signals were equiprobable. In the last condition, automatic and voluntary

processes competed together. On one hand, attention was automatically oriented towards the cued location. On the other hand, however, subjects knew
that the most probable stimulus location was the uncued location. Results
showed that automatic orienting effects were smaller in expert athletes than in
control subjects. These attentional effects, however, were much larger than
those observed when investigating the voluntary orienting of attention, con-
firming previous results (Jonides, 1981). Interestingly, it was shown that automatic and voluntary orienting of attention can either compete or work together
for processing a given stimulus. As shown in Figure 7.2, attentional effects decreased as cue probability decreased. This clearly suggested that automatic
orienting of attention can be partly controlled or modulated (Jacoby, Ste-
Marie, & Toth, 1993) by voluntary orienting. Furthermore, expert athletes
seemed more efficient in exerting an endogenous control on automatic orienting processes. Similar findings were obtained with volleyball players in the
process of attentional focusing on either small or large cued areas (Pesce
Anzeneder & Bösel, in press}. In the less probable cued condition, however,
that is the 20%/80% probability condition, there were still automatic attentional effects, suggesting that automatic orienting is based on stronger unconscious processes than is the voluntary control of attention.

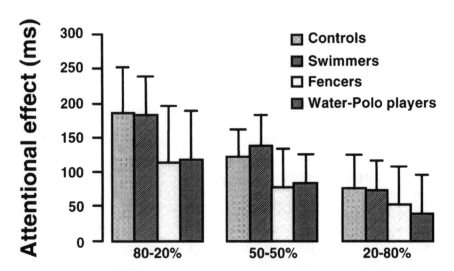

Figure 7.2. Attentional effects for expert athletes (water-polo players,
swimmers, and fencers) and controls, in a paradigm combining an
automatic orienting of attention and a voluntary control of attention.
The voluntary control was manipulated through the probability of
cued and uncued signals (80-20%, 50-50% and 20-80% probability
combinations). Adapted from Nougier et al. (1996).

The Characteristics of Expertise

First of all, it must be emphasized that the effects of expertise on orienting of attention are not systematic. As could be expected, this mainly depends on the attentional characteristics of the situations (i.e., the sport skill) that the subjects frequently face. For example, expert water-polo players or fencers (i.e., open skills) showed optimized attentional processes whereas it was not the case for expert swimmers (i.e., closed skill) who behave as control subjects (Nougier et al., 1996). Furthermore, it has been also shown that deafferented subjects suffering a great impairment in their control of movements because of an absence of proprioceptive reafferences behave as expert athletes in terms of orienting of attention (Nougier et al., 1994). This suggested that subjects daily facing situations requiring a high mental workload, prolonged sustained visual attention, and a continuously changing environment are more efficient in adopting a cost-minimizing strategy to orient attention in the visual space. More precisely, this may suggest that, rather than task specific, the development of expertise is based on general (e.g., basic) *abilities* that can also emerge in laboratory tasks requiring similar abilities.

From another point of view, it has been shown that expert athletes are characterized by a very specific cognitive attentional style (Rossi & Zani, 1991). These authors recorded the latency of some components (N2 and P300) of the event-related brain potentials and reaction times of expert skeet and trap clay-pigeon shooters in an auditory discrimination task. In the skeet competition, the clay-pigeon follows a known trajectory from trial to trial but can be randomly pulled within a delay of 3 seconds. In the trap competition, the claypigeon is randomly pulled without any fixed delay, in one of three different directions and with one of different slopes between 0° and 45°. Thus, the main difference between the two sport skills is the higher degree of uncertainty for the trap competition than for the skeet competition. Results clearly showed that there are important interindividual differences in how the athletes process the easy and difficult tasks. As illustrated in Figure 7.3, there were no differences in RT in the easy task, but significant differences in the latencies of the N2 and P300 event-related components. That is, a different timing subserved the processing of the task. Conversely, in the difficult task, there were longer RTs for the skeet than for the trap shooters, but similar N2 and P300 latencies, suggesting that the underlying processes were similar for both groups but with a longer processing time for the skeet than for the trap shooters.

Similarly, Castiello and Umiltà (1990) found that expert volleyball setters show normal costs and benefits in the horizontal dimension with respect to control subjects. In the vertical dimension, costs and benefits were still normal when the unexpected location lay below the expected one. In contrast, costs

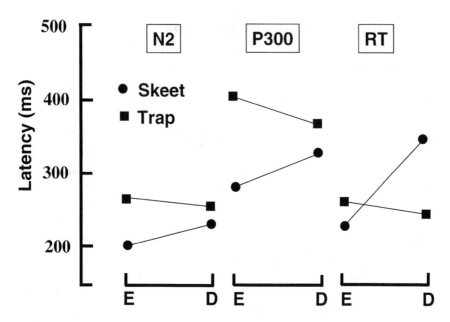

Figure 7.3. N2, P300, and RT latencies for expert skeet and trap shooters as a function of the complexity (E = Easy and D = Difficult) of an auditory discrimination task. In the easy task, subjects had to discriminate between 1000 Hz and 2000 Hz pitch tones. In the difficult task, they had to discriminate between 1000 Hz and 1050 Hz pitch tones. Adapted from Rossi and Zani (1991).

were absent when the unexpected location lay above the expected one. This clearly suggested that expert setters were very fast in reorienting attention upwards, but not downwards, leftwards, or rightwards. In other words, there was a very high specificity of attentional expertise. This suggests that the notion of expertise has to be referred to a specific context (Abernethy, 1993) in which this expertise can be exerted.

These results clearly suggested that, beyond general characteristics of attentional expertise (expertise specific abilities), there also exist more task-specific abilities that are developed according to the precise characteristics of the athletes' sport skill. In other words, attentional expertise in sport seems to be characterized both by the development of general abilities and by the development of specific sport skill abilities. These specific abilities can emerge only when the experimental task simulates the specific requirements of a given sport skill (e.g., vertical vs. horizontal orienting as in Castiello and Umiltà's experiment) or when the constraints of the attentional task increase dramatically (e.g., shorter temporal delays, lower probabilities). Under conditions, significant differences can be observed also between expert athletes who belong to different sport disciplines requiring similar attentional abilities (e.g., water-polo players vs. fencers or volleyball players) and/or between expert athletes of the same sport discipline but having a different role on the field (e.g., goalkeepers vs. defenders or forward players: Rossi, Rudic, & Nougier, 1995). In these experimental situations, interindividual differences can also emerge.

Orienting of Attention and Action

Another aspect of orienting of attention is that this process, mainly involved in increasing the efficiency of sensory information processing, can also play a role at the motor stages of information processing, that is, both during motor preparation and movement execution (Requin, 1985). Indeed, one of the major problems for motor control is interfacing sensory information and motor programs in a common frame of reference (Jeannerod, 1988). During a pointing movement, for example, this may suppose to integrate both visual information about target location and multimodal information about movement commands during reaching.

Thus, some data can be interpreted from an attentional and/or a motor preparation point of view (Nougier, Stein, & Azémar, 1990). For example, it has been shown that subjects can benefit from attending to a feature of a movement that has to be performed (Lépine, Glencross & Requin, 1989; Requin, 1985; Rosenbaum, 1980, 1983). More specifically, in the precueing technique (Rosenbaum, 1980, 1983), the cue provides information about some features of the movement. RTs are analyzed according to the nature and to the number of dimensions of the movement that are known in advance. In the priming technique (Lépine et al., 1989; Requin, 1985), the cued movement has a high probability to be performed and the uncued movements a low probability to be executed. RTs are analyzed according to the nature and number of dimensions that the cued and required movements have in common. This procedure is very similar to the one used for studying orienting mechanisms of attention. In both cases, there are cued and uncued locations. In orienting of attention paradigms, however, a unique motor response is generally required (e.g., pressing a single key) independently of stimulus location. This allows the isolation of the attentional effects by neutralizing motor-preparation effects. Conversely, in motor-preparation paradigms, different motor responses are required according to stimuli locations that subserve different dimensions of the movement. It is assumed that attentional effects are neutralized because they are similar whatever the movement to execute. This similarity of paradigms and effects suggests that attentional processes and motor-preparation processes can either compete or work together.

In the paradigm manipulating automatic orienting of attention that was described above (Nougier et al., 1996), it was possible to study the interaction of attentional and motor-preparation processes. Indeed, the response to cued and uncued stimuli was made with either the left or right hand, according to stimulus location in one of two adjacent boxes, independently of the visual hemifield of presentation (Figure 7.4). When the target occurred in the left box, subjects responded with the left hand; when it occurred in the right box, they responded with the right hand. The probability for responding with either the left or right hand was the same. Furthermore, in order to ensure a complete orientation of attention prior to responding to the cued or uncued signals, subjects had to react to a first stimulus that was always in the cued location, in one of the two adjacent boxes. Subjects responded with either the left or right hand according to the box in which the stimulus was presented. In other words, subjects gave two consecutive hand responses, which can be either a repetition of the same hand response (left or right) or an alternation of the two hand responses (left then right, or right then left). The special interest of this last condition was that on some trials there was a high compatibility between the orientation of attention and the changing hand response. This was the case, for example, when attention was initially oriented towards the left visual hemifield with a first left-hand response, and then reoriented towards the right visual hemifield (uncued attentional condition) with a right-hand response. On other trials, however, there was a high incompatibility between orienting of attention and hand responses. This was the case, for example, when attention was oriented towards the left visual hemifield with a first right-hand response, and then reoriented towards the right visual hemifield (uncued attentional condition) with a left-hand response. In that condition, attention was oriented from the left to the right whereas the motor responses were organized from the right to the left hand.

As illustrated in Figure 7.5, the attentional effects were modulated according to the compatibility between orienting of attention and the two successive motor responses. Reaction time decreased when the compatibility between orienting of attention and the motor response was high. Conversely, reaction time increased when the compatibility between orienting of attention and the motor response was low. These effects were observed for both the valid and invalid conditions. However, they were greater for the invalid than for the valid condition.

These results supported the idea that orienting of attention and motor preparation are based on similar processes, but that the former mainly affects

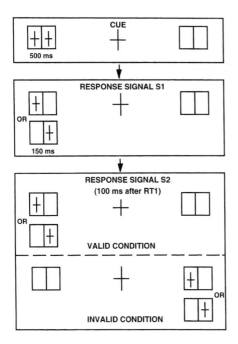

Figure 7.4. Illustration of the sequence of events in the Nougier et al. (1994 ; 1996) paradigm. Subjects responded to the presentation of a first signal with either the left or right hand and then to the presentation of a second signal in the same conditions.

the sensory stages of information processing whereas the latter mainly affects the motor stages of information processing (Requin, 1980). Such a distinction between these two processes, that is, between selective attention (orienting of attention) and intention (motor preparation) has been supported by various neurophysiological evidences (Heilman, Watson, & Valenstein, 1985; Pribram & McGuinness, 1975; Verfallie, Bowers, & Heilman, 1988). For example, Verfallie, Bowers, and Heilman (1988) showed that there were no hemispheric asymmetries for the processing of attentional information whereas they found hemispheric asymmetries for the processing of intentional information related to response preparation.

However, our results also showed that orienting of attention plays a major role in organizing subjects' motor behavior. More specifically, they suggested a hierarchical organization from sensory to motor processes, in terms of orienting of attention. That is, orienting of attention can affect how a movement is prepared (Lépine et al., 1989). In other words, a stimulus (a target) location may subserve specific movement features, for example, in terms of movement direction and amplitude towards this target. When attention is oriented towards the cued stimulus, if no movement is required, attentional processes are involved alone and are dependent on stimulus characteristics. If, however, a movement is required towards what can then be called a target, orienting of attention allows the presetting of the movement features subserved by stimulus location (Allport, 1980).

Orienting of attention can also play a role in the control of movements during their execution. In recent experiments (Boulinguez & Nougier, 1998), we

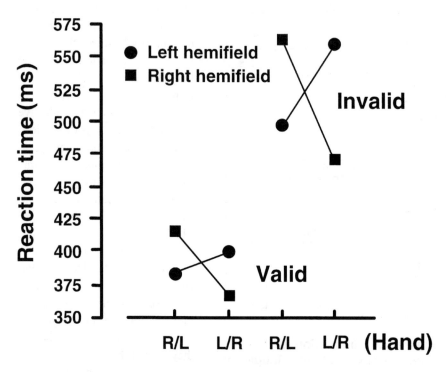

Figure 7.5. Mean RT for successive responses of the right then left (R/L) or left then right (L/R) hands, when valid and invalid signals are presented in either the left or right visual hemifield of presentation. Unpublished data.

asked the subjects to execute pointing movements in a classical double-step paradigm. In 75% of the trials, subjects pointed towards a cued target. On the remaining 25% of the trials, another target was presented during movement execution, requiring a correction of the initial movement. The probability of location for this second target was manipulated such as, when it occurred, movement correction was more or less probable towards a given target with respect to the others. In one block of trials, the movement had to be corrected on 75% of the corrected trials on the left and on the remaining 25% of the corrected trials, on the right. In a second block of trials, the probabilities were inverted. In a last block of trials, the probability of correction towards the left or right was the same (50% for each direction). These probabilities were previously known by the subjects. Results showed that when the probability of correction towards a given target was modified, the kinematic characteristics of the corrected movements were modified too. The greater the probability that a movement was to be corrected towards a given target, the greater was the efficiency of the corrected movement. More precisely, movement trajectory was shorter and less variable, and movement time was shorter too. Also, movement correction occurred earlier and in a shorter time after presentation of the new target, as illustrated in Figure 7.6. This suggested that orienting subjects' attention towards the most probable location for correcting a movement allowed them, if necessary, to optimize their motor behavior by way of a cognitive top-down process. More specifically, orienting attention towards the most probable direction of correction during execution of the initial movement may allow athletes to save time for updating the internal representation of the goal of the movement (Jeannerod, 1988). It remains, however, to investigate to which extent these processes are more efficient in expert athletes trained to execute movements with a high level of constraints.

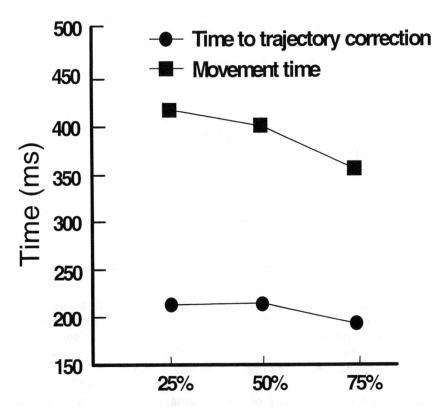

Figure 7.6. Mean time to trajectory inflection and correction time according to the probability of the corrected movement. Adapted from Boulinguez and Nougier (1998).

Conclusion

In summary, it may be emphasized that orienting of attention is not a unique process. It has to be considered as a process that can play a role at different stages of information processing (perceptual and/or motor stages), following different modalities (automatic vs. voluntary orienting). As illustrated in Figure 7.7, it can play a role not only prior to a given movement, but also during its execution and correction by selecting sensory inputs and/or motor outputs.

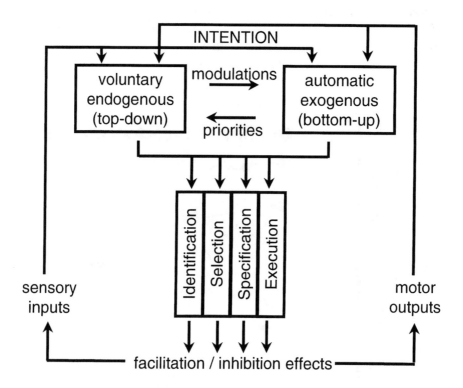

Figure 7.7. Illustration of how voluntary and automatic orienting of attention play a role in the different stages of information processing. Voluntary orienting is an endogenous process mainly under control of subjects' intention whereas automatic orienting is an exogenous process, mainly dependent on the stimulus and movement characteristics. Automatic orienting can be modulated through a voluntary control, but has a priority on the voluntary orienting of attention. These two processes can affect one or more stages of information processing through facilitation and inhibition effects, thus increasing or decreasing subjects' sensory and motor performances.

In other words, attention can be viewed both as a top-down and as a bottom-up process. As a top-down process (voluntary endogenous mode), attention can facilitate and inhibit a priori sources of information, according to the specificity of the task and to the subjects' knowledge of the context (Posner, 1980). It can also modulate automatic orienting effects by either increasing these effects or limiting their amplitude (Jacoby et al., 1993). As a bottom-up process (automatic exogenous mode), attention gives the opportunity to the subject to better process unexpected sources of information, with the counter-part of deviating from the initial center of interest. This means that automatic orienting has a hierarchical priority on voluntary orienting mechanisms. The two processes, however, have similar effects on both sensory inputs and motor outputs. In turn, sensory inputs and motor outputs affect how attention is involved through subjects' intention.

Finally, these two processes also seem to work more efficiently in elite athletes than in control subjects, or more generally in subjects frequently facing highly complex situations in which there is much information to process in a short time. At a more specific level, this greater efficiency can be expressed through a precise attentional style. It remains, however, to go beyond a simple description of expertise effects in order to provide more powerful explanations of how expertise is acquired and how it modifies human brain functions and behavior.

References

Abernethy, B. (1993). The nature of expertise in sport. In S. Serpa, J. Alves, V. Ferriera, & A. Paula-Brito (Eds.), *Proceedings of the 8th World Congress of Sport Psychology* (pp. 18–22). Portugal: Lisboa.

Allport, D.A. (1980). Attention and performance. In D. Claxton (Ed.), *Cognitive psychology: New directions* (pp. 112–153). London: Routledge & Kegan Paul.

Boulinguez, P., & Nougier, V. (1998). Attentional and motor preparation effects on movement control. Manuscript submitted for publication.

Castiello, U., & Umiltà, C. (1990). Size of the attentional focus and efficiency of processing. *Acta Psychologica, 73,* 195–209.

Castiello, U., & Umiltà, C. (1992). Orienting of attention in volleyball players. *International Journal of Sport Psychology, 23,* 301–310.

Eriksen, C., & Murphy, T. (1987). Movements of attentional focus across the visual field: A critical look at the evidence. *Perception & Psychophysics, 42,* 299–305.

Eriksen, C., & St. James, J. (1986). Visual attention within and around the field of focal attention: A zoom-lens model. *Perception & Psychophysics, 40,* 225–240.

Eriksen, C., & Yeh, Y. (1985). Allocation of attention in the visual field. *Journal of Experimental Psychology: Human Perception and Performance, 5,* 583–595.

Heilman, K.M., Watson, R.T., & Valenstein, E. (1985). Neglect and relted disorders. In K.M. Heilman & E. Valenstein (Eds), *Clinical neuropsychology* (pp. 243–293). New York: Oxford University Press.

Henderson, J. M. (1991). Stimulus discrimination following covert attentional orienting to exogenous cue. *Journal of Experimental Psychology: Human Perception and Performance, 17,* 91–106.

Jacoby, L.L., Ste-Marie, D., & Toth, J.P. (1993). Redefining automaticity: Unconcious influences, awareness and control. In A.D. Baddeley & L. Weiskrantz (Eds.), *Attention: Selection, awareness and control: A tribute to Donald Broadbent* (pp. 261–282). Oxford: Clarendon.

Jeannerod, M. (1988). *The neural and behavioral organization of goal-directed movements.* Oxford: Clarendon.

Jonides, J. (1981). Voluntary versus automatic control over the mind's eye movement. In J. Long & A. Baddeley (Eds.), *Attention and performance IX* (pp. 187–203). Hillsdale, NJ: Erlbaum.

Jonides, J., & Yantis, S. (1988). Uniqueness of abrupt visual onset in capturing attention. *Perception & Psychophysics, 43,* 346–354.

Kahneman, D., & Treisman, A. (1984). Changing views of attention and automaticity. In R. Parasuraman & D. Davies (Eds.), *Varieties of attention* (pp. 29–61). New York: Academic Press.

Keele, S., & Hawkins, H. (1982). Exploration of individual differences relevant to high level skill. *Journal of Motor Behavior, 14,* 3–23.

Klein, R.M. (1994). Perceptual-motor expectancies interact with covert visual orienting under conditions of endogenous but not exogenous control. *Canadian Journal of Psychology, 48,* 167–181.

La Berge, D., & Brown, V. (1989). Theory of attentional operations in shape identification. *Psychological Review, 96,* 101–124.

La Berge, D., Brown, V., Carter, M., Bash, D., & Hartley, A. (1991). Reducing the effects of adjacent distractors by narrowing attention. *Journal of Experimental Psychology: Human Perception and Performance, 17,* 65–76.

Lépine, D., Glencross, D., & Requin, J. (1989). Some experimental evidence for and against a parametric conception of movement programming. *Journal of Experimental Psychology: Human Perception and Performance, 15,* 347–362.

Müller, H.J., & Rabbitt, P.M.A. (1989). Reflexive and voluntary orienting of visual attention: Time course of attivation and resistance to interruption. *Journal of Experimental Psychology: Human Perception and Performance, 15,* 315–330.

Nougier, V., Azémar, G., Stein, J.F., & Ripoll, H. (1992). Covert orienting to central visual cues and sport practice relations in the development of visual attention. *Journal of Experimental Child Psychology, 54,* 315–333.

Nougier, V., Ripoll, H., & Stein, J.F. (1989). Orienting of attention with highly skilled athletes. *International Journal of Sport Psychology, 20,* 205–223.

Nougier, V., Rossi, B., Alain, C., & Taddei, F. (1996). Evidence of strategic effects in the modulation of orienting of attention. *Ergonomics, 9,* 1119–1133.

Nougier, V., Rossi, B., Bard, C., Fleury, M., Teasdale, N., Cole, J., Lamarre, Y. (1994). Orienting of attention in deafferented patients. *Neuropsychologia, 9,* 1079–1088

Nougier, V., Stein, J.-F., & Azémar, G. (1990). Covert orienting of attention and motor preparation processes as a factor of success in fencing. *Journal of Human Movement Studies, 19,* 251–272.

Nougier, V., Stein, J.-F., & Bonnel, A.-M. (1991). Information processing in sport and "orienting of attention". In H. Ripoll (Ed.), Information Processing and Decision Making in Sport. *International Journal of Sport Psychology, 3–4,* 307–327.

Parasuraman, R., & Davies, D. (1984). *Varieties of attention.* New York: Academic Press.

Pesce Anzeneder, C. & Bösel, R. (in press). Modulation of the spatial extent of the attentional focus in high-level volleyball players. *European Journal of Cognitive Psychology.*

Posner, M.I. (1980). Orienting of attention. *Quarterly Journal of Experimental Psychology, 32,* 3–25.

Posner, M.I., & Cohen, Y. (1984). Components of visual orienting. In H. Bouma & D.G. Bouwhuis (Eds.), *Attention and performance X* (pp. 531–555). Hillsdale, NJ: Erlbaum.

Posner, M.I., & Snyder, C. (1975). Facilitation and inhibition in the processing of signals. In P. Rabbitt & S. Dornic (Eds.), *Attention and Performance V* (pp. 669–682). London: Academic Press.

Posner, M.I., Snyder, C., & Davidson, B. (1980). Attention and the detection of signals. *Journal of Experimental Psychology: General, 2,* 160–174.

Possamaï, C., (1986). Relationship between inhibition and facilitation following a visual cue. *Acta Psychologica, 61,* 243–258.

Pribram, K., & McGuinness, D. (1975). Arousal, activation and effort in the control of attention. *Psychological Review, 182,* 111–149.

Requin, J. (1980). Toward a psychobiology of preparation for action. In G.E. Stelmach & J. Requin (Eds.), *Tutorials in Motor Behavior* (pp. 373–398). Amsterdam: North Holland.

Requin, J. (1985). Looking forward to moving soon: Ante factum selective processes in motor control. In M. Posner & O. Marin (Eds.), *Attention and Performance XI* (pp. 147–167). Hillsdale, NJ: Erlbaum.

Rosenbaum, D. (1980). Human movement initiation: Specification of arm, direction and extent. *Journal of Experimental Psychology: General, 109,* 444–474.

Rosenbaum, D. (1983). The movement precueing technique: Assumptions, applications and extensions. In R. Magill (Ed.), *Memory and control of action* (pp. 231–274). Amsterdam: North Holland.

Rossi, B., Rudic, R., & Nougier, V. (1995). L'attenzione nel pallanuotista. *Rivista di Cultura Sportiva, 32,* 2–8.

Rossi, B., & Zani, A. (1991). Timing of movement-related decision processes in clay-pigeon shooters as assessed by event-related brain potentials and reaction times. *International Journal of Sport Psychology, 22,* 128–139.

Tsal, Y. (1983). Movements of attention across the visual field. *Journal of Experimental Psychology: Human Perception and Performance, 9,* 523–530.

Verfallie, M., Bowers, D., & Heilman, K.M. (1988). Hemispheric asymmetries in mediating intention but not selective attention. *Neuropsychologia, 26,* 521–531.

8

Information and Movement in Interception Tasks

Reinoud J. Bootsma
University of the Mediterranean and CNRS
Marseille, France

Interceptive actions capitalize on the constraints imposed by relative movement between an actor (the term will we use to denote the individual engaged in action) and his or her environment. In the present contribution we examine four different hypotheses that have been put forward to account for the ability to successfully accomplish interception tasks. These four hypotheses, which we have termed respectively (a) closing the gap, (b) contact prediction by trajectory extrapolation, (c) contact prediction by direct assessment, and (d) contact prospection, allow us to analyze interception performance by considering the different ways in which information and movement have been suggested to be coupled. Each strategy is discussed by focusing first on the information used and subsequently on the way in which this information is used. By drawing on relevant empirical studies where necessary, the feasibility of each strategy is examined.

1. Closing the gap

Perhaps the simplest way in which one can try to intercept a moving object such as a ball is to continuously move toward the current position of the object to be intercepted. All one has to do, then, is to regularly determine the currently required direction of movement and move as fast as possible in that direction. Although this action is both simple and expedient, one should bear in mind that this strategy guarantees success only if the actor is able to maintain a speed greater than that of the object (see Figure 8.1 for an example in which this is not the case). It is thus clear that in many (ball) sports settings such a "guided missile" strategy would not be appropriate. Moreover, experimental work has demonstrated that, even in the situation in which it could work, the spatiotemporal trajectory followed by the actor, even if she or he is a very young child, does not have the curved form predicted by this strategy (Von Hofsten, 1987).

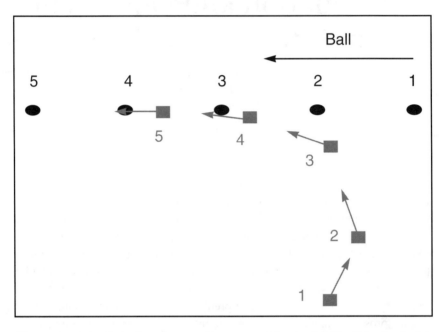

Figure 8.1. The "closing the gap" strategy. The ball (filled black circle) moves from right to left (from position 1 to position 5). Interception is sought after by continuously moving (gray square) towards the current position of the ball. For the conditions presented the velocity of movement is not sufficient to ensure interception.

2a. Contact Prediction I:
Trajectory Extrapolation

In most cases the movement trajectories observed are more or less rectilinear in nature, with the actor moving directly toward the future interception point. This observation has been taken to imply that the actor has determined before movement onset when and where contact is to take place. By extrapolating from the perceived characteristics of the motion of the ball, accomplished through learned procedures referred to as internal models (Bahill & Karnavas,

1993; McBeath, 1990), the future place and time of contact are obtained (Regan, 1997; Saxberg, 1987). Once these have been established, a movement is then prepared to bring the effector to the required position within the required time span. Notwithstanding its wide acceptance perhaps due to its intuitive appeal, the success of this "ballistic missile" strategy depends critically on the capabilities of the actor to obtain accurate information about the future trajectory of the object. As we will come back to the issue further on, it suffices here to remark that the mechanics of the motion of a ball, rolling over the ground or flying through the air, are already quite complicated. Internal models that can adequately account for trajectory extrapolation are therefore complex and rely on a multitude of different inputs.

2b. Contact Prediction II: Direct Assessment

In recent years, the suggestion that trajectory extrapolation, accomplished by means of an internal model, constitutes an appropriate way of accounting for the behaviors observed, has been questioned. It has been argued that invoking the existence of intelligent structures, such as internal models, to explain behavior does not constitute a solution that is scientifically satisfactory (Kugler & Turvey, 1987). Invoking such intermediate structures in fact does not really solve the problem, but merely displaces it, giving rise to (rarely addressed but nevertheless deep) questions with respect to where such structures come from and by what principles they operate.

Moreover, analyses of the optic-flow patterns available to the eye have demonstrated that both the future place and time of contact may be directly available, making the cumbersome extrapolation of these properties from perceived characteristics of the trajectories superfluous. For reasons of mathematical convenience, the geometrical analyses that follow to demonstrate this point are performed utilizing a planar projection technique. The idea is to show that relevant properties, such as the future place and time of contact, are available on a two-dimensional projection surface (such as a television screen). If this proves to be the case, one may assume that these properties are also available to a visual system, albeit in perhaps a somewhat different form due to differences in the shape of the projection surface (Lee, 1974; Todd, 1981).

Consider the situation of relative movement between a point of observation and a ball, as depicted in Figure 8.2. The ball, of diameter R, is currently distance in depth of Z m from the point of observation with a lateral offset of X m. Setting the distance between the projection plane and the point of observation to unity (again for reasons of mathematical convenience), the currently projected size r and the currently projected lateral distance x are equal to

$$r = \frac{R}{Z} \qquad (1)$$

$$x = \frac{X}{Z} \qquad (2)$$

When the ball moves, for instance, along the line indicated by the arrow, both X and Z change. Denoting the time derivative of a variable by a dot above it, we find that the rates of change of the projected size and position are

$$\dot{r} = \frac{R\dot{Z}}{Z^2} \qquad (3)$$

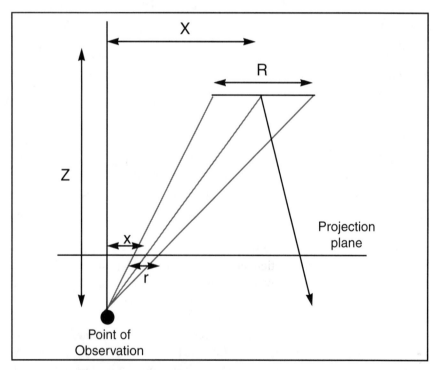

Figure 8.2. Geometrical relations between a ball of size R at current coordinates (X,Z) relative to a point of observation and the projections of its size (r) and lateral offset (x) on a plane.

$$\dot{x} = \frac{\dot{X}Z - X\dot{Z}}{Z^2} \tag{4}$$

Thus, both the rate of change of r (i.e., $\dot{r}$) and the rate of change of x (i.e., $\dot{x}$) are complex functions of the size, current position, and current rate of change of position of the ball. By themselves they cannot, therefore, be used to obtain univocal information about motion of the ball. However, the first-order[1] time remaining until distance $Z = 0$, is directly available in the pattern of optical change as is clear from the combination of (1) and (3):

$$TC_1(Z) = -\frac{Z}{\dot{Z}} = \frac{r}{\dot{r}} \tag{5}$$

First-order time $TC_1(Z)$, being the time until distance Z is reduced to zero by current velocity $\dot{Z}$, is fully specified by the ratio of projected size over the rate of change of projected size. This compound optical variable, often referred to as *tau* (Lee, 1976), may thus be used to obtain information about (first-order) time remaining.

The lateral distance X_L at which the ball will be after time T is defined by

$$X_L = X + \dot{X}T \tag{6}$$

The future passing distance is the distance at which the ball will be at the moment $Z = 0$. The time remaining until $Z = 0$ is provided by (5). Appropriate substitution of (5) for (6) leads to

$$X_L = R\,\frac{\dot{x}}{\dot{r}} \tag{7}$$

Thus the lateral distance at which the ball will pass is specified, in units ball size (i.e., X_L/R) by the ratio of optical displacement velocity over optical expansion velocity.

---

1 The term *first-order* denotes the fact that only the first time derivative is taken into account. First-order time until a given distance is zero as defined by the ratio of current distance over current velocity. If changes in velocity due to a constant acceleration are taken into account, second-order properties are being considered. If changes in acceleration due to a constant jerk are taken into account, third-order properties are being considered. Et cetera.

Hence, both the future time and place of contact are available in the optic-flow pattern generated by the relative movement and do not need, therefore, to be extrapolated (the reader interested in more detail is referred to Bootsma and Peper, 1992), Bootsma and Oudejans (1993), Todd (1981) and Tresilian (1991, 1994)). Note that both the future time and place are obtained without the actor having any explicit knowledge about the current position and/or current velocity of the ball!

Notwithstanding the attractiveness of the shortcut in calculation provided by the direct assessment strategy, both forms of contact prediction, be it by trajectory extrapolation or by direct assessment, ensure a conceptual separation between perception and movement: Perception merely serves to determine the future place and time of contact. Once this has been done, a movement is organized in such a way that the actor arrives at the future place of contact at the desired moment. A number of arguments, both theoretical and empirical, suggest that humans and other animals may in fact not operate in this way.

From a theoretical point of view, it is clear that strategies based on contact prediction can only function when the resulting prediction is almost perfect. Whereas we demonstrated in the foregoing that information specifying the future time and place of contact is available, it is important to bear in mind that this analysis assumed that the current velocity of approach would be maintained. In other words, the analysis only deals with first-order properties of space and time. Given that a genuinely constant velocity of approach is more of an exception than the rule, the contact prediction perspective cannot but consider the variables identified above as approximate (e.g., Tresilian, 1994), and a good number of discussions have been devoted to the conditions under which such approximations are no longer sufficient to guarantee successful performance (cf. Wann, 1996). However, although better approximations could in principle be obtained by considering that changes in velocity may occur (i.e., by considering second-order properties), there is no way in which an actor can take into account all possible (nth-order) changes that may intervene (Bootsma, Fayt, Zaal, & Laurent, 1997). In the framework of the contact-prediction perspective, the actor, therefore, has to learn what type of approximate information is sufficiently accurate to allow successful performance. In such a perspective, expertise is, in part at least, characterized by acquired task-specific procedures of selecting appropriate information sources.

Irrespective of the exact way in which future place and time of contact would be obtained, one of the basic assumptions underlying the contact-prediction perspective is that movement is programmed according to the perceived spatiotemporal requirements. Thus, even if future place and time of contact would have been determined with sufficient precision, performance will be successful only if the movement subsequently produced is of itself not a source of unacceptable variation. This implies that timing accuracy at the moment of onset of movement (i.e., when the program is launched) must be good enough to ensure that timing accuracy by the end of the movement remains satisfactory. Another characteristic of expertise would therefore be the ability to limit the "drift" due to inherent neuro-muscular noise (Tyldesley & Whiting, 1975). Empirical results obtained from analyses of the movement patterns produced by expert table tennis and volleyball players, however, provide a picture that is far removed from the ideas sketched above. Rather than slightly decreasing, timing accuracy was found to increase (i.e., temporal variablity decreases) during the course of movement, reaching maximal accuracy at the all-important moment of contact with the ball (see Tables 8.1 and 8.2). Basically these results, obtained in radically different settings, indicate that a common characteristic of expert movement is not its stability but its flexibility.

Table 8.1. Timing accuracy in milliseconds for five experts performing an attacking forehand drive in table tennis. Data from Bootsma and Van Wieringen (1990).

	Onset of Swing	Contact
S1	20.9	2.0
S2	5.3	2.1
S3	8.7	2.6
S4	4.8	4.1
S5	19.0	4.7

Table 8.2. Timing accuracy in milliseconds for five experts performing a volleyball spike. Data from Sardinha and Bootsma (1993).

	Jump Take-off	Onset of Backward Swing	Onset of Forward Swing	Contact
S1	27.6	9.5	5.3	4.0
S2	19.8	11.9	3.5	3.0
S3	36.6	10.7	4.6	5.0
S4	24.2	9.2	5.2	5.4
S5	32.0	7.6	0.0	4.6

These results, in clear contradiction to the expectations of the ballistic missile strategy, led Peper, Bootsma, Mestre, and Bakker (1994) to further dissect the idea that perception serves to identify the future place and time of contact and that movement is subsequently executed according to these requirements. The task they proposed required participants to catch balls converging along different trajectories to identical interception locations (see Figure 8.3). If catching movements were based on the identification of the spatiotemporal properties of the future interception point, all trajectories converging toward the same point within the same time should give rise to identical movement patterns. As is evident from the (partial) results depicted in Figure 8.4, the nature of the trajectory (notably the angle of approach to the interception point) influenced the kinematics of the catching movements produced, notwithstanding the fact that all balls were caught. Once again, this result does not fit the contact-prediction perspective.

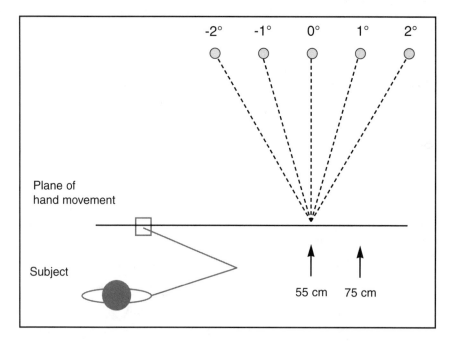

Figure 8.3. Schematic representation of the catching task used by Peper et al. (1994). Subjects caught balls approaching along different trajectories (varying in their of angle of approach) to the same interception point that was located at either 55 or 75 cm from the initial hand position.

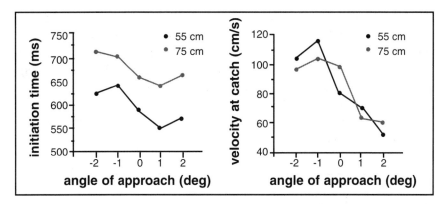

Figure 8.4. Even though all balls were caught at the same interception point (55 or 75 cm from the initial hand position), characterisics of the catching movements produced varied as a function of angle of approach.

Having thus established that timing accuracy increases during the unfolding of the movement and that movement kinematics vary as a function of the characteristics of the approach, we are confronted with the conclusion that future place and time of contact are not estimated prior to movement onset.

3. Contact Prospection

If not through prediction of the future place and time of contact, how then can an actor succeed at intercepting a moving object? The answer to this question is not as complicated as it might seem. Rather than seeking to know when the moving ball will be where, the actor could seek to establish a relation that guarantees that contact will ensue, without needing to know a priori when and where this will be. While this type of contact prospection has received some attention in the domain of locomoting to the position where a fly ball will land (e.g., Chapman, 1968; MacBeath, Shaffer, & Kaiser, 1995; McLeod & Dienes, 1993, 1996; Michaels & Oudejans, 1992), it has not been seriously considered in other domains.

Let us consider the catching tasks used by Peper et al. (1994) in some more detail. Figure 8.5 presents a situation in which the movement of the hand is aligned with the motion of the ball in such a way that the position of the hand continuously coincides with the current lateral position of the ball (obtained through orthogonal projection onto the plane of movement of the hand). If both the ball and hand continue to move as they are currently moving, the hand will meet the ball at the very moment that the ball passes through the plane of movement of the hand. In other words, continuously tracking the lateral position of the ball ensures that contact will occur, without necessitating a priori knowledge of when and where this will be. The tight coupling between the movements of the hand and ball depicted in Figure 8.5 in fact maintains a lateral distance between hand and (projected) ball position equal to zero all along the trajectory. However, the requirement that contact must occur does not necessarily dictate that this distance be zero throughout the trajectory.

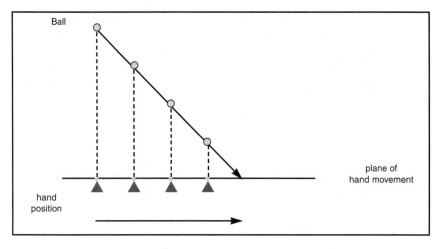

Figure 8.5. Movement of the hand is coupled to the movement of the ball so that the current position of the hand coincides with the projected current position of the ball.

Consider the situation depicted in Figure 8.6 in which the hand does not (yet) move. When the ball is in position 1, the distance ΔX between hand and ball is zero, and hence the hand need not move. This is, however, no longer the case a little later when the ball has reached position 2. In order to guarantee future contact between ball and hand, the hand should, therefore, move so as to cover distance ΔX, and it should do so in the time remaining until the ball passes through the plane of movement of the hand. For reasons that will soon become apparent, first-order time remaining adequately captures the temporal constraint. Thus, at each instant, the situation can be described as giving rise to a currently required velocity of hand movement that is given by the ratio of current lateral distance ΔX over current (first-order) time remaining TC_1. As long as this required hand velocity is smaller than a given threshold, the hand will remain stationary. When the currently required hand velocity exceeds this threshold, hand movement is initiated with acceleration being dependent on the difference between actual and required velocity.

As the ball continues to move, time remaining until passage through the plane of movement of the hand diminishes while current distance ΔX evolves as a function of both continued movement of the ball as well as movement of the hand. In other words, required velocity evolves as a function of movement of both the hand and ball and movement of the hand continuously integrates the current difference between actual and required velocity. For specifics of the dynamical model, the interested reader is referred to Peper et al. (1994) and Bootsma et al. (1997). In the present framework we simply want to point out that the evolution over time of the required velocity of movement is considerably different for the five trajectories depicted in Figure 8.3, even though all five converge toward the same interception point. This is easily understood when one simply considers the different ways in which ΔX evolves over time when the hand is kept stationary at its initial location: For outward moving trajectories (approach angles of -2 and -1°), ΔX is relatively small initially and increases as time runs out, whereas for the inward-moving trajectories (approach angles of 1 and 2°), ΔX is relatively large initially and decreases as time runs out. Movement produced according to the foregoing logic thus predicts that movement initiation should occur earlier for inward-moving trajectories

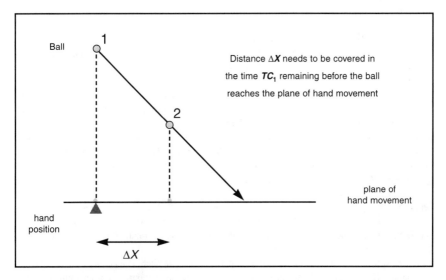

Figure 8.6. Contact is guaranteed by the adoption of the currently required velocity which is given by the ratio of the current distance ΔX over the current time remaining TC_1.

whereas the hand velocity at the moment of contact should be larger for outward-moving trajectories. Inspection of the results obtained by Peper et al. (1994) as depicted in Figure 8.4 reveals that this is exactly what was found.

Conclusion

The intuitive idea that successful performance in interception tasks requires prediction has been challenged in two ways. First, analyses of the movement patterns produced by expert players reveal that the logical implications of prediction strategies are not in agreement with the results obtained. When tested in a specifically designed laboratory catching task, the evidence obtained once again runs counter to a prediction strategy. Second, upon reflection, the possibility to ensure success through prediction is in fact quite limited because the requirement that prediction must be almost perfect is simply not realistic. A mode of functioning in which an evaluation that is continuous over time is used to dynamically shape the movements produced accounts for stability under constant conditions (the same process giving rise to the same results) while at the same time allowing flexibility (changes in the situation give rise to changes in the movement produced).

References

Bahill, A.T., & Karnavas, W.J. (1993). The perceptual illusion of baseball's rising fastball and breaking curve ball. *Journal of Experimental Psychology: Human Perception and Performance, 19,* 3–14.

Bootsma, R.J., Fayt, V., Zaal, F.T.J.M., & Laurent, M. (1997). On the information-based regulation of movement: Things Wann (1996) may want to consider. *Journal of Experimental Psychology: Human Perception and Performance, 23,* 1282–1289.

Bootsma, R.J., & Oudejans, R.R.D. (1993). Visual information about time to collision between two objects. *Journal of Experimental Psychology: Human Perception and Performance, 19,* 1041–1052.

Bootsma, R.J., & Peper, C.E. (1992). Predictive information sources for the regulation of action with special emphasis on catching and hitting. In L. Proteau & D. Elliott (Eds.), *Vision and motor control* (pp. 285–314). Amsterdam: North-Holland.

Bootsma, R.J., & Van Wieringen, P.C.W. (1990). Timing an attacking forehand drive in table tennis. *Journal of Experimental Psychology: Human Perception and Performance, 16,* 21–29.

Chapman, S. (1968). Catching a baseball. *American Journal of Physics, 36,* 868–870.

Kugler, P.N., & Turvey, M.T. (1987). *Information, natural law, and the self-assembly of rhythmic movement.* Hillsdale, NJ: Erlbaum.

Lee, D.N. (1974). Visual information during locomotion. In R.B. McLeod & H. Pick (Eds.). *Perception: Essays in honor of J.J. Gibson* (pp. 250–267). Ithaca, NY: Cornell University Press.

Lee, D.N. (1976). A theory of visual control of braking based on information about time-to-collision. *Perception, 5,* 437–459.

McBeath, M.K. (1990). The rising fastball: Baseball's impossible pitch. *Perception, 19,* 545–552.

McBeath, M.K., Shaffer, D,M., & Kaiser, M.K. (1995). How baseball outfielders determine where to run to catch fly balls. *Science, 268,* 569–573.

McLeod, P. & Dienes, Z. (1993). Running to catch a ball. *Nature, 362,* 23.

McLeod, P. & Dienes, Z. (1996). Do fielders know where to go to catch the ball or only how to get there? *Journal of Experimental Psychology: Human Perception and Performance, 22,* 531–543.

Michaels, C.F., & Oudejans, R.R.D. (1992). The optics and actions of catching fly balls: Zeroing out optical acceleration. *Ecological Psychology, 4,* 199–222.

Peper, C.E., Bootsma, R.J., Mestre, D.R., & Bakker, F.C. (1994). Catching balls: How to get the hand to the right place at the right time. *Journal of Experimental Psychology: Human Perception and Performance, 20,* 591–612.

Regan, D. (1997). Visual factors in hitting and catching. *Journal of Sport Sciences, 15,* 533–559.

Sardinha, L.F., & Bootsma, R.J. (1993). A perception-action approach to the study of the volleyball spike. *Portugese Journal of Human Performance Studies, 9,* 5–29.

Saxberg, B,V,H, (1987). Projected free fall trajectories: I. Theory and simulation. *Biological Cybernetics, 56,* 159–175.

Todd, J.T. (1981). Visual information about moving objects. *Journal of Experimental Psychology: Human Perception and Performance, 7,* 795–810.

Tresilian, J.R. (1991). Empirical and theoretical issues in the perception of time to contact. *Journal of Experimental Psychology: Human Perception and Performance, 17,* 865–876.

Tresilian, J.R. (1994). Perceptual and motor processes in interceptive timing. *Human Movement Science, 13,* 335–373.

Tyldesley, D. A., & Whiting, H.T.A. (1975). Operational timing. *Journal of Human Movement Studies, 1,* 172–177.

Von Hofsten, C. (1987) Catching. In H. Heuer, & A. F. Sanders (Eds.), *Perspectives on perception and action* (pp. 333–347). London: Lawrence Erlbaum Associates.

Wann, J.P. (1996). Anticipating arrival: Is the tau-margin a specious theory? *Journal of Experimental Psychology: Human Perception and Performance, 22,* 1031–1048.

Part IV

Motivation and Emotion

Motivation and emotion are two of the most popular topics in sport psychology. Athletic achievement is substantially affected by such factors as the motivation to practice, the commitment to improve oneself, and the will to attain a high level of excellence. Another critical factor relevant to achievement is the actual state and the quality of the performer's emotions. The four chapters included in this part provide theoretical and practical discussions on motivation in athletes and regulation of emotions during motor performance.

Chapter 9, entitled "Persistence, Excellence, and Fulfillment," provides a general overview of motivation and discusses self-perception of participants in sport settings and their potential to achieve. In addition, typical characteristics of high achievers, as well as important variables related to the achievement motive, are discussed.

In chapter 10, entitled "Intrinsic and Extrinsic Motivation in Sport: Toward a Hierarchical Model," a number of empirical studies supporting the hierarchical model are reviewed. It is also demonstrated how this model may lead to a better under-standing of motivational phenomena found in sport.

A current view of motivation and leadership in sport psychology is presented in chapter 11, entitled "Toward an Integration of Models of Leadership With a Contemporary Theory of Motivation." The chapter attempts to integrate multidimensional models of leadership and goal perspective theory, emphasizing the central links existing between these concepts.

Chapter 12, entitled "The Presentation and Modulation of Emotions," presents recent research on emotion in sports. Selected findings are reviewed, followed by a brief look into strategies of emotional regulation and their effect on motivation and performance.

9

Persistence, Excellence, and Fulfillment

Robert N. Singer and Iris Orbach
Department of Exercise and Sport Sciences
University of Florida
Gainesville, Florida, USA

The level of motivation present within a person influences preferences and selection of activities in a free-choice situation, persistence, effort, and quality of performance. Potential materialistic gain from what one accomplishes can obviously have an enormous motivational impact. As well, perceptions of accomplishment, satisfaction, and fulfillment via the process and outcome serve as powerful directional energy forces. In other words, the ideal world is one in which we like what we are doing, feel good about ourselves, and get rewarded/recognized for our accomplishments.

The motivation to practice, condition, and persevere, with the commitment to improve and attain a level of excellence, is at the heart of achieving. The most successful athletes, those who are successful in numerous competitive events over many years, have learned the value of inspiration, perspiration, and dedication. Continual efforts to do one's best in practice and competition over a long period of time reflect the motivation to persist (Singer, 1984). Invariably, injuries, setbacks, frustrations, and personal problems are overcome to reach levels of performance realized by only a few athletes in any sport. Yet, anyone can attain a reasonable level of satisfaction in and through sport experiences.

Much has been written historically about motivation from behavioristic, humanistic, and cognitive perspectives. Behaviorists have emphasized the importance of external motivational factors, such as rewards and punishments, in stimulating interest, sustaining motivation, and attaining proficiency in particular activities. For humanistic psychologists, self-perceptions are associated with satisfaction, fulfillment, and accomplishment as central factors in sustaining motivation. Cognitive psychologists shift the focus from inner needs and environmental factors to the subjective world of the individual. They are most recognized for their contributions in understanding how mental processes related to appropriate expectancies and attributions influence motivation and, in turn, achievement. Scholars from their particular perspectives have attempted to explain motivation and how it can be influenced as well as function most advantageously (e.g., Covington, 1992; Nicholls, 1992; Weiner, 1995). However, the popular approach today is to examine forces that influence choices, persistence, and achievement from cognitive perspectives. For example, personal perceptions in the form of goals (e.g., Duda, Chi, Newton, Walling, & Catley, 1995), self-determination (Frederick & Ryan, 1995), and explanatory behavior about one's performance (Buchanan & Seligman, 1995) have been determined to be critical in influencing the achievement motive, the desire to persist, and the ability to attain proficiency.

Furthermore, self-perceptions related to self-efficacy, locus of control, coping style, and personal causation also apparently determine level of achievement (Singer, 1984). Putting it simply, how we think influences what we do, how much we do it, and how well we do it. In addition, besides accomplishing, our perspectives about what we do and the outcome of our activities are related to the degree of our sense of self-satisfaction and fulfillment.

Motivation potentially affects behavior in a variety of ways. Of major interest here are the kinds of things athletes can do to elevate and maintain their enthusiasm, drive, and resolve to be the best they can be. In other words, *persistence motivation* will be the primary focus. The underlying theme is that striving and accomplishing are within the grasp of everyone (Ericcson & Charness, 1994). This premise assumes the presence of reasonable capabilities and opportunities, and no overwhelming bad fate, such as severe injuries and health problems, that is impossible to overcome. It also assumes the dedication to practice. Ericcson and Charness have studied expert performance in a number of areas and conclude that the best achievers practice more conscientiously and deliberately than do others. For instance, a highly successful Olympic canoeist has said, "Everything I do, whether it is weights, or running, or the normal training things, or the leisure activities I do, it is all geared toward how it's going to affect my paddling . . ." (Orlick & Partington, 1988, p. 110).

Extrinsic and intrinsic sources of motivation, separately or together, contribute to staying with an activity. However, the primary consideration throughout this paper is the significance of intrinsic factors (Deci & Ryan, 1985): of doing something for the sake of doing it, of enjoying the challenge, of trying to improve and determine self-competence, and of feeling fulfilled through the experiences. Anecdotal and other evidence (Hardy & Parfitt, 1994; Mahoney, Gabriel, & Perkins, 1987; Orlick & Partington, 1988) suggest that many elite athletes do indeed sustain high levels of intrinsic motivation throughout their career. Basic concepts from Deci and Ryan's (1985, 1991) cognitive evaluation theory are pertinent. When a person perceives that he or she has the ability to *cause* things to happen, that behaviors and achievements are *self-determined*, intrinsic motivation prevails. Self-determination is associated with the perception of autonomy. As we proceed, fundamental ideas from cognitive and humanistic psychology will be shown to be related to intrinsic motivation, persistence, and achievement.

Thus, the purposes of this chapter are to (a) provide a general overview about motivation; (b) discuss self-perceptions with implications for analyzing participants in sport settings and their potential to achieve, as well as their will to demonstrate competence; and (c) describe typical characteristics of high achievers while discussing happiness, satisfaction, and fulfillment as important ideal corollary variables related to the achievement motive and appropriate rationale for continuing in sport with the intention of developing excellence.

What Does Motivation Influence?

To begin with a general overview, it is important to realize that motivation is associated with arousal level and energized thoughts and emotions oriented to attaining a goal. In sport, they are typically expressed toward the intent of winning and avoiding losing. Or they can be associated with being the best one can be, with proving one's ability to perform well. Goals have been conceptualized in reference to personal dispositions and have been differentiated as ego (performance outcome) oriented versus task (mastery) oriented (e.g., Ames, 1992; Kavussanu & Roberts, 1996; Nicholls, 1992). The two orientations differ in the comparisons that performers make in order to formulate their perceptions of competence (Duda, 1992). These are not necessarily incompatible goals, although most experts agree that process and mastery goals, associated with intrinsic motivation and self-determination, represent the more desirable category (Frederick & Ryan, 1995). Furthermore, it has been found that ego orientations are likely to lead to high anxiety (Duda, Newton, & Chi, 1990), low self-efficacy (Nicholls, 1992), and a denigration of the role of effort in performance (Duda & Chi, 1989) in those who have a low perception of their own ability. Whatever the source, or reasons, motivation can influence

1. The *selection* of an activity in which to be engaged, assuming free choice;
2. *Continuing* involvement (persistence) in that activity;
3. *Effort* shown—in practice, conditioning, and competition;
4. *Quality* of performance at any time.

The more motivation to achieve in a particular sport, the more likely a person will decide to be involved in it when alternative opportunities are present. Furthermore, training will be sustained over a long period of time. Effort to improve is continually demonstrated. When it is time to display capabilities, as during competition, an *optimal* level of motivation (arousal state) is ideal prior to and during performance. The ideal state depends on the act to be executed, like a dive, or the changing situational dynamics as associated with ball sports. We are becoming more aware of the importance of the athlete's attaining this ideal mental-emotional state. But oftentimes neglected is the consideration of motivation as a driving force to train, and train hard, over many days, months, and years.

Motivation in Perspective

Saying it simply, high-level achievement in a particular sport or in any activity may be viewed as an effect of three variables. A person needs

1. To possess reasonable *capabilities* for *that* activity
2. To *train diligently* to develop these capabilities
3. To learn to be effective when in *evaluation situations*, as in competition.

For an athlete to do well, he or she must have potentials that can be developed. They are to some degree genetically determined. These are predispositions to do well in some endeavor, and they relate to body structure, emotional tendencies, coordination of body parts, and the like. Much contemporary research suggests the relative impact of genetics vs. environment on behaviors (e.g., Bouchard, 1994). In fact, the June 1994 issue of *Science* was devoted to the theme "Genes & Behavior." Early childhood experiences play a significant role in redefining the influence of heredity attributes (Bloom, 1985).

In order for a person with reasonable capabilities to be successful in a particular sport, the next consideration is working purposefully to develop and refine foundational as well as higher order skills and strategies. Conditioning and a healthy lifestyle are prerequisites. The third component is the ability to demonstrate what has been learned. The athlete who executes well in practice must learn how to execute well in contest competition. Ultimately, performance in competition reflects (a) personal potentialities; (b) sincere commitment to practicing, conditioning, and improving; and (c) the ability to do well under the stress of competition.

As an aside, many media specialists and the public at large often neglect the contributions of (b) and (c). Constant reference is made to successful athletes who presumably possess instincts and natural abilities. Commitment to goals as expressed through effective preparation is underplayed. Unfortunately, there are many misconceptions about those who become outstanding in their respective sports. "A lot of people assume it's an overnight success story. It's taken me nine years of hard work in international competition and many years before that" (Kerrin Lee-Gartner, 1992 Olympic Gold medalist in the Women's Downhill Ski Race, quoted in Orlick & Lee-Gartner, 1993, p. 111). It is interesting to hear the comments of well-known athletic figures (Hemery, 1991; Orlick & Partington, 1988). Many make very similar reactions as to what they felt contributed to their success. Few refer to their innate abilities or natural propensity to fare well in the sports in which they chose to compete. Instead, many dwell upon their *dedication to practice*, and to *practice with dedication*: They even look forward to training. They do not attempt shortcuts; they are proud of their many hours of hard work. Oftentimes we may be guilty of assuming that accomplishments come easy, that athletes almost automatically become stars. Genetics help. They set the machinery in motion. But there is no substitution for labor—even a love of labor—in order to become among the best, or actually the best.

An example for the commitment and dedication of elite athletes is Greg Louganis (1995), who was somehow able to deal with a series of tragedies most of his life to become the best diver of all time, winning gold medals at the 1984 and 1988 Olympic Games. His autobiography, *Breaking the Surface*, was published in the beginning of 1995 and reveals that he kept secret that he was diagnosed as having AIDS (HIV-positive) 6 months before the 1988 Olympics in Seoul, Korea. During the Games, he hit his head on the board as he attempted a dive and bled profusely in the pool. Still, he told no one of his AIDS condition, even though AIDS might have been contagious to the other swimmers. Furthermore, he writes in his book of a painful upbringing. Louganis was adopted by an abusive alcoholic father, and was continuously depressed, a heavy drug user, and involved in a stormy six-year homosexual relationship. In spite of such miseries and perhaps in order to conceal them, he obsessively trained as a diver. Louganis' persistence to attain the highest levels of excellence was remarkable in that he was not visibly distracted by all of his personal miseries.

Motivation is such an important contributor to success that it is usually taken for granted. Yet it is the foundation for achievement. Perhaps, in summary, it can be depicted more fully in Figure 9.1.

We believe that an interaction exists between skill level and competitive capabilities. For instance, athletes with similar skill levels will be expected to demonstrate different performance levels depending on their available resources to handle competitive pressure. Furthermore, researchers have fre-

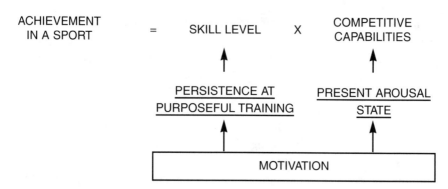

Figure 9.1. The relationship of aspects of motivation to achievement in sport.

quently demonstrated the influence of motivation on persistence and arousal state (see review by Roberts, 1992).

Trying and Trying Again

Many athletes may be afraid of trying too hard for various reasons. They may have a fear of success, of having others depend upon them too much if, in fact, they did well. Or they may shield a terrible fear of failure, of trying hard and worrying about this effort not resulting in proficiency. There are all sorts of reasons for not trying hard, for not persisting consistently at training. *Self-Worth theory* (Covington, 1992) suggests that most of us are searching for self-acceptance. Ability is valued, and failure-avoiding strategies are readily available for those who want to maintain a positive self-image of competency, especially when risking competitive failure. Nothing ventured, nothing lost.

As has been stated, one of the most difficult but necessary ingredients in attaining a degree of proficiency in an activity is the ability to maintain motivation to achieve over a long period of time. Perseverance at practice is demonstrated when high levels of motivation for the activity are present—and sustained continuously. How can this commitment be developed and sustained? Potential to achieve comes closer when the athlete is dedicated to improve and succeed. This commitment is expressed in trying to attain increasingly more challenging goals, as is the case with high achievers.

Self-Perceptions

Accomplishing is facilitated when appropriate self-perceptions are present. What needs to be realized is that hard work pays off. People who are successful in this world in different kinds of endeavors are those who believe in their capabilities and who trust that they are what they are because they helped to make themselves what they are. They expect to do well (Bandura, 1997). Unfortunately, there are many who feel they are not in control of themselves and their destiny. They resign themselves to being victims or pawns in their situations (deCharms, 1968). Perceptions of self-competency and assuredness evolve slowly, but must develop. So do perceptions of an ability to achieve, somewhat independent of the influence of fate, luck, and the influence of others (Weiner, 1995). Personal perceptions of effective strategies and capabilities are associated with motivation and achievement. Four major considerations are discussed next.

Personal Causation / Locus of Control

One characteristic that is not particularly beneficial to achievement is a continual feeling that what happens personally is external, beyond personal control. Two extreme types of individuals may be classified as *origins* or *pawns* (deCharms, 1968). Those who experience being an origin perceive themselves as originating their own behavior. They want something of personal meaning ⇌ learn the characteristics of the relevant situation ⇌ know what to do ⇌ engage in appropriate activities ⇌ be successful often ⇌ and feel personal causation, that they originated their own action. Pawns believe themselves to be pushed around—that they are doomed for failure and have no control on outcomes. Personal causation is thereby defined in terms of perceived locus of causality. Individuals are said to be origins when they perceive their actions to have been initiated by themselves, but pawns when they perceive their actions to have been initiated by events external to themselves (deCharms, 1968). The perception of choice is the important factor.

A similar construct is the locus of control dimension (Rotter, 1966), which considers the relationship perceived by a person between her or his behavior and success or failure realized. Is the connection between what a person does and what happens (like in competition in sport) perceived to be direct? If so, such an individual would be described as having an *internal locus of control*. When no or little relationship is believed to exist, an *external locus of control* prevails.

Research indicates that "internals" tend to be more productive than "externals." To achieve more, one has to be dedicated and believe in a causation relationship: How and what the person does will influence outcomes in situations. Externals tend to feel that factors outside of their control affect their achievement, or lack of it. Programs developed to modify the outlook of externals are geared to have them assume responsibility for their status.

For instance, reinforcement can help shape behaviors. Comments made and actions shown by a person indicating a recognition of the need to work hard to improve might be praised. In the 1970s, McHugh, Duquin, and Frieze (1978) reported that encouraging athletes to make effort attributions increased their pride in success and led to increase in persistence. Furthermore, more responsibility could be given to the person—to set goals and dedicate energies toward reaching these goals. Personally set goals should be more meaningful and motivational than goals established by others. For instance, Garland, Weinberg, Bruya, and Jackson (1988) found that subjects' personal goals were a better predictor of performance than were their assigned ones. Goals attached to specifically stated behaviors can be assessed with regularity. In general, the object is to provide more decision-making experiences and responsibility to the person with an external locus of control. As a result, this person will probably try harder, and most likely achieve more.

Being a pawn and having an external locus of control are both inadequate, but not to the extent that they cannot be worked with to change their attitudes, perceptions, and subsequent productivity—through pertinent experiences. In an extensive training program (deCharms, 1968), teachers and students in inner St. Louis were taught to act as origins. Dramatic alterations in behavior were made. Students' origin feelings were increased as well as their academic accomplishments. They displayed greater feelings of commitment, responsibility, and persistence at school activities (in other words, motivation). Self-perceived pawns can become origins. Origin training can be effective, and parents and coaches should be aware of diagnostic procedures and reshaping possibilities.

Coping Style

Another behavioral dimension underlying motivation is related to the reasons given to explain successes and failures. When studying these situations, it is important to realize that failure is only what one perceives as failure. An athlete may not have won a race in five contests, but his or her time might be improving in each competition. Is this failure? Improvement might be interpreted as personal success, and dedication to improve should be reinforced. Dweck (1975) has identified two coping styles: *mastery oriented* vs. *helpless*. The person with a mastery-orientation style attributes personal failure to not enough effort. The result is to try even harder the next time, for effort is valued. He or she has learned through previous experiences that sustained effort usually brings forth success.

"Learned helpless" individuals (Buchanan & Seligman, 1995) think that their failures are due to a lack of ability. Their perception is that it is not worth it to try harder because it will not make a difference; inadequate ability cannot be overcome. These people generally demonstrate poor motivation as reflected in inadequate persistence levels at challenging tasks, and obviously poor performances (e.g., Seligman, Nolen-Hoeksema, Norton, & Norton, 1988, as cited in Pargman, 1993). Ironically, any successes are attributed to the activity being easy—no credit for ability or effort is assumed.

Attribution training programs, as will be discussed later in the chapter, can help (Forsterling, 1988). Situations need to be created that will help a person to overcome a helpless coping style, to alter the reasons (attributions) given to explain failures or successes. In a typical training program in schools, students in classes are constantly encouraged to try to achieve, to value effort. When effort is shown, reinforcement in the form of praise is given (Dweck, 1975). However, although lack of effort is usually suggested as the best reason to give for failure (Forsterling, 1988), Covington and Omelich (1979) have indicated that individuals who invest greater effort following failure, but still fail, are even more likely to attribute this second failure to ability than they were for the first. Consequently, the preferred attribution for failure in sport, or any other setting, may be to a different controllable factor, such as strategy, rather than to effort (Biddle, 1993).

Furthermore, any activity to be learned can be modified so that everyone has a reasonable chance at success. When succeeding, praise is given for effort, and the level of task difficulty is then increased. Gradually, successes or failures are internalized and attributed more to effort, and it is realized that a mastery coping style is better than a helpless coping style.

Attributions

A related construct to coping styles is attributional style (Weiner, 1979, 1986, 1995). Following performance in an activity, it is fairly typical for an athlete not only to appraise its quality and effectiveness, but also to make personal evaluations as to potential causative factors. This will take place especially when the outcome is negative, unexpected, and/or important (Weiner, 1995). These explanatory behaviors, or reasons, are termed *attributions*.

Why and how do we think about what we did? Causes for perceived success or failure in an act have been described by Weiner (1979) in a three-dimensional classification scheme: locus of control (internal versus external), stability (stable versus unstable), and controllability (controllable versus uncontrollable). Attributions to ability and effort are considered to be internal, that is, under self-control. Task difficulty and luck, two other possible attributions, are examples of factors external to the person. Personal ability and the level of difficulty of the present challenge are viewed as relatively stable factors. They do not change much. Effort and luck are relatively unstable (fluctuating) factors. They can differ considerably from occasion to occasion. It has been recognized that there are other reasons people generate as attributions (Roberts & Pascuzzi, 1979), and these reasons can probably be classified within the three dimensions. Therefore, when discussing attributions and modification of cognitions, it is important to emphasize the dimensions instead of the reasons themselves.

Given certain information, such as success or failure, persons usually make attributions to causes that may influence later achievements. However, high and low achievers presumably have different perceptions of responsibility for performance outcomes (Weiner et al., 1971). The high-need achiever generally believes success is due to both ability and effort and that failure is the result of lack of effort or any other controllable reason (e.g., strategy, technique). The person low in achievement need ascribes no particular attributional preference for success but believes that failure is due to lack of ability. In fact, dysfunctional attributions (internal, stable, and uncontrollable) probably emerge in the face of failure.

These disparate perceptions of responsibility under conditions where success or failure are experienced may have important implications for understanding differences in learning progress and the application of effective motivational techniques. Weiner (1986) has suggested that attributions may enhance or hinder different parameters, such as expectations, emotions, and achievement-related behavior. For example, performers using functional attributions (internal, controllable, and unstable) are reported to be more persistent after failure. This has been interpreted as due to their belief that they can control situations and make things happen in order to succeed. The relationship between the type of attributions made to present performance and level of expectancy of achievement in future attempts may be conceived as presented in Figure 9.2.

Figure 9.2. The relationship of expectancies, attributions, persistence, and potential achievement.

For example, a successful performance may be attributed to ability and effort, which raises the level of expectations for future success in similar tasks (e.g., Wilson & Linville, 1985). In turn, this circumstance produces a greater degree of persistence and effort. Then, when confronted with a competitive situation, high expectations for immediate task success are probable (Orbach, Price, & Singer, 1997). This will result in a better performance. Feedback concerning performance failure may encourage or discourage subsequent persistence and performance, depending on whether failure is viewed as an indication that more effort is required to master a challenge of greater than expected difficulty or failure is viewed as the result of personal limitations.

One of the foremost reasons for discouragement, a loss of sustained interest in sport, and giving up, is perceived failing, especially if this feeling is continuous. However, not everyone quits. A person's analysis of why the failure occurred is an important factor. If the perception is that not doing well is due to an unchangeable factor, such as lack of ability or the difficulty of the sport, the likelihood of quitting is increased (Weiner, 1986). On the other hand, if it is thought that the failure was produced by a readily changeable factor, such as effort shown or luck involved, persistence in spite of failure will probably continue (Weiner, 1986). Of these two attributions, degree of effort is personally controllable and, therefore, thought to be best in promoting success expectancies. As mentioned previously, ineffective attributions when failure is experienced are associated with internal, stable, and uncontrollable dimensions.

To summarize, Weiner's model suggests that in a case that one attributes a failure to an internal, unstable, and controllable reason (e.g., lack of effort), future expectations for success should remain stable. Further, negative emotions may be experienced, such as guilt for not trying hard enough; however, this emotion can be a motivating influence. Thus, there probably will be a continuation to persist and even try harder (Weiner, 1986).

On the other hand, with attributions to failure to an internal, stable, and uncontrollable cause (e.g., natural ability), expectations for future success will decrease, and negative emotions may be experienced, such as shame and humiliation (McAuley & Gross, 1983). Consequently, practice may be discontinued due to a belief that it will not lead to success. As can be seen, the kind of attributions that individuals make is very critical to future persistence and performance.

Of course, of major interest is the degree to which dysfunctional attributions (i.e., attributing failure to internal, stable, and uncontrollable reasons) can be modified and, in turn, achievement increased as well. Attributional training programs have been studied in school settings, and results suggest that they can influence cognitions and behaviors in the predicted directions

(Cavanaugh, 1991; Dweck, 1975; Forsterling, 1985; Fowler & Peterson, 1981; Perry & Magnusson, 1989; Perry & Penner, 1990; Wilson & Linville, 1985). However, attribution training techniques have rarely been of interest to sport researchers, for some strange reason. Recently, however, Orbach and her colleagues have undertaken research in this area. In one study (Orbach, Singer, & Murphey, 1997), college recreational basketball players were oriented to perceive their performance in a basketball skill test as due to (a) controllable, unstable factors; (b) uncontrollable, stable factors; or (c) no specific factors. Condition 1 (a) is associated with an ideal attributions. At the initial testing, all three groups had developed dysfunctional attributions (i.e., attributing failure to an internal, uncontrollable, and stable reason) when experiencing what they perceived to be failure performances. Following training under one of the three conditions, the group administered the ideal attributions (i.e., Condition 1) showed the strongest change toward ideal factors and demonstrated the best improvement in performance.

In another study (Orbach, Price, & Singer, 1997), a similar situation was created with college beginner-level tennis players. Once again, it was shown that it is possible to modify dysfunctional attributions to a more functional ones. Furthermore, results revealed that players who changed their attributions to be more functional had higher expectations for future success than those who did not, and experienced positive emotions. Although not significant, interesting trends were found for the performance and persistence data. Attribution training can apparently provide an important approach that can influence striving to achieve and should be studied more seriously in sport settings in the future.

Self-Efficacy

Self-doubt and anxiety about one's ability to perform well in competition occur on occasion in almost every athlete. When this state occurs too intensely, or worse yet, when it is not overcome at the right time, problems arise in performance. This is why the importance of *self-efficacy* is stressed: A person's conviction that he or she can do what needs to be done, that he or she can perform according to developed capabilities (Bandura, 1982).

The degree of self-efficacy influences choice of activity; the amount of effort expended in those activities; and persistence in the face of aversive stimuli, thought patterns, and emotional reactions (Bandura, 1986, 1997). Obviously, low self-esteem, confidence, and performance expectation in relation to a sport are factors that are not conducive to interest in, persistence at, and achievement in that sport. When faced with stressful stimuli, low-efficacious individuals tend to give up, attribute failure internally, and experience greater anxiety or depression (Bandura, 1982). When perceptions of confidence relate to the possibility of being able to win while fearing losing, much self-doubt and anxiety will probably be present. Yet, if such perceptions relate to being able to do one's best, to perform well, it is easier to feel better about oneself and the situation.

Although Bandura (1982) suggests that judgment of self-efficacy is based on four major sources of information (i.e., performance accomplishment, vicarious experience, persuasion, and physiological state), performance accomplishments have been shown to be the most effective in enhancing self-efficacy beliefs and performance (Brody, Hatfield, & Spalding, 1988; McAuley, 1985). Everyone needs *mastery experiences.* These are associated with the level of challenge (difficulty) in relation to one's degree of skill. An athlete is more likely to realize accomplishments when engaged at a level of challenge in which he or she has a reasonable chance of doing well. Challenges, and personal expectations, should increase as skill improves. Confidence is increased with achievements, as measured more easily through steady improvement and less easily with wins against formidable opponents. As self-efficacy builds, so do personal expectations. Persistence increases as does performance level (Weiss, Wiese, & Klint, 1989).

Based on the above discussion, some advice for coaches can be made:

1. Competition should involve athletes who have a reasonable, equal chance of winning. The possibility of successes should be maximized, related to individual ability levels. This will lead to an increase in self-efficacy.
2. An emphasis on effort evaluations should be made toward *improvement,* rather than win-lose, success-failure, evaluations. This might encourage continuance at an activity because it is under the athlete's control. An effort evaluation of the athlete's performance in relation to personal ability should lead to enhanced self-esteem as progress is experienced.
3. An athlete should be encouraged to realize factors that are under his or her control (e.g., quality and intensity of preparation and training, effort and strategies in a contest) versus those that are not (e.g., the skill level of the opponent, the outcome of the contest). This will lead to the development of a functional attributional style.

It should be evident that unless a person looks forward to improving, it either will not be done, will not be done well, or will not be done for too long. In the sport environment, the athlete is faced with many personal and competitive challenges. The urge to try to be superior to others is related to the achievement motive as is the desire to improve oneself, to determine one's capabilities and competencies. A person's mental and emotional reactions to sport (practice and competition) in the context of intrinsic and achievement sources of motivation will have a great impact on continuance and ultimate accomplishments. Personal satisfaction in overcoming challenges is the ultimate experience. And experiences can, and should, be satisfying.

In summary, perceptions about oneself, what can be accomplished, and what was just done can promote or hinder progress and achievement. Many athletes have the physical potential to do well in sport. However, if psychological processes used to approach practice, conditioning, and competition are not effective, athletic experiences will be disappointing. In summary, a few types of self-perceptions were discussed in this regard, and they are presented in Table 9.1.

Table 9.1. Ideal and ineffective self-perceptions.

Perception	Ideal	Ineffective
personal causation	origin	pawn
coping style	mastery oriented	helpless
locus of control	internal	external
self-efficacy	can do	can't do
attributional orientation	functional	dysfunctional

Characteristics of High Achievers

Many of the ideal self-perceptions just described are somewhat common among high achievers, in any area. So are other types of behaviors. A review of the research in which the behaviors of high achievers have been analyzed would lead to the following observations (Csikszentmihalyi, 1990; Garfield & Bennett, 1984; Gould, Eklund, & Jackson, 1992; Hardy, Jones, & Gould, 1996; Ravizza, 1984). Those who excel in their specialization tend to

1. Demonstrate an extremely high persistence at activities;
2. Exhibit exceptional quality in performance;
3. Complete activities at a high rate;
4. Be task rather than person oriented;
5. Take reasonable risks and enjoy the positive aspects of stress;
6. Like to take personal responsibility for actions;
7. Like to have knowledge of the results of the activity in which they are involved (to judge capabilities in order to develop them further);
8. Have a driving energy to excel, to do things better, faster, and more efficiently than others;

9. Set challenging goals that demand maximum effort and effective plans; automatic or easy success is not satisfying;
10. Find a way to do what needs to be done;
11. Get immersed in what they are doing; time rushes by them as if there is not enough time to do all the things necessary to succeed;
12. Feel pleasure and fulfillment in the process of striving and attaining expertise.

The study of the characteristics in common among high achievers—those who demand, expect, and realize success—is important in order to determine reference standards that can be applied to those who hope to realize similar levels of expertise. Productivity and satisfaction do not necessarily increase because procedures and policies are dictated by others. Personal qualities and aspirations need to emerge. In other words, to start with, an athlete has to be truly intrinsically motivated to want to do well. Then, he or she needs to know what to do in order to accomplish. Strategies adopted, as typically used by high achievers, make everything possible.

Strategic Behavior

It is becoming realized more and more that procedural skills, or how to understand situations and develop enabling skills, greatly contribute to achievement. Newer theories of intelligence suggest three, five, or even seven forms intelligence. For instance, Gardner (1983) proposes seven types of intelligence: linguistic, musical, spatial, logical-mathematical, bodily kinesthetic, interpersonal, and intrapersonal intelligence. Furthermore, Bloom (1985) investigated different domains and pointed out a few necessary skills for expert performance that are likely to be mostly inborn, such as "motor coordination, speed of reflexes, and hand-eye coordination" (p. 546). However, it is believed that the salient aspect of talent is only the potential for achievement; therefore, deliberate training is crucial (Ericsson & Charness, 1994). Typically, the kind of intelligence not taught in classes that a person picks up on his or her own makes a difference in being successful on the job. The significance of understanding how to interact effectively socially and being aware of the "rules of the game," or being "street-wise," is typically underrated (e.g., Sternberg, 1991, 1992).

In sport, the rules of the game are obvious to the athlete. However, it is one matter to want to do well and something else to know "rules" of how to succeed. One consideration is how to function productively in the system, the coach's system. An athlete needs to learn how to get along with the coach as well as with other athletes on a team. Another consideration is to determine how to convert dreams of succeeding to a vision and, in turn, to short- and long-term meaningful, high, but attainable goals of improvement. Continual objective self-evaluations of personal strengths and weaknesses are a necessity. How to train and practice, and how much, must be addressed. A commitment to realizing goals by certain dates leads to structure and organization. Overcoming personal or sport-related problems means understanding alternatives under personal control that can be utilized as occasions warrant. Strategic behaviors play a significant role in contributing to continual improvement and ultimate accomplishments.

For the exceptionally talented athlete, there is a fine line between being a champion and almost being one. The lesser dedicated athlete is doomed. The wrong reasons for competing, too many excuses, a lack of commitment, and nondisciplined training contribute to nonfulfillment of high expectations. Succeeding, being among the best in a sport, is a special experience. It is the outcome of so many potential contributing factors. Among the most significant is a determination to attain dreams that were translated into achievable goals that in turn, were made possible through dedicated meaningful training and practice. Perceptions of being in control of one's destiny and the ability to transform these beliefs into positive action plans are paramount to success.

Achievement and Fulfillment

Sustained efforts at achieving are reinforced when accomplishments/goals are experienced reasonably frequently, as well as when the *process* is challenging, stimulating, absorbing, satisfying, and fulfilling. Csikszentmihalyi (1990, 1993) has termed this the state of flow. Unfortunately, there are many unhappy and very stressed high achievers. The ideal state occurs when intrinsic motivation leads to personally meaningful experiences, and accomplishments, along with whatever materialistic gains are derived with such successes. Although much research seemingly indicates the detrimental effects of rewards on intrinsic task interest, recent literature (e.g., Cameron & Pierce, 1994; Eisenberger & Cameron, 1996) suggests otherwise. Using meta-analysis procedures, Cameron and Pierce revealed that an external reward will be detrimental only under a highly specified set of circumstances that can be easily prevented in sport. More specifically, when a tangible reward (e.g., money, trophy) is given independent of performance quality, it will decrease intrinsic motivation. Both situations, of being intrinsically motivated and being externally rewarded, may be complementary. In other words, a person can do well, be rewarded, *and,* in addition, feel good about the process and experiences.

Unfortunately, many athletes do not seem to enjoy their experiences in sport. Doing something for the sake of doing it—being actively engaged in purposeful activity and attempting to master it—is personally rewarding and fulfilling. In high-level sport, the truly successful athlete is one who attains excellence and also enjoys the process of becoming excellent. Great athletes who have sustained their competitive abilities over long periods of time often talk about how much their sport means to them (Orlick & Partington, 1988). They describe feelings associated with striving to be the best that they can be, of proving to themselves what they can become. "I just did it because I wanted to . . . getting the best out of myself for all the effort I'd put in" (Steve Ovett, 1975 World Cup 800 m champion, and 1977 and 1980 World Cup 1500 m champion quoted in Hemery, 1991, p. 142). Extrinsic rewards and recognitions are motivators. But intrinsic motivation is the source that fuels a happy engine along the difficult, long, and painful road to success, road after road, day after day.

From Dreams to Reality

The path from hopes and dreams to eventual success (see Figure 9.3) is complex and time-consuming, and depends upon capabilities, striving, improving, and good fortune. Yet, a few athletes go all the way to the top; most do not. What makes the difference? Alternative paths, are presented in Figure 9.4.

Figure 9.3. From dreams to achievement (adapted from Singer, 1996).

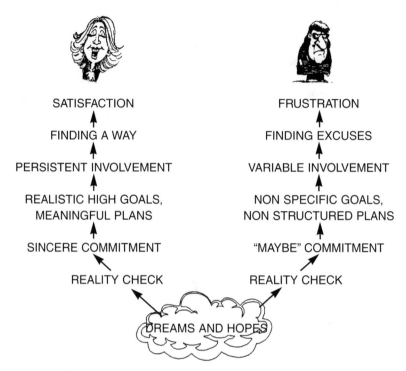

Figure 9.4. Satisfaction vs. frustration (adapted from Singer, 1996).

Dreams and reality check. Wishful thinking is where it all begins. Without dreams of accomplishing and "making it big," we restrict our potential. They give us hope, excitement, and the belief that fantasy can be reality. They stimulate our drives, energize us, and force a reality assessment as to what may be truly possible.

For many, dreams are eventually discarded. Objective assessments usually indicate that hopes far exceed the potential to attain them. Or it may be perceived that the necessary dedication and hard work are not worth the risk of failing. The determination if the risks and payoffs are compatible or too imbalanced is an important variable that separates between those who "do it" and those who do not.

Faced with a reality dilemma, most athletes quit or proceed with ready-to-offer excuses as to why they did not achieve. Bad luck, limited opportunities, not enough time to practice, or other defensive explanations provide an escape route for failing. Obviously, in this way, failing is not perceived as such but rather as "I could have been great, if only—."

And yet, those athletes who surface as the best in their sport are a special breed. They know what they want, they believe they can make it happen, and they establish meaningful goals and workable plans that will most likely contribute to success. They are not afraid to train and practice hard. They learn to sacrifice. Their guiding perspective is being able to say, "I gave it everything I have". If everything does not work out well, there is comfort in being able to be assured that at least a complete effort was made to try to succeed.

Commitment. Proficiency, being among the very best in a sport, requires dedication, effort, and appropriate experiences. It is the outcome of so many potential contributing factors. Among the most significant is a commitment to attain dreams that were translated into achievable goals that, in turn, were made possible through dedicated meaningful training and practice. Perceptions of being in control of one's destiny and the ability to transform these beliefs into positive action plans are paramount to success.

Achievement does not come about accidentally, and it does not come easily. It is earned. Sport is cruel, as there are many more failures (if win-loss ratios are the criterion). However, the right attitude and approach to self and life contribute greatly to the probability of making good things happen. Devotion and purpose allow dreams to become a reality. Because of this, we know that all of us can achieve to some degree—in our own unique special areas.

Goals and purposeful plans. The insecure or noncommitted athlete sets unrealistically high goals that cannot be attained (and, therefore, the ego is protected because expectations for reaching these goals were low) or such low goals that achieving them is meaningless. Furthermore, such athletes do not establish a sufficient structure or plan to really make goals work. Commitment means dedicating time and energy for purposeful training to realize short- and long-term goals.

High achievers set realistically high but attainable goals. They devise training programs that will enable them to fulfill these goals. They believe they are in reasonable control of their destiny—options are available, and hard work will allow them to realize their potential. Their explanatory behavior for how they are doing is couched in objective perceptions that enable them to know when to attribute inadequate performances to lack of effort, prior preparation, or other internally controllable factors. Constructive evaluations contribute to strong self-efficacy, to a belief that a way can be found to overcome and move onward and upward.

Training and preparation. The insincere athlete who is not truly motivated will practice and train in a haphazard manner. Sometimes everything will be great; other times, they are ineffective. Competition performances will be variable—high and low—reflecting approaches to practice and training. Excuses for inadequacy are frequently made. Such attributions protect the ego and provide a convenient rationale for a lack of succeeding.

On the other hand, high-achieving athletes commit to persevering, to working hard, to not relying on "natural" or "instinctive" abilities. They look forward to improving and doing what it takes to have an edge over their competitors. They intuitively know that their future potential success is at least partly contributed to by determination and a belief in themselves. They are not afraid to fail because they learn and become stronger as a result.

Finding a way. When involved in a pursuit for achievement, recognition, and stardom, the fragile athlete who is not really dedicated will readily locate excuses for things that don't go well. Finding excuses is easy—and convenient. They protect insecurity and a noncommitment to doing what it really takes to be special.

The alternative is finding a way. Striving for excellence in sport is fraught with liabilities. Dealing with fatigue, injury, pain, losses, depression, loneliness, and a lack of typical opportunities to socialize is no easy matter. Yet, the great athletes overcome. They do what it takes to cope with competitive stress and personal problems. They keep going, as they are fixated on their goals that represent being special in their sport.

Satisfaction. A person can do well *and* in addition feel good about the process and experiences. The quality of life, optimal experiences, and happiness are what Csikszentmihalyi (1990, 1993) has studied for over two decades. He and his colleagues have collected on-line self-reports with the use of electronic pagers from all kinds of people doing all kinds of things. At the beep, the participants indicated what they were doing, where they were, how hard they were concentrating, how challenging the activity was, and how well they were meeting the challenge.

When things were going well, people talked about being carried away with the activity. It was all-involving, seemingly effortless (because of their being so consumed with it), challenging, and enjoyable. Csikszentmihalyi coined the term, *flow,* to describe this state, these feelings. From the mountain climber to the chess player to the book reader, anyone can experience flow. In fact, Csikszentmihalyi suggested that game situations may be particularly amenable to creating the flow experience because of the structure and nature of the tasks. And, indeed, it can be argued that the study of flow is important to the understanding of elite athletes because it has been shown that athletes perform their best while in flow (Jackson, 1992) and report positive experiences from sport.

According to Csikszentmihalyi (1990), a number of factors seem to be related to being in the state of flow:

- Having sufficient skill, being able to complete a challenging activity
- Absorbing attention completely by the activity
- Setting clear goals and having immediate feedback about how things are going
- Feeling a sense of control, over self and situation
- Losing self-consciousness (consciousness of the self)
- Losing track of time.

Summary

In conclusion, potential motivators to achieve are many and varied. At the beginning of this paper, it was indicated that behavioristic, humanistic, and cognitive psychology perspectives, although contrasting, provide insights into the nature of motivation: how it is influenced and how it in turn influences what we do, how often we do it, and how well we do it. After describing the powerful role of motivation in determining achievement, strategies of high achievers were described. The road to a high degree of success versus alternatives can be negotiated more capably with strong intentions and a knowledge of how to proceed.

Many ideas from cognitive and humanistic psychology were stressed throughout. Self-perceptions, especially locus of control, causation, mastery style, level of efficacy, and attributional orientation, relate very highly to persistence and achievement. However, in the final analysis, the most desirable approach to achieving is through looking forward to meaningful experiences and challenges. These relate to overcoming obstacles, actively pursuing excellence for the sake of proving to oneself what one can accomplish, and finding satisfaction and enjoyment in the process of self-realization. Those who continually actively pursue a healthy lifestyle and expand their knowledge and skills through enriching experiences truly know what the quality of life is all about.

Participation in sport, at any skill level, provides a wonderful medium for this. It is hoped that more people will discover personally rewarding experiences through their active involvement in sport. The potential to achieve—at something—is within the capacities of everyone.

References

Ames, C. (1992). Classrooms: Goals, structures, and student motivation. *Journal of Educational Psychology, 84,* 261–271.

Bandura, A. (1982). Self-efficacy mechanism in human agency. *American Psychologist, 37,* 122–147.

Bandura, A. (1986). *Social foundations of thought and action: A social cognitive theory.* Englewood Cliffs, NJ: Prentice-Hall.

Bandura, A. (1997). *Self-efficacy: The exercise of control.* New York: Freeman.

Biddle, S. J. H. (1993). Attribution research and sport psychology. In R. N. Singer, M. Murphey, & L. K. Tennant (Eds.), *Handbook of research on sport psychology* (pp. 437–464). New York: Macmillan.

Bloom, B. S. (1985). *Developing talent in young people.* New York: Ballantine Books.

Brody, E. B., Hatfield, B. D., & Spalding, T. W. (1988). Generalization of self-efficacy to a continuum of stressors upon mastery of a high-risk sport skill. *Journal of Sport Psychology, 10,* 32–34.

Bouchard, T. J. (1994). Genes, environment, and personality. *Science, 264,* 1700–1701.

Buchanan, M., & Seligman, M. E. P. (Eds.). (1995). *Explanatory style.* Hillsdale, NJ: Erlbaum.

Cameron, J., & Pierce, W. D. (1994). Reinforcement, reward, and intrinsic motivation: A meta-analysis. *Review of Educational Research, 64*(3), 363–423.

Cavanaugh, D. P. (1991). The effects of strategy training and attributional retraining on poor readers. *Dissertation Abstracts International 51*(7), 2328-A.

Covington, M. V. (1992). *Making the grade: A self-worth perspective on motivation and school reform.* New York: Cambridge University Press.

Covington, M. V., & Omelich, C. L. (1979). Effort: The double edged sword in school achievement. *Journal of Educational Psychology, 71,* 169–182.

Csikszentmihalyi, M. (1990). *Flow: The psychology of optimal experience.* New York: Harper Perennial.

Csikszentmihalyi, M. (1993). *The evolving self.* New York: Harper Collins.

deCharms, R. (1968). *Personal causation: The internal effective determinants of behavior.* New York: Academic Press.

Deci, E. L., & Ryan, R. M. (1985). *Intrinsic motivation and self-determination in human behavior.* New York: Plenum.

Deci, E. L., & Ryan, R. M. (1991). A motivational approach to self: Integration in personality. In R. Dienstbier (Ed.), *Nebraska Symposium on Motivation: Vol. 38. Perspectives on motivation* (pp. 273–288). Lincoln, NE: University of Nebraska Press.

Duda, J. L. (1992). Motivation in sport settings: A goal perspective approach. In G. Roberts (Ed.), *Motivation in sport and exercise* (pp. 57–91). Champaign, IL: Human Kinetics.

Duda, J. L., & Chi,.L. (1989, September). *The effect of task and ego involving conditions on perceived competence and causal attributions in basketball.* Paper presented at the meeting of the Association for the Advancement of Applied Sport Psychology, University of Washington, Seattle.

Duda, J. L., Chi, L., Newton, M. L., Walling, M. D., & Catley, D. (1995). Task and ego orientation and intrinsic motivation in sport. *International Journal of Sport Psychology, 26,* 40–63.

Duda, J. L., Newton, M., & Chi, L. (1990, May). *The relationship of task and ego orientations and expectations of multidimensional state anxiety.* Paper presented at the meeting of the North American Society for the Psychology of Sport and Physical Activity, University of Houston, TX.

Dweck, C. S. (1975). The role of expectations and attributions in the alleviation of learned helplessness. *Journal of Personality and Social Psychology, 3,* 287–298.

Eisenberger, R., & Cameron, J. (1996). Detrimental effects of reward: Reality or myth? *American Psychologist, 51*(11), 1153–1166.

Ericcson, K. A., & Charness, N. (1994). Expert performance: Its structure and acquisition. *American Psychologist, 49,* 725–747.

Forsterling, F. (1985). Attributional retraining: A review. *Psychological Bulletin, 98*(3), 495–512.

Forsterling, F. (1988). *Attribution theory in clinical psychology.* Chichester, England: Wiley.

Fowler, J. W., & Peterson, P. L. (1981). Increasing reading persistence and altering attributional style of learned helpless children. *Journal of Educational Psychology, 73,* 251–260.

Frederick, C. M., & Ryan, R. M. (1995). Self-determination in sport: A review using cognitive evaluation theory. *International Journal of Sport Psychology, 26,* 5–23.

Gardner, H. (1983). *Frames of mind: The theory of multiple intelligences.* New York: Basic Books.

Garfield, C. A., & Bennett, H. Z. (1984). *Peak performance: Mental training techniques of the world's greatest athletes.* Los Angeles: Tarcher.

Garland, H., Weinberg, R., Bruya, L., & Jackson, A. (1988). Self-efficacy and endurance performance: A longitudinal field test of cognitive mediation theory. *Applied Psychology: An International Review, 34,* 381–394.

Gould, D., Eklund, R. C., & Jackson, S. A. (1992). 1988 U.S. Olympic wrestling excellence: Mental preparation, precompetitive cognition, and affect. *The Sport Psychologist, 6,* 358–382.

Hardy, L., Jones, G., & Gould, D. (1996). *Understanding psychological preparation for sport.* Chichester, England: Wiley.

Hardy, L., & Parfitt, G. (1994). The development of a model for the provision of psychological support to a national squad. *The Sport Psychologist, 8,* 126–142.

Hemery, D. (1991). *Sporting excellence: What makes a champion* (2nd ed.). New York: Wiley.

Jackson, S. A. (1992). Athletes in flow: A qualitative investigation of flow states in elite figure skaters. *Journal of Applied Sport Psychology, 4,* 161–180.

Kavussanu, M., & Roberts, G. C. (1996). Motivation in physical activity contexts: The relationship of perceived motivational climate to intrinsic motivation and self-efficacy. *Journal of Sport and Exercise Psychology, 18,* 264–280.

Louganis, G. (1995). *Breaking the surface.* New York: Random House.

Mahoney, M. J., Gabriel, T. J., & Perkins, T. S. (1987). Psychological skills and exceptional athletic performance. *The Sport Psychologist, 1,* 181–199.

McAuley, E. (1985). Modeling and self-efficacy: A test of Bandura's model. *Journal of Sport Psychology, 7,* 283–295.

McAuley, E., & Gross, J. B. (1983). Perceptions of causality in sport: An application of the Causal Dimension Scale. *Journal of Sport Psychology, 5,* 72–76.

McHugh, M. C., Duquin, M. E., & Frieze, I. H. (1978). Beliefs about success and failure: Attribution and the female athlete. In C. Oglesby (Ed.), *Women and sport: From myth to reality* (pp. 173–191). Philadelphia: Lea & Febiger.

Nicholls, J. G. (1992). The general and the specific in the development and expression of achievement motivation. In G. C. Roberts (Ed.), *Motivation in sport and exercise* (pp. 31–56). Champaign, IL: Human Kinetics.

Orbach, I., Singer, R. N., & Murphey, M. (1997). Changing attributions with an attribution training technique related to basketball dribbling. *The Sport Psychologist, 11*(3), 294–304.

Orbach, I., Price, S., & Singer, R. N. (1997). *The implications of an attribution training program for achievement in sport: Phase I.* Manuscript submitted for publication.

Orlick, T., & Lee-Gartner, K. (1993). Going after the dream and reaching it: The Olympic downhill. *Performance Enhancement, 1,* 110–122.

Orlick, T., & Partington, J. (1988). Mental links to excellence. *The Sport Psychologist, 2,* 105–130.

Pargman, D. (1993). Individual differences: Cognitive and perceptual styles. In R. N. Singer, M. Murphey, & L. K. Tennant (Eds.), *Handbook of research on sport psychology* (pp. 379–404). New York: Macmillan.

Perry, R. P., & Magnusson, J. L. (1989). Causal attributions and perceived performance: Consequences for college student's achievement and perceived control in different instructional conditions. *Journal of Educational Psychology, 81,* 164–172.

Perry, R. P., & Penner, K. S. (1990). Enhancing academic achievement in college students through attributional retraining and instruction. *Journal of Educational Psychology, 82,* 123–145.

Ravizza, K. (1984). Qualities of the peak experience in sport. In J. M. Silva & R. S. Weinberg (Eds.), *Psychological foundations of sport* (pp. 452–462). Champaign, IL: Human Kinetics.

Roberts, G. C. (Ed.). (1992). *Motivation in sport and exercise.* Champaign, IL: Human Kinetics.

Roberts, G. C., & Pascuzzi, D. L. (1979). Causal attributions in sport: Some theoretical implications. *Journal of Sport Psychology, 1,* 203–211.

Rotter, J. B. (1966). Generalized expectancies for internal and external control of reinforcement. *Psychological Monographs, 81,* 1–28.

Singer, R. N. (1984). *Sustaining motivation in sport.* Tallahassee, FL: Sport Consultants International.

Singer, R. N. (1996). Moving toward the quality of life. *Quest, 48,* 246–252.

Sternberg, R. J. (1991). Theory-based testing of intellectual abilities: Rationale for the Triarchic Abilities Test. In H. A. Rowe (Ed.), *Intelligence: Reconceptualization and measurement* (pp. 183–202). Hillsdale, NJ: Erlbaum.

Sternberg, R. J. (1992). Metaphors of mind underlying the testing of intelligence. In J. C. Rosen & P. McReynolds (Eds.), *Advances in psychological assessment* (Vol. 8, pp. 1–39). New York: Plenum.

Weiner, B. (1979). A theory of motivation for some classroom experiences. *Journal of Educational Psychology, 71,* 3–25.

Weiner, B. (1986). *An attributional theory of motivation and emotion.* New York: Springer-Verlag.

Weiner, B. (1995). *Judgments of responsibility.* New York: The Guilford Press.

Weiner, B., Frieze, I., Kukla, A., Reed, L., Rest, S., & Rosenbaum, R. M. (1971). Perceiving the causes of success and failure. In E. E. Jones, D. E. Kanose, H. H. Kelley, R. E. Nisbett, S. Valins, & B. Weiner (Eds.), *Attribution: Perceiving the causes of behavior* (pp. 95–120). Morristown, NJ: General Learning Press.

Weiss, M. R., Wiese, D. M., & Klint, K. A. (1989). Head over heels with success: The relationship between self-efficacy and performance in competitive youth gymnastics. *Journal of Sport and Exercise Psychology, 11,* 444–451.

Wilson, T. D., & Linville, P. W. (1985). Improving the performance of college freshman with attributional techniques. *Journal of Personality and Social Psychology, 49,* 287–293.

10

Intrinsic and Extrinsic Motivation in Sport: Toward a Hierarchical Model

Robert J. Vallerand and Stéphane Perreault
Laboratoire de Recherche sur le Comportement Social
Université du Québec à Montréal, Canada

Over the past 25 years, much research in psychology in general, and in sport in particular, has focused on two specific types of motivation, namely intrinsic and extrinsic motivation (Vallerand, Deci, & Ryan, 1987). *Intrinsic motivation* refers to engaging in an activity for the pleasures it provides whereas *extrinsic motivation* pertains to doing an activity in order to obtain rewards or to avoid punishment (Deci, 1971). The purpose of this chapter is to present a new theoretical model that allows us not only to integrate the various perspectives inherent in the intrinsic/extrinsic motivation literature, but also to propose new and original testable hypotheses. Such a model takes into consideration the variety of ways motivation can be represented in the individual, how these various representations of motivation are related among themselves, as well as to various determinants and consequences. Before we begin the presentation of this new conceptual model, we would like to inform the reader that the model is not only limited to sport but also makes important predictions with respect to other life contexts, such as interpersonal relations and education (see Vallerand, 1997). In this chapter, a number of empirical studies supporting the hierarchical model will be presented to show how the model may lead to a better understanding of motivational phenomena to be found in sport. Although our emphasis will be on how the model can be applied to sport, we will also attempt to show how sport and other life contexts can influence each other.

A Hierarchical Model of Intrinsic and Extrinsic Motivation

Let's start with an example that should serve to illustrate some of the issues that the model deals with. John is a 12-year-old adolescent. He is the type of person who does things generally because he likes them. Thus, he goes to school and interacts with other people out of fun. Consequently, such activities generally lead him to experience pleasure and satisfaction. However, contrary to the contexts of school and interpersonal relationships, John plays baseball because he feels he has to. In that context, John feels that other people (including his dad—a former baseball player), and especially his coach, force him to do things he would not choose to do. He feels controlled and experiences very little sense of autonomy. Consequently, his performance is not very good, and he generally derives little satisfaction from his sport involvement. However, in the last 3 weeks, things have started to come around. His regular coach has been away and has been replaced by the assistant coach, who is much less controlling. The new coach allows players to express themselves and to try new things. Players are often allowed to lead the warm-up period, and John likes that. More and more, John feels that he is going to practices and games out of choice and, at times, pleasure. Consequently, his performance has started to improve, and he generally feels happier at the park. This afternoon, in the game, the new coach has just asked John if he wants to try to bunt to advance the runner on first base or would rather go for the hit and run. John indicats that he wants to bunt. John experiences feelings of autonomy because the coach let him decide what to do. He focuses on the pitcher, is fully concentrated on his rhythm, and hits the ball just right, allowing the runner on first to advance to second. Although he is declared out at first, John feels good and is very satisfied with himself. After the game, he also experiences an inclination to play some more. So he throws the ball with teammates and practices different things.

The above example underscores several points with respect to motivation. A first point is that humans are motivationally complex. It is, therefore, not sufficient to talk about motivation in general to describe a person. Rather, we should refer to a collection of motivations that vary in types and levels of generality. In the example, John appeared to be intrinsically motivated toward school and interpersonal relationships, but to be extrinsically motivated toward baseball. Each of these different types of motivation represents a part of John, and if we are to understand this particular individual, we need to take into consideration the different motivations that describe him. Of importance is that these different types of motivation exist within the individual at three levels of generality. For instance, in the example, we indicated that John generally does things because he enjoys them. Overall at the global level, John would, therefore, appear to have an intrinsic-motivation personality that would generally predispose him to be intrinsically motivated toward different contexts. Thus, John was depicted as intrinsically motivated toward school and interpersonal relationships. Finally, at the situational level, that specific day at the park, John was intrinsically motivated to bunt. We feel that it is important to distinguish these different levels as such distinctions should lead to a better understanding of motivational processes.

A second issue of interest is that motivation is not only an intrapersonal phenomenon, but also a social phenomenon. Indeed, other people can have a powerful impact on our motivation, just as John's former coach had on his contextual motivation toward baseball. Although John has an intrinsic-motivation personality, he is nevertheless extrinsically motivated toward baseball. Thus, intrapersonal factors (global motivation) are not the sole influences on motivation. Social factors, and in this case, contextual factors, can play an important role as determinants of (contextual) motivation. The same reasoning applies at the situational level. For instance, the assistant coach's supportive approach to let John decide to bunt or to go for the hit and run seems to have had a positive effect on John's immediate (or situational) motivation at that specific time at the ballpark. It thus appears that both intra- and interpersonal forces can influence global, contextual, and situational motivation at their respective level of generality .

Third, motivation leads to important consequences, and these may occur at the three levels of generality. At the contextual level, they may vary from context to context as a function of the relevant contextual motivation. For instance, John generally experiences positive benefits from his engagement in school and interpersonal activities. Such was not the case in baseball, however, because his motivation was extrinsic in nature. There, he felt unsatisfied with the game, and his performance was low. However, with the change of coach (a change in contextual factors), his motivation shifted from extrinsic to intrinsic. Consequently, his performance started to improve, and he felt much happier playing baseball. At the situational level, it was seen that John's intrinsic motivation allowed him to remain focused during the game, to feel good about himself, and to want to keep on playing later that day at the park. Therefore, motivation does not appear to be an epiphenomenon; it can lead to important outcomes.

Finally, it is believed that instances of situational intrinsic motivation, and associated positive benefits such as those experienced by John at the park that afternoon, serve to facilitate contextual intrinsic motivation. It is thus not surprising that John is now more intrinsically motivated toward baseball: Repeated instances of situational intrinsic motivation like the one at the ballpark have had recursive effects on his contextual motivation toward baseball in general.

As we can see, the model pothat motivation results from an ongoing transaction between the person and the environment. Furthermore, the model also integrates the personality and social psychological traditions of motivation. The model is presented in Figure 10.1 and is described below in the forms of five postulates.

POSTULATE 1—A complete analysis of motivation must include intrinsic and extrinsic motivation and amotivation

The first postulate posits that a complete analysis of motivation must deal with three concepts, namely those of intrinsic motivation (IM), extrinsic motivation (EM), and amotivation (AM). Indeed, much research has supported the existence and the usefulness of these types of motivation.

Intrinsic motivation. In general, IM refers to the fact of doing an activity for itself, and the pleasure and satisfaction derived from participation (e.g., Deci, 1975; Deci & Ryan, 1985a). An example of IM is the athlete who plays soccer because he or she finds it interesting and satisfying to learn more about the game. Although most researchers posit the presence of a global IM construct, a tripartite taxonomy of intrinsic motivation has been postulated by Vallerand and his colleagues (Vallerand, Blais, Brière, & Pelletier, 1989; Vallerand et al., 1992, 1993). These three types of IM can be identified as IM to know, to accomplish things, and to experience stimulation.

Extrinsic motivation. Contrary to IM, EM pertains to a wide variety of behaviors where the goals of action extend beyond those inherent in the activity itself. They are behaviors that are engaged in as a means to an end and not for their own sake. Originally, it was thought that EM referred to behaviors performed in the absence of self-determination and thus could be prompted only by external contingencies. However, more recently, Deci, Ryan, and their colleagues (Deci & Ryan, 1991) have proposed that different types of EM exist, some of which are self-determined and may be performed through choice.[1]

External regulation corresponds to EM as it generally appears in the literature. That is, behavior is regulated through external means, such as rewards and constraints. For instance, an individual might say: "I play soccer because my parents force me to."

---

1. Another type of extrinsic motivation is integrated regulation (Deci & Ryan, 1985a). We have not included this particular type of extrinsic motivation because previous research has shown that integrated regulation did not come out as a reason for participating in sport (see, Pelletier et al., 1995). Future research would appear necessary on this issue.

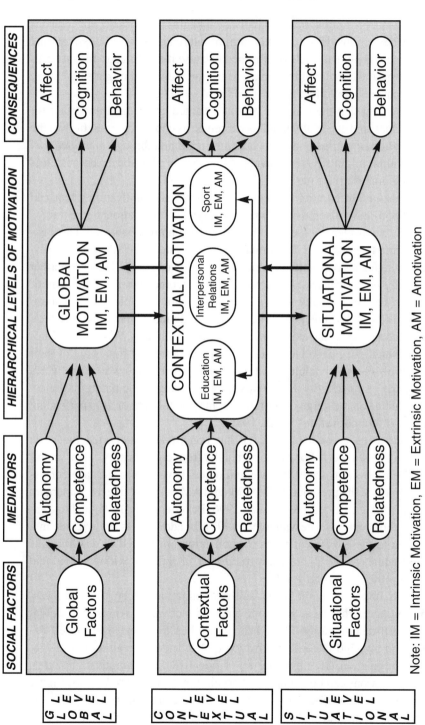

Note: IM = Intrinsic Motivation, EM = Extrinsic Motivation, AM = Amotivation

Figure 10.1. The hierarchical model of intrinsic and extrinsic motivation as applied to sports (based on Vallerand, 1997).

With *introjected regulation,* the individual begins to internalize the reasons for his or her actions. However, this form of internalization, although internal to the person, is not truly self-determined because it is limited to the internalization of past external contingencies. Thus, the individual might say, "I play soccer because I would feel guilty if I didn't."

To the extent that the behavior becomes valued and judged important for the individual, and especially that it is perceived as chosen by oneself, then the internalization of extrinsic motives becomes regulated through *identification.* The individual might say, for instance: "I choose to play soccer because it is something important for me."

Amotivation. In addition to intrinsic and extrinsic motivation, Deci and Ryan (1985a) have also posited that a third type of motivational construct is important to consider in order to fully understand human behavior. This concept is termed amotivation. Individuals are amotivated when they do not perceive contingencies between outcomes and their own actions. They are neither intrinsically nor extrinsically motivated. They become nonmotivated. Amotivation can be seen in many ways as similar to learned helplessness (Abramson, Seligman, & Teasdale, 1978) because the individual will experience feelings of incompetence and expectancies of uncontrollability. When individuals are amotivated, they perceive their behaviors as caused by forces out of their own control. They feel helpless and start asking themselves why in the world they engage in the activity. Eventually they may stop participating in the activity. Athletes on the verge of burning out may be thought of as experiencing a great deal of amotivation (Smith, 1986).

An increasing amount of research has consistently supported the basic premises of Postulate 1. For instance, results from confirmatory factor analyses on the motivation scales that we and others have developed have consistently supported the presence of IM, EM, and AM in sports (Brière, Vallerand, Blais, & Pelletier, 1995; Li & Harmer, 1996; Pelletier et al., 1995) and in a variety of other contexts (see Vallerand, 1997). In addition, as we will see in a later section, these different types of motivation are related to determinants and consequences as theoretically predicted, thereby providing additional support for their construct validity.

Another important point is that self-determination theory (Deci & Ryan, 1985a) proposes that these different types of motivation represent different levels of self-determination. Thus, from the highest to lowest levels of self-determination, we find intrinsic motivation (IM), identified regulation (ID), introjected regulation (IR), external regulation (ER), and amotivation (AM). These motivations can be aligned on a continuum from AM to IM (see Figure 10.2). Because the various forms of motivation are aligned on a self-determination continuum, it also allows us, for sake of brevity, to use a motivational

Figure 10.2. The self-determination continuum (adapted from Deci & Ryan, 1985a, 1991; *from Vallerand et al., 1989,1992).

index integrating all scales. This is called a self-determination index. The more self-determined the index, the more IM and ID, and the less the IR, ER, and AM experienced by the individual. It is this index that has been used in several studies reported herein.

POSTULATE 2—Intrinsic and extrinsic motivation and amotivation exist at three different levels of generality: the global, contextual, and situational levels

Over the past 15 years or so, much research and theorizing on the self have suggested that self-regulation processes are best represented at different levels in a hierarchy. For instance, Carver and Scheier (1981) proposed a hierarchy of self-regulatory processes. Shavelson and Marsh (1986) also proposed three levels of self-concept, the global, the academic and nonacademic self-concepts, and finally the more specific subject self-concept (e.g., English or math). In line with past research on the self, the second postulate posits that the different types of motivation described above (IM, EM, AM) are represented in the individual at three hierarchical levels of generality. From top to bottom, these are the global, the contextual, and the situational levels.

At the global level, it is proposed that the individual has developed a global and general motivational orientation to interact with the environment in an intrinsic, extrinsic, or amotivated way. The work of Deci and Ryan (1985b) with the General Causality Orientations Scale [GCOS], and of Guay, Blais, Vallerand, and Pelletier (1996), who have developed the Global Motivation Scale, is exemplary of such research. These last researchers have reported among other findings that a global intrinsic orientation is associated with higher levels of life satisfaction, as well as global perceptions of competence, autonomy, and relatedness. To the best of our knowledge, no research in sport has been conducted at this level.

Research at the second level of generality, that is at the contextual level, has been particularly popular over the past 15 years. By contexts, we mean a distinct sphere of human activity (Emmons, 1995). Research by Blais, Vallerand, Gasnon, Brière, & Pelletier, (1990b) has shown that the three most important contexts for young adults are education, interpersonal relationships, and leisure, which of course includes sport. In such life contexts, individuals have developed motivational orientations that, although still responsive to the individual's environment, are nevertheless somewhat stable. At this level, individuals' motivational orientations in specific life contexts are assessed and related to various determinants and consequences. The work of Brustad (1988) on the role of parental behavior in the enjoyment of children's sport participation over a season is an example of sport research at the contextual level.

The situational (or state) level represents the third and last level in the hierarchy. Motivation at the situational level refers to the motivation an individual has while he or she is currently engaging in an activity. Motivation at this level of generality has been measured either through a behavioral indicator of how much time the individual spends on the task during a phase subsequent to the experimental phase (the so-called free-choice period; Deci, 1971) or through questionnaires assessing one's interest toward the activity (for a review, see Vallerand & Fortier, 1998). This research has been mainly conducted in the laboratory and has largely focused on the determinants of IM. Thus, research on the effects of rewards, deadlines, performance feedback, and other situational variables on IM, as measured by the time spent on the task or interest toward the activity in that particular setting and at that particular time, have dealt with this level of generality. The work of Orlick and Mosher (1978) on the effects of awards, that of Weinberg and Ragan (1979) on the effects of competition, and of Whitehead and Corbin (1991) on the effects of feedback are exemplary of IM research at the situational level.

In sum, research in the motivation area reveals that motivation exists at three levels of a hierarchy that goes from the global, to the contextual, to the situational levels. It also appears that research in sport has mainly focused on the contextual and situational levels. Furthermore, our recent methodological work has enabled us to develop scales assessing the same motivational constructs at each of the three levels of the hierarchy. Thus, we have developed the Global Motivation Scale (Guay et al., 1996) to assess motivation at the global level. In order to better understand contextual motivation in real-life settings, we have developed scales measuring motivation in education (Vallerand et al., 1989, 1992, 1993), in interpersonal relationships (Blais,

Vallerand, Pelletier, & Brière, 1994), and leisure (Pelletier, Vallerand, Blais, Brière, & Green-Demers, 1996). We also developed the Sport Motivation Scale (Brière et al., 1995; Pelletier et al., 1995) because sport is one very important form of leisure. Finally, in order to measure motivation at the situational level, we have developed the Situational Motivation Scale (Guay & Vallerand, 1995, 1997). All of these scales display high levels of reliability and validity (see Vallerand, 1997). Thus, the methodology needed to test novel hypotheses on human motivation within the context of the hierarchical model is now available.

POSTULATE 3—Motivation at a given level results from two potential sources: (a) social factors and (b) top-down effects from motivation at the proximal level

Postulate 3 deals with the effects of determinants or antecedents on motivation. This third postulate is subdivided into three corollaries.

Corollary 3.1: Motivation at a given level can result from social factors that can be global, contextual, or situational, depending on the level in the hierarchy. By social factors, we refer to both human and nonhuman factors found in our social environment. We distinguish among situational, contextual, and global determinants in the following manner. *Situational factors* refer to variables that are present at a given point in time but not on a permanent basis. For instance, receiving positive feedback at 3:45 of the fourth quarter of a football game represents an example of a situational factor. *Contextual factors* represent variables that are present on a general or recurrent basis in one specific life context (e.g., having a controlling swimming coach) but not in another (e.g., the coach is part of the sport context, but not of the educational context). Finally, *global factors* refer to social factors whose presence is so pervasive that they are present in most aspects of the person's life. A good example of such a global factor is the housing of elite athletes in one location. Being confined to such an environment for an extended period of time may have important consequences on an athlete's global motivation. We feel that it is important to distinguish among the three types of social factors because it then becomes possible to make clearer hypotheses regarding which type of factors should influence motivation at the various levels of the hierarchy. Specifically, social factors should mostly influence motivation at their respective level of the hierarchy.

Recent research has supported this corollary. Research has shown that one type of social factors influences motivation at one level, but not at another level. For example, in a recent study (Vallerand, 1996), we have assessed the effects of a known situational variable, success/failure, on motivation at the situational, context (leisure), and global levels. If our reasoning is correct, failure on the task should have affected only situational motivation (undermining IM especially toward accomplishment and enhancing AM relative to the success condition), but not context (leisure) or global motivation. Results supported this hypothesis.

Corollary 3.2: The impact of social factors on motivation is mediated by perceptions of competence, autonomy, and relatedness. It was posited in Corollary 3.1 that social factors influence motivation. One theoretical perspective that appears to provide a rather complete account of such processes is cognitive evaluation theory (Deci, 1975; Deci & Ryan, 1985a, 1991), a subtheory of self-determination theory. According to this theory, situational factors affect motivation through their impact on people's perceptions of competence, autonomy, and relatedness. This is because these perceptions relate to fundamental human needs that individuals seek to satisfy. Activities that promote such perceptions will be reengaged in freely because they nurture people's fundamental needs.

The need for competence implies that individuals have a desire to interact effectively with the environment in order to experience a sense of competence in producing desired outcomes and preventing undesired events (Connell & Wellborn, 1991; Deci, 1975; Deci & Ryan, 1985a; Harter, 1978; White, 1959). On the other hand, the need for autonomy reflects a desire to be the origin of one's own behavior (deCharms, 1968; Deci, 1975, 1980; Deci & Ryan, 1985a). Finally, the need for relatedness (Bowlby, 1988; Harlow, 1958) involves feeling connected (or feeling that one belongs in a given social milieu; see Baumeister & Leary, 1995; Richer & Vallerand, in press; Ryan, 1993, for recent reviews on belongingness and/or relatedness). Thus, according to cognitive evaluation theory, social factors that facilitate individuals' perceptions of competence, autonomy, and relatedness will facilitate their IM and ID, but undermine their IR, ER and AM (see Deci, Vallerand, Pelletier, & Ryan, 1991).

Much research supports cognitive evaluation theory at the situational level. Noteworthy is the work of Vallerand and Reid (1984). In this particular study, participants engaged in the stabilometer task during a pretest and in a posttest during which independent variables were imposed. Participants received positive, negative, or no performance feedback. Following both the pre- and posttest, subjects completed questionnaires assessing perceptions of competence and intrinsic motivation. Change scores were used in a path analysis. In line with cognitive evaluation theory, results showed that the effects of performance feedback on situational intrinsic motivation were mainly mediated by perceptions of competence. In a more recent study by Blanchard and Vallerand (1996), basketball players completed scales measuring perceptions of personal and team performance, as well as situational perceptions of competence, autonomy, and relatedness, and situational motivation during a game. Results from this study also showed that perceptions of autonomy, competence, and relatedness play a mediational role between personal and team performance and self-determined motivation (as assessed by the self-determination index) during the game.

Similar findings have been reported by Cadorette, Blanchard, and Vallerand (1996) at the contextual level. Individuals (N=208) involved in a weight-loss program completed scales assessing perceptions of the fitness leader's style (autonomy support) and the ambiance of the fitness center, as well as contextual perceptions of competence, autonomy, and relatedness, and contextual motivation (the SMS) toward exercising and dieting. Cadorette et al. (1996) showed through path analysis that perceptions of competence, autonomy, and relatedness mediated the impact of the fitness leader's style and the ambiance of the center on self-determined motivation toward exercising and dieting.

In sum, although much research still needs to be done on the determinants of motivation, it does appear that perceptions of competence, autonomy, and relatedness at the situational and contextual levels represent key mediators of the effects of various situational, and contextual factors on motivation, respectively. The same logic should apply to the global level, although there is no empirical evidence so far to support this claim in sport. These various mediators should, therefore, be included in a model of human motivation.

Corollary 3.3: In addition to the influence of psychological mediators, motivation at a given level also result from top-down effects from motivation at the proximal level higher up in the hierarchy. The third corollary recognizes the potential top-down impact of motivation at higher levels in the hierarchy on motivation at the next lower level. More specifically, it is proposed that motivation at the proximal level should have stronger effects top-down on motivation at the next lower level than on motivation at a distal level. Thus, contextual motivation should have a stronger impact on situational motivation than does global motivation. Similarly, global motivation should have a strong impact on contextual motivation. For instance, one would expect someone with a global intrinsic-motivation orientation to display an intrinsic motivational orientation in different contexts such as sport. Finally, it is also proposed that self-determined motivation at the higher level will facilitate self-determined levels of motivation at the next level down in the hierarchy. Thus, athletes who display a self-determined motivational profile in contextual motivation toward their sport are likely to display a similar motivational profile at the situational level while playing.

Corollary 3.3 is in line with recent conceptual work on self-regulatory processes that has shown that global properties of the self influence more specific aspects of the self (Brown, 1993; Brown & Dutton, 1995; Sansone & Harackiewicz, 1996). To the best of our knowledge, only two studies have tested Corollary 3.3 in sports and exercise. Thus, in two studies with basketball players, Blanchard, Vallerand, and Provencher (1995) were able to show that contextual motivation toward basketball in general, as assessed either just prior to (Study 1) or several weeks before (Study 2) a game, predicted situational motivation experienced during a basketball game. Here again, the more self-determined the athletes' contextual motivation toward basketball, the more self determined their situational motivation. Overall, the findings from the above two studies indicate that motivation can produce top-down effects on motivation at the next lower level in the hierarchy. Although the results of these two studies are encouraging, more studies are needed to test this hypothesis from an experimental perspective.

In sum, research reviewed in this section provides strong support for Postulate 3 and its corollaries. We have seen that it may prove quite heuristic to distinguish among global, contextual, and situational factors. In addition, the role of perceptions of competence, autonomy, and relatedness as psychological mediators of the social factors-motivation relationship was strongly supported, especially at the situational and contextual levels. Finally, we have also shown that motivation at a higher level in the hierarchy can influence motivation at the next lower level.

POSTULATE 4—There is a recursive bottom-up relationship between motivation at the proximal level and motivation at the next level up in the hierarchy

The fourth postulate underscores the bidirectional relationship between motivation at the various levels of the hierarchy. The purpose of this postulate is to specifically take into consideration motivational changes that may occur over time and how the interplay between the different levels of motivation can account for these.

In order to illustrate more clearly this bidirectional effect, let's take a real-life example of a basketball player who participated in the quarter-finals of a high-school basketball tournament. As the leading scorer of the team, the player had to deliver a great performance for his team to have a chance to win the game. Unfortunately, he did not deliver—scored only 16 points—and his team lost by 22 points. Near the end of the game with the team's loss certain, his situational motivation was at its lowest. He did not feel like playing at that moment: He was amotivated. Later that evening he started to think about next season's grueling training camp and boring practices. Then, for the first time in his life, he started wondering if basketball was worth the time investment. Perhaps he had obtained all there was to get from the game. Perhaps it was time to move on. And he did.

How can we explain what this basketball player went through? Let's start explaining his situational motivation near the end of the crucial quarter-final game. He did not play well, and his team lost. These represent two crucial situational factors that had a negative impact on his situational motivation (Corollary 3.1). These factors were so strong that they superseded the impact of the player's intrinsic contextual motivation on his situational motivation and led him to experience a low level of IM and a high level of AM at the situational level (near the end of the game). In turn, this low self-determined situational motivation had a recursive negative effect (Postulate 4) on his contextual motivation toward basketball. With his contextual motivation now being strongly amotivated, the player decided to call it quits (an important behavioral consequence as we will see with Postulate 5).

We have tested the above processes with respect to basketball players. In this study, Blanchard et al. (1995) had basketball players complete the Sports Motivation Scale before a tournament, as well as the Situational Motivation Scale and the Sport Motivation Scale after each of two games of a basketball tournament. Finally, 10 days after the tournament, subjects completed again the Sports Motivation Scale (Pelletier et al., 1995). It was predicted that contextual motivation toward sport (here basketball) would influence situational motivation right after the first game, which in turn would influence subsequent contextual motivation. This cycle was expected to be repeated for the second game. Finally, situational motivation was hypothesized to influence subsequent contextual motivation after the tournament. Results supported the hypothesis. There was a recursive relation between contextual motivation and situational motivation. More specifically, contextual motivation toward basketball influenced situational motivation for Game 1, which in turn influenced subsequent contextual motivation. This cycle was again repeated for Game 2. Finally, situational motivation for game 2 (and also 1) influenced contextual motivation toward basketball 10 days following the tournament. As predicted by the model, the more self-determined the athletes' situational motivation in the tournament, the more self-determined the contextual motivation after the tournament. With respect to our motivational model, as predicted, situational motivation had a recursive effect over time on contextual motivation.

The above reasoning can also be applied to the next level. For example, if for various reasons, an individual displays repeated high levels of IM toward sports, eventually such changes could bring about changes in IM at the global level. This latter hypothesis remains to be empirically tested, however. In sum, not only is there a top-down relation between motivation at higher levels and those below, but there is also a bottom-up effect from lower levels to the next adjacent higher level.

POSTULATE 5—Motivation leads to important consequences

The fifth and last postulate deals with the consequences of motivation. Although some may object to the use of the term *consequences,* we feel it is appropriate to use such a term for at least two reasons. First, from an intuitive perspective, it seems appropriate to see variables as diverse as attention, satisfaction, and behavioral persistence as being influenced by motivation. For instance, an intrinsically motivated athlete should be more attentive during a game than should one who is amotivated. Second, from an empirical perspective, there is evidence that motivation "causes" some of the consequences mentioned above. For instance, Amabile (1985) has shown that inducing extrinsic motivation in writers led to lower quality poems than those produced in the intrinsic motivation or control conditions. Several other studies provide support for the causal effects of motivation on consequences (Curry, Wagner, & Grothaus, 1991; Lepper & Cordova, 1992). It is thus clear that motivation produces some important consequences.

It would also appear useful to conceive of consequences as being cognitive, affective, and behavioral in nature. Concentration, attention, and memory are examples of cognitive consequences that have been studied in the IM/EM literature. Affective consequences have been particularly popular and include the following: interest, positive emotions, and satisfaction. Finally, choice of behavior, persistence at the task, intensity, task complexity, behavioral intentions, and performance represent examples of behavioral consequences that have been studied in the area. It is important to distinguish among the three general classes of consequences because among other things this distinction should lead to a better prediction of which types of motivation will most strongly affect which types of consequence (see below the corollaries on this issue). Thus, by distinguishing among the three types of consequences, it may eventually become possible to chart the motivation-consequences relationship more precisely.

Corollary 5.1: Consequences are decreasingly positive from intrinsic motivation to amotivation. The first corollary on motivational consequences deals with consequences as a function of the type of motivation. The self-determination continuum proposed by Deci and Ryan (1985a) is especially useful in making predictions about motivational consequences. Because IM, ID, IR, ER, and AM are hypothesized to be on a continuum from high to low self-determination (Deci & Ryan, 1985a), and because self-determination is associated with enhanced psychological functioning (Deci, 1980), one would expect a corresponding pattern of consequences. That is, one might expect IM to have the most positive consequences, followed by identification. On the other hand, one might also expect external regulation and especially AM to be associated with negative consequences. Introjection should lead to consequences inbetween those produced by identification and external regulation.

Much research supports this corollary (see Ryan, 1995; Vallerand, 1993, 1997) in various life contexts including work (Blais, Brière, Lachance, Riddle, & Vallerand, 1993), leisure (Pelletier et al., 1996) education (Vallerand & Bissonnette, 1992), and interpersonal relationships (Blais, Sabourin, Boucher, & Vallerand, 1990a). Research in sport has also supported this corollary. For example, research by Pelletier et al. (1995) has shown that behavioral consequences, such as effort and intentions to continue in sport, are positively correlated with the most self-determined forms of motivation (IM and ID) but negatively with AM (the least self-determined form of motivation). Results from this study also found support for the self-determination continuum by demonstrating that a cognitive consequence (distraction in training) was negatively correlated with IM and ID and positively with AM. Please note that the pattern of correlations is reversed because distraction in training is a negative consequence. Although these results appear promising, much work needs to be done in this area, however.

Corollary 5.2: Motivational consequences exist at the three levels of the hierarchy, and the level of generality of the consequences depends on the level of the motivation that has produced them. The second corollary deals with the level of generality of the consequences. In line with the hierarchical model, it is proposed that motivational consequences exist at the three levels of the hierarchy. The level of generality of the various consequences depends on the level of generality of the motivation that engenders them. Thus, consequences of situational motivation will be experienced at the situational level, such as feelings of satisfaction, levels of attention, and persistence displayed at that specific moment. Similarly, consequences at the contextual level will be of moderate generality (e.g., satisfaction and behavior in sport) and will be specific to the context to which they pertain. Finally, consequences at the global level will be of the highest level of generality (e.g., satisfaction with one's life) and will vary as a function of global motivation.

Results from a recent study by Pelletier, Fortier, Vallerand, and Brière (1997) provide support for the above corollary with respect to motivation and one important consequence at the contextual level in sport, namely dropping out. In this study, 368 competitive swimmers completed various questionnaires including perceptions of autonomy support and control from the coach and the Sport Motivation Scale. In the two following years, the authors determined which swimmers persisted and which dropped out. Results from the structural equation modeling analysis (using LISREL) revealed that amotivation and intrinsic motivation had respectively the most negative and positive impact on persistence over the 2 years. Furthermore, using the different motivations allowed the researchers to show that the impact of external regulation on persistence was negligible the first year but negative the second. On the other hand, the impact of introjected regulation on persistence was positive the first year, but negligible the second.

In sum, research reviewed in this section provides strong support for Postulate 5 and its corollaries in that motivation leads to important consequences. These consequences can be cognitive, affective, and behavioral in nature and take place at three levels of generality in line with the motivation that produces them. Finally, consequences are decreasingly positive as we move from the highest self-determined form of motivation (i.e., IM) to the lowest self-determined form of self-determination (i.e., AM).[2]

Future Sport Research on the Hierarchical Model

Overall, a great deal of sport research supports the postulated links of the model. It therefore appears that the model represents a sound framework to explain current knowledge on sport motivation. In addition, we feel that the hierarchical model can lead to important future research in sport. Here are only a few examples.

First, the interactional effects of social factors and contextual motivation on situational motivation need to be further studied. Research has shown that extrinsic factors, such as trophies and awards, have negative effects on situational motivation (Orlick & Mosher, 1978). However, such research has not taken contextual motivation into consideration. What are the effects of extrinsic factors when the contextual motivation is self-determined? When it is non-self-determined in nature? Future research is needed to answer these questions.

---

2. Much research reveals that intrinsic motivation leads to the most positive outcomes (Vallerand, 1997). However, this is not always the case. Identified regulation has been found to lead to more positive outcomes than does intrinsic motivation in the context of politics (Koestner, Losier, Vallerand, & Carducci, 1996) and the protection of the environment (Pelletier, Tuson, Green-Demers, Noels, & Beaton, in press). Vallerand (1997) has suggested that these results may be due to the nature of the task. According to Vallerand (1997), when a task is perceived as not interesting, then identified regulation may become a more important determinant of positive consequences than intrinsic motivation. Although this hypothesis appears plausible, additional research is needed to clarify this point.

Second, additional work on the psychological mediators is also needed. Researchers to this point have considered perceived competence, autonomy, and relatedness as additive. That is, the higher the individual's perceptions of competence, autonomy, and relatedness, the higher one's self-determined motivation. However, it has been suggested that their effects on motivation may be interactive (Ryan, 1993). For instance, it has been posited that perceptions of competence can primarily influence motivation when one is feeling autonomous (Deci & Ryan, 1985a). Ryan (1993) further posits that perceptions of autonomy and relatedness may even clash, especially for teenagers and young adults. Very little research to date has examined this hypothesis.

Third, research involving motivation at more than one level is needed. More specifically, research needs to deal with the recursive effects of motivation at one level on motivation at the higher level up in the hierarchy. We need to find out about how situational motivation produces the recursive effects on contextual motivation. More specifically, what are the processes through which the recursive motivational effects occur? Does situational motivation affect contextual motivation directly? Or are other variables, such as consequences (e.g., positive or negative effect), responsible for these recursive effects? The same question also applies to the recursive effects from contextual motivation to global motivation.

Fourth, we need to investigate how the different contexts may interact among each other. We see at least two interesting possibilities. First, a conflict effect. In the terminology of the model, athletes who display a self-determined motivational profile in contextual motivation toward their sport are likely to display a similar motivational profile at the situational level while playing. What happens to the link between contextual sport motivation and situational motivation toward a sport activity when another contextual motivation (i.e., education) is primed? For instance, what happens when someone is engaged in a sport task and is reminded that there is an exam tomorrow? How will behavior be influenced by these two contextual motivations (sport vs. education motivation)? Will the individual change from the sport task to the educational activity? If so, what are the psychological processes involved? Are some individuals more inclined than others to experience conflictual motivations?

A second issue deals with two opposing effects, the compensation and the infusion effect (Blanchard, Vallerand, & Provencher, 1996). These occur as a function of motivational changes that take place in one context. For instance, what happens when an individual experiences a loss of intrinsic motivation in one context such as sport? The infusion effect would predict that there should be a ripple effect so that all contexts (e.g., education, interpersonal relationships, sport) will be negatively affected. On the other hand, the compensation effect would predict that the individual should be able to regroup and even experience an increase of intrinsic motivation in another domain. There is evidence that both effects do occur for self-relevant variables such as mental health (Linville, 1987; Sheldon, Ryan, Rawsthorne, & Ilardi, in press). These issues appear as especially important from a sport perspective as they would allow us to focus on the whole individual in sport and not strictly the athlete. Thus, future research is definitely encouraged on this topic.

Finally, we need to replicate some of the present findings with different populations. So far, most of the participants in our sport studies have been athletes at the college level. Although we believe that the present findings would also hold with other populations (e.g., professional athletes), this remains to be empirically tested. This would allow researchers to test the external validity of the hierarchical model.

Conclusion

The hierarchical model of motivation allows us not only to integrate the various perspectives inherent in the intrinsic/extrinsic motivation literature, but also to propose new and original testable hypotheses. Such a model takes into consideration the variety of ways motivation can be represented in the individual and how these various representations of motivation are related, as well as the determinants and consequences of these motivational representations. For more than 25 years, researchers have made great advances in our understanding of the psychological processes involved in intrinsic and extrinsic motivation. In this chapter, we have proposed a model that should help us integrate actual knowledge in the area, as well as lead to new avenues of research in the context of sport. In light of the potential scientific value of the model and the findings presented today, we feel optimistic that future research using this model as a starting base should bring us one step closer to a more comprehensive understanding of sport motivation, thereby leading to a more enjoyable and positive sport environment for all.

References

Abramson, L.Y., Seligman, M.E.P., & Teasdale, J.D. (1978). Learned helplessness in humans: Critique and reformulation. *Journal of Abnormal Psychology, 87,* 49–74.

Amabile, T.M. (1985). Motivation and creativity: Effects of motivational orientation on creative writers. *Journal of Personality and Social Psychology, 48,* 393–399.

Baumeister, R.F., & Leary, M.R. (1995). The need to belong: Desire for interpersonal attachments as a fundamental human motivation. *Psychological Bulletin, 117,* 497–529.

Blais, M.R., Brière, N.M., Lachance, L., Riddle, A.S., & Vallerand, R.J. (1993). L'Inventaire des motivations au travail de Blais [The Blais Work Motivation Inventory]. *Revue Québécoise de Psychologie, 14,* 185–215.

Blais, M.R., Sabourin, S., Boucher, C., & Vallerand, R.J. (1990a). Toward a motivational model of couple happiness. *Journal of Personality and Social Psychology, 59,* 1021–1031.

Blais, M.R., Vallerand, R.J., Gagnon, A., Brière, N.M., & Pelletier, L.G. (1990b). Significance, structure, and gender differences in life domains of college students. *Sex Roles, 22,* 199–212

Blais, M.R., Vallerand, R.J., Pelletier, L.G., & Brière, N.M. (1994). *Construction et validation de l'Inventaire des Motivations Interpersonnelles* [Construction and validation of the Inventory of Interpersonal Motivations]. Unpublished manuscript, Université du Québec à Montréal.

Blanchard, C., & Vallerand, R.J. (1996). *Perceptions of competence, autonomy, and relatedness as psychological mediators of the social factors-contextual motivation relationship.* Unpublished manuscript, Université du Québec à Montréal.

Blanchard, C., Vallerand, R.J., & Provencher, P. (1995, October). *Une analyse des effets bidirectionnels entre la motivation contextuelle et la motivation situationnelle en milieu naturel* [An analysis of the bidirectional effects between contextual and situational motivation in a natural setting]. Paper presented at the annual conference of the Québec Society for Research on Psychology, Ottawa.

Blanchard, C., Vallerand, R.J., & Provencher, P. (1996, August). *Une analyse motivationnelle des mécanismes de compensation et de contagion du soi* [A motivational analysis of the compensation and contagion mechanisms of the self]. Paper presented at the first annual conference on social psychology in the French language, Montreal, Canada.

Bowlby, J. (1988). *A secure base: Parent-child attachment and healthy human development.* New York: Basic Books.

Brière, N.M., Vallerand, R.J., Blais, M.R., & Pelletier, L.G. (1995). Développement et validation d'une mesure de motivation intrinsèque, extrinsèque et d'amotivation en contexte sportif: l'Échelle de motivation dans les sports (EMS) [On the development and validation of the French form of the Sport Motivation Scale]. *International Journal of Sport Psychology, 26,* 465–489.

Brown, J.D. (1993). Self-esteem and self-evaluation: Feeling is believing. In J. Suls (Ed.), *Psychological perspectives on the self* (vol. 4, pp. 27–58). Hillsdale, NJ: Erlbaum.

Brown, J.D., & Dutton, K.A. (1995). *From the top-down: Self-esteem and self-evaluation.* Unpublished manuscript, University of Washington.

Brustad, R.J. (1988). Affective outcomes in competitive youth sport: The influence of intrapersonal and socialization factors. *Journal of Sport and Exercise Psychology, 10,* 307–321.

Cadorette, I., Blanchard, C., & Vallerand, R.J. (1996, October). *Programme d'amaigrissement: Influence du centre de condtionnement physique et du style de l'entraîneur sur la motivation des participants.* [Weight loss program: Effects of the fitness center and the instructor on participants' motivation]. Paper presented at the annual conference of the Quebec Society for Research in Psychology, Trois-Rivières, Quebec.

Carver, C.S., & Scheier, M.F. (1981). *Attention and self-regulation.* New-York: Springer-Verlag.

Connell, J.P., & Wellborn, J.G. (1991). Competence, autonomy, and relatedness: A motivational analysis of self-esteem processes. In M.R. Gunnar & L.A. Sroufe (Eds.), *The Minnesota symposium on child psychology: Vol. 22. Self-processes in development* (pp. 43–77). Hillsdale, NJ: Erlbaum.

Curry, S.J., Wagner, E.H., & Grothaus, L.C. (1991). Evaluation of intrinsic and extrinsic motivation interventions with a self-help smoking cessation program. *Journal of Consulting and Clinical Psychology, 59,* 318–324.

deCharms, R.C. (1968). *Personal causation: The internal affective determinants of behavior.* New York: Academic Press.

Deci, E.L. (1971). Effects of externally mediated rewards on intrinsic motivation. *Journal of Personality and Social Psychology, 18,* 105–115.

Deci, E.L. (1975). *Intrinsic motivation.* New York: Plenum.

Deci, E.L. (1980). *The psychology of self-determination.* Lexington, MA: DC Heath.

Deci, E.L., & Ryan, R.M. (1985a). *Intrinsic motivation and self-determination in human behavior.* New York: Plenum.

Deci, E.L., & Ryan, R.M. (1985b). The General Causality Orientations Scale: Self-determination in personality. *Journal of Research in Personality, 62,*119–142.

Deci, E.L., & Ryan, R.M. (1991). A motivational approach to self: Integration in personality. In R. Dienstbier (Ed.), *Nebraska symposium on motivation: Vol. 38. Perspectives on motivation* (pp. 237–288). Lincoln, NE: University of Nebraska Press.

Deci, E.L., Vallerand, R.J., Pelletier, L.G., & Ryan, R.M. (1991). Motivation and education: The self-determination perspective. *The Educational Psychologist, 26,* 325–346.

Emmons, R.A. (1995). Levels and domains in personality: An introduction. *Journal of Personality, 63,* 341–364.

Guay, F., Blais, M.R., Vallerand, R.J., & Pelletier, L.G. (1996). *The Global Motivation Scale.* Manuscript in preparation, Université du Québec à Montréal.

Guay, F., & Vallerand, R.J. (1995, June). *The Situational Motivation Scale.* Paper presented at the annual convention of the American Psychological Society, New York.

Guay, F., & Vallerand, R.J. (1997). *On the assessment of state intrinsic and extrinsic motivation: The Situational Motivation Scale (SIMS).* Manuscript submitted for publication.

Harlow, H.F. (1958). The nature of love. *American Psychologist, 13,* 673–685.

Harter, S. (1978). Effectance motivation reconsidered: Toward a developmental model. *Human Development, 1,* 34–64.

Koestner, R., Losier, G.F., Vallerand, R.J., & Carducci, D. (1996). Identified and introjected forms of political internalization: Extending self-determination theory. *Journal of Personality and Social Psychology, 70,* 1025–1036.

Lepper, M.R., & Cordova, D.I. (1992). A desire to be taught: Instructional consequences of intrinsic motivation. *Motivation and Emotion, 16,* 187–208.

Li, F., & Harmer, P. (1996). Testing the simplex assumption underlying the sport motivation scale: A structural equation modeling analysis. *Research Quarterly for Exercise and Sport, 67,* 396–405.

Linville, P.W. (1987). Self-complexity as a cognitive buffer against stress-related illness and depression. *Journal of Personality and Social Psychology, 52,* 663–676.

Orlick, T.D., & Mosher, R. (1978). Extrinsic rewards and participant motivation in a sport related task. *International Journal of Sport Psychology, 9,* 27–39.

Pelletier, L.G., Fortier, M. S., Vallerand, R. J., & Brière, N.M. (1997). *Perceived autonomy support, motivation, and persistence in physical activity: A longitudinal investigation.* Unpublished manuscript, University of Ottawa.

Pelletier, L.G., Fortier, M.S., Vallerand, R.J., Tuson, K.M., Brière, N.M., & Blais, M.R. (1995). Toward a new measure of intrinsic motivation, extrinsic motivation, and amotivation in sports: The Sport Motivation Scale (SMS). *Journal of Sport & Exercise Psychology, 17,* 35–53.

Pelletier, L.G., Tuson, K.M., Green-Demers, I., Noels, K., & Beaton, A.M. (in press). Why are we doing things for the environment? The Motivation Towards the Environment Scale (MTES). *Journal of Applied Social Psychology.*

Pelletier, L.G., Vallerand, R.J., Blais, M.R., Brière, N.M., & Green-Demers, I. (1996). Construction et validation d'une mesure de motivation intrinsèque, de motivation extrinsèque et d'amotivation vis-à-vis des activités de loisirs: l'Échelle de motivation vis-à-vis les loisirs (EML) [Construction and validation of the Leisure Motivation Scale]. *Loisir et Société, 19,* 559–585.

Richer, S., & Vallerand, R.J. (in press). Construction et validation de l'échelle du sentiment d'appartenance sociale. (Construction and validation of the Perceived Relatedness Scale). *Revue Européenne de Psychologie Appliquée.*

Ryan, R.M. (1993). Agency and organization: Intrinsic motivation, autonomy and the self in psychological development. In R. Dientsbier (Ed.), *The Nebraska symposium on motivation:* Vol. *40,* (pp. 1–56). Lincoln, NE: University of Nebraska Press.

Ryan, R.M. (1995). The integration of behavioral regulation within life domains. *Journal of Personality, 63,* 397–429.

Sansone, C., & Harackiewicz, J.M. (1996). "I don't feel like it": The function of interest in self-regulation. In L. Martin & A. Tesser (Eds.), *Striving and feeling: Interactions between goals and affect* (pp. 203–228). Hillsdale, NJ: Erlbaum.

Shavelson, R.J., & Marsh, H.W. (1986). On the structure of self-concept. In R. Schwarzer (Ed.), *Anxiety and cognitions* (pp. 305–330). Hillsdale, NJ: Erlbaum.

Sheldon, K.M., Ryan, R.M., Rawsthorne, L.J., & Ilardi, B. (in press). "Trait" self and "true" self: Cross-role variation in the Big Five personality traits and its relations with psychological authenticity and subjective well-being. *Journal of Personality and Social Psychology.*

Smith, R. E. (1986). Toward a cognitive-affective model of athletic burnout. *Journal of Sport Psychology, 8,* 36–50.

Vallerand, R.J. (1993). La motivation intrinsèque et extrinsèque en contexte naturel: Implications pour les contextes de l'éducation, du travail, des relations interpersonnelles et des loisirs [Intrinsic and extrinsic motivation in natural contexts: Implications for the education, work, interpersonal relationships, and leisure contexts]. In R.J. Vallerand & E.E. Thill (Eds.), *Introduction à la psychologie de la motivation* [Introduction to the psychology of motivation] (pp. 533–582). Laval, Québec: Etudes Vivantes.

Vallerand, R.J. (1996). [On the effects of success/failure on motivation at three levels of generality]. Unpublished raw data.

Vallerand.R.J. (1997). Toward a hierarchical model of intrinsic and extrinsic motivation. In M.P. Zanna (Ed.), *Advances in experimental social psychology* (pp. 271–360). New York: Academic Press.

Vallerand, R.J., & Bissonnette, R. (1992). Intrinsic, extrinsic, and amotivational styles as predictors of behavior: A prospective study. *Journal of Personality, 60,* 599–620.

Vallerand, R.J., Blais, M.R., Brière, N.M., & Pelletier, L.G. (1989). Construction et validation de l'Echelle de motivation en éducation (EME) [On the construction and validation of the French form of the Academic Motivation Scale]. *Canadian Journal of Behavioural Science, 21,* 323–349.

Vallerand, R.J., Deci, E.L., & Ryan, R.M. (1987). Intrinsic motivation in sport. In K.B. Pandoff (Ed.), *Exercise and sport sciences reviews* (pp. 389–425). New York: Macmillan.

Vallerand, R.J., & Fortier, M. (1998). Measures of intrinsic and extrinsic motivation in sport and physical activity: A rand critique. In J. Duda (Ed.), *Advancements in sport and exercise psychology measurement* (pp. 81–101). Morgantown, WV: Fitness Information Technology.

Vallerand, R.J., Pelletier, L.G., Blais, M.R., Brière, N.M., Senécal, C., & Vallières, E.F. (1992). The Academic Motivation Scale: A measure of intrinsic, extrinsic, and amotivation in education. *Educational and Psychological Measurement, 52,* 1003–1019.

Vallerand, R.J., Pelletier, L.G., Blais, M.R., Brière, N.M., Senécal, C., & Vallières, E.F. (1993). On the assessment of intrinsic, extrinsic, and amotivation in education: Evidence on the concurrent and construct validity of the Academic Motivation Scale. *Educational and Psychological Measurement, 53,* 159–172.

Vallerand, R.J., & Reid, G. (1984). On the causal effects of perceived competence on intrinsic motivation: A test of cognitive evaluation theory. *Journal of Sport Psychology, 6,* 94–102.

Weinberg, R.S., & Ragan. J. (1979). Competition and extrinsic rewards: Effect on intrinsic motivation and attributions. *Research Quarterly, 50,* 494–502

White, R.W. (1959). Motivation reconsidered: The concept of competence. *Psychological Review, 66,* 297–333.

Whitehead, J.R., & Corbin, C. B. (1991). Youth fitness testing: The effects of percentile-based evaluative feedback on intrinsic motivation. *Research Quarterly for Exercise and Sport, 62,* 225–231.

Author notes

Preparation of this paper was facilitated through grants from the Social Sciences and Humanities Research Council of Canada (SSHRC) and Le Fonds pour la Formation des Chercheurs et l'Aide à la Recherche (FCAR, Québec). Reprint requests should be addressed to Robert J. Vallerand, Laboratoire de Recherche sur le Comportement Social, Département de Psychologie, Université du Québec à Montréal, C.P. 8888, Succ. Centre-Ville, Montréal, QC, Canada, H3C 3P8.

11

Toward an Integration of Models of Leadership With a Contemporary Theory of Motivation

Joan L. Duda
Purdue University, USA

Isabel Balaguer
University of Valencia, Spain

Sport research has indicated that the coach has an important influence on the long-term process of sport socialization as well as the creation of a current motivational climate for his or her athletes. Among the various approaches employed for studying the dynamic between the athlete and the coach in sport psychology, models of leadership behavior have played a central role. Two of the most important frameworks that have guided the study of leadership in the athletic domain have been Smith, Smoll, and associates' Mediational Model of Leadership (Smith, Smoll, & Curtis, 1979) and Chelladurai's Multidimensional Model of Leadership (Chelladurai, 1993).

Mediational Model of Leadership

The work of Smith, Smoll, and colleagues (Smith, Smoll, & Curtis, 1978, 1979; Smith, Zane, Smoll, & Coppel, 1983) has made a significant contribution to understanding the social reinforcements provided by coaches and their impact on the quality of the youth sport experience. These researchers developed the Coaching Behavior Assessment System (CBAS) and examined the relationship of coaches' behaviors to young baseball and basketball players' perceptions and attitudes. Their approach consisted of assessing coaches' behaviors through observation, measuring the players' reactions, training the coaches to modify their behaviors, and evaluating the effects of the training program. In general, their results indicated that coaches who provided more mistake-contingent technical information, less general feedback, less punishment, and less controlling behaviors had players who evaluated the coaches more highly, felt better about themselves, liked their teammates more and expressed a higher level of sport enjoyment. In more recent work, Barnett, Smith, and Smoll (1992) have found that athletes who played for coaches participating in effectiveness training were less likely to drop out when compared to their peers who played for control group coaches.

As shown in Figure 11.1, the mediational model (Smoll & Smith, 1989; Smoll, Smith, Curtis, & Hunt, 1978) comprises three basic elements: that is, coach behaviors, player perceptions and recall, and players' evaluative reactions. Also included in the model are individual difference variables and situational factors that may impact the interrelationships between leader behaviors, athletes' interpretations of these actions, and the consequences of perceived coach behaviors for athletes.

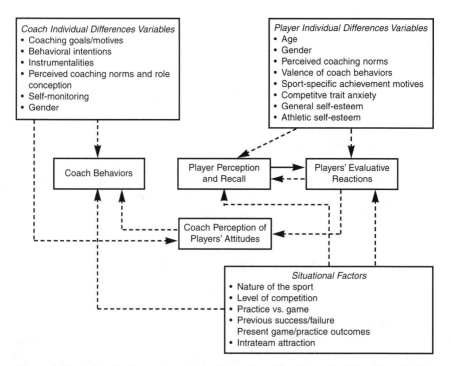

Figure 11.1. Mediational model of leadership (Smoll & Smith, 1989). Reprinted with permission.

With regard to the player-individual difference variables, age (Smoll & Smith, 1989), gender (Smoll & Smith, 1989), and athletes' normative beliefs regarding appropriate coaching behaviors are assumed to influence players' recall and perception of and response to a coach's behavior. According to Smoll and Smith, another important person factor is the players' achievement motivation for performing well. Smoll and Smith argue both a person's desire to succeed and his or her fear of failure need to be considered as potential moderating variables.

It is also assumed in the mediational model that aspects of the sport situation would influence athletes' perceptions of and reactions to the behaviors exhibited by the coach. For example, Smoll and Smith (1989) suggest that level of competition would impact how coaches act and how athletes interpret these actions and subsequently respond.

Multidimensional Model of Leadership

As depicted in Figure 11.2, Chelladurai's (1990, 1993) Multidimensional Model of Leadership assumes three facets of leadership behavior: required, preferred, and actual leader behavior. In contrast to the work of Smoll and Smith (1989), which entails observation of behaviors by external observers, actual leader behavior is operationalized in this case "as the average of the perceptions of members of a team" (Chelladurai & Riemer, 1998, p. 36). Chelladurai and Riemer (1998) indicate that required behavior can be defined as "the average of the preferences of all subjects from a sport" or the "average of the self-reported behaviors of a significant amount of successful coaches in a sport" (p. 38).

In Chelladurai's model, characteristics of the situation, the leader, and the members are held to be determinants of the three aspects of leadership behavior. As exemplified in Chelladurai and Saleh's (1978, 1980) Leadership Scale for Sport, it is further presumed that there are five dimensions of leader behavior, namely, training and instruction, democratic behavior, autocratic behavior, social support, and positive feedback.

It is also proposed in the multidimensional model that group performance and member satisfaction are a function of the congruence between actual leader behaviors, the preferences of athletes, and the requirements of the situation. The model concludes with a feedback loop indicating that actual leader behavior may also be impacted by what the leader observes in terms of group performance and member satisfaction.

The Multidimensional Model of Leadership has provided the foundation for a considerable amount of sport research. Previous studies have determined the influence of selected antecedent variables (e.g., gender, age, ability level,

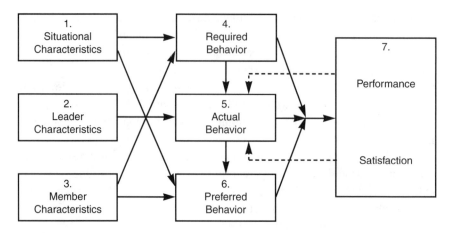

Figure 11.2. Multidimensional model of leadership (Chelladurai,1990). Reprinted with permission.

personality) on preferred and/or perceived leadership (Chelladurai & Carron, 1981, 1983; Chelladurai & Saleh, 1978; Garland & Barry, 1988). Other investigations have examined the congruence between perceived and preferred leadership in relation to satisfaction with leadership and/or team and individual performance (e.g., Chelladurai, 1984; Chelladurai, Imamura, Yamaguchi, Oinuma, & Miyauchi, 1988; Riemer & Chelladurai, 1995; Schliesshman, 1987; Weiss & Friedrichs, 1986). In general, this literature suggests that

> athletes are satisfied with leadership to the extent that the coach emphasizes (a) training and instruction that enhances the ability and co-ordinated effort by members, which in turn contributes to task accomplishment; and (b) positive feedback that recognizes and rewards good performance. (Chelladurai, 1993, p. 654)

Leadership Models and the Tenets of Goal Perspective Theory

Both models (i.e., the Mediational Model of Leadership and the Multidimensional Model of Leadership) have implications for the motivation of athletes, but neither has been systematically related with contemporary theories of motivated behavior. In regard to their leadership model, Smoll and Smith (1989) indicate that "cognitive and affective processes serve as filters between overt coaching behaviors and youngsters' attitudes toward their coach and their sport experience" (p. 1527). However, in their work, these processes are not articulated or couched within a motivational framework. Specific to the coach effectiveness guidelines that stem from the research of Smith, Smoll and colleagues (Smith, Smoll, & Curtis, 1978, 1979; Smith et al., 1983), Chaumeton and Duda (1988) pointed out that the behaviors identified as desirable were more task involving whereas the social reinforcements considered less desirable were more ego involving.

In terms of the mediational model, Chelladurai (1993; Chelladurai & Riemer, 1998) argue for the meaningfulness of the teaching and instruction, social support, and positive feedback dimensions of the Leadership in Sport Scale via Porter and Lawler's (1968) model of motivation. However, the motivational processes by which such leader behaviors might influence the performance and satisfaction of group members have not been discerned. In essence, the mediational and multidimensional models of leadership provide limited insight into *how* and *why* divergent leader behaviors have differential effects in terms of athletes' self-perceptions, emotional responses to sport, and behavior in the athletic domain.

Smith, Smoll, and Curtis (1978, 1979) and Chelladurai and Riemer (1998), however, do propose that the motivational goals held by coaches influence their perceptions of their own behaviors and that players' goals will influence their perceptions of coaches' behaviors. Chelladurai and Riemer (1998) suggest that there should be associations between the goal orientations held by athletes and their views concerning their coaches' leadership style. Specific to the multidimensional model, it is also reasonable to assume that athletes' goals would correspond in a logical way to how they prefer their coaches act.

One theory of motivation that considers individual differences in athletes' goal orientations and perceptions concerning the environment created by the coach is goal-perspective theory (Ames, 1992; Nicholls, 1989). According to this theoretical framework, motivation in achievement settings is influenced by the manner in which individuals construe their level of ability and define success and failure (Nicholls, 1984, 1989). Two primary goals have been identified and are termed *task involvement* and *ego involvement*. These divergent goal perspectives are assumed to impact athletes' behaviors, cognitions, and affective responses in the athletic setting, in short, how they interpret and react to sport.

Task involvement operates when human action is primarily motivated by task mastery and the experience of personal improvement. In this case, success and failure are defined in terms of self-referenced perceptions of one's performance. Ego involvement is characterized by actions that are primarily motivated to demonstrate normatively superior competence. Ego-involved individuals feel successful when they perform better than their peers or similarly with less effort. In terms of predicted achievement patterns, it is expected that a focus on task-involved goals will result in maximal motivation regardless of the individual's level of perceived ability. Ego involvement, however, coupled with doubts about one's competence level, is assumed to result in negative achievement behaviors (e.g., the rescinding of effort, dropping out, performance impairment).

Goal-perspective theory holds that whether a person is in a state of task or ego involvement is a function of dispositional differences and situational factors (Ames, 1984, 1992; Nicholls, 1989). In regard to the former, if is presumed that individuals vary in terms of two orthogonal goal orientations, that is, task and ego orientation. Among a constellation of variables, athletes' degree of task and ego orientation has been found to relate their beliefs about the causes of success, intrinsic interest, perceptions of the purposes of sport involvement, and attitudes toward cheating and aggression (see Duda, 1994, 1996, and Duda & Whitehead, 1998, for recent reviews of this literature).

The majority of research on contextual factors has emphasized how the perceived motivational climate or situational goal structure at hand relates to variations in athletes' self-perceptions, beliefs, and emotional responses. These climates can be more or less task and/or ego involving. Created by significant others such as one's coach, teacher, or parents, the perceived motivational climate is assumed to be a function of the goals to be achieved, the evaluation and reward process, and how individuals are required to relate to each other in the particular setting (Ames & Archer, 1988).

Within the sport setting specifically, Seifriz, Duda, and Chi (1992) were the first to point out that athletes could distinguish between task-involving and ego-involving team climates. On high school male basketball teams that were deemed more task focused, the athletes felt that trying hard was rewarded, players were encouraged by the coach for doing their best and cooperating with teammates, and every player had an important role on the team. In terms of an ego-involving climate, the athletes perceived that teammates were reinforced to try and outdo each other, that players were punished by the coach for mistakes, and that the most talented players received more of the coach's attention.

Seifriz et al. (1992) found athletes perceiving a task-involving climate to report increased levels of enjoyment and a stronger belief that effort leads to success. In contrast, athletes who perceived an ego-involving team climate reported decreased levels of enjoyment and expressed the belief that the possession of superior ability results in success. More recent work in the athletic domain (e.g., Kavassanu & Roberts, 1996; Newton & Duda, in press; Walling, Duda, & Chi, 1993) has extended work on the perceived motivational climate to different samples and additional indices of motivation. In total, this literature suggests that task-involving environments are conducive to motivation whereas strongly ego-involving situations relate to lower satisfaction and confidence and greater stress among athletes.

Links Between Goal Perspectives and Constructs From the Mediational Model of Leadership

Central to the Mediational Model of Leadership (Smoll & Smith, 1989) are the social reinforcements perceived to be provided by coaches. According to goal-perspective theory (Ames, 1992; Nicholls, 1989), this facet of the social environment surrounding athletes has motivational significance. In particular, the nature, frequency, and bases of the social reinforcements exhibited by coaches contribute to their creating a climate that encourages more or less task involvement and ego involvement.

To date, one study has attempted to examine the social reinforcements of coaches according to the Smoll and Smith (1989) protocol and the conceptual lens provided by goal-perspective theory. Employing an adapted version of the CBAS, Chaumeton and Duda (1988) determined variations in coaches' behaviors as a function of the situation (i.e., competition versus practice) and level of competition. Smith and Smoll's CBAS distinguishes between the reactive behaviors of positive and negative reinforcements in regard to positive or negative performance in general. In this study, the CBAS was modified so that the positive reinforcements and punishments given by the coach were distinguished in terms of whether they were directed at the process (i.e., task execution, exerted effort) or outcome (e.g., points scored) of players' desirable and undesirable behaviors. Although the dimensions underlying perceptions of the motivational climate go beyond social reinforcement patterns (Ames, 1992; Duda & Whitehead, 1998), it was suggested that the former bases for reinforcements would promote a task-involving environment whereas a sporting climate marked by outcome-based social reinforcements would foster greater ego involvement among the athletes.

In the Chaumeton and Duda (1988) investigation, four elementary, junior high, and high school boys' varsity basketball coaches were observed during two practices and two competitive games. Given the more evaluative and social comparative nature of competition versus training sessions, it was expected that coach behaviors would vary as a function of the context (as was also found by Horn, 1984, and Wandzilak, Ansorage, & Potter, 1986). In particular, it was hypothesized that more ego-involving social reinforcements would be observed in game situations. A competitive-level effect was also expected. Similar to what has been observed in the classroom (Eccles, Midgley, & Adler, 1984), the demonstration of more ego-involving social reinforcements was predicted for the coaches at the more advanced levels where the "stakes" are assumed to be greater.

Chaumeton and Duda (1988) administered a questionnaire that assessed the coaches' personal emphasis on skill development versus winning and their perceptions of their athletes' concern with such goal criteria. The 124 basketball players also indicated their focus on task- versus ego-involved goals.

The Chaumeton and Duda (1988) findings indicated that among the higher competitive-level coaches (i.e., those at the junior and senior high level), there was a higher frequency of outcome-based reinforcements during competition than during the practice sessions. Regardless of the context, coaches of elementary teams reinforced the athletes' processes more often and reinforced on the basis of outcome less often than did the higher level coaches.

Compatible with the observational data, the goal perspectives emphasized in interscholastic boys' basketball seemed to become more ego involving with an increase in competitive level. In their personal goals and perceptions of their athletes' goals, high school coaches stressed winning more than the junior high and elementary team coaches did. Moreover, junior and senior high basketball players rated winning as a more salient goal than did the elementary-level players.

In general, the results of the Chaumeton and Duda (1988) investigation suggest that the social reinforcements provided by coaches can be examined in a way that has meaning from the standpoint of goal perspective theory. Moreover, as assumed in the mediational model of leadership and the goal perspective framework, there is a consistency between how individuals (in this case, coaches) act and the goals they deem significant in the context at hand.

Links Between Goal Perspectives and Constructs From the Multidimensional Model of Leadership

Recent research has begun to ascertain the links between athletes' goal orientations, their perceptions of the task- and ego-involving features of the team environment created by the coach, and their perceptions of and preferences for leader behaviors. Grounded in goal-perspective theory and the Multidimensional Model of Leadership, Balaguer and her colleagues (Balaguer, Crespo, & Duda, 1996a, 1996b; Balaguer, Duda, Atienza, & Mayo, 1998; Balaguer, Duda, & Mayo, 1997) have examined the associations between goal perspectives, leadership style, subjective performance, satisfaction, and coach ratings in the sports of tennis and handball. In particular, one purpose of their research was to examine both dispositional and situationally emphasized goals in relation to athletes' perceptions of the leadership style exhibited by coaches and their preferences for certain leadership behaviors. A second objective of these investigations was to determine the relationship of the perceived motivational climate created by the coach to athletes' perceptions of improvement, satisfaction and evaluation of their coach.

The sample in the first study (Balaguer, Crespo, & Duda, 1996a, 1996b) comprised 219 tennis players from clubs around Spain (73 females and 116 males) with a mean age of 15.6 ± 2.1 years. These athletes represented the intermediate (32.1%), advanced (56.6%), and professional (11.3%) levels of tennis competition. The subjects in the second study (Balaguer et al., 1998; Balaguer et al., 1997) were 181 female handball players from 14 teams participating in a national handball competition in Spain. The athletes were between 17 and 34 years of age (*M* age = 21.75 ± 3.7 years).

A multi section inventory was administered in both investigations that contained a Spanish version (Balaguer, Castillo, & Tomas, 1996) of the Task and Ego Orientation in Sport Questionnaire (Duda, 1989); a Spanish version (Balaguer, Guivernau, Duda, & Crespo, 1997) of the Perceived Motivational Climate in Sport Questionnaire-2 (PMCSQ-2; Newton & Duda, 1993), which was completed specific to tennis or handball, assessments of perceived improvement, satisfaction, and coach ratings; and the Spanish version (Balaguer, Crespo, & Duda, 1996a) of the 40-item Leadership Scale for Sports (LSS; Chelladurai & Saleh, 1980). Both the preferred and perceived leadership versions of the LSS were completed by the athletes. Across the two studies, factor analyses of the two measures of leadership behavior resulted in two stable dimensions only, that is, Training and Instruction and Social Support. Consistent with the operational definitions provided by Chelladurai (1993), Training and Instruction were defined as coaching behaviors aimed at improving the athletes' performance by emphasizing and facilitating hard and strenuous training; instructing them in skills, techniques, and tactics of the sport; clarifying the relationship among members; and structuring and coordinating members' activities. On the other hand, Social Support was defined as coaching behaviors characterized by a concern for the welfare of individual athletes, a positive group atmosphere, and warm interpersonal relations with members.

Perceived Climate and Perceived/Preferred Leadership

Simple correlations (Table 11.1) indicated that the climate created by the tennis and handball coaches was significantly related to both facets of leadership behavior (i.e., preferred and perceived). When the players perceived that their coach created a more task-involving environment, they perceived that their coach provided higher levels of training and instruction and social support. Athletes in a task-involving environment also indicated a greater preference for their coaches to exhibit such leadership behaviors.

Table 11.1. Correlations between perceptions of the motivational climate and athletes' perceptions of and preferences for dimensions of coaches' leadership style.

	TASK CLIMATE		EGO CLIMATE	
	Tennis	Handball	Tennis	Handball
PREFERRED LEADERSHIP				
Training and Instruction	.36***	.13	-.21**	-.07
Social Support	.38***	.31***	.08	-.11
PERCEIVED LEADERSHIP				
Training and Instruction	.56***	.57***	-.32***	-.35***
Social Support	.46***	.19*	-.21**	-.19**

Note: *$p < .05$; **$p < .01$; ***$p < .001$

Perceptions of an ego-involving atmosphere on the team was negatively associated with the tennis and handball athletes' sense that their coach demonstrated concern for them as a person (Social Support) and was interested in and acted in a way that facilitated performance improvement (Training and Instruction). Among the tennis players particularly, the perception of an ego- involving climate was also negatively associated with the preference for instruction and challenging, strenuous training from their coaches.

Goal Orientations and Perceived/Preferred Leadership

Conceptually logical associations also emerged in terms of the links between individual differences in goal orientations and perceptions of and preferences for leadership behaviors (see Table 11.2). When tennis players were higher in task orientation, they indicated that they perceived and preferred more training and instruction and social support. Highly ego-oriented tennis players indicated a greater preference for a supportive coach.

Consistent with what was observed among the tennis players, task orientation was significantly and positively related to the handball players' preference for training and instruction from the coach.

Perceived Climate, Subjective Improvement, Satisfaction, and Coach Ratings

In Balaguer and colleagues' research focused on tennis and handball (Bala-

Table 11.2. Correlations between goal orientations and athletes' perceptions of and preferences for dimensions of the coaches' leadership style.

	TASK ORIENTATION		EGO ORIENTATION	
	Tennis	Handball	Tennis	Handball
PREFERRED LEADERSHIP				
Training and Instruction	.29***	.27***	-.08	-.03
Social Support	.22	.11	.20*	.09
PERCEIVED LEADERSHIP				
Training and Instruction	.29***	.10	-.04	.03
Social Support	.27***	.07	.01	.10

Note: *$p < .05$; **$p < .01$; ***$p < .001$

guer, Crespo, & Duda, 1996b; Balaguer et al., 1998), players evaluated their improvement over the season specific to the tactical, technical, physical, and psychological dimensions of their game and in terms of their overall competitive results. The athletes' degree of satisfaction with their recent results, level of play, and the instruction received from their coach was also assessed. Because they participate in a team sport, the handball players reported their perceived improvement and satisfaction in terms of their own play and in regard to the team. Finally, both groups of athletes indicated their preference for their present coach and rated his or her importance in their training.

Simple correlations (Table 11.3) indicated that a perceived task-involving climate was positively linked to perceived improvement for the tennis players and, especially, the handball athletes. Specifically, we found that tennis players who perceived that their coaches created a more task-involving environment reported greater tactical, technical, psychological, and overall improvement in their competitive results. A similar and stronger pattern of associations emerged for the handball players in terms of their own and team performance. If the environment created by the coach was deemed to be more task involving, handball players also perceived greater personal and team improvement in the physical aspects of their sport.

In general, the tennis and handball players were more satisfied with their game results, level of play, and their coach (at the individual and team level) when the motivational climate was viewed as more task involving (Table 11.3).

Table 11.3. Correlations between perceptions of the motivational climate and perceived improvement, satisfaction and coach ratings among competitive tennis players and elite women handball teams.

	MOTIVATIONAL CLIMATE			
	TASK CLIMATE		EGO CLIMATE	
	TENNIS	HANDBALL	TENNIS	HANDBALL
PERCEIVED IMPROVEMENT				
TACTICAL	.13*	.38*** *.44****	-.03	-.09 *-.02*
TECHNICAL	.14*	.33*** *.38****	-.10	-.04 *.07*
PHYSICAL	.02	.43*** *.37****	.07	.03 *.12*
PSYCHOLOGICAL	.26***	.29*** *.22***	-.05	-.08 *-.04*
GENERAL RESULTS	.17*	.30*** *.12*	-.07	-.07 *.11*
SATISFACTION				
SATISFACTION WITH RESULTS	.23***	.09	-.16* *.15**	.07 *.20***
SATISFACTION WITH LEVEL OF PLAY	.23***	.21** *.27****	-.13*	.11 *.11*
SATISFACTION WITH THE COACH	.41***	.45*** *.43****	-.41***	-.30*** *-.18**
COACH RATINGS				
COACH THAT IS PREFERRED	.32***	.35***	-.33***	-.30***
IMPORTANCE OF COACH IN TRAINING PROCESS	.32***	.35***	-.35***	-.24**

NOTE: * $p < .05$; ** $p < .01$; *** $p < .001$; Regular = Individual athlete and ***Bold Italic*** = Team

Both groups of athletes were less satisfied with their coach if they perceived the coach-created environment to be ego involving. However, perceptions of an ego-involving climate positively related to handball players' satisfaction ratings regarding the team's competitive results and level of play.

The results of the studies of Balaguer and associates (Balaguer, Crespo, & Duda, 1996a; Balaguer et al., 1998) further reinforced the relevance of the perceived motivational climate in regard to the opinion that athletes have about their coach (Table 11.3). When both groups of athletes perceived that their coaches emphasized a task-involving environment, they were more likely to indicate that their present coach was like the coach they would prefer to have and felt that their coach was important in the training process. On the other hand, perceptions of an ego-involving climate were negatively associated with these two coach ratings for both the tennis and handball players.

Consistent with the proposals of Smith et al. (1978, 1979) and Chelladurai and Riemer (1998), the results of these investigations by Balaguer and colleagues indicate that athletes' goal orientations relate to their perceptions of the actions of their coach and their degree of satisfaction with those actions. Similarly, athletes' degree of task and orientation corresponds to what they would like their coaches to do, particularly in terms of the amount of training and instruction and social support provided. As would be suggested from the tenets of goal-perspective theory (Ames, 1992; Nicholls, 1989), the research by Balaguer and associates further suggests that coaches act differently in environments that should foster task rather than ego involvement. Based on this work, there appears to be a logical congruence between facets of leadership style (as conceptualized in Chelladurai's [1993] model) and situationally emphasized goal perspectives (as conceptualized in goal-perspective theory). In short, when coaches emphasize rigorous training, provide high levels of instruction, and care for the overall welfare of their athletes, they are creating motivational climates that are more task involving and less ego involving.

A Proposed Integrated Model

In Figure 11.3, a model is presented that combines elements, central variables, and predicted relationships emanating from the work of Smith and Smoll (Smith et al., 1979, 1983; Smoll & Smith, 1989), Chelladurai (1993; Chelladurai & Riemer, 1998) and the tenets of goal-perspective theory (Ames, 1992; Nicholls, 1989). Aligned with both the mediational and multidimensional models of leadership, the proposed integrated model places emphasis on athletes' perceptions of the behaviors exhibited by their coaches. It also considers actual coach behaviors (which are objectively assessed by external observers; see Smith et al., 1983). The integrated model incorporates the construct of preferred coach behavior/climate that is fundamental to Chelladurai's (1991) leadership model. As reinforced in Smoll and Smith's (1989) framework, it is assumed that perceptions of the atmosphere created by one's coach mediates the effect of the coach's objective behaviors and the athlete's preferences concerning his or her coach's actions.

A major extension of the two major theories of sport leadership incorporated in the integrated model is that the environment manifested via coaches' actual behaviors, perceived behaviors, and athletes' preferences concerning

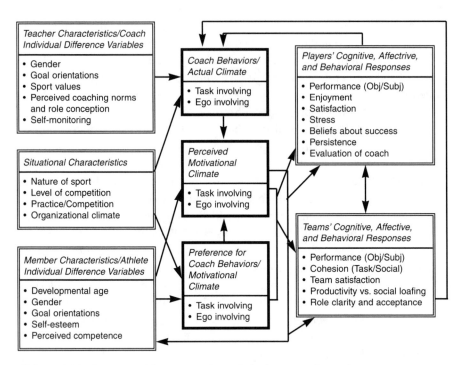

Figure 11.3. Proposed integrated model of antecedents/consequences of coach leadership.

those behaviors is conceptualized in terms of its task- and ego-involving features. It is emphasized that leader behavior should be distinguished in a manner concerning its implications for variability in the cognitive and affective processes that impact athletes' short- and long-term motivated behavior. Stemming from previous research based on the mediational and multidimensional models of leadership and goal-perspective theory, task-involving behaviors exhibited by the coach would include teaching and instruction (especially following mistakes), social support, positive feedback following desirable performance, and social reinforcements tied to the performance process and exertion of effort. In contrast, ego-involving behaviors of the coach would encompass more controlling behaviors, punitive responses to mistakes and, in general, social reinforcements based on outcome criteria.

Compatible with the mediational and multidimensional models of leadership, our proposed integrated framework includes coach individual difference variables/leader characteristics, situational factors, and athlete individual difference variables/member characteristics as critical antecedent variables. The former two are hypothesized to influence the coach's actual behaviors whereas the latter variable is assumed to impact athletes' perceptions of and preferences for their coaches' behaviors. It is indicated that aspects of the situation (e.g., practice versus competition) would also affect athletes' preferences concerning how their coaches should act.

With reference to both the coach and athlete individual difference components, the proposed framework specifically includes the variable of goal orientations. Moreover, pulling from the tenets of goal-perspective theory (Ames, 1992; Dweck, 1986; Nicholls, 1989), athletes' perceived ability is listed as another critical person factor.

The framework depicted in Figure 11.3 acknowledges, as considered in the Chelladurai (1990) model, that the degree of congruence between athletes' preferences for and perceptions of their coaches' behaviors may impact their motivation. However, consonant with goal-perspective theory (Ames, 1992; Dweck, 1986; Nicholls, 1989), it is also assumed that variations in individual and/or team motivational patterns will result as a function of an interaction between athlete individual difference variables (in particular, athletes' goal orientations, perceptions of ability) and perceptions of the motivational climate operating on one's team. Pulling from the research of Newton and Duda (in press), positive achievement patterns should emerge if the athletes are strongly task oriented and/or the perceived environment is definitely task involving. Negative motivation would be expected when ego orientation prevails and the team climate is perceived to be highly ego involving (especially when the athletes doubt their competence). As embedded in the two existent models of leadership behavior, the proposed integrated framework also contains a feedback loop suggesting that the cognitive, affective, and behavioral responses of athletes and teams may influence coaches' subsequent behavior.

Finally, in terms of players'/teams' cognitive, affective, and behavioral responses, the present model includes a listing of variables that have been linked in the literature with situationally emphasized and/or dispositional goal perspectives (see Duda, 1994, 1996; Duda & Whitehead, 1998, for reviews), the social reinforcements of coaches as revealed in the work of Smith, Smoll and associates (Smith et al., 1979, 1983; Smoll et al., 1978), and preferred-perceived leader behavior congruencies as demonstrated in research based on the multidimensional model (Chelladurai, 1993; Chelladurai & Riemer, 1998).

Conclusions and Future Directions

Research stemming from the Mediational Model of Leadership (Smith et al., 1978, 1979) has provided a wealth of information concerning the salience of coaches' social-reinforcement patterns as well as the bases for changing coaches' behaviors so that they will be more effective. Work steeped in the

Multidimensional Model of Leadership (Chelladurai, 1993) affords greater awareness of the dimensions of leadership style and the relevance of particular facets of leader behavior and their interrelationships to athletes' performance and satisfaction. An abundance of studies grounded in goal-perspective theory have informed us concerning the motivational implications of the goals athletes adopt and the role of the coach in promoting task versus ego involvement in sport. A conceptual framework is presented in this paper that attempts to pull together concepts and relationships from the three lines of work. We encourage future investigations that explore, test, and extend the proposed integrated model of leadership and motivation in sport.

References

Ames, C. (1984). Competitive, cooperative and individualistic goal structures: A motivational analysis. In R. Ames & C. Ames (Eds.), *Research on motivation in education: Student motivation* (pp. 177–207). New York: Academic Press.

Ames, C. (1992). Achievement goals, motivational climate, and motivational processes. In G. Roberts (Ed.), *Motivation in sport and exercise* (pp. 161–176). Champaign, IL: Human Kinetics.

Ames, C., & Archer, J. (1988). Achievement goals in the classroom: Students' learning strategies and motivation processes. *Journal of Educational Psychology, 80,* 260–267.

Balaguer, I., Castillo, I., & Tomas, I. (1996). Analisis del Cuestionario de Orientacion al Ego y a la Tarea en el Deporte (TEOSQ) en su traduccion al castellano. *Psicologica, 17,* 71–81.

Balaguer, I., Crespo, M., & Duda. J.L. (1996a). Dispositional goal perspectives and perceptions of the motivational climate as predictor of coach ratings, satisfaction and perceived improvement among competitive club tennis players. *Journal of Applied Sport Psychology, 8* (Supple.), S13.

Balaguer, I., Crespo, M., & Duda, J.L. (1996b). The relationship of motivational climate and athletes' goal orientation to perceived/preferred leadership style. *Journal of Sport and Exercise Psychology, 18* (Supple.), S13.

Balaguer, I., Duda, J.L., Atienza, F.L., & Mayo, C. (1998,August). *Motivational climate as a predictor of individual and team improvement and satisfaction among elite female handball players.* Paper presented at the meetings of the International Congress of Applied Psychology, San Francisco.

Balaguer, I., Duda, J.L., and Mayo, C. (1997). The relationship of goal orientations and the perceived motivational climate to coaches' leadership style in competitive handball. *Proceedings of the IXth World Congress of Sport Psychology* (pp. 94–96). Netanya, Israel: Wingate Institute.

Balaguer, I., Guivernau, M., Duda, J.L., & Crespo, M. (1997). Analisis de la validez de constructo y de la validez predictiva del cuestionario de clima motivacional percibido en el deporte (PMCSQ-2) con tenistas espanoles de competicion. *Revista de Psicologia del Deporte, 11,* 41–57.

Barnett, N., Smith, R.L., & Smoll, F. (1992). Effects of enhancing coach-athlete relationships on youth sport attrition. *The Sport Psychologist, 6,* 111–127.

Chaumeton, N.R., & Duda, J.L. (1988). Is it how you play the game or whether you win or lose? The effect of competitive level and situation on coaching behaviors. *Journal of Sport Behavior, 11,* 157–173.

Chelladurai, P. (1984). Discrepancy between preferences and perceptions of leadership behavior and satisfaction of athletes in varying sports. *Journal of Sport Psychology, 6,* 27–41.

Chelladurai, P. (1990). Leadership in sports: A review. *International Journal of Sport Psychology, 21,* 328–354.

Chelladurai, P. (1993). Leadership. In R. N. Singer, M. Murphy, & L.K. Tennant (Eds.). *Handbook of research on sport psychology* (pp. 647–671). New York: McMillan.

Chelladurai, P., & Carron, A.V. (1981). Task characteristics and individual differences and their relationship to preferred leadership in sport. *Psychology of Motor Behavior and Sport-1982* (p.87). College Park, MD: North American Society for the Psychology of Sport and Physical Activity.

Chelladurai, P., & Carron, A.V. (1983). Athletic maturity and preferred leadership. *Journal of Sport Psychology, 5,* 371–380.

Chelladurai, P., Imamura, K., Yamaguchi, Y., Oinuma, Y., & Miyauchi, T. (1988). Sport leadership in a cross-national setting: The case of Japanese and Canadian university athletes. *Journal of Sport and Exercise Psychology, 10,* 374–389.

Chelladurai, P. & Riemer, H.A. (1998). Measurement of leadership in sport. In J.L. Duda (Ed.), *Advances in sport and exercise psychology measurement* (pp. 227–256). Morgantown, WV: Fitness Information Technology.

Chelladurai, P., & Saleh, S.D. (1978). Preferred leadership in sports. *Canadian Journal of Applied Sport Sciences, 3,* 85–92.

Chelladurai, P., & Saleh, S.D. (1980). Dimensions of leader behavior in sports: Development of a leadership scale. *Journal of Sport Psychology, 2,* 34–45.

Duda, J.L. (1989). Relationship between task and ego orientation and the perceived purpose of sport among high school athletes. *Journal of Sport and Exercise Psychology, 11,* 318–335.

Duda, J.L. (1994). A goal perspective theory of meaning and motivation in sport. In S. Serpa, J. Alves, & V. Pataco (Eds.), *International perspectives on sport and exercise psychology* (pp. 127–148). Morgantown, WV: Fitness Information Technology.

Duda, J.L. (1996). Maximizing motivation in sport and physical education among children and adolescents: The case for greater task involvement. *Quest, 48,* 290–302.

Duda, J.L., & Whitehead, J. (1998). Measurement of goal perspectives in the physical domain. In J.L. Duda (Ed.), *Advances in sport and exercise psychology measurement* (pp. 21–48). Morgantown, WV: Fitness Information Technology.

Dweck, C.S. (1986). Motivational processes affecting learning. *American Psychologist, 41,* 1040–1048.

Eccles, J., Midgley, C., & Adler, T. (1984). Grade-related changes in the school environment: Effects on achievement motivation. In J. Nicholls (Ed.), *The development of achievement motivation* (pp. 280–332). Greenwich, CT: JAI Press.

Garland, D.L., & Barry, J.R. (1988). The effects of personality and perceived leader behavior on performance in collegiate football. *The Psychological Record, 38,* 237–247.

Horn, T.S. (1984). Expectancy effects in the interscholastic setting: Methodological considerations. *Journal of Sport Psychology, 6,* 60–76.

Kavussanu, M., & Roberts, G.C. (1996). Motivation in physical activity context: The relationship of perceived motivational climate to intrinsic motivation and self efficacy. *Journal of Sport and Exercise Psychology, 18,* 264–280.

Newton, M.L., & Duda, J.L. (in press). The interaction of motivational climate, dispositional goal orientation, and perceived ability in predicting indices of motivation. *International Journal of Sport Psychology.*

Nicholls, J.G. (1984). Conceptions of ability and achievement motivation. In R. Ames & C. Ames (Eds.), *Research on motivation in education: Vol. 1 Student motivation.* New York: Academic Press.

Nicholls, J.G. (1989). *The competitive ethos and democratic education.* Cambridge, MA: Harvard University Press.

Porter, I.W., & Lawler, E.E. (1968). *Managerial attitudes and performance.* Homewood, IL: Richard D. Irwin Press.

Riemer, H.A., & Chelladurai, P. (1995). Leadership and satisfaction in athletics. *Journal of Sport and Exercise Psychology, 17,* 276–293.

Schlieshman, E.S. (1987). Relationship between the congruence of preferred and actual leader behavior and subordinate satisfaction with leadership. *Journal of Sport Behavior, 10,* 157–166.

Seifriz, J.J., Duda, J.L., & Chi, L. (1992). The relationship of perceived motivational climate to intrinsic motivation and beliefs about success in basketball. *Journal of Sport and Exercise Psychology, 14,* 375–391.

Smith, R.E., Smoll, F.L., & Curtis, B. (1978). Coaching behaviors in Little League baseball. In F.L. Smoll & R.E. Smith (Eds.), *Psychological perspectives on youth sports* (pp. 173–201). Washington, DC: Hemisphere.

Smith, R.E., Smoll, F.L., & Curtis, B. (1979). Coach effectiveness training: A cognitive-behavioral approach to enhancing relationship skills in youth sport coaches. *Journal of Sport Psychology, 1,* 59–75.

Smith, R.E., Zane, N.W.S., Smoll, F.L., & Coppel, D.B. (1983). Behavioral assessment in youth sports: Coaching behaviors and children's attitudes. *Medicine and Science in Sport and Exercise, 15,* 208–214.

Smoll, F.L., & Smith, R.E. (1989). Leadership behaviors in sport: A theoretical model and research paradigm. *Journal of Applied Social Psychology, 19,* 1522–1551.

Smoll, F.L., Smith, R.E., Curtis, B., & Hunt, E. (1978). Toward a mediational model of the coach-player relationship. *Research Quarterly, 49,* 528–541.

Walling, M., Duda, J.L., & Chi, L. (1993). The Perceived Motivational Climate in Sport Questionnaire: Construct and predictive validity. *Journal of Sport and Exercise Psychology, 15,* 172–183.

Wandzilak, T., Ansorage, C.J., & Potter, G. (1986, April). *Comparison of selected behaviors and the perceptions of behaviors of youth sport coaches between practice and game settings.* Paper presented at the Annual Meeting of the American Alliance for Health, Physical Education and Recreation, Cincinnati, OH.

Weiss, M.R., & Friedrichs, W.D. (1986). The influence of leader behaviors, coach attributes, and institutional variables on performance and satisfaction of collegiate basketball teams. *Journal of Sport Psychology, 8,* 332–346.

12

The Presentation and Modulation of Emotions

Dieter Hackfort
University FD Munich, Germany

Introduction

After a period of time in which psychologists predominantly have been interested in what is going on in unconsciousness and in clarifying what kind of stimuli will lead to what kind of reactions in the '60s, there was a shift in paradigm and a focus on cognitive processes. In the '80s, there seemed to be a neglect of emotions in psychological research and theory, which a few psychologists deplored. However, already anxiety and stress-related emotions are becoming a main focus in research in sport psychology. This fact seems to indicate either that sport psychologists are now up-to-date or that emotions are of special importance in sports settings; perhaps both of these statements are true.

It is a fundamental endeavor of my contributions for a decade (see, e.g., Hackfort, 1989, 1991a, b; Hackfort & Schwenkmezger, 1993) that "positive" as well as "negative" emotions can have both benefits and costs with respect to action regulation and, consequently, performance. I would like to advance these ideas and to provide

1. A brief discussion of what is meant when talking about "positive" and "negative" emotions from an action theory perspective, and
2. Selected findings from actual research on emotion presentation.
3. Finally, a brief hint on a strategy that actually is in the process of development for influencing the emotional state, what we call emotion modulation, and the effects on motivation and performance factors.

The purpose of this contribution is not to give a detailed report on a single study dealing with one special problem but to provide information on our recent research on emotions in sports.

An Action Theory Approach
for a Functional Analysis of Emotions

To talk about "positive" or "negative" emotions is very common in everyday life and language. It refers predominantly to the actual state and the quality of the present feeling—if it is pleasant or unpleasant, comfortable or uncomfortable. In theory, this is somewhat misleading, and emotions must be differentiated with regard to categorical differentiations and their functional meaning with respect to the process of action regulation. The categories "positive" and "negative" on the one hand refer to the emotional state, which is represented by pleasant and unpleasant feelings. On the other hand, "positve" and "negative" refer to processes closely connected with action regulation (organization and control of intentional, purposive behavior). For example, worries as they are characteristic for anxiety may be "negative" for action-regulation processes as they are debilitating or disturbing agents that lead to a loss of concentration, but—at the same point in time—anxiety may be "positive" for action regulation by initiating security strategies and facilitating motivation for further exertion. Figure 12.1 provides an overview of these aspects.

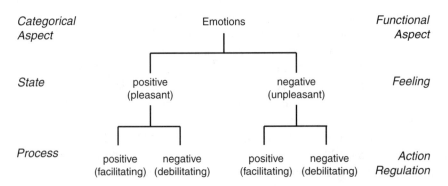

Figure 12.1. Aspects of emotions.

Emotions appear in all three phases of an action: anticipation phase, realization phase, and interpretation phase (see Hackfort, 1991a). Here the focus is on the realization phase and the meaning of emotions when they rise during sports activities. Take, as an example, a soccer player who scores an important goal. Play, then, is influenced by emotions if that soccer player, who is overjoyed about the goal, then neglects his task as a marker. It is often observed in sports that a soccer team that has just scored a goal has to concede a goal shortly afterwards. Or a young athlete who within a very short period of time shows brilliant performance, is praised excessively by the press and celebrated as a new star, but whose performance then drops to average standard. On the other hand there are several reports on athletes "surpassing themselves" if, for example, an audience is wholeheartedly behind them. There are athletes who are able to provoke this audience reaction, for instance, Jimmy Connors, who "orchestrates the crowd," as Gilbert (see Gilbert & Jamison, 1993, p. 19) has called it. When trying to emphasize the functional meanings of emotions as they are illustrated in these examples on the basis of appropriate theoretical approaches, different relations of emotions can be distinguished, for example, emotion and concentration on the task at hand, or emotion and motivation. However, it has to be pointed out that "emotion," "cognition," and "motivation" are categorical classifications and can only be differentiated analytically (for a discussion on definitional problems, see Hackfort, 1987) from a functional-analyses perspective; in real-life situations emotional, cognitive, and motivational processes are interrelated.

Furthermore, a mere differentiation of positive and negative emotions with regard to general functioning is misleading and it is necessary to consider various influences of emotions on the process of organizing and controlling actions. In this respect a certain ("differential" or "fundamental"; see, e.g., Izard, 1977; Plutchik, 1962) emotion may have functional or dysfunctional meaning, facilitating or debilitating influence on action regulation, depending on its intensity and dominance in the regimen of actual emotions. There are very few situations in which only one emotion is experienced and of functional influence in the action-regulation process. Usually in everyday life situations a mixture of different emotions will be experienced. This leads to different influences on the action-regulation process and the process of behavioral organization; and may have synergetic or dissociative effects, or both effects at the same point in time with respect to different subsystems of action regulation (e.g., cognitive and sensorimotor subsystem; for further hints and explanations with special reference to anxiety, see Hackfort, 1987; Hackfort & Schwenkmezger, 1993). For instance, Alpert and Haber (1960) have discussed facilitating and debilitating effects of anxiety focussing on performance outcome but neglecting the process of action regulation. Their contribution initiated discussions not only in test anxiety research but also in research on anxiety in sport psychology (see Hackfort & Schwenkmezger, 1993). Anxiety may have facilitating effects on activation and energy expenditure and debilitating effects on concentration and attention control. Both influences may occur at the same point in time, and the situation will even become more complex when not only anxiety is experienced but also for instance, pride or a mixture of anxiety, anger, and pride.

Emotions are regarded as relatively short-term processes whereas longer lasting states are characterized as mood. Out of a Gestalt psychology perspective the relation between mood and emotion is like that of background and figure: The actual emotion is the figure on the background of mood. Emotions are closely connected with the individual definition of the situation (based on the individual perception and subjective evaluation of the person-task-environment constellation by that person) by the acting person. Further differentiations and theoretical conceptualizations have to consider that emotions are interrelated with cognitions and that there is a large body of evidence for the influence of cognitions on emotional processes and the influence of emotions on cognitive processes. It seems, on the one hand, that the relation between emotion and cognition is not a unidirectional but interdependent one. On the other hand, causality may not be the (only) appropriate concept for explaining the cognition-emotion relationship. Emotions cannot be regarded (only) as causes or effects but (also) as representations of the individual significance of the person-environment-task constellation as it is coming up with the interpretation of that constellation in the situation definition (see Hackfort, 1987).

Research Report

Research on Emotion Presentation

Competitive situations for elite athletes are social situations: how one presents one's self (self-presentation) to spectators and in relation with an opponent is characteristic of these situations. This includes a specific demand (task that might be regarded as a threat or challenge) to the athlete that is closely linked with the experience and expression of emotions. A good example of evidence for this is Boris Becker—the best known German athlete at present. In the final of the Wimbledon tennis championship on July 7, 1991, Boris Becker and Michael Stich, the two German finalists that year, gave an excellent demonstration of experiencing emotions during the match, expressing and not expressing the felt emotions, and influencing oneself and the opponent by doing so. When asked about the reasons for his sensational victory, Michael Stich said that Boris Becker's fits of rage had given him enormous energy. Stich did not demonstrate his emotions during the match; and especially suppressed his upcoming enjoyment, but he did so very much after the match, expressing his enjoyment and demonstrating his pride.

The following report of the results of our investigations on the experience and presentation of emotions is based on differentiations for a functional analysis from an action theory perspective (see Hackfort, 1987, 1991; Hackfort & Schlattmann, 1991), which is outlined in Figure 12.2. The presentation of an emotion is regarded as an intentional expression of that emotion and a suppression of an emotion would be a nonpresentation. Furthermore, not-experienced emotions may be expressed. The presentation of experienced and the intentional expression of not-experienced emotions are regarded as emotion demonstration.

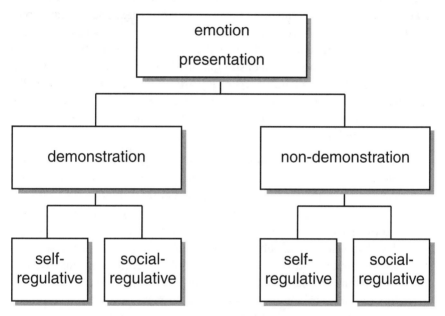

Figure 12.2. Functions of emotion presentation.

The special procedure we used to analyze functional meanings of emotion presentation is the video-stimulated self-commentary method (see Hackfort, 1989). This method is based on videotapes of the preceding actions of the person during a competition. The athlete is confronted with these tapes after the competition (usually some hours, a day, or maximum a week later) and asked to report on his emotions. Further details of this procedure and these studies are reported elsewhere (see Hackfort, 1995; Schlattmann & Hackfort, 1991).

At first it becomes obvious that not only can the personal experience of emotions lead to or contribute to effects that stimulate or restrict an athlete's performance (e.g., the feeling of anger is able to activate further energy and hence improve performance when energy expenditure is necessary to be successful at that task). But, second, also the (maybe even unexpected lack of) perception of emotions of interacting persons influences action regulation and performance (e.g., the perception of anger in the opponent may lead to further motivation, exertion, and performance improvement, whereas the lack of expected expressions of anger may be irritating and reduce achievement motivation). These functional meanings have been reconstructed by the verbal data from the self-commentaries of the athletes who participated in the study and were confronted with videotapes. Therefore, these findings have to be considered as attributions of functional meanings of emotions by athletes with special reference to the presentation of experienced or nonexperienced emotions.

On the background of the action-regulation concept, it was possible to detect a further differentiation in the verbal data with respect to the (attribution of) functional meaning of demonstration or nondemonstration of emotions. For instance, the effusive transports of joy after a successful goal can be differentiated according to the self-regulative (such as diversion of arousal) and the social-regulative functional meaning (such as intimidation of opponents). These two functional aspects can be described as follows:

1. *Self-regulative* emotion presentation is accomplished by demonstrating emotions to reduce arousal, the intensity of that emotion, and to thus modify the quality of the emotion. Sometimes emotions are demonstrated that are different from those that are experienced in a certain situation. This strategy serves to overcome those emotions (e.g., anxiety). The demonstration of self-security or self-confidence seems to be an effective strategy to overcome feelings of insecurity and anxiety. Not demonstrating emotions that are being experienced serves to prevent loss of concentration in an athlete. Furthermore, the public and private (self-) image is protected against doubts.

2. *Social-regulative* emotion presentation is accomplished by demonstrating emotions to provoke special reactions in an opponent (e.g., pity and supportive behavior). Not demonstrating emotions that are being experienced serves to irritate the opponent. By athletes' not demonstrating emotions that are present, opponents are deceived or their motivation is weakened. In addition, athletes sometimes avoid to present an emotion that is not present and thus avoid provoking an impression which they don't like and which they fear to be the reason for undesirable social reactions.

Research on Emotion Modulation

Thus far the social aspect of emotions has been emphasized. In further research we are investigating strategies to influence emotions, or, as we call it, "emotion modulation." That is, we are looking for ways to modulate an ambiguous or even "negative" (unpleasant, discomfortable) emotional state and thus influence further mental processes and physiologic processes. The conceptual links of components activated in the emotional process and emotion modulation are briefly summarized in Figure 12.3.

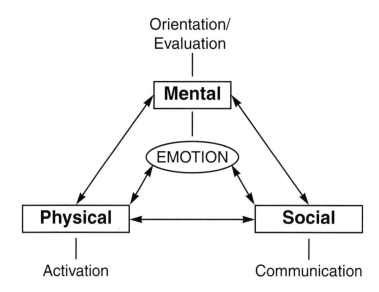

Figure 12.3. Functional components of emotions.

Emotion modulation is different from emotion regulation and emotion control. Emotion regulation is based on feedback processes in a feedback-control system. This feedback refers to a certain emotion or a certain component (e.g., physiological arousal) of that emotion. Emotion regulation may be realized by reducing or intensifying the physiological arousal or activation. Emotion control refers to the intended induction or reduction of a certain emotion by especially organized strategies (e.g., anxiety control strategies; see Hackfort & Schwenkmezger, 1993); that is, emotion control has a monoemotional and (only) quantitative (intensity) orientation. Emotion modulation has a multiemotional and multicomponential (physiological componential, cognitive componential, feeling componential) orientation; that is, it is not only dealing with a single emotion but also with several (sometimes conflicting) emotions, or/and it is dealing with different components and various dimensions. The following three dimensions have to be distinguished: (a) intensity as mintage of one dimension, (b) extensity as effects on different dimensions, (c) persistance as duration of effects.

In this research we are using the video technique as an influencing agent.

We have produced several different video clips regarding sports and emotional quality. We focused on highlights of track and field competitions of various disciplines in the video clip we used for this investigation. The 4.5 minute video clip consists of takes from various precompetition (anticipation phase), in-competition (realization phase), and postcompetition (interpretation phase) situations and was shown in our laboratory to the subjects participating in the study. The study design is illustrated in Table 12.1.

Table 12.1. Design.

Design

t1	t2	t3	t4
Baseline	Performance	and	Ratings
CG	Power	Endurance	Power + Endurance
EG	EMOD + Power	EMOD + Endurance	EMOD + Power + Endurance

CG: n = 10 Students, active in various sports
EG: n = 10 Track and field athletes of various disciplines

The main aim of this investigation was to prove the effectiveness of the strategy of emotion modulation and the consequences for activation (heart rate), mental processes (especially motivation: level of aspiration), and performance. To test this we registered the course of heart rate and collected level of aspiration ratings and actual performance data in an endurance task (ergometer bycycling test; the resistance = watt was raised each 2 minutes by 25 watts, starting with 100 watts) and a power task (weight-lifting test, kilogram was raised by 5 kilograms each step/trial, starting with 30 kilograms). Subjects were male track and field athletes (not top athletes but better than average, n=10, EG), and students competed in a variety of sports (with a sporting experience of ca. 10 years, n=10, CG). There was no age difference between the two groups (M= 25.7, SD= 2.99). An overview of the statistical results is presented in Table 12.2.

Table 12.2. Overview of the statistical results.

	CG		EG		Group		Time		Group x Time	
	M	SD	M	SD	F	p	F	p	F	p
Level of Aspiration (Endurance)	t3: 5,0 t4: 7,5	15,81 23,71	t3 27,5 t4: 32,5	18,45 20,58	9.31	0.01	0.77	0.39	0.09	0.77
Level of Aspiration (Power)	t2: 4,5 t4: 4,0	1,58 5,16	t2: 5,5 t3: 6,5	1,58 3,37	2.67	0.12	0.06	0.81	0.56	0.46
Endurance (watt)	t1: 305,0 t3: 310,0 t4: 307,5	36,89 37,74 47,72	t1: 302,5 t3: 322,5 t4: 322,5	41,58 47,80 47,80	0.11	0.74	5.03	0.04	3.04	0.09
Endurance (sec)	t1: 1038,9 t3: 1056,4 t4: 1034,0	186,51 182,69 212,90	t1: 1032,2 t3: 1113,9 t4: 1116,9	182,55 224,84 209,85	0.19	0.67	4.42	0.05	5.57	0.03
Power (kg)	t1: 63,0 t2: 66,5 t4: 66,0	14,57 14,92 12,20	t1: 63,0 t2: 64,0 t4: 64,5	11,35 11,50 10,92	0.02	0.89	5.83	0.03	0.65	0.43

Recordings of heart rates during the video presentation (continuous data recording with a physio modul system by Natic) showed that the video clip heightened the activation (pulse rate) of the subjects, which firstly is a sign of an activation effect. Even the elevations in HR are not impressive with respect to the absolute amount; in this study the course of heart rate is of importance (and therefore no inferential statistics will be helpful but an inspection of the course of heart rate) especially with respect to curve and its parts corresponding with the phases mentioned above and certain scenes in the videotape. Furthermore, in addition to other effects (verbal reports, expressive behavior that will not be reported here in detail), the course of heart rate gives a hint for an emotion-modulation effect. It may seem surprising, but this effect was repeated in all of the three video sessions (see Figure 12.4); the possible and expected outcome was that there would be a habituation effect instead.

With respect to endurance, the level of aspiration was significantly higher and the performance was higher in the experimental group (see Figure 12.5). This group also improved more than the control group in relation to time (duration) and watt (see Figures 12.6 and 12.7). Both these results are significant.

Course of Heart Rate

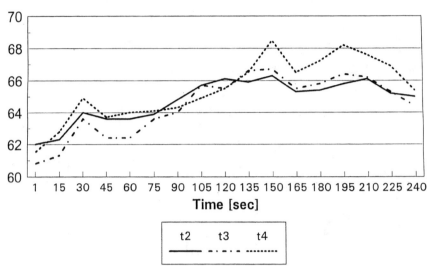

Figure 12.4. Course of heart rate during the three EMOD sessions of the EG.

Level of Aspiration: Endurance

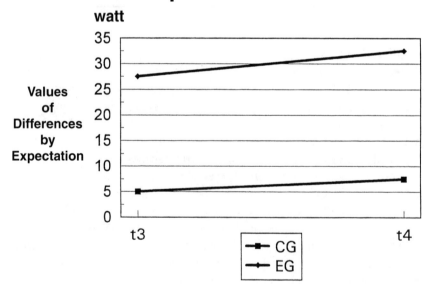

Figure 12.5. Differences in ratings of aspiration with respect to the endurance task.

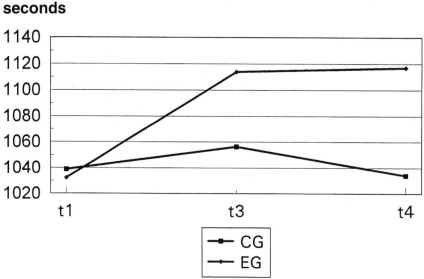

Figure 12.6. Performance in the endurance task (time).

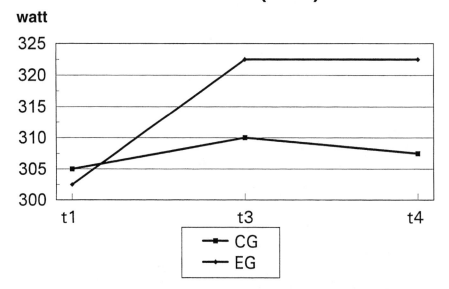

Figure 12.7. Performance in the endurance task (watt).

With regard to power, there was no difference in the level of aspiration between the two groups. No significant changes and no effect of the emotion modulation could be proven, either for motivation or performance (see Figures 12.8 and 12.9). Only a significant effect of time (analyzed by a multiple analysis of variance) indicated that there was an improvement in weight lifting in both groups, which might be attributed to an improvement in technique.

Some results are in line with our hypotheses; some are not. Especially the differential effects in the endurance and power task performance are striking. Before referring to a task specificity and trying to find attributions of possible responsible factors or task characteristics, it should be proven if the differential effects will occur again in comparable studies. Therefore we ran a further study that only should be mentioned as it fits in the research program, which is reported here.

In this study several series of selected slides were tested in their potential for emotion modulation (Hackfort, in press). A series of six slides showing moments of enjoyment in various sports and a further series of six slides showing moments of anger in various sports was selected by experts' ($n=3$) ratings. Each series of slides was shown to students (two groups of 12 male students) who rated the emotional state by a special scale (SBS-scale; Hackfort &

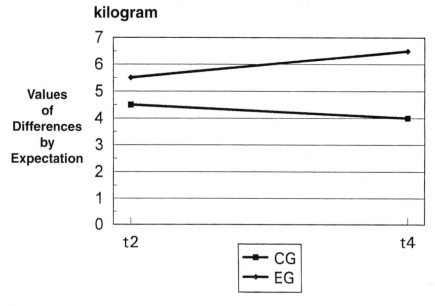

Figure 12.8. Differences in ratings of aspiration with respect to the power task.

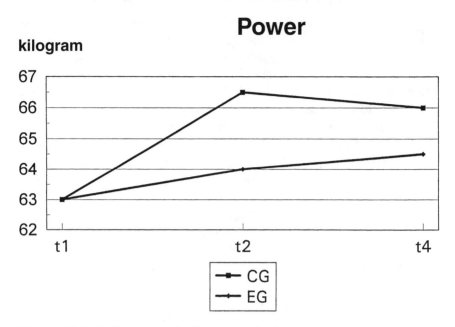

Figure 12.9. Performance in the power task.

Schlattmann, 1995) before and after slide projection to measure emotional changes induced by the slides. After the slide session, the students were asked to remember a situation in which they had feelings like those they saw on the slides. Following the intervention the students had to perform a set of tasks including those reported above (endurance and power task).

The main results of this investigation were (a) that the emotional state could be modulated by this strategy. Especially for enjoyment, strong effects could be proven. (b) Again, performance in the endurance task was heightened (with regard to the baseline testing). This effect was stronger for anger than for enjoyment. (c) No improvement could be proven in the power task, again—neither for anger nor for enjoyment.

Conclusion

In an action theory perspective, the functional meanings of emotions have to be differentiated referring to the process of action regulation in a specific situation. The aspect of emotion presentation has been neglected in sport psychology research on elite athletes despite many top athletes having mentioned this aspect. Our recent studies have given evidence to the self-regulative and social-regulative functional meaning of emotion presentation. Now it is necessary to bring this aspect to the attention of sport psychologists and coaches who work with elite athletes.

A successful strategy to influence emotions can be provided by use of special video clips. The effects on motivation and performance could be proven for track and field athletes regarding level of aspiration and performance in an endurance task. A weight-lifting task did not seem to be an appropriate test to prove the influence of the emotion modulation on power for this group—there was only a slight improvement due to technique. In general, the findings from this study provide evidence that emotions can be influenced by such a strategy (video-induced emotion modulation) and that emotion modulation has positve consequences on motivation and performance with respect to certain tasks. These findings have been supported by an investigation in which emotion modulation has been realized by using slides (slide-assisted emotion modulation). These results should inspire further sport psychology research on emotions and the functional meaning of emotions in sports, as well as on possibilities to influence the experience and presentation of emotions especially according to the application of sport psycholgy considering the various tasks and demands in sports.

References

Alpert, R., & Haber, R.N. (1960). Anxiety in academic achievement situations. *Journal of Abnormal and Social Psychology, 61,* 207–215.

Gilbert, B., & Jamison, S. (1993). *Winning ugly. Mental warfare in tennis—Lessons from a master.* New York: Simon & Schuster.

Hackfort, D. (1987). *Theorie und Analyse sportbezogener Ängstlichkeit [Theory and analysis of sport-related anxiety].* Schorndorf: Hofmann.

Hackfort, D. (1989). Emotion and emotion control in sports: Benefits and costs. In IOC (Ed.), *Proceedings of the First IOC World Congress on Sport Psychology* (pp. 375–379). Colorado Springs.

Hackfort, D. (1991a). Emotion in sports: An action theoretical analysis. In C.D. Spielberger, J.G. Sarason, Z. Kulcsar, & G.L. Van Heck (Eds.), *Stress and emotion* (vol. 14, pp. 65–73). New York: Hemisphere.

Hackfort, D. (Ed.). (1991b). *Research on emotions in sport.* Köln: Strauss.

Hackfort, D. (1995). Emotion in sports: A functional analysis out of the action theory perspective. In F.H. Fu & Mee-Lee Ng (Eds.), *Sport psychology: Perspectives and practices toward the 21st century* (pp. 27–34). Hong Kong: Dept. of Phys. Ed. Hong Kong Baptist University.

Hackfort, D. (in press). Emotion und sportliches Bewegungshandeln [Emotion and sport-related movement actions]. In M. Jerusalem & R. Pekrun (Eds.), *Emotion, Motivation und Leistung [Emotion, motivation, and performance].* Göttingen: Hogrefe.

Hackfort, D., & Schlattmann A. (1991). Functions of emotion presentation in sport. In D. Hackfort (Ed.), *Research on emotions in sport* (pp. 95–110). Köln: Strauss.

Hackfort, D., & Schlattmann, A. (1995). Die Stimmungs—und Befindensskalen (SBS) (The trait- and state-mood scales). *Arbeitsinformation Sportwissenschaft,* Heft 7.

Hackfort, D., & Schwenkmezger, P. (1993). Anxiety. In R. N. Singer, M. Murphey, & L. K. Tennant (Eds.), *Handbook of research on sport psychology* (pp. 328–364). New York: Macmillan.

Izard, C.E. (1977). *Human emotions.* New York: Plenum.

Plutchik, R. (1962). *The emotions: Facts, theories and a new model.* New York: Random House.

Schlattmann, A., & Hackfort, D. (1991). Attributions of functional meanings of "positive" emotions in acting in sport . In D. Hackfort (Ed.), *Research on emotions in sport* (pp. 1–19). Köln: Strauss.

Part V

❖

The Interface Between Behavioral Sciences and Society

Interest in sporting activities has expanded during the past two decades into large and varied sectors of the population. Sport currently occupies much of the spare time of children and youth, the older population, and the disabled. Not only has the number of spectators dramatically increased, but also the number of active individuals and teams has grown. As a result, sport psychology is currently engaged in several issues that reflect these developments. For example, some unique topics that have attracted the attention of researchers and practitioners are moral development and behavior, sex abuse in sport, and psychological characteristics of disabled athletes. These topics are discussed in this part.

Chapter 13, entitled "Character in Action: The Influences of Moral Atmosphere on Athletes' Sport Behavior," presents some important facets of moral issues in sport: commercialization, motivational climate, and game reasoning. In addition, this chapter describes how building a sense of moral community among team members can affect the moral behavior of athletes.

In chapter 14, entitled "Protecting Athletes from Sexual Abuse in Sport: How Theory Can Improve Practice," an attempt is made to establish the current status of knowledge about sex abuse in sport and to explain how theoretical analysis has influenced the practice of protecting athletes—mainly female—from sexual abuse.

Chapter 15, entitled "Disability, Physical Activity, Psychological Well-Being, and Empowerment: A Life-Span Perspective," demonstrates how sport and physical activity can contribute to the well-being of individuals with disabilities throughout their life span. In addition, recommendations for future research and practice in this area are provided.

13

Character in Action: The Influences of Moral Atmosphere On Athletes' Sport Behavior

Brenda Light Bredemeier
University of California at Berkeley, USA

I recently participated in a unique seminar on violence and sport at a major university in the United States. The seminar was unique for several reasons, but primarily because of the circumstances out of which it evolved. The university community had been stunned the previous October when 31 members of its football team drove to a fraternity house near campus, then surrounded and attacked the house and the young men who lived there. Police intervened, but not before several members of the fraternity were badly beaten and their house seriously damaged. The assault was allegedly in retaliation for the expulsion of two players from a private fraternity party the previous Friday night.

Even in an era of escalating violence perpetrated by athletes, this incident was extraordinary because it involved premeditated action that required the coordinated efforts of so many players. The university president, athletic director, and football coach took swift and decisive disciplinary action, dismissing two students from the football program and suspending others pending the outcomes of their criminal cases. The university also forfeited the next football game and compensated their scheduled opponent for lost ticket revenues and concession sales. The pain of this violent incident seared the entire campus community. But it also galvanized the community and spawned a series of educational programs designed to teach conflict-resolution skills and encourage violence prevention—including the seminar of which I was a part.

In trying to make sense of an incident such as this, social scientists have at their disposal a multitude of theoretical lenses, each shedding light on different aspects of the event. For the purpose of this chapter, I will use the lens of moral atmosphere to examine influences on athletes' moral judgment and action, including those that may have been involved in this illustration of sport-related violence.

Kohlberg (Power, Higgins, & Kohlberg, 1989) used the term *moral atmosphere* to refer to a group's shared norms for moral behavior. In this context, the term *norms* has both a descriptive and prescriptive meaning. When norms are shared within a group, they describe the moral behaviors one is likely to observe among group members, and they also serve as prescriptive guidelines for acceptable behavior. Kohlberg, like Durkheim (1925/1961) before him, observed that groups are guided by collective norms that are not reducible to those held by individuals. Over time, groups develop common understandings about rights and responsibilities, privileges and freedoms, and duties and obligations that hold for all who are members of that group.

Sport teams, like all groups, develop a moral atmosphere comprising of collective norms that help shape the moral actions of each group member. For example, I believe that the violent incident described in my introduction was more a product of the moral norms shared by members of the football team than of individual players' characteristics. Collective norms for athletes' moral behavior are influenced by a complex network of perceived values, including (a) broader cultural values; (b) team values that include values within the general domain of sport, the particular sport being played, and the specific group of individuals who are associated with a team; and (c) personal values held by individual athletes.

In this chapter, I will discuss three important influences on the moral atmosphere of sport: commercialization, motivational climate, and game reasoning. These three represent examples of cultural, team, and personal influences respectively. Each has contributed to a sport climate where violence, cheating, and other "bad sport" behaviors are often seen as acceptable, sometimes even necessary or desirable. After discussing these interrelated influences, I'll discuss how building a sense of moral community among team members can encourage athletes' moral behavior.

Commercialization

Across cultures and throughout history, sporting events have entertained observers and stimulated economic interests. Yet contemporary social scientists agree that sport has never been as commercialized as it is today in North America. The evolution of professional and Olympic sport, intercollegiate and interscholastic sport, even youth sport, into new forms of commercial entertainment has had a profound impact on the moral atmosphere of sport. In the commercial sport industry, values are shaped primarily by the ethics and standards of profit making; the economic bottom line rules over any moral accounting of personal or social needs and responsibilities. Sport commodification has wide-ranging moral implications for spectators, athletes, even sport psychologists.

The success of any commercial entertainment depends on its mass appeal. To attract a mass audience of spectators who have varying degrees of sport interest and knowledge, sport must be "packaged" in a way that "hooks" spectators. Coakley (1990) has noted that because many people don't have technical knowledge about the complex athletic skills and strategies used by players and coaches,

> they tend to focus on things they can easily understand. For example, they enjoy situations in which players take risks and face clear danger, they are attracted to players who are masters of dramatic expression or who are willing to go beyond their normal physical limits to the point of endangering safety and well-being; and they like to see players committed to victory no matter what the personal cost. (p. 255)

Owners and sponsors of commercial sport depend on the interest of a mass audience, and they believe that economic rewards depend on their ability to "produce" what they believe spectators want to see. Thus, as sport becomes more commodified, it becomes more like a spectacle that can be sold for profit to spectators who wish to "consume" it. As an example, consider the words of National Hockey League president, John Ziegler, when asked if he had a responsibility to curb fighting in NHL hockey.

> It doesn't matter to me. What matters to me is providing a product that people enjoy and want to see . . . because I am in the entertainment business, and the measure to me is: Are people going to pay money to see . . . [fighting]? And are they going to say yes to it? . . . So if it ain't broke, don't fix it. (Quoted in Sage, 1990, p. 108)

Sport commercialization influences the meaning participants attach to their sport experience and the values they associate with it. Athletes and coaches come to see themselves and their teams or franchises as commodities that can be bought, owned, manipulated, and sold in order to maximize the profits of media giants, major universities, or team owners. When sport participants experience this depersonalization and devaluing of personal development, family, and community, it is difficult for them to retain their intrinsic valuing of sport and to see themselves and others as moral beings. They begin to accept behavioral norms based on their perceptions of what spectators expect and what commercial interests dictate: norms that require playing with pain, sacrificing one's body, and risking serious injury, not for the love of the game, but for the sake of a job or a scholarship or an endorsement; norms that require aggression and cheating against opponents; norms that embody the popular slogan "winning isn't everything, it's the only thing."

The depersonalizing nature of sport commercialization also has important moral implications for the way an athlete's body is viewed. When sport is experienced in its more playful form, the athlete's body is a nexus of diverse and complex experience. It is a source of pleasure and power, discipline and devotion, spontaneity and skill, excitement and ecstacy. It is also a means of expressing who one is and what one values. But when commercial interests come to dominate sport experience, the body of the comes to be viewed instrumentally. The commodified body is seen as a machine that pumps out athletic performances, inviting scientific and technological manipulation to optimize its functioning. When its performance is not as machinelike as is desired, drugs (legal and illegal) are administered, nutritional supplements dispensed, even psychological skills taught so that the body may sustain a training regime or perform at a level not possible without intervention. The commodified body is seen also as a weapon, particularly in high-contact and combative sports, inviting a confusion between excellence and violence that rewards the most aggressive athletes with greater status and more media attention. And the commodified body is seen as the epitome of commercial success, inviting efforts to sell anything an athlete wears, eats or drinks, drives, plays with, likes, associates with, or stands for!

The moral ramifications of sport commercialization are closely tied to the dominant theme of entertainment sport: "the thrill of victory and the agony of defeat." When the outcome—victory or defeat—becomes more important than the process—playing fairly, developing excellence, having fun—almost any action in the pursuit of victory becomes acceptable. In fact, such acts as rule violations, trash talk, and challenges to the authority of umpires can add an element of excitement and suspense for the audience, making these actions desirable from a commercial standpoint regardless of their game implications. And to add insult to injury, those who most exemplify such activities are rewarded with endorsements and book deals.

The commercialization of sport has encouraged participants to behave in ways that are counter to sport's moral underpinnings. Let us keep in mind that the concepts of fairness and freedom are central to the very structure and spirit of sport. Without fairness, sport dissolves. Without freedom, sport transforms into compulsory work. Sport derives from the free choice of participants to engage in the same or similar set of physical activities, activities that have been designed carefully to balance offense with defense, challenge with potential, risk with safety. And all activities are carried out under scrupulously equalizing conditions. But when commercial interests begin to dominate, both freedom and fairness are threatened. Winning, regardless of the means employed, supersedes all other values.

Motivational Climate

A second influence on moral atmosphere is a team's motivational climate. The concept of motivational climate is rooted in the fact that sport is an achievement activity that can elicit, give expression to, and influence participant motivation. Stated differently, sport provides an opportunity for participants to develop and demonstrate competence. The desire to experience and display competence may not be the only motivational dynamic related to sport involvement, but it certainly is a major one.

Ames and her colleagues studied how young students' interpretations of the achievement goals most salient in their learning environment can evoke two distinct motivational trends (Ames & Ames, 1984; Ames & Archer, 1988). Extending this work, Duda and her colleagues (Duda, 1989; Duda, Olson, & Templin, 1991) have developed a measure to assess mastery-oriented and performance-oriented motivational climates in sport.

Team members who experience a mastery-oriented climate tend to demonstrate competence by mastering new tasks and excelling beyond previous levels of performance. In contrast, team members who perceive the sport climate as performance-oriented tend to define competence through a process of social comparison. Competence is equated with outperforming the opponent, and success is defined in terms of competitive victory.

One way that motivational climate influences a team's moral atmosphere is by helping to shape how sport participants view competition. In a mastery-oriented climate, participants tend to interpret competition—in keeping with the etymology of the word—as a process of "striving with" others. Competitors are seen as cocreators of an experience that enables both parties to test limits, and to excel beyond what can be done without the worthy challenge provided by the other. In contrast, when sport is characterized by a performance-oriented motivational climate, athletes tend to see competition as a process of "striving against" others, a valued image in commercialized sport. This climate encourages a derogatory, depersonalized picture of the competitor as a mere obstacle to be overcome in the quest for victory, an object to be dominated and defeated, an opportunity for "proving" one's superior competence. Competitors become the mere canvas upon which one paints self-glorifying self-portraits.

The relationships among motivation and moral variables have been examined more fully with the construct of dispositional motivational orientation than with motivational climate.

Significantly, Nicholls (1989) maintained that "different motivational orientations are not just different types of wants or needs" (p. 102). He believed that each orientation corresponds to a specific set of attitudes, beliefs, and values that informs a person's worldview, including his or her personal philosophy about the meaning and purpose of achievement activities, and perceptions about what is acceptable behavior in the context of that activity. For example, a person with a strong ego orientation, characterized by motivation to demonstrate competence via a performance that is superior to that of others, is likely to have little concern about issues of justice and fairness. Nicholls (1989) claimed, "When winning is everything, it is worth doing anything to win" (p. 133). On the other hand, a person with a strong task orientation is concerned with self-referenced success and improving task performance, and is more likely to emphasize fair play and compliance with the rules.

Duda and her colleagues (Duda, 1989; Duda, Olson, & Templin, 1991; Huston & Duda, 1992) were the first to test these intuitive relationships empirically. In a study involving high school athletes, Duda (1989) found that task orientation was positively related to the belief that sport should teach participants to try their best, to value cooperation, to obey the rules, and to be a good citizen. Ego orientation, on the other hand, was correlated with beliefs that sport should enhance participants' self-esteem and status, and teach them how to get ahead in a "dog-eat-dog world." Duda and her colleagues (Duda et al., 1991; Huston & Duda, 1992) also found that athletes who were more task oriented endorsed less cheating behavior and expressed greater approval of "good sport" behaviors. Ego-oriented athletes were more likely to endorse unfair sport behaviors and to judge acts of athletic aggression as legitimate.

It is quite possible that the relationship of individual motivational orientations with personal attitudes about such moral issues as aggression and cheating parallels the association between a team's motivational climate and its collective moral norms. Though there has been little research on the relationship between sport teams' motivational climates and their moral variables, one recent study does lend tentative support to the associations proposed. In a study of 9- to 14-year-old female soccer competitors, Stephens and Bredemeier (1996) found that players who described themselves as more likely to aggress against an opponent also were more likely to (a) estimate that a larger number of teammates would aggress in a similar situation and (b) perceive their coach as placing greater importance on performance-oriented goals. These results suggest that young athletes' aggressive behavior is related to their team's moral atmosphere and motivational climate. The likelihood of player aggression against an opponent was best predicted by—not players' own moral judgments or motivational orientations—but rather, players' perceptions of team norms for athletic aggression and players' interpretations of their coaches' performance-oriented achiegoals.

Clearly we need to explore these relationships more fully, examining associations across genders, ages, sport areas, and levels of competition. We need to push beyond establishing correlations to determining patterns of causality, and we need to check for ecological validity because people may say one thing and do another. But although we need more empirical information about the relationship between motivational and moral variables, these preliminary results suggest that a team's mastery-oriented climate may enhance its moral atmosphere.

Before moving on to the third influence on moral atmosphere, let me briefly recap what we have covered thus far. I began by suggesting that a team's moral atmosphere, their shared norms regarding appropriate behavior, is a powerful influence on the actions of sport participants. I also proposed that we examine examples of three levels of influence on the moral atmosphere of contemporary sport teams. The first was the influence of commercialization. I proposed that the packaging of sport for mass appeal has promoted a bottom line that elevates commercial values over moral values. I then went on to suggest that a team's motivational climate also impacts on its moral atmosphere, partly by shaping athletes' perceptions of the purpose and meaning of competition, and partly by influencing athletes' motivational orientations and moral judgments about appropriate behavior. Finally, I discussed the linkage between commodified sport and a team's performance-oriented climate, emphasizing the common emphasis on winning at all costs. I now turn to the third influence on moral atmosphere: game reasoning.

Game Reasoning

To discuss the third influence on moral atmosphere, game reasoning, we need to consider the ways sport is "set apart" from other spheres of daily life. Of course this does not mean that sport is disconnected from, uninfluenced by, or irrelevant to broader culture. In fact, our discussion of commercialized sport illustrated some of the ways sport is shaped by the norms and values of broader culture. Yet it is also the case that sport is a "world within a world." Philosophers and social scientists (Bateson, 1955; Schmitz, 1976; Sutton-Smith, 1971) have suggested that sport exists in a unique sphere, separated from the rest of life, and that entry into that sphere requires cognitive, attitudinal, and value adjustments. Firth (1973), for example, discusses how rituals and conventions serve to mark sport's spacial and temporal boundaries, and to symbolize the reconstitution of people into players and players into people.

The separateness of sport may have significant implications for the moral atmosphere within which sport is experienced. Ennis (1976) describes sport as an institution of release, a zone where participants are freed from the usual challenges and responsibilities of daily life. We have postulated that sport also temporarily frees participants from their typical moral obligation to consider equally the interests and needs of all persons. In other words, sport participation can involve a "bracketed morality" that legitimates a narrow focus on self-interest.

Several features of sport help create and legitimate the "brackets" that separate sport morality from the morality of everyday life. First, spacial and temporal boundaries underscore the separateness of sport and emphasize its temporary nature; people enter the world of sport, athletes compete, and then winners and losers return to their normal lives. A second structural feature of many sports is the concentration of moral decision making and responsibility in the roles of coaches and officials, thus limiting the moral accountability of athletes. Finally, game rules, intended to provide consensual external regulation, provide several moral functions: They guarantee conditions of fairness and equal protection from harm, they specify legitimate success strategies, and they identify appropriate penalties for rule violations. These formal properties of sport allow for the development of a moral atmosphere that is characterized by a greater degree of personal freedom, of moral latitude, than the moral atmosphere of most other spheres of life.

If entry into sport involves bracketed morality, then it is reasonable to hypothesize that moral reasoning undergoes some structural change as well. Indeed, a series of empirical investigations support this hypothesis. In a study of 120 high school and college basketball players, swimmers and nonparticipants in interscholastic or intercollegiate sport, we analyzed moral reasoning responses to hypothetical dilemmas set in sport-specific contexts and in other spheres of daily life (Bredemeier & Shields, 1984). We found that when people thought about moral issues in everyday life, they used reasoning that was significantly more mature in its structure than when the same individuals thought about moral issues in sport. Cross-sectional analyses revealed that the sport-life reasoning divergence was greater for males than females, for athletes than nonathletes, and for college athletes than high school athletes; male intercollegiate athletes' sport-life reasoning patterns were most divergent.

Similar analyses were conducted on the moral reasoning of 110 girls and boys who were 8 to 13 years of age (Bredemeier, 1995). It was found that the sport-life reasoning divergence began around ages 11 and 12. Younger children didn't demonstrate context-specific reasoning patterns.

We have coined the term *game reasoning* to refer to that form of moral reasoning that arises from and reflects the bracketed moral interactions within sport (Shields & Bredemeier, 1995). It is a sport-specific form of reasoning about moral issues that parallels less mature, more egocentric forms of moral reasoning. As one intercollegiate athlete explained:

> In sports you can do what you want, in life it's more restricted. The pressure is different in sports and life. It's harder to make decisions in life because there are so many people to think about, different people to worry about. In sports you're free to think about yourself. (Quoted in Bredemeier & Shields, 1984, pp. 262–263)

Often game reasoning seems to reflect a "legitimated regression" (Shields & Bredemeier, 1984) to a form of reasoning resembling more immature levels. After all, competition demands some degree of egocentrism, and the unique ethical structures of sport (such as the existence of balanced and equalizing rules, and external moral regulation through use of sport officials) function to legitimate it. Focus on self-interest is not only allowed in sport, it is presupposed.

Yet sport is not a moral free-for-all. The term bracketed morality connotes a form of moral action that is nested within a broader, more encompassing morality—the morality of everyday life. Players remain people, and moral responsibility cannot be completely set aside. We believe that mature moral reasoning sets limits on the exercise of egocentric game reasoning. To remain legitimate, one can only "play" at egocentrism, for game reasoning is a "playful" adaptation to the "playful" dimension of sport.

It is important to remember that sport is premised on each party single-mindedly pursuing self-interest. If players do not want to win, which is to say to seek their own gain over the other, then the game dissolves. Sport play requires egocentrism, and game reasoning is a playful moral adaptation to this reality. But the whole structure of sport is set up and designed for the mutual benefit, enrichment, and enjoyment of all participants. When the broader purposes of sport are no longer kept in mind, then sport ceases to be playful, and game reasoning degenerates into moral rationalization. This point needs elaboration.

Sport, of course, is by no means a pure form of play. In fact, my discussion of commercialized sport and motivational climate emphasized the ways sport is precariously balanced between the somewhat contradictory demands of play and work. Sport balances intrinsic motives with extrinsic motives; it between the spontaneous world of play and the driven world of spectacle. This double identity of sport, I believe, creates a high degree of ambiguity with regard to the appropriateness and reach of game reasoning. Game reasoning can all too easily degenerate into ugly forms of moral hedonism that rationalize athletic aggression, illegal use of performance-enhancing drugs, or other efforts to gain an unfair advantage for the sake of victory.

The ambiguity involved in game reasoning may be one of the most important contributors to the moral problems of contemporary sport. Game reasoning can be "play" morality, but therein lies the catch. Commercialized sport may have many of the trappings of play, but it has become increasingly serious and instrumental. A motivational climate that emphasizes performance outcome over mastery also minimizes the "playful" nature of sport. These two influences on moral atmosphere have important consequences for the ways in which game reasoning gets "played out" in sport.

Let me offer a brief aside at this point. Ironically, game reasoning—a context-specific form of moral reasoning—may transcend the world of sport in surprising and sometimes disturbing ways. I would hypothesize that game reasoning is sometimes elicited in other domains of life by the use of sport analogies and metaphors and that this is done, perhaps unintentionally, to legitimize egocentric morality in situations that are nonplayful and that lack the protective moral structures of sport. For example, the use of sport terminology in political circles may elicit game reasoning, leading to morally questionable behaviors that politicians judge to be legitimate when framed by a metaphor that defines others as either "on our team" or "opponents."

Another example of game reasoning transcending the direct world of sport is, perhaps, more germane to the present topic. I believe that when athletes socialize together, particularly if they play on the same team, it is sometimes tempting to employ game reasoning to legitimate otherwise unacceptable behavior outside the world of sport. Game reasoning can influence the collective norms of the social group just as it influences the sport team. The football scenario I described at the beginning of this paper is only one example of athletes aggressing as a group against others.

Creation of a Positive Moral Atmosphere

The moral atmosphere experienced in sport is a product of cultural, team, and personal influences. Sport commercialization, motivational climate, and game reasoning are examples of each of these influences. Up to this point, I have emphasized how these various influences might create conditions ripe for moral failure on the part of athletes, such as the incident I mentioned in my introduction. Yet this anecdote also offers a prescription for creating a more positive moral atmosphere. Leaders in the athletic department came together and said, essentially,

"This action is not acceptable. Some members of our community have stepped over a line; we must all reflect on what has happened, consider the reasons and the consequences, and identify ways to conduct ourselves—within and outside sport—that conform to our moral values."

The athletic department became committed to creating a positive moral atmosphere on their football team by (among other strategies) prescribing reflective action in a context of mutual care and concern. I want to conclude my chapter by briefly addressing the significance of mutual care and reflective action for sport psychologists who wish to help create a positive moral atmosphere for the athletes with whom they work.

Moral atmosphere can be thought of as a kind of culture within which athletes develop both muscles and morals. Typically, social scientists use the term *culture* to refer to a system of symbols and shared meanings, norms, and values. And, indeed, this is part of what comprises a moral atmosphere. But I would also like us to borrow from our colleagues in the biological sciences. For them, a culture is literally a medium in which living things grow. We can use the biological definition of culture metaphorically to emphasize that a team's moral culture is more than a system of symbols and shared meanings, norms, and values. It is a medium within which athletes' moral qualities can grow and flourish.

Power et al. (1989) write:

> The word "culture" is derived from the Latin "cultura," meaning to cultivate or till the soil. Culture thus expresses a process of development of acculturation which takes into account both natural growth and conscious efforts to promote or enhance that growth by the one(s) doing the cultivating or tilling. (p. 104)

So how do we as sport psychologists help to cultivate a moral culture? After reviewing studies of moral atmosphere, Power et al. (1989) identified the development of a strong sense of community as a principal element of moral atmosphere. Moreover, they found that group members' sense of moral community sprang from a shared norm of caring. Again, let me quote, this time substituting language for a sport team:

> caring provides the social glue within a team. It is the norm that binds all member of the team to each other. On sport teams, athletes are usually obliged to care for their teammates only to the degree that it facilitates winning contests. In a moral community, however, caring is a function of the communal bond that unites all members of the team. This norm of caring doesn't mean that all team members have to be close friends. It does mean that team members must treat each other not only with respect, but with real concern. (Power et al., 1989, p. 104)

How could we as sport psychologists promote this shared norm of caring? To develop such a norm would involve going counter to the trend of commercialism. It would require that every person associated with a sport team view every other participant as a multidimensional human being with a host of interests and yearnings not reducible to athletic prowess.

What would it mean for us as sport psychologists to care in this way? How would it influence the choices we make, the ways we teach and listen and respond to athletes, the interpretations we offer in the face of victory and defeat, the methods we use to motivate? How would this shared norm of caring influence our temptation to see "winners" as somehow superior beings, "better" people than those athletes who lost?

Sage (1990) points out that although it may be a worthy sport science goal to help athletes run faster, jump higher, and throw farther, it is also the case that many of these efforts have been appropriated to serve commodified sport interests. He warns that

> High performance sport has increasingly become a project in human engineering whose objective is producing high levels of performance with seemingly little understanding—or even interest in—what the consequences might be for the personal and social development of the athlete. This approach to sport tends to implicitly validate enhancing performance, employing scientific findings, and using technological techniques as unproblematic—there is an unreflecting and uncritical attitude about ends in sport. . . . In their desire for status, recognition, and entry into the rarified environment of elite sports, sport scientists have been unwilling to criticize what coaches and athletes are doing in the name of achieving records and winning championships. (p. 104)

Caring may be the wellspring for moral culture, but as Sage points out, it's also important for us as sport psychologists to reflect on our own motives and on the consequences of our most well-intended actions. To help develop a positive moral culture, athletes (and those associated with athletes) must reflect on their actions. Especially those who have leadership roles within these communities need to practice guided, reflective action. What I mean by this is really very simple—at least in theory. We must break the code of silence. We need to talk about moral issues as they arise in sport. We need to encourage athletes to interpret their experience in moral as well as athletic terms, to see the moral ramifications of their sporting interactions with others.

I'd like to close with a challenge to the popular Nike slogan, "Just Do It!" We must, in fact, if we are to encourage a positive moral atmosphere in sport, do the opposite. We must all—athletes, coaches, administrators, sport psychologists—reflect on the motives and consequences of our actions, so that in the future we cannot "Just Do It," but rather, "Do It Justly!"

References

Ames, C., & Ames, R. (1984). Systems of student and teacher motivation: Toward a qualitative definition. *Journal of Educational Psychology, 76,* 535–556.

Ames, C., & Archer, J. (1988). Achievement goals in the classroom: Students' learning strategies and motivation processes. *Journal of Educational Psychology, 80,* 260–267.

Bateson, G. (1955). A theory of play and fantasy. *Psychiatric Research Reports, 2,* 39–51.

Bredemeier, B.J. (1995). Divergence in children's moral reasoning about issues in daily life and sport specific contexts. *The International Journal of Sport Psychology, 26,* 453–463.

Bredemeier, B.J., & Shields, D.L. (1984). Divergence in moral reasoning about sport and life. *Sociology of Sport Journal, 1,* 348–357.

Coakley, J.J. (1990). *Sport in society: Issues and controversies* (4th ed.). St. Louis: Times Mirror/Mosby.

Duda, J.L. (1989). The relationship between task and ego orientation and the perceived purpose of sport among male and female high school athletes. *Journal of Sport and Exercise Psychology, 11,* 318–335.

Duda, J.L., Olson, L.K., & Templin, T.J. (1991). The relationship of task and ego orientation to sportsmanship attitudes and the perceived legitimacy of injurious acts. *Research Quarterly for Exercise and Sport, 62,* 79–87.

Durkheim, E. (1961). *Moral education.* New York: Free Press. (Original work published 1925)

Ennis, P.H. (1976, April). *Expressive symbol systems and the institutions of release.* Paper presented at the Third Annual Conference on Theory and the Arts, State University of New York, Albany.

Firth, R. (1973). *Symbols public and private.* New York: Cornell University Press.

Huston, L., & Duda, J. (1992). *The relationship of goal orientation and competitive level to the endorsement of aggressive acts in football.* Unpublished manuscript.

Nicholls, J.G. (1989). *The competitive ethos and democratic education.* Cambridge, MA: Harvard University Press.

Power, F.C., Higgins, A., & Kohlberg, L. (1989). *Lawrence Kohlberg's approach to moral education.* New York: Columbia University Press.

Sage, G. (1990). *Power and ideology in American sport: A critical perspective.* Champaign, IL: Human Kinetics.

Schmitz, K. (1976). Sport and play: Suspension of the ordinary. In M. Hart (Ed.), *Sport in the sociocultural process* (pp. 35–48). Dubuque: W.C. Brown.

Shields, D., & Bredemeier, B. (1984). Sport and moral growth: A structural developmental perspective. In W. Straub & J. Williams (Eds.), *Cognitive sport psychology* (pp. 89–101). Lansing, NY: Sport Science Associates.

Shields, D., & Bredemeier, B. (1995). *Character development and physical activity.* Champaign, IL: Human Kinetics.

Stephens, D., & Bredemeier, B. (1996). Moral atmosphere and judgments about aggression in girls' soccer: Relationships among moral and motivational variables. *Journal of Sport and Exercise Psychology, 18,* 158–173.

Sutton-Smith, B. (1971). Boundaries. In R. E. Herron & B. Sutton-Smith (Eds.), *Child's play* (pp. 103–109). New York: John Wiley & Sons.

14

Protecting Athletes From Sexual Abuse in Sport: How Theory Can Improve Practice

Celia H Brackenridge   and   Sandra Kirby
Cheltenham & Gloucester College   Department of Sociology,
of Higher Education, United Kingdom   University of Winnipeg, Canada

Recognizing the Problem

Recent legal cases against senior sports coaches in Britain, the United States and Canada have caused widespread concern in the sporting community and given impetus to the debate about how to protect athletes, especially children, from sexual abuse in sport. The attitude that "it couldn't happen here", which was common until the mid 1990s, has now shifted to an acceptance that abuse cases are not simply isolated but *could* and *do* happen across a range of situations at every level of sport, from recreational to elite. Findings from studies in Canada (Kirby & Greaves, 1996), the United States (Pike Masteralexis, 1995; Volkwein, 1996) and Britain (Brackenridge, 1997b) challenge those organisations who continue to deny the existence of sexual abuse in sport. Indeed, there have been several distinct shifts in the institutional responses to this issue, first from denial to obstruction/resistance (Finkelhor, 1994), then from resistance to reluctant acceptance, then from acceptance to the formulation and dissemination of advocacy and intervention programmes (Crouch, 1995; National Coaching Foundation *et al.*, 1996). Although empirical data are still sparse, it is increasingly clear that harassment and abuse in sport constitute a problem which demands responses from sports organisations and sport professionals, including sport psychologists, at the level of both policy and practice. This chapter sets out the current state of knowledge about this problem and explores how theoretical analysis has begun to inform practice to protect athletes, particularly girls and women, from sexual abuse.

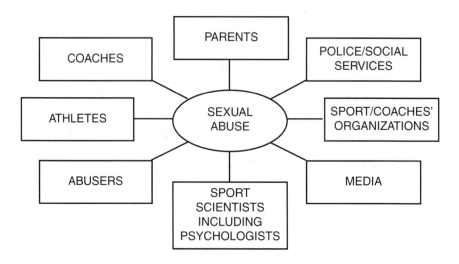

Figure 14.1. Major stakeholders in sexual abuse in sport.

The task of protection includes shielding or guarding athletes from sexual danger. Some sport organisations, notably the Canadian Centre for Ethics and Sport (CCES), have defined this responsibility in terms of an ethic of care

> ensuring the protection of the well-being, health and safety of young people whose welfare, by virtue of their participation in sport, must be entrusted to others. Consequently, when such duty is not fulfilled, or when such trust is breached, we must be concerned with the best interests of those who are harmed by this failure of care. (Lachance, 1997, p. 3)

Many individuals and agencies have a role to play in the perpetration of or protection from sexual abuse in sport. These include parents; coaches; peer athletes; social and legal services; advocacy groups, such as feminists and sexual assault centre workers; sport organisations; and coaches' organisations (see Figure 14.1).

In addition there are a number of critical support professionals who hold positions of authority and who facilitate athlete development, such as sports physicians, athletic therapists and athletic trainers and sport psychologists. Sport psychologists represent an important stakeholder group: They may well uncover sexual abuse before others because they come into close personal contact with athletes in the course of their work, because they have special responsibilities for diagnosing and helping to address psychological problems and because they do important research on the issue. In addition, the work of the sport psychologist encompasses the understanding and enhancement of athletes' moral development, emotional well-being, management of stress, positive body image, all with the effect of improving athletes' effort, tenacity and achievements and their perceptions of themselves (President's Council on Physical Fitness and Sports, 1997). Sport psychologists may also confront ethical, legal and humanitarian difficulties as part of their work because they have access to what is called 'guilty knowledge' (Fetterman, 1989), in other words, information that could incriminate others. Other sport science professionals, including physiotherapists and medical practitioners, have already identified sexual abuse as a feature of the case histories of some troubled athletes. However, although we may now be able to recognise the symptoms of sexual abuse, we know far too little about its causes.

It is important to accept that we are all part of the network of stakeholders in this issue and that it is not helpful to 'point the finger' or accuse particular individuals because the whole system is itself at risk or vulnerable. Where sport takes place largely in voluntary settings, away from the legal protections of the statutory sector, or away from the gaze and surveillance of public life, these risks are increased. Research from the cognate fields of social work and day care has already shown that abusers may be coaches, instructors, chaperones, parent-helpers, bus drivers, other athletes, or anyone with access to young athletes, so it is important not to assume that any individual or group is necessarily immune from blame just because of their status (Finkelhor & Williams, 1988). However, sports research and protection work has focused so far on coaches and other "authority figures" (Kirby & Greaves, 1996) simply because we have knowledge about abusive coaches and because some sport organisations concerned about coaching (such as the National Coaching Foundation in Britain and Athletes CAN and the Coaching Association of Canada) have been amongst the first to address the issue.

Defining the Problem

According to the National Society for the Prevention of Cruelty to Children (NSPCC) the term abuse includes emotional, physical and sexual abuse as well as neglect (Crouch, 1995). In the work developed by Brackenridge (1996, 1997a), sexual harassment and sexual abuse are identified stages along a continuum of sexual violence (see Figure 14.2) but there is, as yet, no set of universally agreed definitions. However, there *is* agreement that sexual harassment is *unwanted attention of a sexual nature* and that it may even occur without physical touch: the short-hand definition 'invasion without consent' might be used. In practice, emotional, physical and sexual abuse are usually

SEX DISCRIMINATION ◄──►	SEXUAL HARASSMENT ◄──►	SEXUAL ABUSE
"the chilly climate"	*"unwanted attention"*	*"groomed or coerced"*

MAINLY INSTITUTIONAL .... *MAINLY PERSONAL*

- vertical & horizontal job segregation	- written or verbal abuse or threats	- exchange of reward or privilege for sexual favours
- lack of harassment policy and/or officer or reporting channels	- sexually oriented comments	- rape
	- jokes, lewd comments or sexual innuendoes, taunts about body, dress, marital situation or sexuality	- anal or vaginal penetration by penis, fingers or objects
- lack of counselling or mentoring systems		- forced sexual activity
- differential pay or rewards or promotion prospects on the basis of sex	- ridiculing of performance	- sexual assault
	- sexual or homophobic graffiti	- physical/sexual violence
	- practical jokes based on sex	- groping
- poorly/unsafely designed or lit venues	- intimidating sexual remarks, propositions, invitations or familiarity	- indecent exposure
- absence of security		- incest
	- domination of meetings, play space or equipment	
	- condescending or patronising behaviour undermining self-respect or work performance	
	- physical contact, fondling, pinching or kissing	
	- vandalism on the basis of sex	
	- offensive phone calls or photos	

Figure 14.2. The sexual discrimination-sexual abuse continuum.

experienced as an interrelated set of traumas, and attempts to distinguish between them are of little relevance to victims.

The focus of this chapter is on sexual abuse and on its effects on girls and young women in sport because we know most about this and have good reason to believe that girls and women, in sport as in general social settings, suffer such crimes disproportionately when compared with boys and men (Doyle, 1994; MacMillan *et al.*, 1997). However, it is important to acknowledge that there is a large literature about sexual abuse of boys and men (Christopherson *et al.*, 1989), and a lengthening list of such accounts in the context of sport, for example, multiple cases which emerged from the Maple Leaf Gardens scandal in Canada during 1997 (Grange, 1997). It is also known from social work studies that most victims are female and the vast majority of abusers are male, although there is growing evidence of abuse by females (Elliott, 1993; Matthews, Matthews, & Speltz, 1989).

Figure 14.2 indicates that an important defining feature of sexual abuse is that it is groomed or coerced. Grooming is the process by which a perpetrator isolates and prepares an intended victim: The entrapment may takes weeks, months or years and moves steadily so that the abuser can maintain secrecy and avoid exposure (see Brackenridge, 1997a). Grooming is important for several reasons, not least of which is that it brings about the appearance of apparent co-operation from the targeted individual, making the act of abuse appear to be consensual.

Different studies of sexual abuse use different definitions and operational measurements, hence, it is very difficult to come to an agreed position on prevalence and incidence figures (see Brackenridge, 1992). Some researchers set a five year age difference between victim and abuser as a minimum interval below which sexual relations cannot be defined as abusive (Finkelhor, 1984). Some studies report as abuse only those actions which involve physical sexual touch of some kind. Given the variation in approaches to these concepts, and the consequences that different definitions have for official recognition and treatment of survivors of abuse, it is all the more important that sport psychologists familiarise themselves with the subject, for practices that might fail to meet official or *objective criteria* for abuse may well be *subjectively experienced* as trauma.

Research Findings

There are very few quantitative studies of sexual abuse in sport. Our starting point, therefore, is statistics from cognate fields, notably social work. Data from such studies in Britain indicate that perhaps one in four girls and one in six boys are sexually abused before adulthood, and that approximately 14% of cases occur *outside* the family (Creighton, 1989), which, of course, includes voluntary sport organisations (Russell, 1984). Reports from North America indicate even more worrying prevalence figures (MacMillan *et al.*, 1997; Whetsell-Mitchell, 1995).The work of feminists in researching interpersonal violence has been significant in moving forward political and policy debates on such issues as marital rape, female circumcision, so-called 'date rape' and the state costs of sexual violence (Bart & Geil Moran, 1993; Fawcett, Featherston, Hearn, & Toft, 1996; Haskell & Randall, 1993). It is not surprising therefore that, with the exception of Crosset (1986) and Donnelly (1997), both from North America, feminist researchers have been the prime movers in addressing sexual abuse in sport (Brackenridge, 1994, 1996, 1997a,b,c; Kirby, 1995; Kirby & Greaves, 1996; Lenskyj, 1992, Pike Masteralexis, 1995; Volkwein, 1996).

In the first national study of this problem, a survey of the total population of Canada's high-performance and recently retired Olympic athletes (N=1200), Kirby and Greaves (1996) found that sexual harassment and abuse by authority figures in sport were fairly widespread practices. Although the response rate of 22.2% in this study might lead us to regard the figures with some caution, it was achieved *without* the usual follow-up procedures to increase survey returns. This was a deliberate tactic to guarantee confidentiality to participants. Canadian athletes were asked to report on unwanted sexual experiences only within the sporting context. Twenty-one and eight tenths percent of the 266 respondents replied that they had had sexual intercourse with persons in positions of authority. Additionally, 8.6% reported they had experienced *forced* sexual intercourse, or rape, with such persons which, by whatever standard, is a startling figure. Twenty-three respondents were under 16 years of age at the time of the sexual assault, in other words experienced child sexual assault (defined as rape in some countries). In the same study, sexual harassment and abuse were differentially experienced by females and males with the females demonstrating a higher degree of vulnerability, higher awareness of the issues, more instances of abuse and harassment, and wider variation in the types of abuses they experienced. Three and two tenths of athletes in the Canadian research reported that, when under 16 years of age, they had been upset by a flasher (someone exposing their genitals) in a sporting context. Two and six tenths of athletes experienced unwanted sexual touching prior to the age of 16 years. It is not clear how many of the athletes surveyed in this project entered sport after the age of 16 or whether these data are additive, that is, related to experiences of sexual harassment and abuse reported *outside* the sporting context, particularly in the family (figures for which are reported in Brackenridge, 1994, 1996). However, we have reason to believe that athletes who, for whatever reason, have endured negative experiences of sexual, physical or emotional abuse, bring added vulnerability into the sport context. This vulnerability is compounded by their intense commitment to sporting goals. They are particularly easy targets for coaches or other authority figures with motivations to abuse and are more likely to be singled out for the grooming process whereby individuals are targeted and prepared for abuse.

Descriptive studies utilising qualitative methods are now emerging. A recent qualitative study involving in-depth interviews with female victims of sexual abuse in elite sport in the Netherlands indicates that family neglect and abuse is a stronger predictor of vulnerability to sexual abuse in sport at the recreational level, whereas dependence on the coach appears to be more strongly related to susceptibility to abuse at the elite level (Cense, 1997). Brackenridge (1997c) carried out a qualitative study in which former female athletes gave detailed accounts of the sexual abuse they had suffered from their coaches; and Volkwein (1996) reports extensive concerns amongst campus athletes and non-athletes about acts of sexual harassment generated by student athletes. Systematic analysis of descriptive information provided by athletes is providing useful insights not only into how sexual abuse is experienced but also what needs to be done to eradicate it.

Theoretical Explanations

There are several explanations of sexual abuse; what might be termed *structural explanations* suggest that children and young people are less powerful in our society than adults and that they depend on adults for security, shelter and care. Children, especially, find it difficult to report their concerns to sport organisations, which are run by adults. Adults have power and authority over children who, in turn, place their trust in adults. This trusting relationship is at the core of effective coaching, and it is, therefore, devastating for the young athlete when that trust is violated or exploited. The diagnostic literature on sexual abuse is currently dominated by medical, psychiatric and therapeutic analyses, most of which individualize the problem and fail to set it in a social context (see, for example, Marshall, Laws, & Babaree, 1990). Feminist researchers are among those critical of such deterministic approaches and insist on the recognition of the social context of gender power relations in any attempt to understand sexual abuse (Lewis Herman, 1990; Bart & Geil Moran, 1993).

Theoretical explanations of sexual abuse within sport are limited, and at this point, sport researchers have been evaluating theories drawn from the child sexual abuse literature and from organisational analyses. Their use as theoretical applications, we suggest, is somewhat limited because of the unique nature of the sport context. For example, early research by Brackenridge used two theories from social work. First, Finkelhor's Four Factor Theory (1984) shows how motivation to abuse must be resisted or overcome both personally and externally before actual abuse takes place, as can be seen in Figure 14.3. This model is interesting because it includes external and social factors, as well as internal motivational and personal factors. However, this useful but relatively simplistic account of abuse as a linear process may be insufficient for effective intervention and treatment. Because sport psychologists work almost exclusively with the preparation of athletes for competition, they are unlikely to come into regular contact with coaches or other authority figures in sport and, thus, are unlikely to become engaged in treating offenders. For their purposes, then, the *external inhibitors* (policies, systems and prevention procedures) and the *resistance of the child* are the key areas for intervention work.

Secondly, Wolf's cycle of abuse (describes in Fisher, 1994, p.19) plots a sequence of offender behaviour which is self-reinforcing (see Figure 14.4). The theory focuses attention on sexual abuse as an individual disturbance rather than one with sociocultural paramaters. The theory suggests that the abuser lacks personal confidence, retires from normal social contact, starts to use

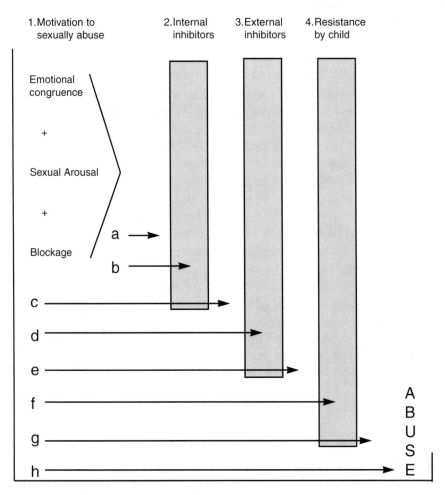

a = internal inhibitors effective
b = internal inhibitors challenged but hold
c = internal inhibitors overcome; external inhibitors effective
d = external inhibitors challenged but hold
e = external inhibitors overcome but resistance by child effective
f = resistance by child challenged but holds
g = resistance by child overcome
h = no resistance by child

Figure 14.3. Finkelhor's four preconditions of sexual abuse (1984, adapted).

sexual fantasies and perhaps pornography, then targets a potential victim or victims. Offenders use secrecy, rewards and the cover of trust to groom the athlete and secure their cooperation. When Wolf's theory of paedophile abuse is

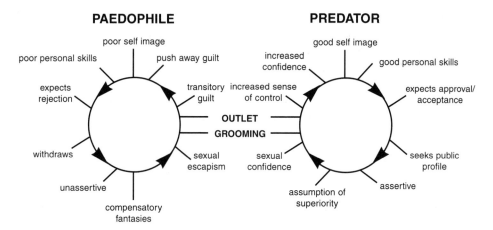

Figure 14.4. Two cycles of offending: the paedophile (Wolf cited in Fisher, 1994) and the predator (Brackenridge, 1996).

applied to sport, it helps to identify the responsibilities of sport organisations which, we argue, lie within the area of the cycle concerned with grooming and actual abuse, rather than with the whole cycle. Because, by this interpretation, the origins of abuse are pathological, there is little that sport organisations can do to prevent certain individuals from becoming sexually aroused by children; however, there is much that they can do situationally to protect young athletes from grooming and actual abuse.

If, as many would argue, it is the case that sport is centred on the well-being of the athlete, then sport psychologists, along with other professionals, have a role to play in ensuring that they and their colleagues uphold the standards of the profession in reporting sexual abuse if it occurs and in supporting athletes in their attempts to deal with abuse. In sum, sport psychologists are key players in guaranteeing the quality of the sport experience for participants. Herein lies a dilemma for the sport psychologist; interventions aimed at child athletes or external inhibitors deal only with the *symptoms* or with the strategies for coping with sexual abuse. Interventions aimed at the *causes* (the sexual arousal and motivation of the offender) lie, in the main, beyond the day-to-day scope of the sport psychologist because the causes are logically prior to sport-related incidents. We believe that is it critical for sport psychologists to decide exactly where the limits of their expertise lie and to be ready to work with other professionals, that is, to refer to, or work with, clinical therapists or others specialists if they feel that the behavior of a coach or other authority figure warrants this. We contend that it is beyond the scope or expertise of sport organisations, and indeed most sport psychologists, to work *outside* this segment of the paedophile cycle. Although sport psychologists cannot stop the motive to abuse, they *can* contribute to more effective prevention by helping to increase athletes' resistance to grooming.

In addition to the paedophile cycle proposed by Wolf, recent research has indicated that a second cycle of abuse, the mirror image of the first, is evident within many reported cases (Brackenridge, 1997c): This has been called the *predator cycle*. Here, the abuser uses the power of his authority to dominate the potential victim through autocratic coaching and strict, hierarchical regimes based on unequal power relations. Abusers in sport often benefit from the alibi of status: The club or squad becomes like a *surrogate family* in which compliance to patriarchal authority systems leads to oppression of athletes. Brackenridge (1997a) describes the building of a sense of primary group, or surrogate family, in sport based on the assumption of a hierarchical family structure, with the coach as head of the family unit. Kirby and Greaves (1997) add that this "familism" in sport provides fertile ground for a staggering number and types of abuse because authority figures have ready access to athletes as sexual partners. According to Brackenridge (1996) the abuse is *virtual incest*.

Exactly where, how and why the confidence and social competence of the sports coach lead him into sexually transgressive behaviour has yet to be established. This violation of the sexual, ethical and interpersonal boundaries which normally constrain coach/athlete relations resembles the breaking of other social taboos and has been much researched in other, cognate settings, such as abuse by clergy and therapists (Gonsiorek, 1995). Unlike the paedophile cycle, where we have argued that sport psychologists have a restricted role, they have an important role to play in challenging and ameliorating the effects of the predator because predatory sexual practices are associated with the social structural features of sport (harsh competition, the emphasis on success, power and physical strength, subordination to the authority of the coach and so on). Sport shares some of these features with the workplace, yet its almost unique legitimation of the physical sets it apart from either the family (where most paedophilia occurs) or the workplace. Coaching and leadership styles have been intensively researched in sport psychology, and psychologists are well-equipped with both knowledge and skills to work with coaches on the development of democratic styles and to use other interventions to help empower athletes and thus reduce the potential for exploitation.

As mentioned earlier, in their study of abuse amongst elite sportswomen, the Netherlands Olympic Committee/Netherlands Sports Confederation have found that coach dependency is a major predictor of risk of abuse (Cense, 1997). This work challenges the notion of the predator cycle by suggesting that apparent-predators exhibit the qualities of paedophiles as well, in other words, that the predator is a subtype of the paedophile. Only through further work of this kind in the context of sport will the validity and reliability of such cycles be established.

The consequences of abuse for the individual athlete are stark; they include social embarrassment, emotional turmoil, psychological scars, loss of self esteem and negative impacts on family, friends and the sport. Many athletes are victimised during or after abuse, usually by the abuser but often, additionally, by peer athletes and, as a result, they may suffer life-long trauma. Thus far, research has not discovered any major differences between the trauma suffered by victims of sexual abuse in sport and those found in studies of abuse in the general population (see Figure 14.5). It is too early to say whether those athletes interviewed and surveyed about their experiences represent a 'typical' group, or whether those who have either dropped out of sport or chosen not to disclose their experiences might yield any different results. Certainly, those who are able to speak out show strength of character and a positive will to survive. The personal costs of sexual abuse to an athlete may be too hard to bear for many, who simply disappear from their sport. The cost to sport is immeasurable. Reports of absenteeism, lower trust, higher turnover, lower team morale and lower energy abound (Kirby, 1995). The extent of lost talent is impossible to calculate.

— Suspicious, unable to trust others
— Afraid, unable to stand up for own opinions
— Blames self for everything bad that happens
— Feels guilty and ashamed even when there is no reason
— Withdraws, does not want to spend time with others
— Feels "different" from others
— Feels hurt by others a lot of the time
— Lonely, bored and empty inside
— Suicidal
— Feels like a perfectionist, cannot tolerate mistakes
— Constantly feels sorry for self
— Feels angry all the time
— Closes off feelings, unable to tolerate emotional pain
— Not caring about appearance
— Feels out of control of life
— Depressed and sad
— Afraid of change
— Feels trapped, like nobody understands
— Feels stupid, less capable than others
— Ashamed of sexual feelings

Figure 14.5. Consequences of sexual abuse for female athletes (from Rodgers, 1995).

Abusers use a number of personal coping strategies to deal with accusations against them: These include (after Rodgers, 1995):

- denying—"It didn't happen."
- minimizing—"It was only a bit of fun."
- blaming the victim—"She was asking for it."
- presenting the victim as unreliable, worthless, mad, manipulative, vindictive—"You can't believe someone like her."

Comments such as these are all too often heard in the sporting context.

Assessing the Risk of Sexual Abuse to Young Athletes

Although some policy interventions have begun to increase *apparent* safety levels within sport, there is no empirical evidence of their *actual* efficacy because there is so little knowledge about the baseline prevalence and incidence levels for sexual abuse in sport. However, a risk-assessment and risk-management approach to sexual abuse in sport is beginning to prove fruitful for those keen to improve protection systems and procedures. Practice in the area of child/athlete protection is currently based on the best knowledge currently available from social work, together with emerging analyses of risk in the specific context of sport.

Risk-factors analysis in sport to date has been based on the limited qualitative and quantitative studies reported above. In particular, Brackenridge (1997b) has provided a set of risk factors for sexual abuse in sport based on interviews with abused former athletes. These are divided into Coach Variables, Athlete Variables and Sport Variables (see Figure 14.6). The risk factors are not predictors in the statistical sense, where for example, percentages of risk can be calculated, but they offer a general picture of warning signs that might be taken into account by practitioners, parents, coaches and sport psychologists. It is important to stress that the risk factors are seen as groups or patterns and not as isolated or causal variables. Where there is a degree of 'saturation' or data confirmation around a factor (Glaser & Strauss, 1967; Kirby & McKenna, 1989), a comment is made in brackets beside the variable: where there is still uncertainty but risk is hypothesised, then a question mark appears. As more and more data are collected and analyzed, so the emerging picture of risk will clarify. For example, a database of over 100 accounts of sexual abuse in sport is currently being compiled on which statistical tests will be run to check the frequency of occurrence of these factors. A mixture of inductive and deductive approaches, then, will gradually construct the knowledge base. Thus far, the risk factors have resonated with audiences and have proved exceptionally useful communication tools.

COACH VARIABLES

— sex [male]
— age [older]
— size/physique [larger/stronger]
— accredited qualifications [good]
— rank/reputation [high]
— previous record of SH [unknown/ignored]
— trust of parents [strong]
— standing in the sport/ club/community [high]
— chances to be alone with athletes in training, at competitions, at coach's home, and away on trips [frequent]
— commitment to sport/national sport-specific codes of ethics and conduct [weak]
— use of car to transport athletes [frequent]

ATHLETE VARIABLES

— sex [female]
— age [younger]
— size/physique [smaller/weaker]
— rank/status [potentially high]
— history of sexual abuse [unknown/none]
— level of awareness of SH [low]
— self-esteem [low]
— medical problems especially disordered eating [medium/high]
— relationship with parents [weak]
— education and training on SH and abuse [none]
— devotion to coach [complete]
— dependence on coach [total]
— puberty relative to sport age/ stage of imminent achievement [at or before]

SPORT VARIABLES

— amount of physical handling required for coaching [?]
— individual/team sport [?]
— location of training & competitions [?]
— opportunity for trips away [many]
— dress requirements [?]
— employment/recruitment controls/ vetting [weak/none]
— regular evaluation including athlete screening and cross-referencing to medical data [none]
— use of national and sport-specific codes of ethics [weak]
— existence of athlete and parent contracts [none]
— climate for debating SH [poor/non-existent]
— coaches association codes of ethics/conduct [weak/none]

Note: Comments in brackets indicate emerging trends from interview data. Where bracket contains question mark further research is required.

Figure 14.6. Risk factors for sexual abuse in sport (updated from Brackenridge, 1997b).

Theory development is a slow process: It must be based on sound data, make sense to sport participants, and stand the challenge of new data. In sport research, it is not yet clear how closely the personal and social parameters of sexual abuse in sport settings match those outside sport. If we are right that the sports club functions as a *surrogate family* and that, therefore, sexual abuse is *virtual rape* (Brackenridge, 1997c), then the social and interpersonal processes leading to abuse, especially those affecting the prepubescent or pubescent athlete who is below the legal age of consent, may well be identical to those in family settings. Sport researchers may, therefore, find fruitful avenues in studying the family abuse/therapy literature. In making the transition from the relatively security of the family to the 'occupational' world of sport, the young athlete arguably faces inherent dangers associated with change, such as psychological adjustments and adaptation to new mentors, which add to situational vulnerability. It is possible that research into abuse in sport may help to refine theoretical tools for analyzing and understanding abuse in other voluntary sport settings, such as music clubs, church and youth groups, and in non-sport contexts (church, military, Big Brothers, caring professions with misconduct problems). However, until systematic studies have been carried out on large samples, many research questions will remain and the links between abuse in sport and nonsport settings will continue to be unclear.

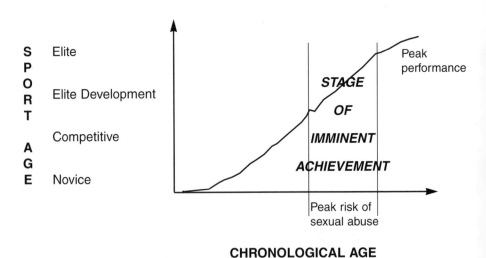

Figure 14.7. Sport age, risk of sexual abuse, and stage of imminent achievement.

Where sport is distinctive from general leisure activities is in its emphasis on skilled, gross motor performance. In this connection a theoretical idea is emerging that may assist psychologists and others to target safety programes more effectively. Building on Kirby's concept of *sport age* (1986), the notion of a *stage of imminent achievement* (SIA) has been developed to indicate that stage of an young athlete's development when top level performance is almost but not quite attained (Brackenridge & Kirby, 1997). The SIA represents that stage when the athlete has the most to lose from dropping out as she or he has invested the most, in terms of time, effort and dedication and has the most to gain from remaining. We hypothesize that, *where the SIA coincides with or precedes the period of puberty or sexual maturation, then the athlete is at peak risk of sexual abuse* (see Figure 14.7). Under this description, there is the possibility that the dynamics of sexual abuse for these athletes differ from those for athletes who have completed puberty and who may be approaching or beyond the minimum legal age of consent.

The dominance of medical and allied sciences in the current diagnostic literature about sexual abuse means that there is undue emphasis on individualized behavior and treatment, whether for the abuser or the victim (Marshall *et al.*, 1990). This pathologises sexual abuse, drawing attention away from important cultural and situational factors being raised by critical social researchers, including feminists. Clearly, what is needed is a *contingency theory* of sexual abuse in sport that addresses the interaction of coach motivation, sport context and athlete susceptibility (see Figure 14.8) based on a collaboration of researchers and practitioners, sport psychologists and social activists,

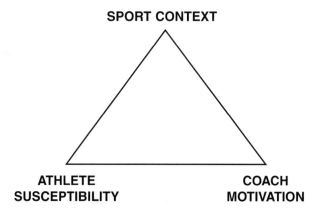

Figure 14.8. Elements of a contingency theory of sexual abuse in sport.

	COACH (Perpetrator)	
ATHLETE (Victim)	MALE	FEMALE
MALE	Increasing numbers; some paedophile but almost no cases recorded with adult victims	Very few women coaches or recorded cases
FEMALE	Almost all recorded cases including many predator	No systematic research yet but anecdotal evidence

Figure 14.9. Current state of research knowledge of sexual harassment and abuse in coach/athlete relationships in sport.

grand and grounded theorists. The tools of sport psychology are already available to contribute to such a theory but it will also be important to draw upon microsociological perspectives from discourse analysis, feminism, process sociology, structuration theory, and elsewhere if we are to develop a comprehensive understanding of this problem and to implement effective prevention and protection.

1. Establish/disseminate and advise on *Codes of Ethics and Conduct*
2. Offer systematic *grievance and disciplinary systems*
3. Investigate the costs and benefits of *registers and criminal record checks*
4. Make *child protection modules* compulsory in coach education
5. Distribute *information* for parents, athletes and coaches
6. Establish simple *contracts* between parents, athletes and coaches
7. Set up an *independent listener/helpline outside* the main sport organisations
8. Adopt *child-centred and democratic coaching styles*
9. Strengthen *links with child protection agencies*
10. Provide *support* for the victim and the accused
11. Disseminate and reward *good practice*
12. Encourage *debate*
13. Commission *research* to increase knowledge

Figure 14.10. Action plan for sport organisations.

Challenges to Sport Psychology

There is always the danger that those of us in the positions of power, whether coaches, parents or sport scientists, will protect ourselves more than the athletes in our charge but athletes, especially those who are still children, are the most vulnerable and must be prioritised. Within the range of stakeholders identified in Figure 14.1, those with the least power to act—children—are those with the most to lose. In this chapter we have tried to explain how knowledge about sexual abuse in sport matches or differs from that in other domains. In particular, we have attempted to set down some challenges to sport psychologists to develop and apply theory in ways which will minimize the risks of abuse to athletes.

The research agenda on the theme of sexual abuse in sport is assuming increasing prominence in sport science (see Figure 14.9). Sport psychologists have entered the field relatively late, following early groundwork by feminist sport sociologists. There is ample scope for a multidisciplinary approach to this problem because no single discipline can ever resolve the many problems which it poses. Indeed, work in the field of sexual abuse in sport necessarily integrates theory, research and application (Vealey, 1997).

Despite conventional wisdom that coaches always put the athlete/child first and that care is central to the ethos of sport, there is great pressure on the coach to push beyond this for performance enhancement, especially where results are at stake. However, it should be accepted that the athlete/child is a total person who has a life not only *after* sport but also *during* sport, and therefore, that his/her development should always come first. The emerging risk factors for sexual abuse in sport shown in Figure 14.2 offer clues to the sport psychologist for research collaboration and for detection and prevention of such abuse. Using these, together with knowledge of the stage of imminent achievement, the sport psychologist also has a major contribution to make in ameliorating the effects of autocratic coaching styles and, by so doing, minimizing the chances of sexual abuse by predatory coaches or other authority figures in sport (see Figure 14.10).

References

Bart, P.B., & Geil Moran, E. (1993). *Violence against women: The bloody footprints*. London: Sage.

Brackenridge, C. (1992, July). *Sexual abuse of children in sport: A comparative exploration of research methodologies and professional practice*. Paper presented to the Pre-Olympic Scientific Congress, Malaga, Spain.

Brackenridge, C. (1994). Fair play or fair game: Child sexual abuse in sport organizations. *International Review for the Sociology of Sport, 29*, 287–299.

Brackenridge, C. (1996). Sexual abuse in sport - whose problem? In C. Brackenridge (Ed.), *Child protection in sport; policies, procedures and systems*. Report of a conference held at Cheltenham & Gloucester College of HE, UK.

Brackenridge, C. (1997a). *Dangerous relations: Men, women and sexual abuse in sport*. Unpublished inaugural professorial lecture, Cheltenham & Gloucester College of HE, UK.

Brackenridge, C. (1997b). He owned me basically: Womens experience of sexual abuse in sport. *International Review for the Sociology of Sport, 32*, 115–130.

Brackenridge, C. (1997c). Researching sexual abuse and sexual harassment in sport. In G. Clarke & B Humberstone (Eds.), *Researching women in sport* (pp. 126–141). London: MacMillan..

Brackenridge, C., & Kirby, S. (1997). Playing safe: Assessing the risk of sexual abuse to elite young athletes. *International Review for the Sociology of Sport, 32*, 407–418.

Canadian Council for Ethics and Sport. (1997). *Notes on discharge of ethic of care*. Victor Lachance, Ottawa, January 29.

Cense, M. (1997). *Rode Kaart of Carte Blanche: Risicofactoren voor seksuelle intimidatie en seksueel misbruik in de sport*. Amsterdam: Netherlands Olympic Committee*Netherlands Sports Federation/TransAct.

Christopherson, J., Furniss, T., O'Mahoney, B., & Peake, A., with Armstrong, H., & Hollows, A. (1989). *Working with sexually abused boys: An introduction for practitioners*. London: National Childrens Bureau.

Creighton. (1989). *Child abuse trends in England and Wales 1983–1987*. London: National Society for the Prevention of Cruelty to Children.

Crosset, T. (1986, July). *Male coach/female athlete relationships*. Paper presented at the First International Conference for Sport Sciences, Sole, Norway.

Crouch, M. (1995). *Protecting children: A guide for sportspeople*. Leeds: National Coaching Foundation/NSPCC.

Donnelly, P., with E. Casperson, L. Sargeant, & B. Steenhof (1993). Problems associated with youth involvement in high-performance sport. In B.R. Cahill & A.J. Pearl (Eds.), *Intensive participation in childrens sports* (pp. 95–126). Champaign, IL: Human Kinetics.

Doyle, C. (1994). *Child sexual abuse : A guide for health professionals*. London: Chapman & Hall.

Elliott, M. (Ed.). (1993). *Female sexual abuse of children: The ultimate taboo*. Harlow, Essex: Longman.

Fawcett, B., Featherstone, B., Hearn, J., & Toft, C. (Eds.). (1996). *Violence and gender relations: Theories and interventions*. London; Sage.

Fetterman, D. M. (1989). *Ethnography step by step*. Applied Social Research Methods Series, Vol. 17. Newbury Park, CA: Sage.

Finkelhor, D. (1984). *Child sexual abuse: New theory and research*. New York: Free Press.

Finkelhor, D. (1994). The backlash and the future of child protection advocacy. In J.E.B. Myers (Ed.), *The backlash: Child protection under fire* (pp. 1–16). London: Sage.

Finkelhor, D., & Williams, L. M. (1988). *Nursery crimes: Sexual abuse in day care*. London: Sage.

Fisher, D. (1994). Adult sexual offenders: Who are they? Why and how do they do it? In T. Morrison, M. Erooga & R.C. Beckett (Eds.), *Sexual offending against children: Assessment and treatment of male abusers* (pp. 1–24). London: Routledge.

Glaser, B., & Strauss, A. (1967). *The discovery of grounded theory*. Chicago: Aldine.

Gonsiorek, J.C. (Ed.). (1995). *Breach of trust: Sexual exploitation by health care professionals and clergy*. London: Sage.

Government of Canada. (1993). *Changing the Landscape: Ending Violence—Achieving Equality*. Final report of the Canadian Panel on Violence Against Women. Ministry of Supply and Services, Canada.

Grange, M. (1997, Feb. 25). Gardens Stops Short of Apology. *Globe and Mail*, pp. A1–A4.

Haskell, L., & L. Randall. (1993). The Womens Safety Project. In Government of Canada, *Changing the landscape: Ending violence—achieving equality* (App. A:A5). Final report of the Canadian Panel on Violence Against Women. Ministry of Supply and Services, Canada.

Kirby, S. (1986). *High performance female athlete retirement*. Unpublished PhD dissertation, University of Alberta, Edmonton, Canada.

Kirby, S. (1995). Not in my back yard. *Canadian Woman Studies, 15*, 58–62.

Kirby, S., & Greaves, L. (1996, July). *Foul play: Sexual abuse and harassment in sport*. Paper presented to Pre-Olympic Scientific Congress, Dallas.

Kirby, S., & Greaves, L. (1997). Le jeu interdit: Le harcélement sexuel dans le sport. *Recherches Féministes,10*, 5–33.

Kirby, S., &. McKenna, K. (1989). *Experience research social change: Methods from the margins*. Toronto: Garamond.

Lachance, V. (1997). *Notes on discharging the ethic of care*. Montreal: Canadian Center for Ethics in Sport.

Lenskyj, H. (1992). Sexual harassment: Female athletes experiences and coaches responsibilities. *Sport Science Periodical on Research and Technology in Sport, 12*, Special Topics B-1.

Lewis Herman, J. (1990). Sex offenders: A feminist perspective. In W.L. Marshall, D.R. Laws & H.E. Barbaree (Eds.), *Handbook of sexual assault: Issues, theories and treatment of the offender* (pp. 177–194). New York: Plenum Press.

MacMillan, H., Fleming, J., Trocomé, E.N., Boyle, M.H., Wong, M., Racine, Y.A., Beardslee, W.R., & Offord, D.R. (1997). Prevalence of child physical and sexual abuse in the community. *Journal of the American Medical Association, 278*(2).

Marshall, W.A., Laws, D.R., & Babaree, H.E. (Eds.). (1990). *Handbook of sexual assault issues, theories and the treatment of the offender*. New York: Plenum Press.

Matthews, R., Matthews, K.J., & Speltz, K. (1989). *Female sexual offenders*. Orwell: The Safer Society Press.

National Coaching Foundation/NSPCC/Amateur Swimming Association of Great Britain. (1996). *Guidance for national governing bodies on child protection procedures*. Leeds: National Coaching Foundation.

Presidents Council on Physical Fitness and Sports. (1997). *Physical activity and sport in the lives of girls*. Minnesota, University of Minnesota: Centre for Research on Girls and Women in Sport.

Pike Masteralexis, L. (1995). Sexual harassment and athletics: Legal and policy implications for athletic departments. *Journal of Sport and Social Issues, 19*, 141–156.

Rodgers, S. (1995, March). The clinical therapists perspective. Paper presented to *Guilty Knowledge*, a workshop of the British Association of Sport & Exercise Sciences, held at Cheltenham & Gloucester College of HE.

Russell, D.E.H. (1984). *Sexual exploitation: Rape, child sexual abuse and workplace harassment*. London: Sage.

Vealey, R. (1997, July). *From information to knowledge: Beyond dualism in sport psychology research and practice*. Keynote paper presented at the IX Congress of the International Society of Sport Psychology, Wingate Institute, Israel.

Volkwein, K. (1996, July). *Sexual harassment in sport perceptions and experiences of female student-athletes*. Paper presented at the Pre-Olympic Scientific Congress, Dallas.

Whetsell-Mitchell, J. (1995). *Rape of the innocent: Understanding and preventing child sexual abuse*. London: Accelerated Development/Taylor & Francis.

15

Disability, Physical Activity, Psychological Well-Being, and Empowerment: A Life-Span Perspective

Yeshayahu Hutzler
The Zinman College of Physical Education and Sport Sciences,
Wingate Institute, Israel

Claudine Sherrill
Department of Kinesiology of the Texas Woman's University,
Denton, Texas, USA

Disability in this chapter, is limited to individual differences in physical or sensory structure, function, appearance, or performance that are perceived as undesirable by self and/or others and thus affect psychological well-being (Sherrill, 1997, 1998). This chapter excludes intellectual and learning difficulties and focuses on amputations, blindness, cerebral palsy, spinal cord injury, and other conditions that result in impaired coordination or ambulation. These conditions historically have been known by many names (e.g., handicap, impairment, defects), but today *disability* and *people with disabilities* are the preferred terms, having arisen by consensus from within the disability community, the international disability sport movement, and various psychological organizations (American Psychological Association, 1994; DePauw & Gavron, 1995; Shapiro, 1993). The terms *handicap* and *impairment* (World Health Organization [WHO], 1980) increasingly are perceived as offensive by many people, because they (a) emphasize disturbance, loss, and other negative aspects of being and (b) imply standards of normalcy that ignore individual differences (Barton, 1993; Davis, 1995; Wendell, 1996).

Some disciplines and some areas of the world do continue to use WHO (1980) terms to differentiate between levels and conditions (i.e., *impairment* as a disturbance at the organ level, *disability* as a limitation at the personal level, and *handicap* as a socially constructed phenomenon). However, this chapter uses only the term *disability,* in support of the stance taken by the leaders in both the disability rights and the disability sport movements.

The American Psychological Association (1994) recommends that *disability* be used to refer to an attribute of an individual and that *handicap* be used to refer to various kinds of barriers that require removal. This recommendation is based on multidimensional identity, personal meaning, and other psychological theories, which emphasize that disability is not a global construct and thus should be treated as only one of many attributes that comprise an individual (Sherrill, 1997; Wendell, 1996; Wright, 1983; Yuker, 1988). Psychological well-being and empowerment depend largely on recognition that the whole self is not disabled, that disability is a dynamic, ever-changing condition, and that individuals have the power to socially construct themselves to become whatever they want to be.

Social construction of psychologically healthy persons occurs through the life-span process of social interactions between self and others that maximize strengths and resources and minimize barriers to self-actualization. Physical activity facilitates psychological well-being and empowerment by helping individuals to gain access to knowledge and resources that, in turn, allow control over their bodies and related life events (Sherrill & Williams, 1996). Figure 15.1, which is based on a comprehensive review of literature (Hutzler & Bar-Eli, 1993), presents a model suggesting that empowerment, as both a process and product of social emancipation during sport participation, is linked to constructs associated with psychological well-being, such as self-efficacy, self-competence, internal locus of control, self-esteem, and self-actualization. The empowerment model serves to introduce the content of this chapter and provide background for the salutogenesis model, also presented in this chapter.

The purpose of this chapter is to demonstrate how sport and physical activity contribute to the life-span well-being and empowerment of individuals with disabilities. Terminology issues related to adapted physical activity, disability sport, psychological well-being, and empowerment are discussed first, followed by (a) an overview of the literature in this field and (b) a focused analysis of selected recent studies. The overview includes results of a computerized search and identification of review articles and chapters in this area. The focused analysis reviews literature on psychological well-being and empowerment under the following topics : (a) physical activity during childhood and adolescence, (b) onset of disability, (c) athletes with disabilities, and (d) retired athletes with disabilities.

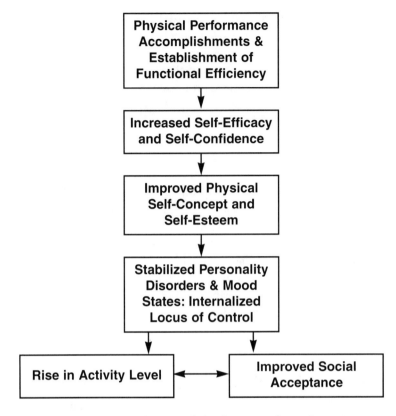

Figure 15.1. An integrative model of sports-based empowerment: positive psychological constructs.

Adapted Physical Activity and Disability Sport

Adapted physical activity and *disability sport* are the terms used in the scholarly literature pertaining to the contribution of sport and physical activity to the well-being and empowerment of people with disabilities. The profession that generates this literature is called *adapted physical activity;* this profession addresses individual differences in psychomotor function or physical appearance that interfere with healthy, active lifestyle and/or goal achievement in sport, dance, and aquatics (Sherrill, 1998; Sherrill & DePauw, 1997). The philosophy that guides *adapted physical activity* emphasizes a strong association between healthy, active lifestyle, psychological well-being, and empowerment. *Disability sport* is a subspecialization within adapted physical activity that encompasses (a) top-level international elite sport like Paralympics; (b) competitive organized sport at the club, school, and national levels; (c) recreational sport performed for personal pleasure; and (d) health sport prescribed for medical, prevention, and fitness purposes (Council of Europe, 1987).

Adapted physical activity professionals are guided by the International Federation of Adapted Physical Activity (IFAPA) with regional affiliates on every continent. Members include sport personnel, educators, psychologists, therapists, and physicians who are committed to facilitating physical and psychological well-being through involvement in physical activity. The official journal of IFAPA is *Adapted Physical Activity Quarterly,* published by Human Kinetics since 1984, but several other journals also pertain to adapted physical activity (e.g., *Palaestra: Forum of Sport, Physical Education and Recreation for Those With Disabilities,* and *Clinical Kinesiology).*

The nature of adapted physical activity service delivery varies throughout the world, but a growing number of universities employ professors with doctoral degrees in this specialization to train direct-services personnel in schools, exercise facilities, rehabilitation centers, and sport clubs and to conduct research concerning disability and physical activity. In some countries, adapted physical activity is primarily a school-based profession that assumes responsibility for socializing children with special needs into healthy, active lifestyles. In other countries, adapted physical activity is a life-span service with specialists employed by all kinds of facilities.

Psychological Well-Being and Empowerment

Feeling well is a relative term, as is *feeling bad.* For one person, climbing a mountain is perceived as a joyful challenge that is worth his or her efforts whereas for another it may be perceived as a boredom that should be avoided. The subjective feeling of well-being is closely related to *"quality of life"* and describes a person's positive orientation towards his or her life, including cognitive, evaluative as well as affective components (Berger, 1996). This orientation is affected by a complex network of factors, which is well illustrated by the salutogenesis model.

Antonovsky's (1987) *salutogenesis* model provides a comprehensive explanation for the interplay of these factors. The model shows that sports participation affects certain factors, which may be viewed as the classical risk factors (malnutrition, smoking, overweight, low fitness, psychological overstress) mediating *distress* and *disease.* However, one of Antonovsky's major contributions is the formulation of protection factors (generalized resistance resources) mediating *"eustress"* and *ease* (i.e., relaxation, comfort, *well-being*). The simplified model presented in Figure 15.2 includes a personal evaluative component (labeled as *sense of coherence*) providing cognitive and

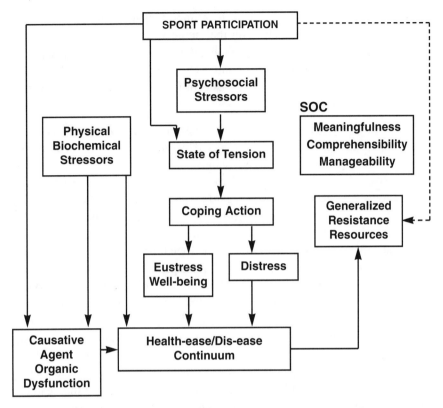

Figure 15.2. The Salutogenic model of health from a sports scientific point of view (SOC = sense of coherence).

affective appraisal of one's orientation towards life as well as psychosocial and physiological continuation of risk and protection factors. Based on a salutogenic physical activity research paradigm, Boes, Woll, Oja, Suni, and Hutzler (1995) found improved psychological well-being of physically active compared to nonactive individuals in relation to increased risk factors, such as age above 40. Studies related to other concepts, such as psychosomatics and hardiness, provide further evidence for the protective function of physical activity. Roth and Holmes (1985) have demonstrated that improved fitness has a significant effect in individuals coping with increased stress and illness. Kobasa, Maddi, and Puccetti (1982) found exercise to decrease illness when interacting with stressful life events. Hutzler (1986, 1990) reported statements made by individuals with a disability suggesting a similar trend. For example, a male athlete with quadriplegia (HK) said,

Particularly for the quadriplegic it is important to be fast again . . . through the fast movement with the racing wheelchair one is equally appraised again. The positive phenomenon in sports is the ability to perform better with the wheelchair and with life in general. Thus the self-confidence increases and the self-esteem is raised. (quoted in Hutzler, 1986, p.176)

Living with a physical disability is a lifelong experience of coping with being different, disadvantaged, and often rejected by others. In contrast to early generalized beliefs of personality psychologists that disability is associated with poor self-esteem and psychological well-being, contemporary rehabilitation psychologists are cautious in this regard (Trieschmann, 1988; Wright, 1983). Self-esteem and psychological well-being increasingly are linked with success in coping. Individuals with congenital disabilities typically cope with overprotective conditions limiting their social interactions (Katz, 1981), whereas individuals with acquired disabilities generally cope with difficulties such as changed roles and attitudes of family members and important others (Goffman, 1963; Wright, 1983; Yuker, 1988). Sport is one vehicle through which coping and related skills can be learned (Crocker, 1993; Sherrill, 1998).

Success in coping with life demands, when accompanied by a state of psychological well-being, leads to empowerment of individuals with disabilities. Empowerment, within the adapted physical activity context, refers to gaining control over one's life and assuming responsibility for changes that lead to a healthy, active lifestyle and positive mental health. Control over the body, gained through disciplined exercise and participation in sport, is for many people a first step toward controlling and improving life in general. Losing weight, developing strength and endurance, and achieving mental toughness to display their bodies in public sport settings all contribute to a changing image that affects attitudes of self and others. Gaining increased control over the body enables better mind-body integration, which impacts on many other areas of life, including improved self-esteem and social acceptance. The process of empowerment is facilitated by both self and others; the process is different in every individual. This chapter highlights people with disabilities who choose exercise and sport as their initial or major vehicle to empowerment; We realize that many people with disabilities choose other means. For people willing to engage in the hard training and discipline needed to become athletes, increasing opportunities at all levels (including national and international) enable empowerment and contribute to psychological well-being.

Research Literature Pertaining to Disability Sport, Well-Being, and Empowerment

A fairly extensive body of literature on psychosocial perspectives of disability sport has evolved over the past 15 years, with research reported primarily in two journals, *Adapted Physical Activity Quarterly* and *Palaestra* (Reid & Prupas, 1998). Proceedings of conferences (e.g., Sherrill, 1986; Steadward, Nelson, & Wheeler, 1994) and textbooks with chapters on disability sport psychosocial perspectives (e.g., DePauw & Gavron, 1995; Shephard, 1990; Sherrill, 1990) have also contributed to the critical mass. Existing research is reviewed on the following pages under these headings: (a) computerized searches, (b) review articles and chapters, and (c) selected individual studies.

Computerized Searches

Hutzler and Felis (1998) conducted a computerized search of the disability sport literature reported in *Medline* (Index Medicus) and SIRC (Sport Database) over the past 15 years (1983-1997), whereas Reid and Prupas (1998) used SIRC and a manual search to identify disability sport literature from 1986 to 1996. Findings were similar. Hutzler and Felis (1998) reported that 29% of the total articles pertained to psychology and sociology disciplines, whereas Reid and Prupas noted that social/psychological aspects of sport ranked third highest in number of publications out of seven disability sport priorities.

Specifically, Hutzler and Felis (1998) visually analyzed a database of 253 records and searched for frequencies of records matching the following categories: (a) scientific discipline, (b) age group, (c) research vs. review or commentary articles, and (d) type of disability. A descriptive analysis was performed, summing up the records cited by discipline over each 5-year interval. Results revealed that physiology accounted for 41% of the records, followed by psychology (29%) and biomechanics (22%). Sociology, which accounted for 9%, included some records related to attitudes that may be referenced also under psychology. Overall, 70% of all the records and 58% of the records regarding psychology included scientific research. The findings related to major population criteria in terms of age, gender, and disability are described in Table 15.1.

From the data in Table 15.1, it is evident that the most frequently researched groups are wheelchair users (55%) and adults (73%). Female participants were included in very few articles. The number of scientific publications in psychology has increased over the years whereas no growth is evident in other disciplines (Table 15.2).

Table 15.1. Distribution of population criteria (frequency and % in brackets)*.

Population Age (& Gender)		
Age/Gender Group	All Records	in Psychology
children	26 (10%)	8 (11%)
youth	12 (5%)	7 (9%)
adults	190 (73%)	49 (65%)
elderly	11 (4%)	4 (5%)
general	27 (10%)	7 (9%)
women**	4 (2%)	1 (1%)

Population Disability		
Disability Group	All Records	in Psychology
wheelchair user	142 (55%)	24 (32%)
amputee	25 (10%)	5 (7%)
cerebral palsy	17 (7%)	5 (7%)
visual	6 (2%)	3 (4%)
non-specific	55 (21%)	27 (36%)
multiple sample	28 (11%)	11 (14%)

* % calculated out of 253 references. Matching of more than one category possible
**studies exclusively related to females

Review Articles and Chapters

Several reviews described data-based research related to the psychological aspects of disability and physical activity (e.g., Benson & Jones, 1992; Crocker, 1993; Hutzler & Bar-Eli, 1993; Porretta & Moore, 1996/1997; Sherrill, 1986, 1990, 1997; Sherrill & Williams, 1996). Although there is some overlap in the studies reviewed, different perspectives are explored. For example, Sherrill (1986) reviewed research relating to (a) stigmatization and prejudice, (b) selected theories (motivation, participation, and social learning), and (c) spectators. A few years later, Sherrill (1990) organized her review by data-collection instruments noting (a) that most research was based on the Sixteen Personality Factor Questionnaire (16PF), Profile of Mood States (POMS), State-Trait Anxiety Inventory (STAI), Personal Orientation Inventory (POI), Test of Attentional and Interpersonal Style (TAIS), and Locus of Control Scales; (b) that validity and reliability of instruments for use with people with disabilities was not adequately addressed; and (c) that research was mostly atheoretical and weak. The approach of Hutzler and Bar-Eli (1993) was to posit an integra-

Table 15.2. Distribution of SIRC and MEDLINE citations exclusively defined by scientific discipline and publication year.

Discipline	1983–1987	1988–1992	1993–1997
Physiology	24	39	40
Biomechanics	4	25	26
Psychology	20	24	30
Sports Medicine	1	1	5
Sociology	8	7	7
Motor Behavior	3		

tive model of sports-based empowerment (Figure 15.1), and then to review research related to the components of this model: performance accomplishments and functional efficiency, perceived self-efficacy, self-concept, and self-esteem, mood states, locus of control, and activity level and social acceptance. Hutzler and Bar-Eli concluded that sports activities contribute to significant psychological gains, which help people with disabilities to restore their action competencies as depicted in the empowerment model. This conclusion was based on comprehensive reviews of 25 studies conducted between 1967 and 1986.

Many of the recent literature reviews have been organized around theories and models. Crocker (1993), for example, discussed the usefulness of three psychological theories for advancing adapted-physical-activity knowledge: transactional stress theory (Lazarus & Folkman, 1984), attribution theory (Weiner, 1985), and planned-behavior theory (Ajzen, 1985). Sherrill (1997) reviewed only studies related to the social construction of disability and the development of self-esteem and perceived competence. Sherrill and Williams (1996) focused only on inclusion and integration as they related to sport participation.

In the most comprehensive review to date, Porretta and Moore (1996/1997) analyzed research published since 1980 under the specific disabilities studied: blindness and visual impairment, neuromuscular conditions/amputations, cerebral palsy, and mental retardation. Like other reviewers, they noted that the results of sport psychology research on persons with disabilities are similar to those on persons without disabilities. Porretta and Moore emphasized, however, that most existing research has little direct application for enhancing sport performance, and recommended that research in the future focus on goal setting, self-regulation, visual rehearsal, relaxation training, and motivator identification. Implementation of this recommendation requires that sport-specific psychological instruments be used in future research.

Selected Individual Studies Across the Life-Span

Psychological research prior to the 1990s was largely atheoretical and typically relied on instruments developed for able-bodied persons. Validity and reliability of these instruments for specific disabilities were seldom addressed; thus, findings must be viewed with caution. Nevertheless, data consistently suggest that (a) sport participation by individuals with disabilities is linked with psychological well-being and empowerment, and (b) few significant differences on global psychosocial measures exist between athletes with and without disabilities. Unexpectedly, a substantial number of researchers have reported that athletes with disabilities score significantly better than the norms for able-bodied persons as outlined in test manuals, particularly on self-esteem and mood-state measures. This finding has been named the *growth-through-adversity phenomenon*, suggesting that coping with disability may develop personal strengths that contribute to high scores on self-esteem and perceived mood states, indicative of good mental health (Sherrill, 1997).

In the following section, research based on questionnaire and in-depth interview results is discussed. The individual studies were selected according to their relationship with vulnerable phases across the life-span.

Physical Activity During Childhood and Adolescence

The level of physical activity participation among children with physical disabilities is markedly lower than that of their able-bodied peers (Longmuir & Bar-Or, in press). Moreover, a significantly smaller percentage of youth with disabilities believe that regular exercise is important to overall health and well-being. Barriers to physical activity most often cited by youth with disabilities are "not being good enough" and "the activity being too hard" (Longmuir & Bar-Or, in press). Both of these barriers, which are not generally mentioned by able-bodied youth, relate to perceived competence in sport activities.

Actual and perceived physical competence. The perceived-competence theory of Harter (1978) has been tested on children and adolescents with disabilities more than any other psychological theory. Perceived competence is domain-specific self-esteem that is related to ability or skill in eight important life areas, including athletic competence. Cross-sectional research indicates that being an athlete makes a difference on how adolescents with and without disabilities score in various domains (Sherrill, 1997). Adolescents with disabilities who are not athletes score significantly lower than test-manual norms for able-bodied peers on Harter's scales of athletic, social, and scholastic competence and on romantic appeal (King, Shultz, Steel, & Gilpin, 1993). In contrast, adolescent athletes with disabilities score similarly to able-bodied norms on all of Harter's scales (Sherrill, Hinson, Gench, Kennedy, & Low, 1990).

These findings seem to support a link between psychological well-being and involvement in competitive sport.

Based on Harter's approach, an investigation was carried out in Israel involving a cross-sectional design searching a link between motor performance and psychological well-being in children with neuromuscular disabilities. This study was a collaborative effort within the European Masters Program in Adapted Physical Activity (Berendsen & Ottevanger, 1996). In this study, the relationship between (a) self-perceived competence (SPC) measured by a version of Harter and Pike's (1984) pictorial scale of perceived competence adapted to children with cerebral palsy (Vermeer, Lanen, Hendriksen, Speth, & Mulderij, 1994), (b) observed actual performance measured by the Functional Motor Assessment Scale (FMAS; Vermeer, Kruithof, & Zoggel, 1995), and (c) functional capacity as perceived by parents and caregivers by means of the Pediatric Evaluation of Disability Inventory (PEDI; Haley, Coster, Ludlow, Haltiwanger, & Andrellos, 1992) were studied in 32 young children (age range 5-11) with cerebral palsy (CP). A low and nonsignificant correlation ($r = .32$) was obtained between the SPC and FMAS, but a significant relationship occurred between SPC and PEDI ($r = .74$, $p<.001$). This finding suggests that relationships between perceived competence and actual performance in children may vary, depending on the measure in which performance is scored and whether professionals or parents are scoring.

Social support, self-determination, and fun. Among factors important to psychological well-being and empowerment of children with and without disabilities are social-support systems (Martin & Mushett, 1996; Varni & Setoguchi, 1991), range of self-determination related to participation in physical activity (Ferris, 1987; Martens, 1996), and degree of fun experienced during activity (Longmuir & Bar-Or, in press; Martens, 1996). During a retrospective in-depth interview related to physical activity history (Hutzler, Almosny, Bergman, Yaakov, & Getz (1998), a retired international female swimmer with cerebral palsy (age 30) described some of her experiences related to these factors during her childhood: "I was afraid of water. At the beginning it was a catastrophe. I didn't like the exercise and wanted to get rid of it as fast as possible."

This attitude is supported in interviews with other individuals socialized into sports during their childhood as part of their rehabilitation program. Most respondents reported perceptions of exercise as "work" rather than "fun." However, perceptions of physical activity changed over time as illustrated by the athlete's summary statement: "In retrospect, it helped me to overcome fears, to become more independent, in my self-image and in coping strategies I have developed" (quoted in Hutzler et al., 1998).

Early participation in sport is affected by the considerable time and efforts of parents who accompany the child to the sport center and to competitions. This increased parental attention may contribute to psychological well-being. On the other hand, increased parental support may increase tension among siblings. One retired athlete recalls her sister accusing:

> Parents are always with you; everything you want you get; Dad goes with you from morning to evening to 'Spivak' (the sport center) and, whenever there is a competition, all of us must come with you. (quoted in Hutzler et al., 1998)

Depending on age, friends are often acknowledged as providing primary support to sport participation of individuals with disabilities (Martin & Mushett, 1996; Wheeler et al., in press). However, friends represent a mixed collective, including individuals affiliated with the neighborhood and school setting as well as those encountered during exercising. Research indicates that athletes report losing friends of the first type because of their investment in physical activity; however, athletes also report gaining new friends, some of them becoming their best friends or even life-partners later on (Wheeler et al., in press; Wuerch & Sherrill, 1998).

Segregated vs. integrated performance setting. The degree of inclusion (i.e., integration within one's own community) varies among children with disabilities, providing different psychological atmospheres. Sherrill and Williams (1996) noted that individuals with and without disabilities share responsibility for making the inclusion process work in many different kinds of sport settings: (a) predominantly able-bodied, (b) unidisability, (c) multi- or cross-disability, (d) parallel involvement, and (e) adapted activities designed specifically to promote social inclusion. The psychological well-being and empowerment of individuals with disability depend largely on motivation to be involved, personal-social skills, overall readiness for inclusion, and receptiveness of able-bodied administrators. Although much research has been conducted in regard to inclusion in academic settings, almost none exists concerning sport settings. Illustrative of the few studies on inclusion in sport settings is the work of Hedrick, a prominent wheelchair athlete himself. In two studies, Hedrick (1985, 1986) explored the particular impact of integrated vs. separate performance settings in the case of wheelchair tennis instruction. In the first study, Hedrick (1985) investigated practical acquisition of tennis skills, perceived efficacy related to tennis skills, perceived global competencies in several domains, and state anxiety during a learning session. Fifteen children and adolescents with lower-limb disabilities (age range 10-18) participated in this study and were randomly assigned to three learning/performance conditions with 15 able-bodied age- and gender-matched children. These conditions were (a) integrated learning and performance, (b) integrated learning and separate performance, and (c) separate learning and performance. Learning was assessed over eight tennis skill development lessons and four sets of tennis doubles. Hedrick concluded that introducing able-bodied coactors is appropriate only after participants with disabilities attain a competitive level of ability.

In the second study, Hedrick (1986) investigated the impact of an integrated program on able-bodied children and found that their perceptions of peers with disabilities significantly improve after the exposure. Based on these findings, different service-delivery options seem applicable for different objectives (i.e., separate conditions for initial skill development and semi-integrated conditions for efficacy and physical competence development). Anxiety should be controlled at all stages.

Relationship of Onset of Disability

From a salutogenic perspective, a mature orientation to life emerges during adolescence and young adulthood, sometimes as late as age 30 (Antonovsky, 1987). Further, stressful life events may contribute to shifts in one's sense of coherence and resource reservoirs. Thus, it may be suspected that growing up under disabling conditions may have an impact on the individual's well-being. Several researchers have examined the relationship of age at onset of a disability and psychological well-being. Hopper (1986), who measured self-esteem in 87 athletes with either a spinal cord injury or amputation, concluded that self-esteem is significantly better in individuals injured after the 17th birthday. Campbell (1995), after assessing mood, anxiety, self-esteem, and mastery in wheelchair athletes with congenital ($n = 50$) and acquired ($n = 43$) disabilities, reported that athletes with acquired disabilities had significantly better scores on all measures of psychological well-being compared to athletes with congenital disabilities. Two different explanations have been suggested: (a) Individuals disabled earlier in life may lack independence, ego identity, and personal skills compared to those who have undergone "normal" socialization (Sherrill, 1998; Wright, 1983); and (b) individuals who acquired their disability later in life may have developed coping mechanisms to adjust to their disability leading to enhanced well-being (growth-through-adversity phenomenon; Glueckauf & Quittner, 1984; Sherrill, Silliman, Gench, & Hinson, 1990). Another possible explanation is that perhaps individuals with congenital disabilities who manage to establish a competent psychological structure have been motivated by parents and professionals to excel in life domains not limited by physical disability (Wright, 1983).

Adult Athletes With Disabilities

The psychological well-being of athletes with disabilities is well established. There appears to be no need to discuss studies summarized in the various review articles and chapters described earlier. However, the variables that contribute to psychological well-being and empowerment are not yet fully understood, nor are the variables that attract individuals with disabilities to sport and keep them involved. The proportion of individuals with disabilities who participate regularly in sport continues to be far less than the proportion of able-bodied individuals who participate (Sherrill & Williams, 1996).

Some evidence exists that different factors are operative in active lifestyle adherence among individuals with and without disabilities (Shifflett, Cator, & Megginson, 1994). Perceived competence is less of a factor for most adults with disabilities than for those without disabilities, but perceived barriers is more of a factor (Shifflett et al., 1994). However, perceived competence is extremely important to elite athletes with disabilities, who almost universally explain that their attraction to sport was based on significant others telling them they were good and on their own feeling that they were good in a particular sport (Hutzler, 1990; Sherrill, Buswell, Piletic, Hilgenbrinck, Schnell, & Frey, 1998; Wuerch & Sherrill, 1998).

Barriers frequently reported are (a) no companion or friend with whom to share experiences, (b) lack of money (c) lack of transportation or time, (d) lack of specific skills, (e) unavailability of desired activities, and (f) insufficient supports (Sherrill et al., 1998). Barriers affecting participation vary by disability (Ferrara, Dattilo, & Dattilo, 1994) and by degree of athletic eliteness (Sherrill et al., 1998; Wuerch & Sherrill, 1998).

The empowerment concept was initially supported by Hutzler (1990) based on interviews with 15 elite wheelchair athletes. This concept is increasingly popular for describing processes and outcomes related to the well-being of athletes with a disability. Based on in-depth interviews with 9 female elite wheelchair road racers (ages 18 to 35), Wuerch and Sherrill (1998) developed a paradigm to describe empowerment through sport. They noted that initial involvement (*first level*) was a matter of balance between coping with barriers and affirming potential through reciprocal interactions with significant others. The *second level* was growth through learning, feeling, persevering, and deriving meaning from sport, linked with intense internal motivation and high goal orientation. *The third level*, leading directly to empowerment, was actualization of strong self-determination, self-esteem, and self-efficacy behaviors. The life-span empowerment of these three attributes began at Level 1 as road racers sought to understand and overcome barriers.

Self-actualization behaviors of Paralympic athletes with various disabilities were investigated by Sherrill and associates (Sherrill & Rainbolt, 1988; Sherrill, Silliman, et al., 1990; Sherrill, Gench, et al., 1990) from 1984 through 1992. Findings from these studies are reviewed in Sherrill and Williams (1996), suggesting that

1. Psychosocial perspectives with regard to the meaning of sport and its relationship to empowerment are unique to each athlete's evolving biography and ecosystems.
2. Time of onset of disability (congenital or acquired) and severity of disability are the two most important variables that continuously interact in shaping disability sport meanings and careers.
3. The growth-through-adversity phenomenon is a central influence in the sport careers of many athletes.
4. Stigmatization, prejudice, and ambiguity in human relations influence the development of athletes and contribute to their need to see sport as empowering.
5. The meaning of sport for elite athletes with disabilities is inextricably linked with the ongoing processes of self-actualization and self-empowerment.

Interview data on approximately 50 Paralympic athletes collected in Atlanta during the 1996 Paralympic Games (Sherrill et al., 1998) support the findings of Wuerch and Sherrill (1998) that overcoming barriers and assertively taking advantage of support systems are ongoing processes that motivate beliefs, attitudes, and practices that lead to selection on Paralympic teams and continuing goal fulfillment as elite athletes. Athletes almost universally see elite sport as a means of empowerment that generalizes to multiple facets of life.

Blinde and McClung (1997) expanded the research scope to addressing outcomes of participation in recreational sports. Using a content analysis of in-depth interviews with 11 women (ages 19 to 54) and 12 men (ages 20 to 36) with physical disabilities, they concluded that recreational sport impacts participants' perceptions of their physical and social selves. Their findings indicate that

1. Participation impacts the *physical self* through (a) experiencing the body in new ways, (b) enhancing perceptions of physical attributes, (c) redefining physical capabilities, and (d) increasing confidence to pursue new activities.
2. Participation impacts the *social self* by (a) expanding social interactions and (b) enabling initiation of social activities in other contexts.

According to data revealed by Kirby, Cull, and Foreman (1996), no association exists between pre- and postlesion participation in sports among 116 individuals with acquired spinal cord injury. Authors reported that 48% of individuals who were not active in sports prelesion participated postlesion, whereas 57% of the ex-participants became sedentary postlesion. These findings, which have implications for recruitment of new participants, support the salutogenic approach and the growth-through-adversity phenomenon. It appears that efficient coping strategies are essential to psychological well-being and empowerment.

Retired Athletes With a Disability

Disabling conditions at all ages may have an impact on the natural adaptation process throughout the life cycle. Schlossberg's (1981) transition model describes how an individual copes with change in life. She suggests that successful transition represents a balance between assets and liabilities (i.e., protective and risk factors) incorporated in personal, environmental, and transition variables. Utilizing this concept, Wheeler, Malone, Van Vlack, Nelson, and Steadward (1996) suggested a three-phase transition model underlying disability sport including (a) initiation, (b) competition, and (c) retirement from elite sport.

Very limited research has been conducted in regard to retirement from disability sports. Wheeler, Hutzler, Bergman, and Schaefer (1996) have performed in-depth retrospective interviews, identifying physical and psychosocial benefits (gaining personal competence, social appreciation, and travel opportunities) and risks (chronic injury and conflicts between sport activity and other domains of life) incorporated in sport competition. Further, they have identified coping mechanisms utilized by retired athletes to manage transition, particularly channeling their energy into other life domains, such as their family and career. A too-strong personal commitment seems, in this context, to risk continuity of an athlete's career rather than to support it. Illustrative of the power of such a commitment is the following citation:

> Now sport is my life . . . everything revolves around sport. When I am not racing, I think about it all the time. It takes up at least 90% of my time. I love it. I spend all my time living, thinking, breathing it.
> (quoted in Wheeler, Malone et al., 1996, p. 389)

The risk to psychological well-being displayed by excessive personal commitment is supported by findings of Hopper (1986), who reported an inverse relationship between personal commitment to participation in sport and degree of participants' global self-esteem. Lack of support from organizational agencies is another important barrier to disability sport participation, while family and friends are perceived as most important during competition and retirement (Wheeler, Hutzler et al., 1996).

Practical Recommendations and Considerations for Future Research

In summary, the relationship between physical activity, psychological well-being, and empowerment is based on research that is predominantly qualitative or cross-sectional. Cause-effect relationships have not been adequately investigated. Longitudinal research is warranted to address this problem. An alternative cross-sectional approach to this cause-effect problem would be a comparison of psychological well-being and empowerment in athletes with acquired disabilities who were and were not active in sports prior to acquiring their disability. Another area that should attract investigators is comparative psychological outcomes of different exercise/sports programs. Finally, research should be designed to examine the effects of specific exercise, particularly in the presence of risk factors such as increasing age and more severe impairment (e.g., individuals with quadriplegia compared to paraplegia). Triangulation of qualitative and quantitative methods is desirable, in order to acquire a broad basis for discussion and interpretation.

Finally, several recommendations for incorporating teaching and coaching practices across the life-span may be identified:

1. Coaches and instructors, as well as parents, should be advised to find the appropriate challenge regarding the optimal zone of fun and arousal (Martens, 1996). Exercise should be pleasing, enjoyable, and relaxing; hardships should be avoided or at least carefully managed (Berger, 1996).
2. Coaches and instructors of youth and adolescents should be encouraged to incorporate social interaction and peer-support systems in their programs, as these resources have particular relation to an individual's perception of self-efficacy and self-esteem (Martin & Mushett, 1996; Varni & Setoguchi, 1991).
3. Initial sport participation of athletes with acquired disabilities is affected by interpersonal differences and preferences. Although one individual may immediately be willing to pursue a sport practiced prior to onset of disability, another may find participation frustrating (Hutzler, 1986).
4. Gains through sports activity should not be overemphasized, and parallel development in professional career and partnership relations should be acknowledged and encouraged. Otherwise, losses in these domains may overstress the individual and prevent him or her from excelling in the sport domain (Wheeler et al., in press).
5. Sport organizations should strive to create an atmosphere of responsibility and commitment, as dropouts and early retirement from physical activity are often associated with negative interpersonal relations and lack of institutional support (Wheeler, Hutzler et al., 1996).

6. When approaching retirement from competitive sport, individuals with disabilities should consider turning to recreational activities more applicable for their current lifestyle, such as health-promoting exercise, kayaking, and other adventure activities, rather than giving up physical activity.

References

Ajzen, I. (1985). From intentions to actions: A theory of planned behaviour. In J. Kuhl & I. Beckman (Eds.), *Action control: From cognition to behaviour* (pp. 11–39). Heidelberg: Springer-Verlag.

American Psychological Association (1994). *Publication manual* (4th. ed.). Washington, DC: Author.

Antonovsky, A. (1987). *Unraveling the mystery of health.* San Fransisco: Jossey Bass.

Barton, L. (1993). Disability, empowerment, and physical education. In J. Evans (Ed.), *Equity, empowerment, and physical education* (pp. 43–54). Lewes, England: Falmer.

Benson, E., & Jones, G. (1992). Psychological implications of physical activity in individuals with physical disabilities. In T. Williams, L. Almond, & A. Sparks (Eds.), *Sport and physical activity: Moving towards excellence* (pp. 278–283). London: Spon.

Berger, B.G. (1996). Psychological benefits of an active lifestyle: What do we know and what do we need to know. *Quest, 48*, 330–353.

Berendsen, B. & Ottevanger, C. (1996). *Perceived competence and actual performance in young Israelian children with cerebral palsy.* MA thesis, Free University of Amsterdam.

Blinde, E.M., & McClung, L. (1997). Enhancing the physical and social self through recreational activity: Accounts of individuals with physical disabilities. *Adapted Physical Activity Quarterly, 14*, 327–344.

Boes, K., Woll, A., Oja. P., Suni, J. & Hutzler, Y. (1995). Health and sports. *Issues in Special Education and Rehabilitation, 10*, 5–18.

Campbell, E. (1995). Psycho-social well-being of participants in wheelchair sports: Comparison of individuals with congenital and acquired disabilities. *Perceptual and Motor Skills, 81*, 563–568.

Council of Europe. (1987). *European charter on sport for all: Disabled people.* Strasbourg: Author.

Crocker, R.R.E. (1993). Sport and exercise psychology and research with individuals with physical disabilities: Using theory to advance knowledge. *Adapted Physical Activity Quarterly, 10*, 324–345.

Davis, L.J. (1995). *Enforcing normalcy: Disability, deafness, and the body.* New York: Verso.

DePauw, K., & Gavron, S. (1995). *Sport and disability.* Champaign, IL: Human Kinetics.

Ferrara, M., Dattilo, J., & Dattilo, A. (1994). A crossdisability analysis of programming needs for athletes with disabilities. *Palaestra, 11*, 32–42.

Ferris, B.F. (1987). Reflections on the physical activity patterns of disabled Canadians: Challenges for practitioners. *Journal of Leisurability, 14*, 18–23.

Glueckauf, R.L., & Quittner, A.L. (1984). Facing physical disability as a young adult: Psychological issues and approaches. In M. Eisenberg, L. Surkin, & M. Jansen (Eds.), *Chronic illness and disability through the life span* (pp. 167–183). New York: Springer.

Goffman, E. (1963) *Stigma: Notes on the management of a spoiled identity.* Englewood Cliffs, NJ: Prentice Hall.

Haley, S.M., Coster, W.J., Ludlow, L.H., Haltiwanger, J.T., & Andrellos, P.J. (1992). *Pediatric evaluation of disability inventory (PEDI): Development, standardization and administration manual.* Boston: New England Medical Center Hospitals Inc.

Harter, S. (1978). Effectance motivation reconsidered—toward a developmental model. *Human Development, 21*, 34–64.

Harter, S., & Pike, R. (1984). The pictorial perceived competence scale for young children. *Child Development, 55*, 1969–1982.

Hedrick, B. (1985). The effect of wheelchair tennis participation and mainstreaming upon the perceptions of competence of physically disabled adolescents. *Therapeutic Recreation Journal, 19,* 34–45.

Hedrick, B. (1986). Wheelchair sport as a mechanism for altering the perceptions of the nondisabled regarding their disabled peers' competence. *Therapeutic Recreation Journal, 20,* 72–84.

Hopper, C.A. (1986). Socialization of wheelchair athletes. In C. Sherrill (Ed.), *Sport and disabled athletes* (pp. 197–202). Champaign, IL: Human Kinetics.

Hutzler, Y. (1986). *The movement action of wheelchair users.* Unpublished doctoral thesis, University of Heidelberg.

Hutzler, Y. (1990). The concept of empowerment in rehabilitative sports. In G. Doll-Tepper, C. Dahms, B. Doll, & H. V. Selzam (Eds.), *Adapted physical activity: An interdisciplinary approach* (pp. 44–51). Heidelberg : Springer.

Hutzler, Y., Almosny, Y., Bergman, U., Yaakov, T., & Getz, M. (1998). *Inclusion of children with physical disabilities.* Manuscript in preparation.

Hutzler, Y., & Bar-Eli, M. (1993). Psychological benefits of sports for disabled people: A review. *Scandinavian Journal of Medicine and Science in Sports, 3,* 217–228.

Hutzler, Y., & Felis, O. (1998). *A computerized search of scientific disability sport literature.* Manuscript submitted for publication.

Katz, I. (1981). *Stigma: A social psychological analysis.* Hillsdale, NJ: L. Lawrence Erlbaum.

King, G.A., Shultz, I.Z., Steel, K., & Gilpin, M. (1993). Self evaluation and self concept of adolescents with physical disabilities. *American Journal of Occupational Therapy, 47,*132–140.

Kirby, R.J., Cull, J., & Foreman, P. (1996). Association of prelesion sports participation and involvement in whellchair sports following spinal cord injury. *Perceptual and Motor Skills, 82,* 481–482.

Kobasa, S.C., Maddi, S.R., & Puccetti, M.C (1982). Personality and exercise as buffers in the stress-illness relationship. *Journal of Behavioral Medicine, 5,* 391–405.

Lazarus, R.S., & Folkman, S. (1984). *Stress, appraisal and coping.* New York: Springer.

Longmuir, P. & Bar-Or, O. (in press). Physical activity levels of youth with and without physical disabilities. *Adapted Physical Activity Quarterly.*

Martens, R. (1996). Turning kids on to physical activity for a lifetime. *Quest, 48,* 303–310.

Martin, J.J., & Mushett, C.A. (1996). Social support mechanisms among athletes with a disability. *Adapted Physical Activity Quarterly, 13,* 74–83.

Porretta, D., & Moore, W. (1996/1997). A review of sport psychology research for individuals with disabilites: Implications for future inquiry. *Clinical Kinesiology, 50,* 83–93.

Reid, G., & Prupas, A. (1998). A documentary analysis of research priorities in disability sport. *Adapted Physical Activity Quarterly, 15,* 168–178.

Roth, D.L., & Holmes, D.S. (1985). Influence of physical fitness in detemining the impact of stressful life events on physical and psychological helath. *Psychosomatic Medicine, 47,* 164–173.

Schlossberg, N.K. (1981). A model for analyzing human adaptation to transition. *The Counseling Psychologist, 9,* 2–18.

Shapiro, J.P. (1993). *No pity: People with disabilities forging a new civil rights movement.* New York: Times Books/Random House.

Shephard, R. (1990). *Fitness in special populations.* Champaign, IL: Human Kinetics.

Sherrill, C. (Ed.). (1986). *Sports and disabled athletes.* Champaign, IL: Human Kinetics.

Sherrill, C. (1990). Psychosocial status of disabled athletes. In G. Reid (Ed.), *Problems in movement control* (pp. 339–364). New York: Elsevier.

Sherrill, C. (1997). Disability identity and involvement in sport and exercise. In K. Fox (Ed.), *The physical self* (pp. 257–286). Champaign, IL: Human Kinetics.

Sherrill, C. (1998). *Adapted physical activity, recreation and sport: Crossdisciplinary and life-span* (5th ed.). Dubuque, IA: WCB/McGraw-Hill.

Sherrill, C., Buswell, D., Piletic, C., Hilgenbrinck, L., Schell, B., & Frey, G. (1998). *Psychosocial perspectives of Paralympians on sport and empowerment.*. Unpublished research monograph.

Sherrill, C., & DePauw, K. (1997). Adapted physical activity and education. In J.D. Massengale & R.A. Swanson (Eds.), *The history of exercise and sport science* (pp. 39–108). Champaign, IL: Human Kinetics.

Sherrill, C., Gench, B., Hinson, M., Gilstrap, T., Richir, K., & Mastro, J. (1990). Self-actualization of elite blind athletes: An explanatory study. *Journal of Visual Impairment & Blindness 82*, 55–60

Sherrill, C., Hinson, M., Gench, B., Kennedy, S.O., & Low, L. (1990). Self-concepts of disabled youth athletes. *Perceptual and Motor Skills, 70*, 1093–1098.

Sherrill, C., & Rainbolt, W. (1988). Self-actualization profiles of male able-bodied and cerebral palsied athletes. *Adapted Physical Activity Quarterly, 5*, 108–119.

Sherrill, C., Silliman, L., Gench, B., & Hinson, M. (1990). Self actualization of elite wheelchiar athletes. *Paraplegia, 23*, 252–260.

Sherrill, C., & Williams, T. (1996). Disability and Sport: Psychosocial perspectives on inclusion, integration and participation. *Sport Science Review, 5*, 42–64.

Shifflett, B., Cator, C., & Megginson, N. (1994). Active lifestyle adherence among individuals with and without disabilities. *Adapted Physical Activity Quarterly, 11*, 359–367.

Steadward, R.D., Nelson, E., & Wheeler, G. (1994). *Vista '93—The outlook: Proceedings from the Vista '93: An international conference on high performance sport for athletes with disabilities.* Edmonton, Alberta, Canada: Rick Hansen Centre.

Trieschmann, R.B. (1988). *Spinal cord injuries: Psychological, social and vocational rehabilitation* (2nd ed.). New York: Demos Publications.

Varni, J.W., & Setoguchi, Y. (1991). Correlates of perceived physical appearance in children with congenital/acquired limb deficiencies. *Developmental and Behavioral Pediatrics, 12*, 171–176.

Vermeer, A., Kruithof, H., & Zoggel, B.V. (1995). The 'Functional Motor Assessment Scale' for children with Cerebral Palsy. *Journal of Rehabilitation Sciences, 8*, 94–98.

Vermeer, A., Lanen, W., Hendriksen, J., Speth, L., & Mulderij. (1994). Measuring perceived competence in children with cerebral palsy. In J.H.A. van Rossum & J.I. Laszlo (Eds.), *Motor development: Aspects of normal and delayed development* (pp. 133–144). Amsterdam: UV Uitgeverij.

Weiner, B. (1985). An attributional theory of achievement motivation and emotion. *Psychological Review, 92*, 548–573.

Wendell, S. (1996). *The rejected body: Feminist philosophical reflections on disability.* New York: Routledge.

Wheeler, G., Hutzler, Y., Bergman, U., & Schaefer, U. (1996). *Results and findings: Canadian and Israeli athletes with a disability samples.* Poster presented at the Rick Hansen Centre. Edmonton, Alberta: The Rick Hansen Centre.

Wheeler, G., Legg, D., Hutzler, Y., Campbell, E., Johnson, A., & Steadward, R. (in press). Competition and retirement experiences in athletes with a disability: The search for competency and identity. *Adapted Physical Activity Quarterly.*

Wheeler, G., Malone, L., VanVlack, S., Nelson, E.R., & Steadward, R.D. (1996). Retirement from disability sport : A pilot study. *Adapted Physical Activity Quarterly, 13*, 382–399.

World Health Organization. (1980). *International classification of impairments, disabilities and handicaps: A manual of classification relating to the consequences of disease.* Geneva, Switzerland: Author.

Wright, B.A. (1983). *Physical disability: A psychosocial approach* (2nd ed.). Philadelphia: Harper & Row.

Wuerch, G., & Sherrill, C. (1998). *Sport as empowerment: Perspectives of women wheelchair road racers.* Unpublished research monograph.

Yuker, H. (Ed.). (1988). *Attitudes toward persons with disabilities.* New York: Springer.

Subject Index